Transforming the Chinese Economy

Social Scientific Studies in Reform Era China

Editor

John Fitzgerald

Volume 2

BEIJING
2010

Transforming the Chinese Economy

Edited by

Cai Fang

BRILL

LEIDEN • BOSTON
2010

This book is the result of a copublication agreement between Social Sciences Academic Press and Koninklijke Brill NV. These articles were translated into English from the original <<中国经济转型>> (Zhongguo jingji zhuanxing) with financial support from China Book International, supported by the General Administration of Press and Publication and the Information Office of the State Council.

This book is printed on acid-free paper.

Library of Congress Cataloging-in-Publication Data

Transforming the Chinese economy = Zhongguo jing ji zhuan xing / edited by Cai Fang. — 1st ed.
p. cm. — (Social scientific studies in reform era China ; 2)
Includes bibliographical references and index.
ISBN 978-90-04-18421-3 (hard cover : alk. paper) 1. China—Economic policy—2000– 2. China—Economic conditions—2000– 3. Women in development—China. I. Cai, Fang. II. Title: Zhongguo jing ji zhuan xing. III. Series.

HC427.95.T73 2010
330.951—dc22

2010008656

ISSN 1879-7539
ISBN 978-90-04-18421-3

PRINTED BY A-D DRUK BV - ZEIST, THE NETHERLANDS

CONTENTS

LIST OF FIGURES

LIST OF TABLES

PREFACE

Cai Fang

The Master said, "If a truly royal ruler were to arise, it would still require a generation for virtue to prevail." According to one of the authoritative annotators of the Analects of Confucius, one generation means a thirty-year period of time. So, Confucius meant it would take thirty years for the government to effectively implement a policy focusing on people's livelihood. Last year was the thirtieth year since China launched its reform and opening campaign, initiated at the Third Plenary Session of the Eleventh Central Committee of the Communist Party of China (the Central Committee) in 1978. During this period, China underwent dramatic changes unseen in its thousands of years of history and only rarely seen in the history of the world economy. Meanwhile, these thirty years were also a peak period of economic globalization. During this time, many developing countries attempted to leverage this round of globalization as an opportunity to catch up economically; transitional countries also hoped to capitalize on the opportunity to carry out economic transition. However, when results are evaluated in terms of economic growth rate or per capita income growth rate, not many countries have achieved success in catching up and transitioning, especially in terms of growth sustainability and stability.

Assessed from any angle or by using any statistical indicator of economic growth and institutional transition, China has realized a dramatic transition—from pervasive poverty to common affluence, from the countryside to the cities, from a centrally-planned to a market system, from public ownership to diverse forms of ownership, and from a closed economy into an open economy engaged in economic globalization. This simple truth has become the general consensus of both domestic and foreign observers.[1] Now the world is marveling at China's economic miracle. Summarizing experiences and lessons from

[1] Brandt, Loren, and Thomas G. Rawski, eds. *China's Great Economic Transformation*, 2008: 3.

the thirty years of reform and opening crusade helps China fine-tune its reform and development policy and provides a valuable reference for other developing and transitional countries.

There has been a great deal written by domestic and foreign economists and financial reporters summarizing and dissecting China's economic reform. Individual authors have their own comparative advantages in analyzing China's reform experiences. The reform experiences summarized by local Chinese economists are of special significance. Local economists, who focus on domestic economic reform issues, are closer to the real world practice of reform and as a result they are in a better position to portray the truth of the process without being unduly influenced by any Western theory or doctrine. A huge gap may arise with any reform, both between its goals and its implementation as well as between its implementation and its documentation. But if scholars, acting as the instigators and observers of reform, conduct a rational review of the process, the information divide between the goals and the implementation of any reform initiative can be minimized or eliminated. As stated by some economists, China's economic reform has progressed so quickly that the systems tracking economic statistics have simply been unable to keep up.[2] Local economists, who are directly engaged in the process of reform, have been able to gain a deep understanding of the statistics from China's transitional period and they can rebalance and reinterpret these figures based on their own empirical experience as well as rational analysis. By contrast, foreign economists are often confused with figures and unable to see the truth in them.[3] Therefore, it is not an exaggeration

---

[2] Ravallion, Martin and Shaohua Chen. "When Economic Reform is Faster Than Statistical Reform: Measuring and Explaining Income Inequality in Rural China."

[3] Many foreign economists are often confused with statistical figures. For example, Johnson found the labor quantity used in agriculture inconsistent with statistical figures (Johnson, D. Gale. *Zhongguo nengfou tongguo zainongcun chuangzao feinonggongzuo zhiwei lai zhuanyi dabufen nongye laodongli* 中国能否通过在农村创造非农工作职位来转移大部分农业劳动力 [*By Creating Non-agricultural Work, Can China Change Labor in the Countryside*], 2004); Rawski was baffled by the statistical inconsistency between the economic growth rate and employment growth rate and raised doubt over the former (Rawski, Thomas G. "What's Happening to China's GDP Statistics?" 2001); Spence expressly stated that only local Chinese economists were able to remove the logical doubt as to how labor productivity growth and employment expansion occurred simultaneously in China's manufacturing industry (Spence, A. Michael. "Zhongguo gaigekaifang de chenggong jingyan he xintiaozhan 中国改革开放的成功经验和新挑战 [The Successes and Future Challenges of China's Reform and Opening]" (Chinese Translation, 2008).

to say that the authors of this book, Chinese economists with direct experience in China's reform process, are best qualified for the job of summarizing China's economic reform experiences.

I. *China's Economic Reform, Opening, and Development*

The Fourteenth National Congress of the Communist Party of China (the National Party Congress) set forth the objective of economic reform to establish a socialist market economy. The success of reform should therefore be measured in terms of the degree of transition from a planned economy to a market economy and ultimately judged in terms of the positive effects of reform and opening on economic and social development. Specifically, the success of reform can be evaluated using major economic indicators. For instance, Assar Lindbeck[4] examine the changes in China's economic system in nine respects: (1) enterprise ownership; (2) asset ownership; (3) economic decision-making method; (4) operational processes of the economy; (5) enterprise incentive mechanism; (6) individual incentive mechanism; (7) degree of competition facing enterprises; (8) degree of competition facing individuals; and (9) degree of opening to the outside world. The most important dimensions of the economic system are covered by these nine indicators. However, this is merely a descriptive analysis of China's economic system. Although alluding to the interrelationships and inherent relationships between these indicators, Lindbeck fails to clearly reveal their hierarchical and logical relationships.

In their work, Justin Lin, Cai Fang, and Li Zhou[5] build model of the economic system model based on four logically interlinked factors. The first is the economic development strategy chosen by a country. In general, there are two options available to each country: the comparative-advantage-defying strategy and comparative-advantage-following strategy.[6] The second factor is the macroeconomic policy environment created to implement a particular development strategy. If a country chooses to implement a comparative-advantage-following

[4] Lindbeck, Assar. "Economic—social Interaction in China," 2008.

[5] Lin, Justin Yifu 林毅夫, Cai Fang 蔡昉 and Li Zhou 李周. *Zhongguo de qiji: fazhan zhanlüe yu jingji gaige (zengdingban)* 中国的奇迹：发展战略与经济改革（增订版） [*China's Miracle: Development Strategy and Economic Reform (Revised Edition)*], 1999.

[6] See Chapter 6 of this book.

strategy, the prices of products and production factors reflect the equilibrium between supply and demand and the relative scarcity of these products and factors. The macroeconomic policy environment under the comparative-advantage-defying strategy results in the distortion of product and factor prices, which are often artificially depressed to reduce the costs of heavy industry development. The third factor is the resource allocation mechanism selected within a specific development strategy. When prices are not distorted, resources are allocated primarily through market mechanisms; otherwise, resources are mainly allocated through central planning. The fourth factor is the microeconomic management mechanisms used with the aforementioned economic policies and system. Under the price-distorted and centrally planned macroeconomic environment created by adoption of the comparative advantage-defying strategy, the microeconomic system is typified by a lack of autonomy for enterprises, soft budget constraints, lack of competition because of government protection, and lack of mechanisms to create incentive. The comparative advantage-following strategy is typified by autonomous firms competing in a market under hard budget constraints and mechanisms for economic incentive.

When China's economic system took shape in the 1950s, the development strategy adopted gave top priority to heavy industry. However, this strategy engendered a contradiction between the economic development target and the resource endowment structure. In other words, the capital intensity and massive investment required by heavy industry development was contradictory with the capital-scarce development stage. Therefore, the macroeconomic policy focused on artificially depressing the prices of capital and other factors of production. When the prices of scarce factors were depressed, resources were allocated under the central planning system and the roles of the market mechanism and price signal were ignored. To ensure production units invested and reinvested resources in heavy industry, as required by the development strategy, the state-owned industry and commune-based agriculture became the logical institutional arrangement. This was the logic of China's traditional economic system that took shape in the late 1950s.

This economic system had a number of symptoms of inefficiency, including the lack of technical efficiency at the micro level and the lack of allocation efficiency at the macro level. To resolve major issues such as the inefficiency of resource-allocation inefficiency and deficiencies of economic-planning, reform would need to turn the entire system around in a short period of time. But for China, a country that shunned the market, had a low level of economic development, and could not afford any drastic economic recession, it would be difficult for the traditional reform through "shock therapy" to be successful. Instead, China launched economic reform at the micro level by allowing grass-roots industrial and agricultural production units to directly tackle micro-incentive and efficiency issues. Reform measures included introducing the household contract responsibility system in the agriculture sector and implementing the power-delegating and profit-sharing schemes for state-owned enterprises. This paved the way for reform to advance along a path with unique Chinese characteristics. It seems that such a model of reform is in opposition to the economic model described above, but logically, it was an approach compatible with the laws of development.[7]

Looking at the results of China's economic reform, economists have often discussed reform target models (the "Washington Consensus" and the "Beijing Consensus"), the approaches to reform (such as incremental or radical reform), and the relationships between governments and the market (authoritarian regimes versus neutral government). Interestingly, scholars often draw starkly different or completely contradictory conclusions about the same experiences, mainly because China's reform has had the following characteristic: the goals of reform have been fixed but the target models and methods of attaining the targets were fluid and blended diverse forms.[8] In spite of this complex phenomenon, China's economic reform can nonetheless generally be described as having the following characteristics:

First, reform has been gradual in nature. In order to resolve institutional deficiencies at the micro level, agriculture and enterprise reform directly addressed such issues as the lack of incentives and inefficiency by introducing simple reforms, such as the contract responsibility system, to instantaneously boost production and bolster economic growth. When such reform yielded instant effects, it restored public confidence and spurred more work units to seek and invest production

---

[7] Lin, Cai Fang, and Li Zhou, *China's Miracle*, 1999.

[8] For example, rural reform and labor market reform are a combination of incremental and radical reform methods and a blend of incremental and stock reform methods. Please refer to Cai Fang 蔡昉, Wang Dewen 王德文 and Du Yang 都阳. *Zhongguo nongcun gaige yu bianqian—30 nian lichen he yingyan fenxi* 中国农村改革与变迁—30 年历程和经验分析 [*Reform and Change in Rural China—Analysis of the Experiences of 30 Years*], 2008; and Chapter 3 of this book.

factors outside of state planning, thereby improving allocation efficiency and boosting profits and worker income. It was therefore natural for reform to enter the field of resource allocation, leading to the creation of market mechanisms outside the system of planning. Reform continued expanding the scope and scale of market influence over commodity distribution and allocation of factors of production. Along with the expanding role of markets in determining the allocation of commodities and production-factors, prices also began to cast off the yoke of state planning and control, becoming determined by market supply and demand. As prices gradually reached their market-determined level, the foundations of the heavy industry-oriented development strategy became insecure. Thus economic growth and structural change were increasingly being pointed in the direction dictated by comparative advantage.

Second, reform has been incremental in nature. Reform began with a focus on resolving the issues with incentives and micro-efficiency without making any premature adjustments, thus avoiding harming any vested interest groups in the traditional system. When studying economic transition, economists often pay special attention to how to mitigate the damage to vested interest groups in order to minimize the political costs and risks of reform.[9] In China, a significant number of the so-called vested interest groups were actually low-income residents. For example, breaking the "iron-rice-bowl" compensation system of state-owned enterprises affected low-wage and older employees whose educational level and skills were not competitive in the labor market. Those affected by commodity price deregulation were low-wage earners unable to easily sustain major lifestyle changes. Therefore, insisting on the principle of incremental reform and granting moderate protection for vested interest groups (or underprivileged groups) were consistent with the objective of using reform to raise people's living standards.

Third, reform has promoted development. Many foreign observers and researchers have noted that China's incremental economic reform started without an overall blueprint and proceeded in a stage-like manner by solving urgent problems and seeking immediate results. Although the goal of establishing a socialist market economy was officially announced at the Fourteenth Party National Congress in 1992,

---

[9] Roland, Gérard. "The Political Economy of Transition," 2002.

China still proceeded with the form of reform characterized as "feeling the stones to cross the river." For instance, many reform tasks had no timetable for completion, the sequence of reform was intentionally left undetermined, and the methods for implementing reform varied depending on time and place. When evaluating the effects of China's reform from the dogma of economics, Western economists tend to make comparisons using a fixed system as their frame of reference[10] but often find that this is not the system followed and pursued in China. This is a philosophical difference between China and other countries regarding reform. In other words, the purpose or aim of China's reform is not to reach a specific target model but to raise the people's standards of living and boost national strength. Proceeding from this purpose, China has gradually explored and blazed a trail of reform with unique Chinese characteristics to realize the transition from a planned to market economy. However, the market system has not become an independent model and instead it is a means to an end, with the end being improving people's livelihood and boosting national strength. The difference in philosophy and purpose of reform has prevented the reform in China from falling into any *a priori* dogmas.[11] The principle that the goal of reform is to enhance productivity, improve living standards, and boost national strength was explicitly laid down at the outset and will remain unchanged forever. Under the guidance of this principle, reform, development, and stability have become an integrated whole: reform aims to promote development but shall subordinate itself to stability; development results are used to examine the correctness of the reform approach; stability creates conditions for further reform.

Lastly, reform in China is integrated in nature. Although China does not publish an overall reform blueprint, the economic system itself is an integral whole. Each part of the economic system should

---

[10] For example, a book published in the United States to discuss China reform was named "How Far Across the River" after Deng Xiaoping's motto "feeling the stones to cross the river" (Hope, Nicholas C., Dennis Tao Yang and Mu Yang Li (eds.). *How Far Across the River: Chinese Policy Reform at the Millennium*, 2003.)

[11] Some economists attribute China's reform success to its correct application of standard economic theories (that is, by observing the "Washington Consensus") (see Yao Yang 姚洋. *Zuowei zhidu chuangxin guocheng de jingji gaige* 作为制度创新过程的经济改革 [*Economic Reform, a Process of Institutional Creativity*], 2008). Actually, this viewpoint confuses the two different concepts of "prescription" and "therapeutic effect." Regarding Chinese reform, there is no evidence on what theoretic doctrines it has followed. What the world is seeing are actual, delivered results.

operate in a unified and mutually adaptive way. In addition, implementation of reforms in China has been done in a spontaneous way. Therefore, the reform process has not been random or arbitrary, but logical.[12] But in characterizing China's reform as a gradual and incremental evolution process, people have also often observe that reform in some areas lags behind that in others. For example, the transition and development of the market for production factors, including the labor market, is regarded as an area in which reform lags behind that of the commodity market.[13] But the question is: if the implementation of such an important part of reform is lagging behind and as a result, the system is uncoordinated, then why have the overall effects of reform still been so pronounced, manifested by thirty years of rapid economic growth, productivity gains, and significant improvement in living standards? An in-depth analysis of the processes and logic of China's economic reform shows it advancing quite radically in certain periods, stages, and areas while proceeding in an incremental and gradual way as a whole. The form and sequence that reform takes depends on the adaptability of the system as a whole as well as their social affordability. Regardless of whether reform is viewed from the perspective of a certain area or a certain stage, in truth, reform has been implemented as a whole and there are no substantially leading or lagging areas.

After thirty years of reform and opening, China has achieved unprecedented accomplishments in all economic and social sectors. These accomplishments can be examined in multiple respects: the degree of China's participation in economic globalization; the development of a commodity market and a production factors market; the transformation of government functions; the degree of coordination between economic development and social development; structural adjustment; reforms in areas of employment, the social security system and income distribution; and developments related to people's livelihood. This volume intends to demonstrate, from multiple angles, the successes of economic and social development through reform and opening, draw upon and analyze the relevant experiences and lessons, identify and suggest new directions of reform, and discuss the value of China's experiences as a reference for other countries and the potential contribution of China's economic success to economic theories.

[12] Lin, Cai Fang, and Li Zhou, *China's Miracle*, 2008.
[13] Lardy, 1994, pp. 8–14.

II. *The Economics of Chinese Reform, Opening, and Development*

As asserted by Lin and Wang,[14] development is a process full of uncertainty and subject to influence of the unique natural, political, cultural, and historical background of a country. While China studies and implements economic reform, opening, and development, Chinese economists have, at the same time, taken it upon themselves to study modern economics. Such learning includes two processes: learning from books and the experiences of other countries; and, learning by understanding the unique characteristics of China's economy. The role economists play in economic development and reform has remained an issue of controversy, but their influence can be understood in a broad. Economists can influence the policymaking process in a number of ways, including publishing economic research outlining policy implications, directly becoming decision-makers, participating in designing institutions as consultants, indirectly participating in policy formulation by exerting influence on public opinion, and influencing policy when their academic standpoints are accepted by policymakers. From this broad perspective, economists in China—and in other countries—do have some influence over economic development and institutional change.[15]

In his work, Zhang Shuguang[16] reviews and comments on the key direction and achievements of China's economic policy over thirty years in eight respects: (1) hypothesis of economic man; (2) enterprise theory; (3) theory of institutional evolution; (4) discussion of the "Needham Puzzle"; (5) macroeconomic theory; (6) discussion of the theory of deflation; (7) research on RMB exchange rate issues; and (8) progress in analytical methods used in income distribution research. The perspectives from which he engages in his analysis and the works cited indicate that he continues to summarize the progress and development of Chinese economics in respect to the framework of Western economics and thus the content of his analysis is incomplete and repetitive.

---

[14] See Chapter 6 of this book.

[15] McMillan, John. "Impact of Modern Economic Theory on Policy and Empirical Research," May 2003. Cai Fang 蔡昉. "The Roles of Chinese Economists in the Economic Reform," 1998.

[16] Zhang Shuguang 张曙光. "Zhongguo jingjixue yanjiu 30nian: fansi yu pinglun 中国经济学研究 30 年：反思与评论 [30 Years of Economics Research in China: a Review and Commentary]." *Zhongguo renwen shehui kexue sanshinian: huigu yu qianzhan*, 2008.

Nevertheless, he pays special attention to China's unique experiences in economic development. Overall, these unique experiences, and the challenges to mainstream economics that they embody, are attributed to the fact that development, reform, macroeconomic management, and government functionality, all with unique Chinese characteristics, have refuted a series of mainstream economic hypotheses that have long been taken for granted in Western countries. In which areas have China's economic reform, opening, and development experiences posed challenges to Western mainstream economic schools of thought? In other words, in which areas are China's experiences unique? We will try to answer both of these questions in the following section.

China's economic reform is unique due to the fact that in the midst of ongoing comprehensive economic reform, and the development that has resulted from such reform, China has also been immersed in two other important transitions.

The first transition relates to change in the dual economic structure. The dualistic model of economic development, developed by W.A. Lewis,[17] has long been criticized and ignored by the leading neoclassical economics.[18] Lewis's hypotheses that the wage disparity between urban and rural labor sectors cannot be avoided and that, in agriculture, the massive surplus of labor would continue to exist has been strongly criticized. However, Lewis's hypothesis can be easily understood by anyone who understands why China chose to establish the *hukou* system in the 1950s, and how that system, during the period of the planned economy and even the reform period, separated the urban and rural labor markets as well as the formal and informal urban labor markets. But in fact, for the entire reform period, economic development has been a process of gradually weakening the dualistic economic structure until the unlimited labor supply is eliminated, at which point China will reach the Lewis point, and enter a new stage of development.[19] Therefore, while neoclassical economics assumes that economic development is homogeneous and unitary, it finds itself too

[17] Lewis, W.A. "Economic Development with Unlimited Supplies of Labor," 1954.

[18] Ranis, Gustav. "Arthur Lewis' Contribution to Development Thinking and Policy," August 2004.

[19] Cai Fang 蔡昉. *Liuyisi zhuanzhedian—Zhongguo Jingji Fazhan Xinjieduan* 刘易斯转折点—中国经济发展新阶段 [*The Lewis Point—The New Step of China's Economic Development*], 2008.

cumbersome to explain or understand China's economy, which was more classically dualistic than even the Lewis model.

The second transition is the systematic transition from planned to market economy. Based on mainstream Western economic theory, transition of economic systems usually needs to follow some fixed doctrine—namely, the so-called "Washington Consensus." Joseph Stiglitz shed light on the true meaning of the "Washington Consensus": a development strategy with privatization, liberalization, and macro-economic stability (mainly price stability) as its major features, and a series of policies based on staunch faith in the free market and aimed at weakening and even minimizing the role of government.[20] Of the countries that laid out a blueprint before reform started, none were lucky enough to escape the influence of the so-called "Washington Consensus" and in consequence all opted for radical "shock therapy" reform options.[21] However, more and more study of economic theory as well as reform experiences has shown that the "Washington Consensus" is not applicable to many countries unique circumstances, and that adopting it often results in derailing the process of reform and development.[22] Even Jeffrey Sachs, who created and implemented the famous "shock therapy" in Latin America and Eastern Europe, has acknowledged that China's gradual reform is far more successful. When delivering an address in Sao Paulo in November 2003, he sighed that the economic development of Latin America compared to that of East Asia represented by China was poles apart.[23]

At the outset of reform in China, there was no blueprint or implementation time table. Therefore, with the exception of some political support from high-level decision-makers, reform in China has not been a "top down" process. It is precisely this characteristic that has given China's reform its pragmatic and gradual nature. However, China's reform also cannot be classified as simply a "bottom up" process. In 1978, Party leadership and theorists launched a grand debate on the criterion of truth. The Third Plenary Session of the Eleventh

---

[20] Stiglitz, Joseph. "The Post Washington Consensus Consensus" (Chinese translation), 2005.

[21] For the "shock therapy" reform practices under this doctrine, please refer to Lipton, David and J. Sachs. "Privatization in Eastern Europe: The Case of Poland," 1990.

[22] Stiglitz, Joseph. "More Instruments and Broader Goals: Moving Toward the Post-Washington Consensus," 2005.

[23] Sachs, Jeffrey. "Lessons for Brazil from China's Success," November 5, 2003.

Central Committee reaffirmed the ideological line of emancipating the mind and seeking truth from facts, thereby providing staunch political support for reform to proceed. In Western discussion regarding the political economy of reform, it has been pointed out that there are two major tasks facing any reform: (1) removing the political constraints in order to start the reform process and (2) advancing reform by relaxing political constraints imposed after the reform starts. Both of these issues are related to the difficulty of compensating the potential losers of reform.[24] The determination to undertake reform and theoretical consensus among the Chinese leadership, coupled with the people's desire for reform and their exploration into its possibilities, together formed a path that combined top-down and bottom-up approaches. It has been the interaction between these two directions that have continued to move the process forward, resolving the pair of difficulties facing reform efforts. In other words, at the reform startup stage and at each stage of implementation, political stability and unwavering commitment to reform have encouraged and empowered the government to follow the principle of "Pareto efficiency" to the maximum extent possible by comprehensively coordinating the pace of reform. Meanwhile, reform has aimed to unleash the potential of efficient organization and, by increasing the size of the economic pie, enable people to benefit. This combined approach has put reform on an irreversible path.

Some have attributed China's reform success to its correct application of standard economic theories,[25] pointing to the fact that China has maintained macroeconomic stability throughout the reform process, which is precisely what many Eastern European and Latin American countries were unable to achieve. However, contrary to the logic underpinning this conclusion, China's macroeconomic stability is based on its own national characteristics, creating a system of macroeconomic management with Chinese characteristics.

Western mainstream economists engage in macroeconomic analysis based on the following assumptions: labor is limited; there are diminishing returns to capital; there is no price distortion for factors of production; technological progress is an innate result of economic growth; etc. Under such assumptions, any problems in the business-cycle issue are mainly issues involving aggregate supply and demand or the

[24] Roland, Gérard. "The Political Economy of Transition," 2002.

[25] Yao, *Economic Reform, a Process of Institutional Creativity*, 2008: 1.

money supply. The methods for resolving such problems are therefore routine macroeconomic policies and primarily monetary policy tools. But for a considerable period of time in China, none of these assumptions applied. Even currently, the characteristics of China's economy are starkly different from those of developed market economies. For example, labor has been far from scarce; capital returns have shown no signs of diminishing; the systematic price distortion of production factors has not been removed; total factor productivity has made significant gains but still failed to become the key driver of economic growth; the economic growth pattern has not yet become a type that inherently generates technological progress.[26] Under these conditions, simply applying Western economic theories to the business cycle or systematically adopting Western-style macroeconomic policy tools is misguided.

It is worth noting that Chinese economists do not deserve much credit in causing China to defy the macroeconomic canons of Western economics. Quite the opposite, the majority of theories and policy recommendations in China fall neatly into the category of mainstream Western macroeconomics. However, China has a group of non-mainstream economists who have continued to engage in analysis based on China's unique circumstances and who have counteracted the influence of pro-Western theorists. In addition, lobbying by various central government agencies and local governments has also played an important role in encouraging macroeconomic policy fit to China's specific framework. Such uniquely Chinese macroeconomic policies include the ingenious coordination between monetary policy and fiscal policy; the methods for implementing monetary policy; striking the right balance between promoting employment and building a social

---

[26] Young and Krugman (Krugman, Paul. "The Myth of Asia's Miracle," 1994) strongly criticized the growth pattern of East Asian economies, arguing that these economies will eventually suffer from diminishing returns and unsustainable growth by purely relying on capital accumulation and labor inputs while lacking productivity progress. This judgment was delivered using the assumptions of labor shortage and diminishing returns to capital typical in Western countries. The increase in the proportion of the working age population and the decrease in dependency ratio due to demographic transition before these economies reached a relatively large TFP contribution share, however, generated the demographic dividend and sustained the fast economic growth for a considerably long period of time (Bloom, David, and Jeffrey Williamson. "Demographic Transition and Economic Miracles in Emerging Asia."; Williamson, Jeffrey. "Growth, Distribution and Demography: Some Lessons from History.").

safety net in policy promoting employment; and the stability of the RMB exchange rate.

The transformation of the government's economic functions has also been quite unique. China's thirty-year journey of reform has happened to coincide with the rise of neo-liberalism in modern economics and economic policy. According to the rules of neo-liberal economics, one would predict that the dominant role of central and local governments in China's reform, opening, and development should naturally lead to disaster. But this prediction simply runs afoul of reality. Despite its problems and abuses, whether one is talking about local government efforts to promote economic growth or the central government formulating plans, enforcing macroeconomic management, coordinating local and departmental interests, and implementing key development strategies,[27] China's model is different from any "consensus" or doctrine and has been widely acclaimed. This has prompted some to search for new explanations to account for this discrepancy between theory and reality.[28]

A transitional economy usually has some features different from those of a steady-state market economy. Such differences also impose special requirements on the government's economic functions different from those for a steady-state economy. First of all, in a country that has long been remote from the market economy, mechanisms for market-driven resource allocation will not be well-established even if the country has started the transition to a market economy.[29] If development of the market has not reached a level where it is able play the role of resource allocation in a completely hassle-free way, allowing the remaining features of the planned economy to play a supplementary role will naturally cause an enormous clash between these different mechanisms of resource allocation. Conversely, using a particular government function to make-up for deficiencies in the market will not

---

[27] For example, Wu (Wu Jinglian 吴敬琏. *Zhongguo zengzhang moshi jueze* 中国增长模式抉择 [Selecting China's Growth Model], 2005) attributes the difficulty facing the transformation of economic growth pattern to excess government power in resource allocation and the simultaneous existence of the three issues of the government "overstepping, mis-stepping, and short-stepping."

[28] Oi, Jean C. "Local State Corporatism," 1999; Walder, Andrew. "Local Governments as Industrial Firms," 1995.

[29] For example, some researchers constructed and used "market memory" as a variable to explain the performance of economic reform (de Melo, Martha, Cevdet Denizer, Alan Gelb, and Stoyan Tenev. *Circumstance and Choice: the Role of Initial Conditions and Policies in Transition Economies*, 1997).

cause any fundamental impediment to future transition. For example, during a transitional period, the credit system required for the market economy is not well established. In the absence of credit assurance, the market cannot automatically take up the task of protecting the interests of both parties to a transaction. Also, for the institutional vacuums that result from the transition from a planned to market economy, in the absence of credit guarantee, corresponding government functions are needed to supplement and maintain market transactions. To maintain the health of the market, the government needs to step in to guarantee credit for enterprises and individuals. At the initial stage of market development, entrepreneurs do not have the human capital required to operate on all fronts under market economic conditions. In this case, it is necessary for the government to take on a more proactive role in the economy supplementing entrepreneurship. Thus, it is not difficult to understand why many local government officials have played a pivotal role in project solicitation and negotiation. Of course, these facts do nothing to change the fact that it is necessary to fundamentally overhaul the government's economic functions as the market system improves. It is an urgent task, and one that has a long, rough road ahead.

III. *Contents and Structure of This Volume*

As mentioned in the previous section, an important achievement of China's economic reform has been the advancement of a uniquely Chinese economic theory. Not only is it an economic theory closely related to the implementation of economic reforms and transition from a dual economy, it is also a theory that has been branded by China's efforts to manage the economy's transition and development and the labor economics related to the people's livelihood. The Chinese economists who have contributed articles to this book are the best representatives of the ongoing research into every area of economic theory and policy. They are not only the leading economists working at the forefront of economic research, but also participants in and observers of China's economic reform. Some authors have directly participated at the highest level in formulating reform strategies and development policies. This book, co-written by this high-echelon of authors, will present, from a broad range of perspectives, a complete picture of the thirty years of reform and opening. Their writings are not only observations of symptoms on the surface, but also a summary of root causes at the theoretical level. In addition, their work presents a review and analysis of China's reform and opening process from the perspective of decision-makers.

This book attempts to summarize reform experiences through a seamless integration of theoretical and historical reasoning. In China, each economic sector has undergone thirty years of reform, so it is very difficult to arrange the sequence of articles in historical order. As discussed earlier, China's economic reform has proceeded in a hands-on fashion without prioritizing or sequencing reform by area or sector. The chapters of this book are therefore arranged in a sequence that begins with the initial areas of reform and proceeds from micro to macro level reform and from specialized to comprehensive topics. Readers may notice that the writing style varies from chapter to chapter but such variation is to be expected. Given the unique backgrounds and experiences of these authors, we have no desire to impose a uniform style or format that might restrict them from leveraging their expertise in the areas of policy, theory, and empirical study; to do so would only impede the goal of offering readers the most authoritative commentary on China's economic reform.

In China, issues relating to agriculture, rural communities, and farmers are all consolidated as "tri-agrarian" issues to facilitate research by scholars and consideration by policymakers. Chen Xiwen writes Chapter 1 from the tri-agrarian perspective. This chapter presents a thorough review and summary of the formation of China's rural reform policy to keep readers abreast of the progress of reforming the basic agricultural management system, the distribution system for agricultural products, the unified urban and rural employment system, the rural taxation system, and the rural financial system. It also addresses the changes in rural social development, cooperative economic organization, and mechanisms for village governance. China's achievements in these areas can mainly be attributed to consistent efforts to: (1) safeguard the economic interests of farmers and respect their democratic rights; (2) measure the success of reform by the standards of whether agriculture has been developed, whether farmer income has increased, and whether the countryside remains stable; (3) respect the collective wisdom of farmers and their extensive experience at the grassroots level; (4) implement reform in urban and rural areas in a unified, coordinated, and guided manner; (5) accurately delineate governmental functions; (6) strengthen public services available to agriculture and the countryside; (7) increase the protection and reasonable utilization of natural resources needed for agricultural production; and (8) bolster social administration in rural areas. So long as China continues to uphold the above principles, we will be able to gradually establish and refine the rural and policy systems that can meet the challenge or any tri-agrarian issues that arise in the future.

Reform of the industrial sector started almost simultaneously with rural reform. China's thirty years of industrial reform has not only consisted of establishing and refining the socialist market system with unique Chinese characteristics, but has also been the largest-scale industrialization in human history. As a result of industrial reform, China's economy has gradually evolved into a "tripartite," consisting of state-owned enterprises, private enterprises, and foreign-invested enterprises. Opening to the outside world has advanced China's industrial reform, boosted the vitality of industry, and accelerated the pace of China's industry's development toward the international division-of-labor system. Chen Jiagui and Wang Qin have long been engaged in observing and analyzing China's industrial reform. Having gleaned experience from the remarkable accomplishments achieved by China in industrial reform and opening, in Chapter 2 they outline seven main characteristics of industrial reform: (1) reform has consistently been market-oriented; (2) China's industrial reform, opening, and development have been pushed forward by both state-owned and non-state-owned enterprises; (3) China's industrial reform has focused on rejuvenating enterprises; (4) China's industrial reform has proceeded by an incremental approach using pilot projects before making changes widespread; (5) the power of local governments has been fully leveraged in China's industrial reform and development; (6) China has synchronizing industrial economic reform with actual industrialization; and (7) China has pursued industrial reform and opening in an integrated way.

Cai Fang has long been engaged in research on the labor market. In Chapter 3, he presents a review of the process and features of urban and rural labor market development and conducts an examination of urban and rural employment expansion. Based on research and analysis, he casts doubt over the prevailing viewpoint that labor market development lags behind reform in other areas and that economic growth is not accompanied by employment growth. This chapter examines the effects of labor market development with respect to the changing landscape of rural labor distribution, reveals the fact that the surplus of rural labor has been shrinking, and argues that the Chinese economy will soon reach the Lewis point. And, by analyzing the reform of the employment system, Cai examines the relationship between reform of the labor market and expansion of employment throughout the reform process (including the stage of radical reform). He finds that diversified employment channels have taken shape and the labor market has become an important mechanism for allocating labor resources. Cai then summarizes the distinctive features of the labor market's transition and development. He holds that reform will expand employment by deploying multiple reform tools such as labor market transition, incremental adjustment, and stock adjustment; conducting simultaneous quantitative and price (wage) adjustment; simultaneously using "bottom-up" and "top-down" reform methods; and abolishing obsolete laws and regulations while enacting new ones. Based on the analysis of the reasoning and results of reform, he also identifies the key areas of future labor market reform.

Reform of the banking sector is an important part of China's transition from a planned to market economy. Unraveling the logic behind banking sector reform is of great significance to demystifying China's whole economic transition. Yi Gang is a renowned financial expert working at the People's Bank of China. In Chapter 4, he presents a review of the thirty years of market-oriented reform in China's banking sector and summarizes the reason of reform by referencing features of the market economy (*i.e.* clearly defined property rights, separation of government and business, state governance under the rule of law, economic incentives, and social supervision) as the frame of reference. The process of reform has been a journey from one institution to many, from only the People's Bank of China, to the formation of the Industrial and Commercial Bank of China, the Agricultural Bank of China, the Bank of China, and the China Construction Bank, as well as ten other shareholding banks; it has also seen the emergence of independent legal entities such as urban commercial banks and rural credit cooperatives, as well as the gradual entry of foreign-funded banks after the financial sector was opened to foreign investors. In this process, the People's Bank of China removed itself from the securities and insurance industries that had previously been under its jurisdiction. The China Securities Regulatory Commission and China Insurance Regulatory Commission were established in 1992 and 1998 respectively to take over the regulatory functions for these sectors. The author shows that during this one-to-many process, the characteristics of the market economic have gradually become very pronounced. At the same time, the author points out the unfinished tasks and challenges facing China's banking sector reform and development.

The core of China's multi-faceted transition is governmental transition. This transition has been one of gradually boosting reason, cooperation, and power-sharing in the relationship between government and society, developing a specifically Chinese model for societal transition and development. Hu Angang has closely observed the transformation of China's government as well as the construction of public finance for a long time. In Chapter 5, he presents an in-depth analysis of the transformation of the government's development objectives as well as the government's functionality, decision-making mechanisms, financial system, and the public revenue and expenditure systems. Based on analysis of the changes in the objectives of the development strategy set in the five-year plans between 1981 and 2010, the author points out the transition from the national decision-making system to the public decision-making system, a change that is apparent in transition of the focus of government evaluation from economic development indicators to public service indicators. Meanwhile, he also examines the historical path and reasons behind the change from an omnipotent nationalistic government into a national-development-(economic construction) oriented government and then to a public-service-oriented government. He also analyzes the changing style of government financial revenue and expenditure, examining how state finance is changed into public finance based on patterns of fiscal revenue, fiscal expenditure, and fiscal transfer payment. In addition, he identifies the future development trends going forward.

Chapter 5 is coauthored by Justin Lin and Wang Yan, who are World Bank experts currently dedicated to promoting learning between countries belonging to the so-called "Global South" and transferring the experiences and lessons of reform from China and other fast-growing countries to developing countries. In their work, they maintain that development is a process replete with uncertainty and dependent on the unique natural, political, cultural and historical background of every country. Given such uncertainty and uniqueness, development is naturally a process of learning, selective adaptation, and industrial upgrading. This chapter summarizes the experiences and lessons from China's reform and opening process, and examines the fundamental reasons behind China's success in trade expansion and economic growth. It shows how China started with homegrown, second-rate institutions, and has embarked on a long journey of reform, experimentation, and learning through experience. During the process, it has shifted its development strategy from a "comparative advantage-defying strategy" to a "comparative advantage-following strategy." China has been rapidly catching up with advanced countries by accumulating factor endowments and upgrading industries, and by some measures has already achieved partial success. Despite enormous challenges such as more unequal income distribution, excessively capital-intensive and energy-intensive industrial structure, and environmental deterioration, China is much better positioned to solve these problems today than it was thirty years ago. This chapter presents a review of the driving forces behind China's own learning and trade integration processes, and attempts to provide experiences and lessons for developing countries with diverse types of factor endowments.

Since the launch of reform and opening, China has sustained rapid economic growth for three decades under a growth model characterized by resource spending sprees and export-driven growth. With the passage of time, China has encountered a plethora of issues such as resource bottlenecking, environmental deterioration, internal and external macroeconomic imbalance, and the accumulation of risk in the financial system. Changing this model for economic growth has become one of the focal points in China's economic policy. Wu Jinglian has long been engaged in research on such topics and has loudly appealed to the public through various media outlets. Chapter 7 is coauthored by Wu Jinglian and Fan Shitao. This chapter presents an in-depth analysis of the zigzag evolution of China's growth model from the time when the pattern changed (upon the advent of economic restructuring), to the time when problems once again intensified, to the time when export-oriented policy was enacted only to be followed by a period of worsening performance. They argue that China's economic growth model has changed since the reform and opening policy was launched, but that this change is not stable because the grown pattern dependent on factor (particularly capital) investment has not fundamentally changed the Chinese economy. The crux of the issue is that reform has not done what is needed to firmly establish the market economic system. Under the existing system, the market for production factors has not been sufficiently developed, commodity and production factor prices are still distorted, rent-seeking behavior has become rampant; and economic entities lack incentive to participate in the innovation process. To resolve these issues, the authors recommend further improving the market economic system by: deploying policies beyond those used to achieve the so-called "East Asia miracle"; changing the export-oriented strategy and policy; reducing government intervention characterized by industrial policy and administrative guidance; allowing factor prices to adjust to their natural levels; developing the factors market; deregulating market access; restructuring the foreign exchange formation system; employing aggregate quantity tools to maintain economic stability; and motivating economic entities to proactively participate in transforming China's growth model by investing in creativity and factor productivity.

One notable phenomenon during China's reform and opening process has been the increasing income disparity, which has widened when measured by any means. This is thought to have already begun to negatively influence the societal results of reform. Li Shi is an expert specializing in income distribution issues. In Chapter 8, he provides a brief description of the relationship between China's economic growth and income distribution and provides a detailed explanation of some features of income disparity change using Kuznets curve, famously put forward by Simon Kuznets. The result of his analysis, though, shows that there is not enough evidence to show that the Kuznets' is an accurate depiction of China, implying that China's income distribution change has its own characteristics. In addition, he also explores multiple dimensions of the factors affecting China's income disparity, including economic development, economic transition, and government policy. This chapter also presents an empirical analysis of income disparity by deconstructing income disparity into rural income disparity, urban income disparity, and urban-rural income disparity. This analysis sheds further light on the nature and characteristics of income disparity. Finally, the author shows that, in spite of the difference of opinion among scholars on the changing trends of income distribution, most policy suggestions in this area have the support of a majority of scholars.

Zhang Linxiu has long focused on rural reform development from the perspective of gender. In Chapter 9, she examines the relationship between the development of the rural labor market and women's participation in the work force. In particular, she observes the reform process and its results from the perspective of gender. This chapter examines rural women's non-farm employment rate and income, assesses how women's participation in the agricultural sector impacts efficiency, and in looks at whether women have benefited from their participation during the thirty years of reform. Her conclusion is that the role of women in the labor force has changed dramatically along with the development of the rural labor market. For example, the female employment rate has grown faster than the male employment rate; among the young labor force, the employment rate is almost equal between males and females. The reason for such change is a decrease in manager's gender preference and women's competition in a free labor market, all of which has provided women with more employment opportunities. In addition, the number of female-specific jobs has increased along with the development of certain industries and the division of labor. Through this process, women's non-farm income has increased and their status has risen, thus they have made gains. At the same time, there is no evidence indicating that the changing labor market has enabled women to play a special role in agriculture. That is, no feminization trends have been noticed in the agricultural sector. Women still assume some role in agriculture, but their employment ratio in this sector has not increased. In addition, this chapter also reviews the evolution of the labor market and shows the structural change of China's economy from agriculture-based to non-agriculture-based. Last but not least, the author reveals a series of gender-related issues that have appeared in the rural labor market as an increasing number of people travel from rural to urban areas for better paying jobs.

Bibliography

Bloom, David, and Jeffrey Williamson. "Demographic Transition and Economic Miracles in Emerging Asia." *NBER Working Paper Series*, Working Paper no. 6268 (1997).

Brandt, Loren, and Thomas G. Rawski, eds. *China's Great Economic Transformation*. Cambridge University Press, 2008.

Cai Fang 蔡昉. "The Roles of Chinese Economists in the Economic Reform." In *Contemporary Economic Issues: Proceedings of the Eleventh World Congress of the International Economic Association, Tunis, Volume 1, Regional Experiences and System Reform*, edited by Justin Yifu Lin 林毅夫, Macmillan/St. Martin in association with International Economic Association, 1998.

——. *Liuyisi zhuanzhedian—Zhongguo Jingji Fazhan Xinjieduan* 刘易斯转折点—中国经济发展新阶段 [*The Lewis Point—The New Step of China's Economic Development*]. Beijing: Social Sciences Academic Press, 2008.

Cai Fang 蔡昉, Wang Dewen 王德文 and Du Yang 都阳. *Zhongguo nongcun gaige yu bianqian—30 nian lichen he yingyan fenxi* 中国农村改革与变迁—30 年历程和经验分析 [*Reform and Change in Rural China—Analysis of the Experiences of 30 Years*]. Shanghai: Truth and Wisdom Press, People's Press, 2008.

de Melo, Martha, Cevdet Denizer, Alan Gelb, and Stoyan Tenev. *Circumstance and Choice: the Role of Initial Conditions and Policies in Transition Economies.* The World Bank and International Finance Corporation, October 1997.

Hope, Nicholas C., Dennis Tao Yang and Mu Yang Li (eds.). *How Far Across the River: Chinese Policy Reform at the Millennium.* Stanford, Calif.: Stanford University Press, 2003.

Huang, Jikun, Otsuka, Keijiro, and Rozelle, Scott. "The Role of Agriculture in China's Development," In *China's Great Economic Transformation*, edited by Loren Brandt and Thomas Rawski. Cambridge University Press, 2008.

Johnson, D. Gale. *Zhongguo nengfou tongguo zainongcun chuangzao feinonggongzuo zhiwei lai zhuanyi dabufen nongye laodongli* 中国能否通过在农村创造非农工作职位来转移大部分农业劳动力 [*By Creating Non-agricultural Work, Can China Change Labor in the Countryside*], (Trans. into Chinese by Justin Lin Yifu 林毅夫). Beijing: The Commercial Press, 2004.

Krugman, Paul. "The Myth of Asia's Miracle." *Foreign Affairs*, November/December (1994).

Lewis, W.A. "Economic Development with Unlimited Supplies of Labor." *The Manchester School of Economic and Social Studies* no. 22 (1954): 139–191.

Lin, Justin Yifu 林毅夫, Cai Fang 蔡昉 and Li Zhou 李周. *Zhongguo de qiji: fazhan zhanlüe yu jingji gaige (zengdingban)* 中国的奇迹：发展战略与经济改革 (增订版) [*China's Miracle: Development Strategy and Economic Reform (Revised Edition)*]. Shanghai: People's Press, 1999.

Lindbeck, Assar. "Economic—social Interaction in China." *Economics of Transition* 16, no. 1 (2008): 113–139.

Lipton, David and J. Sachs. "Privatization in Eastern Europe: The Case of Poland." *Brookings Papers on Economic Activities* no. 2 (1990): 293–341.

McMillan, John. "Impact of Modern Economic Theory on Policy and Empirical Research." *AEA Papers and Proceedings*, May 2003.

Oi, Jean C. "Local State Corporatism." In *Rural China Takes Off: Institutional Foundations of Economic Reform*, edited by Jean C. Oi. Berkeley, Calif.: University of California Press, 1999.

Ranis, Gustav. "Arthur Lewis' Contribution to Development Thinking and Policy." *Yale University Economic Growth Center Discussion Paper* no. 891 (August 2004).

Ravallion, Martin and Shaohua Chen. "When Economic Reform is Faster Than Statistical Reform: Measuring and Explaining Income Inequality in Rural China." *Oxford Bulletin of Economics and Statistics* no. 61(1) (1999): 33–56.

Rawski, Thomas G. "What's Happening to China's GDP Statistics?" *China Economic Review* no. 12(4) (2001): 298–302.

Roland, Gérard. "The Political Economy of Transition." *Journal of Economic Perspectives* no. 16(1) (2002): 29–50.

Sachs, Jeffrey. "Lessons for Brazil from China's Success." Speech transcript, São Paulo, November 5, 2003.

Spence, A. Michael. "Zhongguo gaigekaifang de chenggong jingyan he xintiaozhan 中国改革开放的成功经验和新挑战 [The Successes and Future Challenges of China's Reform and Opening]" (Chinese Translation). *Bijiao* 比较 [*Comparisons*] Vol. 38 (2008).

Stiglitz, Joseph. "More Instruments and Broader Goals: Moving Toward the Post-Washington Consensus." The 1998 WIDER annual lecture, January 7, 1998.

——. "The Post Washington Consensus Consensus" (Chinese translation). In *Zhongguo yu quanqiuhua: huashengdun gongshi haishi beijing gongshi* 中国与全球化：华盛顿共识还是北京共识 [*China and Globalization: the Washington Consensus or the Beijing Consensus*]. Beijing: Social Sciences Academic Press, 2005.

Walder, Andrew. "Local Governments as Industrial Firms." *American Journal of Sociology* no. 101(2) (1995): 263–301.

Wu Jinglian 吴敬琏. *Zhongguo zengzhang moshi jueze* 中国增长模式抉择 [Selecting China's Growth Model]. Shanghai: Far East Press, 2005.

Williamson, Jeffrey. "Growth, Distribution and Demography: Some Lessons from History." *NBER Working Paper Series*, Working Paper No. 6244 (1997).

Yao Yang 姚洋. *Zuowei zhidu chuangxin guocheng de jingji gaige* 作为制度创新过程的经济改革 [*Economic Reform, a Process of Institutional Creativity*]. Shanghai: Truth and Wisdom Press, People's Press, 2008.

Zhang Shuguang 张曙光. "Zhongguo jingjixue yanjiu 30nian: fansi yu pinglun 中国经济学研究 30 年：反思与评论 [30 Years of Economics Research in China: a Review and Commentary]." In *Zhongguo renwen shehui kexue sanshinian: huigu yu qianzhan* 中国人文社会科学三十年：回顾与前瞻 [*Thirty Years of Social Sciences in China: Taking Account and Looking Forward*]. Fudan University Press, 2008.

ACKNOWLEDGEMENTS

The year 2008 marks the thirtieth anniversary of the implementation of the reform and opening policy in China. This book is a collection of papers written by Chinese economists examining the major features and processes of this reform. As editor of this book, I am greatly indebted those who contributed to its completion. Because most of them are not only researchers but also senior advisors to the decision-makers in China, the authors—whose names are actually familiar to experts even outside China—are most qualified to review the progress of reform. The English version of the book will therefore be extremely useful for English language readers interested in understanding China's reform process. More importantly, since China is both a developing and transitional country, its successful reform and resulting economic growth might provide lessons for other developing and transitional countries.

Because this book features work by a collection of authors, the opinions expressed and style of each chapter are not necessarily the same. Nonetheless, I hope that together all the chapters can provide a comprehensive picture of the process of Chinese reform and its future prospects. As China further integrates into the global economy, most observers would agree that China's economic growth in next decade will substantially reshape the structure of the world economy. Thorough understanding the past thirty years of reform and development allows greater insight into the future.

Professor Andrew Watson, former representative of Ford Foundation's Beijing Office, was the to propose the idea of assembling this book and provided financial support for the publication of the Chinese version. His successor, Professor John Fitzgerald, has continued to support the publication process. Mr Xie Shouguang, the President of Social Sciences Academic Press (SSAP) has provided constant encouragement through the editing process, providing support during the most frustrating times. I am also grateful to Ms Guo Rongrong and Qiu Yang at SSAP, Matt Kawecki at Brill, and many colleagues at the Institute of Population and Labor Economics at the Chinese Academy of Social Sciences, which I work for. Any remaining errors are my responsibility alone.

Cai Fang
December 17, 2009
Beijing

LIST OF CONTRIBUTORS

Throughout this volume, Chinese names are always ordered according to standard practice in China, with surnames preceding given names. To clarify this ordering, surnames are in small capital letters in the following list of contributors.

Cai Fang, Ph.D. in Economics, is from Pingxiang of Jiangxi Province. He graduated from Renmin University and from the Graduate School of the Chinese Academy of Social Sciences. He is currently a member of the Standing Committee of National People's Congress and the director of the Institute of Population and Labor Economics at the Chinese Academy of Social Sciences. He is the author of "The Economics of Poverty" and "Scientific Development and Sustainable Growth," as well as the co-author of "The China Miracle," "The Chinese Economy," and "The Transformation and Growth of the Chinese Labor Market." He is also the chief editor of the report series "Chinese Population and Labor Issues." He received the second annual Zhang Peigang Prize for Outstanding Achievement in Development Economics and was named as one of the "Top 100 People in Chinese Development" in its fourth listing.

Chen Xiwen is from Danyang in Jiangsu Province. He graduated from the Department of Agricultural Economics at Renmin University in Beijing. Currently, he is Deputy Director of the Central Finance Leading Group, Director of the Central Rural Work Leading Group, Deputy Director of the Economic Committee of the Chinese People's Political Consultative Conference (CPPCC) National Committee, and a professor at China Agricultural University. He recieved the Sun Yefang Prize for Economics for three consecutive years. He has also been honored with the third annual National Prize for Progress in Science and Technology and was named as one of the "Top 100 People in Chinese Development" in its fourth listing.

Chen Jiagui is from Yuechi County of Sichuan Province. He attended Renmin University in Beijing and the Graduate School of the Chinese Academy of Social Sciences, where he received his master's and doctoral degrees. Currently, he is a member of the Standing Committee of National People's Congress and Vice-president of Chinese Academy of Social Sciences, where he is also a member and the Director of the School of Economics; he is also a doctoral student advisor. He holds concurrent posts as President of the Chinese Enterprise Management Research Association, Vice-chairman of the Economic and Social Council (ECOSOC), Vice-chairman of China Federation of Industrial Economics (CFIE), and member of the Assessment Group of the State Council's Academic Degrees Committee. He has many years of research experience in areas such as industrial economics and business management.

WANG Qin is from Nanyang of Henan Province. He is a doctor of management science as well as a associate research fellow and research director at the Business Administration Research Division of the Institute of Industrial Economics at the Chinese Academy of Social Sciences. In 2001–2002, he studied as a foreign student at Tilburg University in Holland. He is the author of more than sixty academic articles, published in periodicals such as *Chinese Industrial Economy* and *Reform*, and two books. His work received the third annual prize from the Jiang Yiwei Academic Fund for Enterprise Reform and Development. His research interests include competitive analysis, strategic management, and management innovation.

YI Gang received his doctoral degree in economics from the University of Illinois in 1986. He formerly held positions as Deputy Director and a professor at the China Center for Economic Research at Peking University. Currently, he is Vice President of the People's Bank of China. His research interests include econometrics, monetary economics and banking, and international finance. His more than twenty papers have been published in a variety of international academic periodicals and eleven have been compiled as part of the *Journal of Economic Literature*, available for electronic search.

HU Angang is Director of the Tsinghua University Research Center for Contemporary China (RCCC) of the Chinese Academy of Sciences and professor and doctoral student advisor at the School of Public Management at Tsinghua University. In 1991, he was awarded as a "Chinese Doctoral Scholar with Outstanding Contributions" by the State Education Commission and the Academic Degrees Committee of the State Council. His work also received the ninth annual Sun Yefang Award for Papers on Economics. As of April 2008, he had already contributed to fifty-five academic works regarding contemporary China and its development (including fourteen Chinese-language works, fifteen as a co-author, nine as chief editor, seven as an editor, six in English, and four in Japanese). Since 1999, he has had a total of 124 works included in the Chinese Social Sciences Citation Index (CSSCI) and been cited in a total of 1,696 different instances (excluding self-citation), the most within China's human and social sciences.

Justin Yifu Lin received his doctoral degree in economics from the University of Chicago in 1986. At present, he concurrently serves as the World Bank's Chief Economist and the Senior Vice President in charge of development economics. He formerly served as the Director of the China Center for Economic Research (CCER) at Peking University, where he also served as a professor and doctoral student advisor. He served as a member of the CPPCC National Committee during its seventh, eighth, ninth, and tenth sessions and as the Vice Chairman of CPPCC Economic Committee. Currently, he serves as a member of the National People's Congress and as Vice-chairman of the All-China Federation of Industry and Commerce (ACFIC). In 2005, he was selected as academician of the academy of sciences of the developing world (TWAS). His research interests include development economics, agricultural economics, and institutional economics.

Wang Yan received her doctoral degree in economics from Cornell University in 1989. She is currently a senior economist and project manager at the World Bank. At the associated World Bank Institute, she is in charge of several research and capacity training projects in such areas as quality of growth, financial risk management, and international trade. She is the recipient of several awards, including the Sun Yefang Prize for Economics, and author of a broad range of academic work.

Wu Jinglian graduated from the Department of Economics of Shanghai's Fudan University in 1954. At present, he concurrently serves as a researcher at the State Council's Development Research Center, the Vice-chair of the Advisory Committee for National Informatization, the Baogang Chair Professor of Economics at the China Europe International Business School (CEIB), and professor at the Chinese

Academy of Social Sciences and Peking University. He is chief editor of *Comparisons* and the *Journal of Economic Studies*, committee member of the Fifty-person China Economic Forum, and a consultant for the International Economic Association. He has received the Sun Yefang Prize for Economics five times; in 2003, he was awarded the "Award for Outstanding Achievements" from the International Management Institute (IMI); in 2005 he was honored with the first "Award for Outstanding Contributions to Chinese Economics;" he has been granted honorary degrees from both Hong Kong Baptist University and the University of Hong Kong.

Fan Shitao studied at the Department of Economics of Renmin University from 1994 to 1997 and graduated from the Department of Agricultural Economic Management at Nanjing Agricultural University in 2001. Afterwards, he held a post at the China Center for Information Industry Development (CCID). In 2006–2007, he served as the Deputy Director of the Institute of Industrial Policy Research, and at the end of 2007 transferred to the State Council Informatization Office. In July, 2008, he moved again to the Department of Informatization at the Ministry of Industry and Information Technology. He has participated in researching and formulating China's informatization development strategy and electronic signature law. He has authored over twenty academic articles, including "Informatization, Structural Change, and Economic Growth," and has worked on the translation of such books as *The Silicon Valley Edge, Design Rules*, and *Wealth, Poverty, and Politics*.

Li Shi is from Bo'xing of Shandong Province. He received his master's degree from the Department of Economics at Peking University in 1984. Currently, he concurrently serves as a professor at Beijing Normal University, Director of the Income Distribution and Poverty Research Center, researcher for the German Institute for the Study of Labor (IZA), adjunct professor in the department of economics at Zhejiang University, member of the Academic Committee of the Unirule Institute of Economics, researcher for the Center for Human and Economic Development Studies at Peking University, and project expert for the World Bank, the Asian Development Bank, the United Nations Trade and Development Board, and the National Development and Reform Commission. He has served as the manager of major projects of the National Social Sciences Foundation, the State Natural Sciences

Foundation, and the Chinese Academy of Social Sciences, many general projects, and many projects financed by overseas foundations. He has worked as chief editor for the publication of eight works in both Chinese and English and published more than fifty academic papers at home and abroad.

ZHANG Linxiu received her doctoral degree in agricultural economics from the University of Reading in the United Kingdom. She is currently the deputy director, researcher, and doctoral student advisor of the Center for Agricultural Policy Studies at the Chinese Academy of Sciences. She has been engaged in research on agricultural economics for many years. She has published many academic articles in both international and domestic publications, of which more than twenty have been included in the Science Citation Index (SCI) or Social Sciences Citation Index (SSCI). In 2003, she received a prize for outstanding work by young scholars issued by the Natural Science Foundation of China (NSFC) and in 2007 was awarded as part of the "Hundred People Plan." She serves as a policy assessor and council member of many international agencies, including the United Nations, the World Bank, and the Consultative Group on International Agricultural Research (CGIAR).

CHAPTER ONE

FORMATION OF CHINA'S RURAL REFORM POLICY

Chen Xiwen

China's reform began in rural areas. At the Third Plenary Session of the Eleventh CCP Central Committee in 1978, the central government made the historical decision to launch the reform and opening campaign. Languishing at the bottom rung of the social ladder, rural residents were naturally unable to understand the profound changes happening politically. Nevertheless, they could still feel the change in the relatively relaxed social environment two years after the end of the brutal Cultural Revolution. In some areas, farmers began to retool the people's commune system by fixing farm output quotas for each household. Because of China's vast rural acreage and the scattered residences of farmers nationwide, rural reform in China took place quietly, without being noticed by urban residents.

Since the beginning of this reform thirty years ago, China has achieved substantial breakthroughs in critical areas of rural reform. In order to speed up the refinement of rural institutions and mechanisms to be fully compliant with the requirements of the socialist market economy, a thorough review of the thirty years of rural reform and the its key policies was necessary. At the Third Plenary Session of the Seventeenth Central Committee, which ended in October 2008, policymakers presented an executive summary of the thirty years of achievements in rural reform and development with a view to lay out the tasks of rural reform and development for the next twelve years. In light of the thoroughness of this executive summary, this chapter merely attempts to provide a narrative description of the formulation of key policies enacted during the thirty years of rural reform and development. Before beginning this narrative, there are two caveats worth noting: first, key reform policies concerning rural development were not necessarily formulated in chronological order but were criss-crossed and applied an interactive way; second, each reform policy fell far short of reaching its ideal state and China must continue to deepen reform and refine institutions and mechanisms.

The *Draft Decisions of the Central Committee on Speeding up Agricultural Development* (中共中央关于加快农业发展的决定(草案)) was approved at the Third Plenary Session of the Eleventh Central Committee, held December 18–22, 1978. The decision was the prelude to the central government launching rural reform and enacting new rural policy. The rural reform policies enacted in the ensuing thirty years can be summarized in the following respects.

I. *Changes to the Rural Economic System and Governance Structure*

A. *Basic Rural Management Systems Based on Household Contract Management*

Farmers are always key participants in the development of agricultural and rural areas. Whether their enthusiasm, initiative, and creativity can be fully mobilized in rural development and production has a direct bearing on the development process. Whether their interests can be recognized and protected dictates whether their strength can be mobilized. From the 1950s to the dawn of the reform and opening, China's agricultural management system focused on exploring how to arouse the farmers' enthusiasm for production. But the efforts during this era failed to do so due to the fact that even exploratory efforts were constrained by the premise of not changing the system of people's communes.

In the autumn of 1978, eighteen farmers from Xiaogang village in Fengyang County, Anhui province, ventured to contract out the production team's land using a contract system that fixed a plot of land for each household. This was an important event because it went beyond the popular reform model of output quotas for each household. Fixing output quotas was similar to fixing plots of land for each household in the sense that, under both systems, the agricultural production process was contracted to rural households. However, there were also fundamental differences. The system of fixing output quotas for each household took the form of a contract between the production team and the household, under which collective land was contracted to rural households and the annual output quota for each household was determined based on the size of land contracted; each household turned over all the agricultural products it produced to the collective; for fulfilling the output quota, the household would receive a specific amount of remuneration for their allocated by the collective under contractual terms; in the event of exceeding the output quota, the household would receive a specific proportion of output as specified in the contract; in the event of failing to fulfill the output quota, the collective would reduce the amount of remuneration allocated to the rural household. It is clear that, in fixing the output quotas for each household, the subject matter of household contract was the output of land but the right to products produced on the land still rested with the collective. Therefore, fixing farm output quotas for each household did not change the fundamental role of the collective as the management and distribution entity. However, compared with the previous system of work being evaluated and points being allotted by the collective, the output quota system was more in conformity with the principle of income being linked to work. Therefore, the full name of the "fixing farm output quotas for each household" system is the "production responsibility system with remuneration linked to output after contracting collective land to each household."

Contracting out land to each household (as opposed to setting quotas) was quite a different story. After collective land had been contracted to each household, the system required farmers to "turn over the required amount of output to the state, contribute a sufficient amount of output to the collective, and take what remains for their own disposal." In "fixing a plot of land for each household," the collective no longer assumed the role of overall manager and distributor. Instead, the collective only collected "retention money or accumulation funds," which collected based on the size of the contracted land plot and were used to fund the collective's internal management and provide public services. As a result, in the entire agricultural production process, rural households became autonomous entities that made their own management decisions and assumed full responsibility for their profits and losses.

The differences between these two systems cannot be ignored. Had rural reform continued to operate within the confines of "fixing output quotas for each household," the people's commune system might have persisted for years more. Fortunately, the "output quotas" reform model was not implemented for long. As a matter of fact, it had not yet been introduced to many regions before it was replaced by the "contracted plot of land" model. At that time, there was fierce debate regarding the strengths and weaknesses of these two reform models. One viewpoint held that "fixing output quotas for each household" was a production responsibility system for the collective economic organization but that "fixing a plot of land for each household" was not. In truth, it was virtually impossible to pinpoint what the debate was truly about. On May 31, 1980, Deng Xiaoping delivered a keynote speech regarding rural policy issues, reaffirming his firm support for both reform models. In regard to this, he stated, "Generally speaking, the crux of the problem in rural work is that the emancipation of minds has not been completely achieved among our cadres." As a result, farmers did not meet with much resistance when they continued to go ahead with the simpler system of contracting land instead of fixing output quotas.

In hindsight, one may understand that the rapid replacement of output quotas by fixed plots of land took place in part because of an oversimplified understanding of the differences between the models of reform at the time. It was not until 1999 that the Constitution was amended, making the difference more clear. The Constitution's former phrasing, "The state shall improve the two-level operation system of the household contract responsibility system supplemented by unified management, based on household contract management," was replaced with, "The state shall stabilize the rural responsibility system, the main form of which is the household output-related contract responsibility system; and improve the two-level operation system of the household contract responsibility system supplemented by unified management." The land contracting system was not a simple operation and certainly was not as easy as the output system to administer and track. But it was nonetheless preferred, chiefly for the following points:

First, as mentioned earlier, it was "fixing a plot of land" rather than "fixing output quotas" that enabled rural households to become independent operating entities. And it was only when rural households became independent business entities and production teams were no longer directly involved in the management of agricultural that the people's commune system could be abolished.

Second, it became possible for rural households to gradually accumulate their own productive assets only after they had become independent business entities (and after they produced enough for personal consumption). Thus, the system was a major breakthrough of decisive significance for both urban and rural laborers, who under the planned economy could only acquire means of consumption. Thus, under the system of contracting collective land, rural households acquired the right to accumulate their own assets, which widened the scope of rural reform from its original intentions, of reforming the business management system, to reforming the entire system rural property relations.

Third, when agricultural production was contracted to households, production teams no longer managed or scheduled work in a unified way, thus rural labor became emancipated. When this newly-freed labor force was combined with the accumulated assets of rural households, rural areas began to experience a dramatic change and far-reaching transition of ownership structure, industrial structure, employment structure, and income structure. As the supply of agricultural products rapidly increased, township enterprises suddenly emerged; self-employed farmers and private businesses sprang up "like mushrooms after the rain;" migrant rural laborers gathered in cities like a raging storm. Contracting land to households thus sparked the fire of rural economic transition, giving rise to a plethora of rural micro-business entities. It is therefore no exaggeration to say that the "fixing plots of land" system played an enzyme-like role in laying the foundations to the socialist market economy, featuring the simultaneous development of enterprises with different forms of ownership, with public ownership playing a dominant role.

By the end of 1983 China had—on the basis of not changing the collective ownership system—essentially implemented the household contract management as the basic organizational system for rural business operation. From then on, household operation became the main form of agricultural production in China. This greatly aroused the productive enthusiasm of hundreds of millions of rural residents and spurned an extraordinary growth in agricultural production. Grain output surged from 305 million metric tons in 1978 to 407 million metric tons in 1984.

After the contract management system was universally adopted in rural areas, the central government began to consider how to stabilize this system. The CCP Central Committee's 1984 "No. 1 Document" (一号文件)[1] stated that "the land contract shall, in general, be for a period of fifteen years or more." This eliminated farmers' doubts concerning the stability of the system. After this stability was ensured, the rural household contract management system advanced steadily

[1] "No. 1" documents are released by the Central Committee. Their content relates to issues concerning farmers, agriculture, or rural areas.

and stably. The *Notice on the Central Committee and the State Council on 1991 Agricultural and Rural Work*[2] (中共中央、国务院关于一九九一年农业和农村工作的通知) expressly stated that "this management system boasts extensive adaptability and strong vitality; it shall be maintained as a basic organizational system in rural areas for a long time and improved on a continuous basis." This was the first time it was expressly stated in a central government document that the household contract management system would exist on a long-term basis.

The system progressed into the 1990s, and the fifteen-year contract period approached its expiration. To solidify the complete implementation of the household contract management system and stabilize the contracted land relationships, the government released the *Policy Measures of the CCP Central Committee and the State Council Concerning Agricultural and Rural Economic Development*[3] (中共中央、国务院关于当前农业和农村经济发展的若干政策措施) which called for "extending the contracts for arable land for another thirty years after the original term expires." The *Opinions of the Central Committee and the State Council Concerning the 1998 Agricultural and Rural Work*[4] (中共中央、国务院关于 1998 年农业和农村工作的意见) further emphasized "unconditionally extending the land contract for another thirty years in areas where the first-round contract term is set to expire." In the summer of 1998, Jiang Zemin, then-secretary general of the Party Central Committee, visited Xiaogang village in Fengyang County, Anhui province. During his visit, Jiang Zemin reaffirmed the message sent by earlier government documents, "The central government is sure on its position regarding the land contract policy; this is policy is that the system will not change for thirty years. Even after thirty years, the central government sees no reason to change this policy." In the fall of 1998, the Third Plenary Session of the Fifteenth CCP Central Committee was held, where participants approved the *Decisions of the CCP Central Committee on Several Key Issues Concerning Agricultural and Rural Work* (中共中央关于农业和农村工作若干重大问题的决定). This modified the wording of previous policy statements regarding the rural management system, changing the "focused on the household contract responsibility system," which was based on the output quota contract system,

---

[2] *Zhong Fa* 中发 No. 18 (1990).
[3] *Zhong Fa* 中发 No. 11 (1993).
[4] *Zhong Fa* 中发 No. 2 (1998).

to "based on household contract management," which reflected the autonomy of the new system. In addition, the document reiterated that it was "imperative to adhere to the household contract management on a long-term basis."

By the end of 2000, land contracts had been solidified for another thirty years in 93 percent of village organizations nationwide. On August 29, 2002, the *Law of the People's Republic of China on Land Contract in Rural Areas* (中华人民共和国农村土地承包法) was ratified at the Twenty-ninth Meeting of the Standing Committee of the Ninth National People's Congress, codifying the household contract management system. From then on, there was a legal basis for safeguarding the land contract management system. By the end of 2005, 98.7 percent of village organizations had extended the contracts for another thirty years and over 80 percent of rural households had obtained land contract management certificates.

The *Decisions of the CCP Central Committee on Several Key Issues Relating to Pushing forward Rural Reform and Development* (中共中央关于推进农村改革发展若干重大问题的决定) was approved at the Third Plenary Session of the Seventeenth CCP Central Committee on October 12, 2008. This ruling dramatically advanced the stability of the basic management system and imposed the clear requirement that "the household contract management system is adapted to the socialist market economy, conforms to the characteristics of agricultural production, and forms the bedrock of the Party's rural policy. This system shall be unwaveringly upheld to endow farmers with more sufficient and assured rights to land contract management and the existing land contract relationship shall be kept stable and unchanged on a long-term basis." This further demonstrated the resolve of the central government to stabilize the system in rural areas.

B. *The Development of Farmers' Cooperative Economic Organizations*

Chinese farmers are one of the best organized workforces in the world. Upon the establishment of the people's commune system, all farmers belonged to the same collective economic organization. As part of this system, China also established rural credit cooperatives in all townships and villages across the country. To ensure adequate supply of means of production to rural areas and supply farmers with daily necessities, China also established cooperative supply and marketing organizations at all levels from the central government to down to people's communes. These three cooperative systems played a central role in ensuring orderly production as well as protecting the livelihood of farmers under the planned economy.

However, these three systems were clearly not conducive to the development of a market economy. After the people's commune system was abolished, the functions of the collective economic organizations were taken over by village committees. As a result, in most localities, the collective economy organizations have since become internally-oriented social management and service organizations; but in the process, the collective lost the ability to provide production-related services to farmers. The development of some communities' through use of joint-stock cooperatives over the past decade indicates that the development of the socialist market economy can perhaps only be ensured by allowing independent organizations to assume the economic functions of the old commune system.

Due to lack of clear separation between policy-oriented businesses and commercial businesses, ill-defined property rights, flawed governance structure, and low quality management, rural credit cooperatives have suffered from perennial losses and struggled to stay afloat. Thus enhancing the vitality of rural credit cooperatives and boosting their ability to provide agricultural and rural services has become an increasingly pressing policy issue. In spite of the substantial progress of reform around the time, rural credit cooperatives still shoulder heavy burdens and lack competitiveness. There is an urgent need for further reform.

Due to ill-defined property rights, an inflexible mechanisms, heavy staff burdens, and internal mismanagement, a significant portion of rural supply and marketing cooperatives were once on the verge of being eliminated by market forces. But after reform and systematic restructuring over the past decade or so, the cooperatives are basically out of difficulty at present. Currently, however, they still face the basic problem of how to adapt to the needs of reconstructing rural China as well as expanding their own space for continued survival and development.

After the economic functions of the community collective economic organizations were taken over by village committees, it became urgently necessary to develop an economic organization that specialized in providing services for agricultural production, particularly a cooperative economic organization that would enable farmers to serve themselves.

After implementing household contract management, the central government recognized the property rights of farmers, which greatly boosted their enthusiasm for production. However, in the areas of production and distribution, individual households still faced significant limitations. In the 1990s, the farmers took it upon themselves to organize a large number of their own cooperative organizations. But after entering the new millennium—along with the increasing speed and breadth of adjustments to the rural and agricultural economy—the need to provide the services of such cooperatives became more and more clear. In 2002, the Ministry of Agriculture selected 100 special cooperative organizations from across the country, six districts, and Zhejiang province to conduct trial operations. In 2003, the central government began to appropriate funds to support the training of the cooperatives. Meanwhile, they began to gain support through improvement of the policy and legal environment. The *Law of the People's Republic of China on Farmers' Specialized Cooperatives* (农民专业合作社法) was ratified at the Twenty-fourth Meeting of the Standing Committee of the Tenth National People's Congress on October 31, 2006. The law contained comprehensive description of the provisions for membership, organization, financial management, and policy support for farmers' specialized cooperatives. The cooperatives have since been granted legal person status. The *Opinions of the CCP Central Committee and the State Council on Proactively Developing Modern Agriculture and Concretely Pushing forward the Building of Socialist New Rural Areas* (中共中央国务院关于积极发展现代农业扎实推进社会主义新农村建设的若干意见)[5] called for "vigorously developing farmers' specialized cooperative organizations, meticulously implementing *The Law on Farmers' Specialized Cooperatives*, and supporting accelerated development of these cooperative organizations."

By the end of September 2008, China had 79,600 farmers' specialized cooperatives (including branches) that were registered as legal entities and received legal entity certificates. There were 32,300 cooperatives specialized in crop farming, accounting for 27.63 percent of the total, and 25,900 cooperatives specialized in livestock breeding, accounting for 22.51 percent of the total. Developing the cooperatives greatly remedied the functional deficiencies of community collectives and built a bridge for rural residents to enter the increasingly

[5] *Zhong Fa* 中发 No. 1 (2007).

globalized market. It was also indicative of the continuous improvement and sophistication of the rural market economy.

C. *Major Changes in Township and Village Governance Mechanisms*

After the agriculture cooperation movement, China continued to implement the people's commune system featuring the "integration of government administration with commune management" in rural areas until the 1980s. China's township and village governance structure has since undergone two stages of drastic changes.

1. *Stage One (1983–2005)*

In China, the people's commune system was established in the late 1950s; it was subsequently adjusted multiple times, but all without changing its basic characteristics. In regard to the management mechanism, the most salient feature of the people's commune system was the integration of government administration with commune management. The people's commune was in charge of everything from production, construction, finance, and marketing to civil administration, culture, and education, public security, and the armed forces. This system dovetailed neatly with the planned economy and played a fundamental role in supporting industrial development in urban areas and pushing industrialization forward throughout China. When China implemented the "contracting by plot of land" system for households nationwide, the traditional people's communes lost the basis for their existence. In October 1983, the CCP Central Committee and the State Council issued the *Notice on Separating Government Administration from Commune Management and Establishing Township Government* (关于实行政社分开建立乡政府的通知). According to the requirements of the Notice, under the leadership of township Party committees, the township governments became the lowest level of government, fulfilling various functions assigned by higher-level governments.

At the same time, the relationship between townships and villages was fundamentally changed. Under the requirement of separating government administration from commune management, production brigades were changed into the village committees. The *Notice on Separating Government Administration from Commune Management and Establishing Township Government* (关于实行政社分开建立乡政府的通知) stated that "the village committee is a self-governed community organization at the grassroots level and it shall be established in accordance with the villagers' residence status. The village committee shall actively handle affairs relating to the village's welfare and public business and assist the township People's Government in properly carrying out the village's administrative work, production work, and construction work." The 1984 "No. 1 Document" called for each rural area to "set up a regional cooperative economic organization based on the principle of public ownership of land" and stated that "the cooperative economic organization can be separate from the village committee or operated under a separate name yet with the same entity." The *Organization Law of Village Committees (Trial)* (村民委员会组织法(试行)) took effect in 1988. The law expressly stated that the village committee was an autonomous mass organization of villagers responsible for management, education, and service at the grassroots level. It established a systematic framework characterized by democratic elections, democratic decision-making, democratic management, and democratic supervision. After enacting the *Village Committee Organization Law* (村民委员会组织法) and amending it in 1998, the state began to focus on establishing and refining a dynamic mechanism under which villagers could govern themselves with leadership by the village Party committee; it also introduced the general election system for village committees and further strengthened the self-governing mechanisms in villages.

2. *Stage Two (2006–Present)*

In 2006, after years of trial reforms of the rural tax and fee system, China finally repealed its agricultural tax. The resulting budget shortfall for county and township governments and village organizations was subsidized by the central government through fiscal transfer payments. The repeal of the agricultural tax had an enormous impact on the governance structure of townships and villages.

First of all, the functions of township governments have been undergoing a transformation. Prior to the tax reform, collecting taxes was one of the major functions of township governments. In the time right after the reform, fiscal transfer payments from the central government were not able to fully compensate for the decrease in fiscal revenue resulting from the repeal of the taxes and fees. As a result, many townships suffered fiscal deficits. In addition, a large number of township employees all the sudden had nothing to do, which put township governments in an awkward position.

Second, township and village governments have become alienated. Prior to tax reform, most township cadres worked in villages to press them to fulfill production targets and collect taxes and fees.

After reform, the tax and fee were scrapped. Studies have characterized this transition as one from a 'blood-sucking' government to a 'suspended' government.

In addition, the internal governance structure of villages are also undergoing dramatic changes. Stripped of power to apportion charges among rural residents, the villages face difficulty raising money to fund internal public affairs such as education, health, roads, water conservancy, and public security. Since tax and fee reform, the "One case, one meeting" (一事一议) system has been difficult to maintain. More often than not, cases are discussed without reaching a solution or a solution is reached but cannot be implemented. Furthermore, the transfer payment funds from the central government barely reach villages at the lowest level. In consequence, rural areas have faced a severe fund shortage of public funds and public services.

In face of these new problems, China needs to address the most pressing issues first, identifying the root causes and formulating effective solutions. Policies regarding township and village governance must be enacted in accordance with actual situations in order to realize lasting social and political stability in rural areas.

The first and foremost problem relates to the transformation of township government functions. The Fifth National Congress of the Communist Party of China defined the government's functions as "economic control, market supervision, social management, and providing public services." However, this definition may not be applicable to township government. At the township level, the government rarely plays a role in economic control and an insignificant role in market supervision. At the same time, it plays a weak role in terms of public services and social management. Social management and providing public services should become the main functions of township governments. The township government level should not be abolished, but transformed to concentrate on rebuilding China's rural areas.

Second, China should properly sort out the relationship between village committees and economic organizations. The 1984 "No. 1 Document" set forth the requirement that "regional cooperative economic organizations shall be established based on the public ownership of land." In reality, however, the village committee has gradually replaced the cooperative economic organization at the village level. The committees have become grassroots rural organizations directly led by township governments with government administration integrated with commune management, thereby causing villagers to be economically attached to village committees. Looking at the real circumstances in rural China, it is clear that autonomous community organizations are absolutely necessary, but that these organizations are internally-oriented and administrative in nature. To develop the economy, however, farmers are also in urgent need of an externally-oriented economic organization capable of leading them to the marketplace. Thus, the *Law of the People's Republic of China on Farmers' Specialized Cooperatives* (农民专业合作社法) was enacted to vigorously develop farmers' specialized cooperatives and other economic organizations and to carry forward and enhance their economic functions. In areas where conditions permit, it is imperative to proactively explore specific ways to separate village committees from community collective economic organizations and delineate the duties and functions of different organizations in order to strengthen social management, increase access to public services in rural areas, and enable farmers' cooperative economic organization to develop in a productive way.

II. *Deepening of Reform of the Agricultural Product Distribution System*

According to the thinking behind China's rural reform, after the successful implementation of the household contract management system, the second step of reform is to reform the agricultural product distribution system and improve the agricultural product marketing system.

In 1953, China began to impose a state monopoly over the purchase and marketing of agricultural products. The first product put under state monopoly was cotton; the second was grain; and along with the increasingly large demand facing limited supply, more products were subsequently added to the list. In the early 1960s, there were 240 agricultural products put under state monopoly; in 1978, the number was over 170. Under this agricultural product distribution system, it was impossible for the market mechanism to play a role in allocating resources. And due to the severe constraints on production and development created by the people's commune system, agricultural products were in short supply. To ensure an urban supply, the central government had no alternative but to continue increasing the scope and quantity of agricultural products purchased and marketed by the state. However, this further stifled farmers' enthusiasm for production. The unfortunate result of this was that China got stuck in a vicious cycle of state control leading to shortage, then shortage leading to stiffer state control.

Breaking the vicious cycle required increasing supply. At the Third Plenary Session of the Eleventh CCP Central Committee held in 1978, policymakers decided to raise the purchase prices of 18 agricultural and sideline products such as grain, fuel, and cotton beginning in March 1979, while at the same time pushing forward reform of the agricultural management system. The average price increased 24.8 percent. Starting in the summer grain harvest in 1979, the state not only raised grain purchase prices at the basic level, but also decided to raise state purchase prices by another 50 percent for the excess amount over targets.

The price increase policy stimulated farmers' enthusiasm for production and significantly boosted the supply of agricultural products, thereby creating the conditions for relaxing controls over the agricultural product market. The *Minutes of Meeting on Rural Work* (全国农村工作会议纪要),[6] circulated by the CCP Central Committee, stated that, concerning products whose production exceeded targets, some amount or percentage of the excess would still be purchased by the state, while the remaining amount would be handled by the commune, brigade, and farmer at their own discretion. The purchase prices for the excess amount of products over targets were allowed to fluctuate within a specific range based on market supply and demand. As a result, the market began to play an increasingly important role in determining prices. By 1983, agricultural product output had grown rapidly, pushed along by the universal implementation of the contract system and the increased prices of agricultural products. Subsequently, the scope of market-determined prices was expanded further. In 1983, the central government suggested that "the purchase and sales prices of agricultural and sideline products beyond the scope of purchase quotas shall be allowed to rise or fall based on supply and demand forces of the market."

One of the basic characteristics of the state monopoly over the purchase and marketing of agricultural products was that purchase and sales prices were set by the government. During the initial stage of overhauling this policy, the focus of reform was to gradually increase or deregulate the prices for purchase of agricultural products from

[6] *Zhong Fa* 中发 No. 1 (1982).

farmers while still holding the prices of agricultural products sold to urban residents at their original level. As a result, there was a gap between the purchasing price and the sales price for the prices of agricultural products, which made it necessary for the government to further subsidize the purchase and sale of agricultural products, which created financial pressure. The need to reform the distribution system and allow the market to determine prices became increasingly clear. In 1984, the central government allowed the prices of agricultural surpluses that exceeded purchase targets to be fully determined by the market. The *Ten Policies on Further Revitalizing the Rural Economy* (关于进一步活跃农村经济的十项政策)[7] stated that "from this year on, the state will no longer issue agricultural product purchase tasks to farmers except for a specific number of products. The state will undertake purchase by contract or market purchase as needed in different situations." With that, the thirty-one-year-old agricultural product purchasing system came to an end.

To maintain and encourage farmers' enthusiasm for production and sales, in 1986 the central government decided to "reduce the quantity of goods purchased at contract prices and expand the proportion purchased at market prices." Subsequently, the vast majority of agricultural products were sold on the market and the prices were determined by supply and demand. More agricultural products were removed from the scope of state purchase. At this point, the wide variety of food stamps—such as coupons for grain, non-staple foods, oil, and cotton—that had dominated people's lives for decades, were at last done away with, leaving the historical stage. Meanwhile, China developed a market for agricultural products whose prices were determined by the supply and demand of the market; the market mechanism began to play an increasingly important role in allocating agricultural resources.

Starting in 1985, grain output stagnated for four consecutive years, but market prices rose year by year. Seeing this rise, farmers became much less enthusiastic about turning over grain to the state at contract prices. In 1985, the state fulfilled only 60 percent of its grain purchase target. In subsequent years, it was difficult for the state to keep grain purchases and sales in balance. In 1990, the state again raised the grain purchase prices by a large margin. However, under this "buy

---

[7] *Zhong Fa* 中发 No. 1 (1985).

high, sell low" strategy, the state treasury faced increasing pressure. Between 1986 and 1991, government subsidies for grain, cotton, and oil totaled RMB 136.3 billion. Meanwhile, state-owned grain enterprises suffered increasing losses, totaling RMB 54.5 billion by the end of 1991, including RMB 48.6 billion of policy losses. To bring purchase and sales prices into balance and reduce the state's subsidy, on May 1, 1991, the Department of Commerce raised the retail prices of grain and edible oil (for that rationed to urban residents) by 68 percent and 170 percent, respectively. The state raised the grain prices again on April 1, 1992. As a result of these two rounds of price increases, the retail prices for these items rose over 120 percent. At the end of 1991, the State Council issued the *Notice on further Revitalizing the Distribution of Agricultural Products* (关于进一步搞活农产品流通的通知). The *Notice* required deregulating grain prices while guaranteeing the fulfillment of state purchase targets. In April 1992, Guangdong took the lead in deregulating grain prices by allowing purchase and sales prices to be determined by the market. By the end of 1993, over 98 percent of counties (cities) announced the deregulation of grain prices, completely removing the need for food coupons.

After the Fourteenth National Congress of Communist Party of China set the objective of establishing the socialist market economic system, the grain purchase and sales system became increasingly market-oriented. In February 1993, the State Council issued the *Notice on Speeding up the Reform of the Grain Distribution System* (关于加快粮食流通体制改革的通知), setting out the market-oriented roadmap of relaxing price controls, deregulating market operations, boosting the vitality of grain enterprises, and alleviating the government's fiscal burden. The *Policy Measures of the CCP Central Committee and the State Council Concerning the Development of Agriculture and Rural Economy* (中共中央、国务院关于当前农业和农村经济发展的若干政策措施)[8] was issued in November 1993. In this document, the central government declared the end of state monopoly over the purchase and marketing of grain and decided to guarantee the quantity of grain purchased by the state by relaxing price controls beginning in 1994. To guarantee quantity, the state implemented the grain price protection system and established the grain risk fund and reserve system.

[8] *Zhong Fa* 中发 No. 11 (1993).

In 1994, amid surging grain prices, guaranteeing grain supply once again became a key priority. In March 1994, the State Council issued the *Notice on Deepening the Reform of the Grain Purchase and Sales System* (关于深化粮食购销体制改革的通知) and announced that the state should purchase at least 90 billion kg of grain at bargain or market prices and that the state-owned grain system should control 70–80 percent of the grain supply. The *Notice* also called for the establishment and improvement of a grain supply and reserve system at central and local levels. In June 1994, the state began to sharply raise grain purchase prices. In particular, the state raised the average purchase price of wheat, rice, cotton, and soybeans to RMB 52 per 100kg, representing an average increase of 40.4 percent in purchase prices. Meanwhile, state-owned grain enterprises resumed unitary control over the grain supply chain from purchase to wholesale.

The provincial grain responsibility system was first put forward in 1995 in the *Notice of the State Council on Deepening the Reform of the Grain, Cotton and Fertilizer Purchase and Sales System* (国务院关于深化粮食棉花化肥购销体制改革的通知). The central government raised grain purchase prices again in 1996. The purchase prices of medium-quality wheat, rice, cotton, and soybeans were raised 42 percent over the 1994 price level. Subsequently, market grain prices dropped sharply as grain output rapidly rose. On May 19, 1998, the State Council issued the *Decisions of Further Deepening the Reform of the Grain Distribution System* (关于进一步深化粮食流通体制改革的决定) and called for the implementation of the "Three Policies, One Reform Initiative" (三项政策,一项改革). The goal of this initiative was to, by streamlining the sales process and authorizing the Agricultural Development Bank of China to operate purchase funds in a closed loop, to purchase surplus grain from farmers at protected prices and deepen the reform of state-owned grain enterprises. The goal of this reform was to enable grain purchase and reserve enterprises to gradually regain their cumulative losses while also protecting the interests of farmers. Statistics show that open-ended purchase commitments played a significant role in protecting the farmers' interests. However, as the state purchased an increasingly large amount of grain, the state-owned grain system faced unprecedented pressure in terms of funds and warehouse capacity. At the same time, the excessively high state protected prices made it difficult to pass on the costs to consumers, causing state-owned enterprises to suffer ballooning losses.

In the spring of 2000, with the approval of the State Council, Zhejiang province became the first province to undertake trial market-oriented reforms of the grain purchase and sales system. In 2001, the State Council issued the *Opinions on Further Deepening the Reform of the Grain Distribution System* (关于进一步深化粮食流通体制改革的意见)[9] and expanded the scope of reform nationwide, with a focus on the eight regions of Zhejiang, Shanghai, Guangdong, Fujian, Hainan, Jiangsu, Beijing and Tianjin. The *Opinions* condensed reform into sixteen Chinese characters: "expanding sales areas, protecting production areas, putting governors in charge, strengthening control" (放开销区、保护产区、省长负责、加强调控). In 2004, the CCP Central Committee and the State Council issued the *Opinions of the CCP Central Committee and the State Council on Promoting Farmers to Increase Income* (中共中央、国务院关于促进农民增加收入若干政策的意见),[10] expressly requiring the complete opening of the grain purchase and sales market. Also in 2004, the State Council issued the *Opinions on Further Deepening the Reform of the Grain Distribution System* (关于进一步深化粮食流通体制改革的意见),[11] resulting in a comprehensive arrangement for grain system reform. Fully opening the grain purchase and sales market marked the fundamental change in the grain distribution system. Before the spring planting season in 2004, the state enacted the minimum purchase price policy and released the minimum rice purchase price plan. This practice was systematized in the *Opinions of the State Council on Further Deepening the Reform of the Grain Distribution System* (国务院关于进一步深化粮食流通体制改革的意见).[12] The *Opinions* state that "if necessary, the State Council may decide to introduce minimum purchase prices to grain production areas for key varieties of grain that are in shortage." This system played a pivotal role in stabilizing grain production and markets, protecting the interests of farmers, and keeping grain production and markets stable, which they remained for five consecutive years.

[9] *Guo Fa* 国发 No. 28 (2001).
[10] *Zhong Fa* 中发 No. 1 (2004).
[11] *Guo Fa* 国发 No. 17 (2004).
[12] *Guo Fa* 国发 No. 17 (2004).

III. *Change and Integration in the Urban-Rural Relationship*

A. *Integration of Employment Systems in Urban and Rural Areas*

After the reform and opening policy was launched, rural residents began to spend an increasing amount of time boosting their income by engaging in a diverse set of economic activities. Some joined the legion of rural migrant laborers working away from home and doing business in urban areas. In response to this situation, the CCP Central Committee issued the *Notice on 1984 Rural Work* (中共中央关于一九八四年农村工作的通知),[13] stating that "in 1984, each province, autonomous region, and municipality may select some towns to operate pilot programs, under which the government allows rural residents working away from home, doing business, and providing services in urban areas to settle down in towns." This poked a hole into the airtight barrier between urban and rural areas. As urban economic reform deepened, the urban economy became increasingly dynamic with an increasing number of job opportunities. By the late 1980s, China had over thirty million rural migrant workers and was in the midst of a massive "labor migration" from rural to urban areas. This migration put pressure on the transportation infrastructure, family planning, and education system of urban areas. Not all local governments (particularly the governments of places where migrant workers moved to) or local people supported rural residents seeking employment in urban areas, which made rural residents' road to urban employment all the more difficult.

In the 1990s, state-owned enterprises restructured operations in a series of massive layoffs, and barriers began to be established by cities to block rural residents from seeking employment in urban areas. On February 13, 1995, the Shanghai Department of Labor issued the *Administrative Measures of Shanghai Municipality on the Classification of Rural labor Used and Employed by Employers* (上海市单位使用和聘用外地劳动力分类管理办法). This regulation classified industrial jobs into three categories: (1) jobs in which employers were allowed to use rural labor; (2) jobs in which using rural labor was restricted; and (3 jobs in which employers were prohibited from using rural labor. For any industry in which enterprises and institutions were prohibited from using rural

[13] *Zhong Fa* 中发 No. 1 (1984).

labor, the employers were forced to remove any rural laborers they had hired. When an employer was found using rural labor without government permission, the employer was ordered to dismiss the rural laborer within a prescribed time and pay a fine of RMB 500–2000 per worker in addition to making a supplementary payment for management of the system. Subsequently, other provincial capitals followed suit and—on the pretext of optimizing the local industrial structure and boosting competitiveness—imposed stringent requirements on rural migrant workers in regard to access to education and residence qualification. Beset with artificial barriers and complex formalities for employment, low wages, and wage arrears, as well as the difficulties of receiving public services (education, training, health, and social security), rural residents were thereby discouraged from working away from home to earn more money.

After the turn of the new millennium, the state enacted a series of policies aimed at lifting employment restrictions, strengthening protection for migrant workers' rights and interests, and creating a favorable environment for rural residents to work in urban areas. The *Decisions of the CCP Central Committee on Several Key Issues Concerning Agricultural and Rural Work* (中共中央关于农业和农村工作若干重大问题的决定) was approved at the Third Plenary Session of the Fifteenth CCP Central Committee. The *Decisions* required "expanding the paths of employment in rural areas and guiding rural labor to flow into urban areas in a reasonable and orderly manner to meet the employment needs of towns and developed areas." Regarding the systemic barriers and discriminatory regulations established in some localities to restrict rural labor from seeking employment in urban areas, the *Opinions of the CCP Central Committee and the State Council on Well Handling Agricultural and Rural Work in 2002* (中共中央、国务院关于做好 2002 年农业和农村工作的意见)[14] expressly state that rural migrant laborers shall be fairly treated, reasonably guided, well managed, and have access to public services. The *Opinions* called for regions to remove their unreasonable and arbitrary restrictions on rural migrant workers and rectify the malpractice of brutally expelling migrant workers. It called for the development of various intermediary labor organizations and the gradual establishment of a unified urban-rural labor market; finally, it called for improving the labor contract management

[14] *Zhong Fa* 中发 No. 2 (2002).

for rural migrant laborers and safeguarding their legitimate rights and interests. The *Opinions of the CCP Central Committee and the State Council on Well Handling Agricultural and Rural Work* (中共中央、国务院关于做好农业和农村工作的意见)[15] provided specific arrangements for migrant workers and required "strengthening management and services for rural migrant laborers and safeguarding their legitimate rights and interests." In 2006, the State Council issued the *Several Opinions on Solving Problems Related to Migrant Workers* (关于解决农民工问题的若干意见),[16] aimed at cleaning up wage arrears, adjusting minimum wage standards, boosting labor contract management, supervising enterprises to improve occupational safety and health conditions, safeguarding the laborers' rights and interests, cracking down on the use of child labor, strengthening employment guidance and services, conducting skills and safety training, pushing forward work injury and critical illness insurance, exploring suitable ways of providing pension and social security, endowing the children of migrant workers with the right to receive education, intensifying family planning management, including migrant workers and their children in the scope of prevention and control and planned immunity against infectious diseases, and improving the employment environment for migrant workers. To concretely solve problems related to migrant workers, the 2007 "No. 1 Document" further required "strengthening employment training for rural residents and protecting their rights and interests." The 2008 "No. 1 Document" expressly required "strengthening assurance and protection for the rights and interests of migrant workers in an all-around way."

To concretely protect the rights and interests of migrant workers, the State Council established the mechanism of joint meetings by thirty-one ministerial government agencies to tackle issues related to migrant workers. Meanwhile, similar joint meeting mechanisms were established in thirty-one provinces (autonomous regions and municipalities), with provincial governors responsible for convening a joint meeting to tackle issues related to migrant workers on a regular basis. This has improved the coordination mechanism and employment environment for migrant workers, strengthened protection for the rights and interests of migrant workers, and jumpstarted a new stage of rural labor

[15] *Zhong Fa* 中发 No. 3 (2003).
[16] *Guo Fa* 国发 No. 5 (2006).

transfer and employment. By the end of 2007, China had over 130 million migrant laborers (excluding their dependents) working away from home for over half a year, accounting for approximately 26 percent of the total labor force in rural areas.

IV. *Historical Breakthroughs in Rural Tax and Fee Reform*

In the early days after the formation of the People's Republic of China, the central government gave top priority to developing industry and promoted industrial development by artificially depressing agricultural product prices. Under this policy, farmers contributed enormously to industrial development while assuming a heavy economic burden. In the mid-1980s, the central government gradually relaxed control over agricultural product prices and alleviated this hidden burden of farmers. At the same time, however, the central government bombarded farmers with a plethora of taxes, fees, and surcharges. At that time, you might often hear farmers chanting a catch phrase: "The first tax is light, the second is heavy, and charges become a bottomless pit." In recent years, this problem has received utmost attention from the central government. The *Several Issues Concerning Rural Economic Policies* (当前农村经济政策的若干问题)[17] made it "imperative to trim government headcount, reduce government expenditure, eliminate waste, and alleviate the farmer's burden."

The *Decisions of the CCP Central Committee on Further Strengthening Agricultural and Rural Work* (中共中央关于进一步加强农业和农村工作的决定)[18] pointed out that, "At present, farmers assume excess burdens other than taxes but arbitrary charges are still on the rise. This has directly affected farmers' ability to boost agricultural investment and severely harmed the relationship between governments and farmers." The *Decisions* expressly required that "all provinces, autonomous regions, and municipalities clean up the fees and arbitrary charges on farmers and formulate specific regulations in connection to this." The *Policy Measures of the CCP Central Committee and the State Council Concerning the Current Development of Agricultural and the Rural Economy* (中共中央、国务

[17] *Zhong Fa* 中发 No. 1 (1983).
[18] *Zhong Fa* 中发 No. 21 (1991).

院关于当前农业和农村经济发展的若干政策措施)[19] required "working consistently and persistently to supervise and manage the farmer's burden" and "resolutely implementing a series of policies enacted by the CCP Central Committee and the State Council to protect the interests of farmers and alleviate their burdens. All regions and departments must fully carry out the decisions of the People's Government at central and provincial levels regarding: the abolition of agriculture-related fundraising fees, funds and charges; the cessation of erroneous fee collection and management methods; and the suspension of fees on hold."

In subsequent years, central government documents have reiterated the goal of alleviating the farmers' burden, as it still remained unresolved. The *Opinions of the CCP Central Committee and the State Council on Agricultural and Rural Work in 1998* (中共中央、国务院关于 1998 年农业和农村工作的意见)[20] pointed out that the "excess burden on farmers remains the dominant issue affecting rural stability." The central government enacted the policy of "assessing the farmer's burden at a reasonable level and keeping it unchanged for three years." However, some local governments exacerbated the non-tax burdens of farmers by falsifying their income. As a result, the central government once again failed to achieve its objective of alleviating farmers' burdens.

The *Opinions of the CCP Central Committee and the State Council on Well Carrying out the Agricultural and Rural Work in 1999* (中共中央、国务院关于做好 1999 年农业和农村工作的意见)[21] required "urgently studying and implementing the scheme of reform for the rural tax and fee system, legislating and standardizing the administration of taxes and fees in rural areas, and completely eliminating any unreasonable burdens on farmers." This policy statement demonstrated the resolve of the central government to solve the problem at the root level and marked the beginning of tax and fee reform in rural areas.

In 2000, the CCP Central Committee and the State Council issued the *Notice of the CCP Central Committee and the State Council on Reforming the Rural Tax and Fee System on a Piloting Basis* (关于进行农村税费改革试点工作的通知)[22] with a focus on: scrapping administrative fees and government charges collected from farmers to finance rural education

[19] *Zhong Fa* 中发 No. 11 (1993).
[20] *Zhong Fa* 中发 No. 2 (1998).
[21] *Zhong Fa* 中发 No. 3 (1999).
[22] *Zhong Fa* 中发 No. 7 (2000).

at the township level; repealing the hog slaughter tax; eliminating voluntary labor or labor for public accumulation of funds; adjusting the agricultural tax policy and taxes on special agricultural products; and reforming the way of collecting and using village reserve funds. Rural tax and fee reform was first started on a trial basis in Anhui province and in a number of selected counties and cities in other provinces. In 2001, Jiangsu launched a province-wide trial program of rural tax and fee reform on its own, which made remarkable progress. Subsequently, the scope of rural tax and fee reform was rapidly expanded nationwide. The 2004 "No. 1 Document" proposed scrapping the agricultural tax on a trial basis in Jilin and Heilongjiang provinces and reducing the agricultural tax rate by 2 percent in other provinces (autonomous regions and municipalities). The 2005 "No. 1 Document" proposed continuing the trial program of agricultural tax reform in Jilin and Heilongjiang provinces and reducing the agricultural tax rate by another 3 percent in other provinces (autonomous regions and municipalities). At the end of 2005, the Standing Committee of the National People's Congress adopted the motion submitted by the State Council to repeal the agricultural tax beginning from 2006. From then, the "Imperial Grain Tax," known by its modern incarnation as the "Agricultural Tax," which had existed for more than 2,600 years in China, was abolished. The repeal of the agricultural tax reduced farmers' financial burden by RMB 125 billion. Meanwhile, the departments of treasury at central and provincial levels ratcheted up transfer payments to county and township-level governments and increased fiscal subsidies to village organizations to ensure the normal operation of government agencies and organizations at the grassroots level.

V. *Evolution of the Rural Financial System*

To push forward the market-oriented economic and financial development in rural areas, since the market-oriented reform was started in 1979, China has launched a series of reform initiatives to restructure the rural financial system. The rural financial system has undergone the following four stages of reform:

A. *Stage One (1979–1993)*

The measures and policies of reform at this stage were chiefly intended to reinstitute or reestablish financial institutions and provide a relatively relaxed financial regulatory environment. The Agricultural Bank of China was reinstituted in 1979 with a new mission of vigorously supporting the rural commodity economy and increasing the returns on loans. At this stage, the state lifted control over private credit by allowing the free flow of credit to the private sector and the formation of private cooperative financial institutions. In addition, the state sanctioned the coexistence of diverse financing methods, including deposits, loans, bond, stocks, funds, discounted notes, trusts, and leases.

B. *Stage Two (1994–1996)*

The most salient characteristic of this stage was that the state focused on establishing the financial system to provide timely and effective services for agricultural and rural economic development, and shaped up the tripartite balance of power among commercial financial institutions (mainly the Agricultural Bank of China), cooperative financial institutions (mainly rural credit cooperatives), and policy-oriented financial institutions (mainly the Agricultural Development Bank of China). In 1994, the central government transferred the vast majority of policy-oriented financial business from the Agricultural Bank of China and rural credit cooperatives to the Agricultural Development Bank of China. Meanwhile, the banking regulatory authority accelerated the pace of commercializing the Agricultural Bank of China by introducing, for instance, management responsibility system, encouraging large-scale operation of credit funds, and centralizing the loan approval authority. The State Council made a decision on financial system reform in 1994. The decision required pushing forward the commercialization of rural credit cooperatives, setting up county-level credit cooperatives in 1994, and establishing a large number of rural credit cooperative banks in 1995. Meanwhile, rural credit cooperatives were no longer managed by the Agricultural Bank of China. Instead, rural credit cooperatives at the grassroots level were required to be managed by rural credit cooperatives at the county level. In addition, the People's Bank of China was directly responsible for supervising and managing the financial activities of rural credit cooperatives.

C. *Stage Three (1997–2005)*

The most distinctive characteristic of this stage was the exit of commercial financial institutions from rural areas and the advancement of rural credit cooperative reform. Subsequent to the Asian Financial Crisis, the central government put controlling financial risk control at top of its agenda while also deepening the reform of the financial system. In 1997, the Central Financial Work Conference mapped out the basic strategy of "merging county or lower-level financial institutions into state-owned commercial banks, developing small and medium-sized financial institutions, and supporting local economic development." In particular, state-owned commercial banks, including the Agricultural Bank of China, began to take over financial institutions at the county level or lower. By the end of 2005, commercial banks had 31,900 outlets at the county level or lower and employed 431,400 people, representing a reduction of 26,200 outlets and 179,000 people from the levels at the outset of the Fifteenth-Five-Year Plan period. The focus of rural financial system reform was shifted to restructure rural credit cooperatives. Reform initiatives included relaxing restrictions on the band of interest rate fluctuation for rural credit cooperatives, increasing state capital infusion to make up for losses from the non-performing assets of rural credit cooperatives, and pushing and deepening the reform of credit cooperatives. During this period, the state successfully strengthened management of financial risks but provided only meager financial support for rural areas.

D. *Stage Four (2006–Present)*

Since 2005, to provide adequate financial support for rural areas, China has enacted a series of rural financial policies, including, for example, the restructuring of the management system of rural credit cooperatives. In addition, the People's Bank of China provided discount note support for credit cooperatives, expanded the business scope of the Agricultural Development Bank of China, established the China Postal Savings Bank, relaxed the access threshold of rural financial institutions, set up village and township banks on a trial basis, promoting the trial operation of small-sum credit businesses, widened the range of interest rate fluctuation in rural areas, and boosted policy-oriented agricultural insurance on a trial basis. Generally speaking, these policies played a positive role in strengthening financial support for the agricultural sector and rural areas and brought about a significant increase in rural loans. Nevertheless, there were still some obstacles preventing rural households from accessing large-sum credit loans and it was very difficult for small and medium-sized rural enterprises and farmers' specialized cooperative economic organizations to receive loans. Loan difficulty was still one of the major issues constraining the development of rural China as a whole.

In recent years, the rural financial problems have received special attention from academia and inspired debate on a host of issues such as the direction of rural financial reform and development, the formation and organizational structure of financial institutions, and the role of the market mechanism, interest rates, support policy, social responsibility, and the regulatory mechanism. To enhance rural financial reform and development, in 2007 the state established a rural financial reform and development taskforce led by the Banking Regulatory Commission. The taskforce is specifically responsible for conducting research on issues arising from or pertaining to rural financial reform and development. To address the issue of insufficient financial support for rural areas, the central government reached a decision at the Third Plenary Session of the Seventeenth CCP Central Committee to establish a modern rural financial system as one of the six major systems dedicated to rural reform and development. The decision called for: (1) speeding up the formation of a rural financial system that combines commercial finance, cooperative finance, and policy finance, and enables adequate capital, functionality, superior service, and safe operation; (2) boosting policy support for rural finance and widening the channels of financing; (3) mandating financial institutions to actively support rural reform and development and instructing financial institutions at the county level to lend new deposits to local borrowers; and (4) encouraging the development of micro-financial services catering to rural characteristics and needs. To develop the rural insurance industry, the participants of the plenum expressly required refining the policy-oriented agricultural insurance system and accelerating the establishment of an agricultural reinsurance and catastrophe risk diversification mechanism. The 2009 "No. 1 Document" provided specific arrangements for carrying out these requirements laid down by the plenum.

VI. *Social Development in Rural Areas*

Economic development is the basis and prerequisite for social development. Social development is the starting point and foothold of economic development and it also creates a favorable social environment for economic development. Since the Sixteenth National Congress of Communist Party of China, China has sped up social development in rural areas. The Third Plenary Session of the Sixteenth CCP Central Committee singled out the integration of economic and social development as an important part of the ideological mission to establish and implement the scientific outlook on development. In recent years, the central government has reiterated the requirement that new fiscal appropriations for education, health, and culture be mainly used in rural areas. This has accelerated the pace of social development in rural areas. At the Third Plenary Session of the Seventeenth CCP Central Committee, policymakers made it clear that "to build socialist new rural areas and promote the integration of economic and social development in urban and rural areas, it is imperative to expand the coverage of public finance in rural areas and develop public utilities in the countryside so as to enable farmers to be well educated, well paid, well housed, well pensioned, and have good healthcare."

A. *Rural Education*

1. *Improving the Fund Assurance Mechanism for Rural Compulsory Education and Realizing Compulsory Education*

Since the launching of reform and opening until 1995, when the tax sharing system was implemented, China used a rural compulsory education system under which schools were run by governments at all levels (especially at township and village levels). When rural economic development stagnated in the mid- to late-1980s, however, township governments could hardly make ends meet and it found difficult to fund rural education. After the tax sharing system was implemented, China introduced a rural compulsory education system under which schools were administered primarily by county government and secondarily by township government and financed through multiple fund-raising channels. Given their financial difficulties, however, county and township governments were actually incapable of funding the enormous education expenditures. As a result, rural compulsory education expenditures and investments were only able to be financed by levying arbitrary charges on farmers or borrowing from banks.

In 2000, the state decided to reform, on a trial basis, the rural tax and fee system and scrap administrative charges and funds collected by government from rural residents to fund rural education. As a result, the nine-year compulsory education expenditure at the township and village levels came to be funded by governments at all levels through budgetary arrangement. Thus, governments at higher levels were under tremendous pressure. In 2001, the state issued the *Decisions on Basic Education Reform and Development* (关于基础教育改革和发展的决定), requiring governments to take over responsibility from rural residents for rural compulsory education and to replace township government by county government as the key party responsible for rural compulsory education. The *Opinions of the State Council on Reforming the Rural Tax and Fee System on a Piloting Basis* (国务院关于全面推进农村税费改革试点工作的意见) mandated that "county governments pay wages for teachers working at elementary and high schools in rural areas and make up for any shortfall of funds required to maintain normal operation of elementary and high schools in rural areas." In 2003, the *Decisions of the State Council on Further Strengthening Rural Education Work* (国务院关于进一步加强农村教育工作的决定)[23] made it clear that rural compulsory education was to be administered primarily at the county level but should be funded jointly by governments at all levels. The *Decisions* stressed that the provincial government shall fulfill its financial responsibility for rural compulsory education. For counties facing financial difficulties, the provincial government shall define the responsibilities of governments at all levels for transfer payment. In December 2005, the State Council issued the *Notice on Deepening the Reform of the Budget Assurance Mechanism for Rural Compulsory Education* (关于深化农村义务教育经费保障机制改革的通知). The *Notice* required funding rural compulsory education through public finance under the basic principle of "defining the responsibilities of governments at all levels, apportioning the costs between central and local governments, increasing fiscal investment, raising the funding assurance level, and proceeding in a stage-wise fashion."

---

[23] *Guo Fa* 国发 No. 19 (2003).

The new *Compulsory Education Law* (义务教育法) was deliberated and passed by the Standing Committee of the National People's Congress in September 2006. Based on the "county based" management system, the legislation further increased the provincial government's responsibility for funding rural compulsory education. Under the new law, all expenditures for rural compulsory education are to be shared by the People's Governments at all levels according to ratios set by the State Council on an item-by-item basis. The additional outlays from 2006 to 2010 for rural compulsory education under the public funding assurance mechanism were estimated to increase from the original amount of RMB 218.2 billion to RMB 265.2 billion. Of this total, the central government shall cover approximately RMB 160.4 billion and local governments approximately RMB 104.8 billion.

In the midst of increasing investment by the departments of treasury at all levels in rural compulsory education, China launched a series of reform initiatives to retool the rural education system. First of all, China adopted the "two waivers, one stipend" (两免一补) policy. In 2007, full tuition waivers were offered to 150 million elementary and high school students in rural areas; free textbooks were offered to 38 million students from economically disadvantaged rural households; stipends were offered to 7.8 million boarding students from economically disadvantaged rural households. As a result, China truly realized compulsory education in rural areas. Second, the central and local governments increased fiscal appropriations on a *pro rata* basis for rural elementary and high schools. By 2010, China increased public expenditure on compulsory education rural elementary and high schools to RMB 300 and RMB 500 per student, respectively. Third, China improved the conditions of rural compulsory education elementary and high schools. From 2001 until 2005, China planned to renovate the dilapidated buildings of 60,833 elementary and high schools in rural areas. During this period, China renovated 78 million square meters of dilapidated school buildings and moved over 34 million teachers and students out of dangerous school buildings. From 2003 to 2007, the central government appropriated RMB 10 billion to support building or renovating over 7,700 rural boarding schools in western regions. Meanwhile, the central and local governments arranged RMB 10 billion to improve the educational conditions in mid-western regions. Fourth, China consolidated and improved the wage assurance mechanism for the teachers of elementary and high schools in rural areas.

2. *Expediting the Development of Occupational and Technical Education in Rural Areas and Training High Quality Laborers and Practical Talents*

Since launching the reform and opening, China has gained remarkable progress in occupational education. The *Decisions of the State Council on Vigorously Pushing forward the Reform and Development of Occupational Education* (国务院关于大力推进职业教育改革与发展的决定)[24] took occupational education as an important part of China's education system and an important basis of national economic and social development. The *Decisions of the State Council on Further Strengthening Rural Education* (国务院关于进一步加强农村教育工作的决定)[25] required "vigorously developing employment-oriented occupational education in rural areas." In 2005, the State Council issued the *Decisions on Vigorously Developing Occupational Education* (关于大力发展职业教育的决定),[26] expressly requiring "occupational education to serve the transfer of rural labor and the building of socialist new rural areas." The *Decisions* also mapped out specific arrangements for developing occupational education and presented new development opportunities for occupational and technical education in rural areas. In 2007, there were 14,832 occupational secondary schools with an enrollment of 8,100,200 students, accounting for 49.1 percent of senior middle schools. Seventy percent of occupational secondary school students came from rural areas. Occupational education played a very important role in promoting the employment of rural residents and increasing their income.

3. *Steadily Developing Senior Middle School Education and Improving the Education Level of Rural Residents*

China has made remarkable progress in senior middle school education since it launched the reform and opening-up policy. Rural senior middle school education has been significantly improved in quantitative and qualitative terms. Between 2000 and 2007, the number of senior middle schools increased 7.53 percent from 14,600 to 15,700; the enrollment increased 77.74 percent from 4,726,900 to 8,401,600; the number of existing students increased 110 percent from 12,012,600 to 25,224,000. Thanks to their rapid economic growth and robust

[24] *Guo Fa* 国发 No. 16 (2002).
[25] *Guo Fa* 国发 No. 19 (2003).
[26] *Guo Fa* 国发 No. 35 (2005).

financial strength, some developed regions have begun to provide free senior middle school education on a trial basis.

Along with the development of senior middle school education, an increasing number of rural students have been admitted to colleges. In addition, China has made remarkable progress in adult training and anti-illiteracy education in rural areas and paid increasing attention to preschool education and special education.

B. *Medical and Health Services in Rural Areas*

The rural healthcare system has faced severe challenges since the launching of economic reform. The difficulty and costliness in seeing a doctor for rural residents has received widespread social attention. In the 21th century, local governments have begun to set up new rural healthcare cooperatives on a trial basis under the support of the central government. After the Sixteenth National Congress of Communist Party of China—under the requirement for coordinated economic and social development in urban and rural areas—the state boosted investment in rural healthcare services and accelerated reform of the rural healthcare system. China has, to date, made historical progress in rural healthcare.

The *Opinions on the Establishment of the New Rural Cooperative Healthcare System* (关于建立新型农村合作医疗制度的意见)[27] was jointly issued by the Ministry of Health, the Ministry of Finance, and the Ministry of Agriculture in 2003 to lay down the principle and policy framework for the implementation of China's new rural cooperative healthcare system. At the trial stage, the financial contribution to the cooperative healthcare system was very low (about RMB 30 per participant) and equally split among the central government, local government, and rural residents. In 2006, the financial contribution increased to RMB 50 per participant (RMB 10 from each rural resident was matched by RMB 20 each from the central and local governments). The National Rural Cooperative Healthcare Work Conference in 2008 set the target of increasing the per capita contribution to new rural cooperative healthcare services from RMB 50 to RMB 100 within two years. By the end of March 2008, the number of counties (cities and

[27] *Guo Fa* 国发 No. 3 (2003).

prefectures) that had established the new rural cooperative healthcare system reached 2,679, accounting for 98.17 percent of all localities that should have established the cooperative healthcare system and 93.57 percent of the total number of localities in China. Over 800 million people participated in the new rural cooperative healthcare system, reaching a participation rate of 91.05 percent.

In recent years, China has made progress in several areas, including: ramping up efforts to establish the rural health service system at county, township, and village levels; and gaining significant progress in building the rural healthcare supervision network and rural healthcare supply network. At present, China has established the national basic medicine system and provided strong support for medical and health services in rural areas. In addition, China has, over recent years, made remarkable progress in public health and family planning in rural areas and further improved the public health emergency response mechanism, thereby laying a solid foundation for raising the standard of health of rural residents.

VII. *Flourishing Cultural Development in Rural Areas*

During the three decades since the reform policy was launched, the ruling party and government have accorded top priority to enhancing cultural development in rural areas. During the past thirty years, the central government has built milestone cultural projects, organized diverse rural cultural activities, actively developed the rural cultural market, and extensively promoted culture in the countryside. As a result, the farmer's spiritual and cultural lives have been improved and culture has been developing in a healthy way across rural China. The *Opinions on Further Strengthening Cultural Construction in Rural Areas* (关于进一步加强农村文化建设的意见) was jointly issued by the general offices of the CCP Central Committee and the State Council on November 7, 2005. The *Opinions* set out a five-year target of establishing a new rural cultural landscape in accordance with the socialist market economic system, socialist spiritual construction, and the need to rebuild the countryside. In recent years, the central government has boosted universal radio and TV coverage in rural areas, improved rural information services, promoted the publication and circulation of books on "three-dimensional rural problems," vigorously developed rural cultural works, and organized mass cultural activities in rural areas. As a result, the rural cultural undertakings are developing in a healthy and rapid way.

A. *Improving the Social Security System in Rural Areas*

First of all, the minimum living allowance system has been established universally in rural areas. The 2007 "No. 1 Document" encouraged further improvement of the minimum living allowance system in areas where it had been established, supported establishing the system in areas where it had not been established, and offered subsidies for areas suffering financial difficulties. By the end of 2007, the system had been universally established across rural China. In 2007, the departments of treasury appropriated RMB 12 billion of rural minimum living allowance funds and disbursed RMB 10.91 billion to 35,663,000 people (16,085,000 households).

Second, China has explored ways to develop the pension insurance system in rural areas. In 1986, China introduced the social pension insurance system in rural areas on a trial basis. At the end of 2007, China had 51.71 million participants in the rural pension insurance scheme. In 2007, the number of rural residents who received pension benefits reached 3.92 million, representing an increase of 370,000 people over the prior year. The annual pension payment totaled 4 billion in 2007 and the rural pension insurance fund had a cumulative balance of RMB 41.2 billion. The 2009 "No. 1 Document" required formulating opinions on the establishment of a new rural social pension insurance based on personal contribution and supplemented by collective and government subsidy. This marked the entry of the rural pension insurance system into a new stage of development.

Third, China introduced a system of rewarding and supporting for rural households using family planning. In February 2004, the General Office of the State Council circulated The *Opinions of the National Population and Family Planning Commission and the Ministry of Finance on Implementing the System of Reward and Support for Rural Households using Family Planning on a Piloting Basis* (人口计生委财政部关于开展对农村部分计划生育家庭实行奖励扶助制度试点工作的意见).[28] Under the system, the central and local governments offer a reward and assistance

[28] *Guo Ban Fa* 国办发 No. 21 (2004).

of no less than RMB 600 per person per year for any couples, after they reach the age of 60 until they are deceased, who have one boy or two girls. In 2004, China introduced this system on a trial basis in Sichuan, Chongqing, Yunnan, Gansu, and Qinghai. In 2006, the central and local governments appropriated RMB 476 million and RMB 634 million respectively to fund the reward and support system. There were 1,866,000 beneficiaries, 1,346,600 of whom were directly supported by the department of treasury at the central level and 519,400 were supported by the departments of treasury at local levels.

Fourth, China has improved the social assistance system and social welfare. In 2006, the state amended the *Regulations Concerning Work on Providing "Five Guarantees" in Rural Areas* (农村五保戶供养条例) and transformed the "Five Guarantees" from the model of mutual aid between rural residents into a model of government assistance. By the end of 2007, there were 5,257,000 elderly rural residents (4,924,000 households) entitled to the benefits under the "Five Guarantees" assistance program, representing an increase of 8.5 percent from a year earlier. The average annual benefits under the "Five Guarantees" program were RMB 1,432.0 for each beneficiary who lived at home and RMB 1,953.0 for each beneficiary who lived in an alms house. In 2007, expenditure for the rural medical assistance fund totaled RMB 2.97 billion, up 98 percent from a year earlier; the number of beneficiaries reached 6,070,000, up 77 percent from the prior year; the amount of assistance totaled 29,572,000, up 99.8 percent from the previous year. In recent years, China has been dedicated to building a harmonious society with a focus on people. Accordingly, China has made remarkable progress in providing assistance to the victims of disasters and the disabled in rural areas, developing the pension system, enhancing the orphan assistance program, and carrying out charity missions across rural China. As a result, China has improved the living conditions of the victims of disasters, the disabled, the elderly, and orphaned children as well as helped them merge into society and protect their legitimate rights and interests.

B. *Boosting Poverty Reduction Efforts in Rural Areas*

Massive poverty reduction is one of the most remarkable accomplishments in China's economic and social development and an exemplary model recognized worldwide. Between 1980 and 2000, China's poverty reduction program has undergone three stages: (1) the institutional reform-driven poverty reduction stage (1978–1985); (2) the massive development-oriented poverty reduction stage (1986–1993; and (3) the key poverty reduction battle stage (1994–2000). The work priority, the poverty reduction mechanism, and the number of poor people lifted out of poverty have varied significantly from stage to stage because of the considerable differences in the economic foundations and institutional backgrounds of different stages. During this period, China realized the *Seven-Eight National Poverty Reduction Plan* (八七计划) and virtually solved the problem of inadequate food and clothing for rural people living in poverty. Between 1978 and 2007, China reduced the number of rural residents living in extreme poverty from 250 million to 14.79 million and realized all-round economic and social development in poverty-stricken regions. In accordance with the decision reached at the Third Plenary Session of the Seventeenth CCP Central Committee, the 2009 "No. 1 Document" laid down the principle of development-oriented poverty reduction and provided effective measures for the seamless integration of the rural minimum living allowance system and the poverty reduction program. China has adopted a new poverty line and implemented the poverty alleviation policy for the poor and low-income people living in rural areas. At present, China is focusing on getting people well fed and well clothed and lifting them out of poverty as quickly as possible by boosting the self-development capability of rural people living in poverty. This marks a new stage in China's efforts to alleviate rural poverty.

VIII. *Summary*

Over three decades China has achieved remarkable success in agricultural and rural development primarily because of the following reasons: insisting on the principle of safeguarding the economic interests of rural residents and respecting their democratic rights and interests; pursuing reform for the sole purpose of realizing, safeguarding and enhancing the fundamental interests of people; taking practice as the sole criterion for finding the truth (judging the success or failure of reform based on whether agriculture has been developed, farmers have earned more money, and rural areas have remained stable); respecting farmers' creativity and experience accumulated at the grassroots level; allowing people to try things whose acceptability cannot be determined for the time being and examining their acceptability solely based on the results of practice; paying attention to the relationship between reform and development; proceeding in a coordinated and orderly fashion with reform in urban and rural areas; correctly leveraging the government's functions, strengthening support and protection for agriculture and farmers, boosting the provision of public services for the agricultural sector and rural areas, enhancing protection for and reasonable utilization of agriculture and natural resources and ramping up social administration in rural areas, while letting the market mechanism play an increasingly important role.

The above reasons are both a crystallization of thirty years of invaluable experience and important guidelines that China must follow going forward in rural reform and development. The most important factor for success is that we have consistently upheld the cardinal principle laid down at the Third Plenary Session of the Eleventh CCP Central Committee that "economically, the government should earnestly protect the material interests of farmers; politically, the government should concretely safeguard the democratic rights of farmers." China will definitely be able to establish a rural institutional and policy system that meets the requirements of the socialist market economy as long as it insists on the ideological guideline of seeking truth from facts, does in-depth analysis of new situations, studies newly emerged problems, and pursues organizational and institutional innovation based on the stage-wise characteristics of economic and social development by catering to the general expectations of all farmers across China.

Bibliography

Guo Ban Fa 国办发 No. 21 (2004).
Guo Fa 国发 No. 28 (2001).
—— No. 16 (2002).
—— No. 19 (2003).
—— No. 3 (2003).
—— No. 17 (2004).
—— No. 35 (2005).
—— No. 5 (2006).
Zhong Fa 中发 No. 1 (1982).
—— No. 1 (1983).
—— No. 1 (1984).
—— No. 1 (1985).
—— No. 18 (1990).
—— No. 21 (1991).
—— No. 11 (1993.
—— No. 11 (1993).

—— 中发 No. 2 (1998).
—— 中发 No. 3 (1999).
—— 中发 No. 7 (2000).
—— 中发 No. 2 (2002).
—— 中发 No. 3 (2003).
—— 中发 No. 1 (2004).
—— 中发 No. 1 (2007).

CHAPTER TWO

THE REFORM, OPENING, AND DEVELOPMENT OF CHINA'S INDUSTRIAL ECONOMY

Chen Jiagui and Wang Qin

The thirty-year reform, opening, and development process of China's industrial economy has largely been a process of establishing and refining the socialist market economy with Chinese characteristics. At the same time, it has also showcased to the world an industrialization process of the largest scale in human history. China's industrial economy (the key constituent of secondary industry) is the largest of the three industrial sectors (primary, secondary, and tertiary industries) and has made the single largest contribution to China's national economic development. In addition, it is also had the fastest pace of development and the highest degree of internationalization.

I. *Reform of China's Industrial Economy*

A critical part in the reform of China's economic system has been industrial economic reform, which is centered on enterprise reform. Industrial enterprise reform has consisted of two major components: (1) reform of state-owned enterprise, which has aimed to gradually transform state-run enterprise from production units implementing the state plan into market entities; this has involved a strategic adjustment of the state-owned economy; and (2) encouraging the development of non-state-owned enterprise, such as private (individual and otherwise) enterprise as well as foreign-funded enterprise. After thirty years of industrial reform, a balance among the "tripartite of forces" of state-owned, private, and foreign-funded enterprise has gradually taken shape.

A. *The Process of Reforming State-Owned Enterprise*

For thirty years, China has experienced ups and downs in state-owned enterprise reform. Based on the different objectives, theoretical bases,

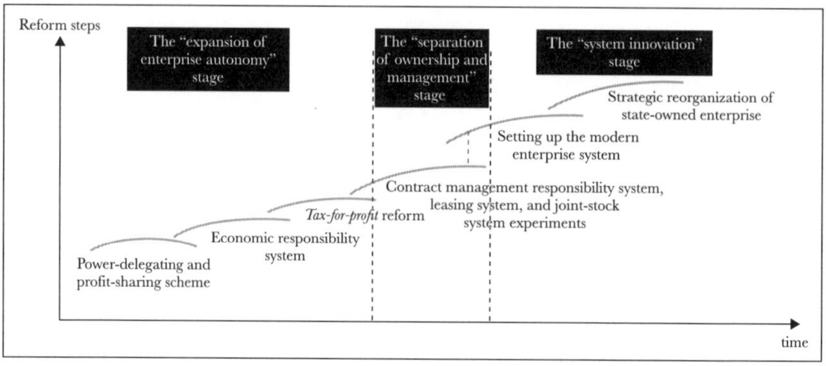

Figure 2.1. The Roadmap of Reforming China's State-Owned Industrial Enterprise.

and key measures of reform at different stages, the thirty-year reform process can be divided into three stages: Stage 1 (December 1978–September 1984) was a stage of reform aimed at expanding enterprise autonomy by way of delegating power and sharing profits; Stage 2 (October 1984–October 1998) was a stage of reform focused on the transformation of enterprise' operational mechanism, characterized by the separation of ownership and management; finally, Stage 3 (November 1998-present) has been a stage of reform focused on establishing a modern enterprise system and carrying out strategic reorganization (see Figure 2.1).

1. *The Stage of Reform Aimed at Expanding Enterprise Autonomy By Way of Delegating Power and Sharing Profits*

The power that should have been exercised by enterprise had long been concentrated in the hands of government at all levels, thereby reducing enterprise to administrative subordinates and severely stifling the productive enthusiasm of enterprise and laborers. As a consequence, enterprise lacked vitality. In this situation, delegating power, sharing profits, and expanding enterprise autonomy were all breakthroughs in the market-oriented reform of China's state-owned enterprise. The key initiatives introduced at this stage include power-delegating and profit-sharing schemes, the economic responsibility system, and tax-for-profit reform.

(1) Power-Delegating and Profit-Sharing Scheme

In October 1978, Sichuan selected six representative enterprises from different industries to take the lead in expanding enterprise autonomy on a trial basis. Subsequently, the six government agencies, including the State Economic and Trade Commission, further expanded the scope of this trial. In July 1979, the State Council issued five documents, including *Several Regulations on Expanding the Operation and Management Autonomy of State-Run Industrial Enterprise* (关于扩大国营工业企业经营管理自主权的若干规定) and *the Provisions for Profit Retention in State-Run Enterprise* (关于国营企业实行利润留成的规定). The number of trial-run enterprise was expanded to 4,200 by the end of 1979 and then to 6,000 in 1980, accounting for approximately 16 percent of industrial enterprise included in the state budget and for 60 percent and 70 percent of output value and profits, respectively.[1]

(2) Implementing the Economic Responsibility System

The power-delegating and profit-sharing scheme inspired enterprise enthusiasm for exceeding the plan and increasing production and income. As a result, the ability of enterprise to accumulate assets and direct their own development increased. In 1979 and 1980, however, China suffered huge fiscal deficits two years in a row. To escape from this deficit crisis, China introduced an economic responsibility system under which industrial enterprises were responsible for reaching their respective profit targets. In October 1981, the State Council approved and forwarded *Several Opinions on Implementing the Industrial Production Responsibility System* (关于实行工业生产责任制若干问题的意见). By the end of 1982, more than 80 percent of industrial enterprise had implemented the economic responsibility system.[2]

(3) Implementing Tax-for-Profit Reform

After implementing the economic responsibility system, some enterprise increased production and income within a short period of time. The vast majority of enterprise, however, failed to register a substantial increase in economic benefits. Meanwhile, the phenomenon of industry leaders being punished also put a damper on firms' desire to make significant changes. In response, the State Council decided to rescind the profit contribution system and replace it with the "tax-

[1] Zhou Shulian 周叔莲. "20nian zhongguo guoyouqiye gaige jingyan de lilunfenxi 20 年中国国有企业改革经验的理论分析 [A Theoretical Analysis of 20 Years of State-owned Enterprise Reform in China]," 2000.

[2] Zhang Dicheng 张迪诚. Zhongguo guoyouqiye gaige biannianshi 中国国有企业改革编年史 (1978–2005) [*The Annals of China's State-Owned Enterprise Reform (1978–2005)*], 2006.

for-profit" scheme. In 1983, China introduced the first part of the "tax-for-profit" scheme, under which an enterprise must pay taxes and contribute profit at the same time. In September 1984, China introduced the second part of the tax-for-profit scheme by adjusting the original tax categories and rates and enabling state-run enterprise to transition from a system of paying "tax plus profit" into the system of paying "tax in lieu of profit." This made it so that, after paying taxes, enterprise had full authority over their after-tax profits.

2. *The Stage of Reform Based on Transforming the Operational Mechanism for Enterprise*

The *Decision of the CPC Central Committee on Economic System Reform* (中共中央关于经济体制改革的决定) was ratified at the Third Plenary Session of the Twelfth CPC Central Committee in October 1984, suggesting that state-owned enterprise reform moved from the stage of decentralization into a new stage underscoring the separation of government and business, the separation of ownership and management, and the transformation of firms' operational mechanism. The key initiatives introduced at this stage include: introducing the contract management responsibility system for state-owned large- and medium-sized industrial enterprise, adopting the lease management responsibility system for state-owned, small-sized industrial enterprise, and conducing joint-stock system trials at a number of large and medium-sized industrial enterprise where conditions permitted.

(1) Corporate Contract Management Responsibility System

Among the large-sized collectively-owned enterprise, the Shougang Group Co. took the lead in implementing the contract responsibility system. Based on the successful experiences of Shougang and the Second Auto Works (now known as Dong Feng Motor Corporation) in introducing the contract management responsibility system, the State Council issued the *Several Opinions on Deepening Enterprise Reform and Boosting Enterprise Vitality* (关于深化企业改革增强企业活力的若干规定) in December 1986, requiring state-owned enterprise to implement various forms of the contract management responsibility system and granting sufficient autonomy to operators. In 1990, the first-round contracting period of over 90 percent of contracted enterprise expired and the second round of contracting commenced. By the end of the first quarter of 1991, more than 90 percent of enterprise whose contract term expired entered into contracts for the second round of contracting.[3]

(2) Leasing System
As economic system reform deepened, many small-sized industrial enterprises in 1984 began to implement, on a trial basis, the lease management responsibility system. These enterprises achieved, to some extent, the separation of management and ownership. A survey of 43,935 state-owned, small-sized industrial enterprise found that by the end of 1988 the number of enterprise adopting the leasing system and other operation approach reached 24,660, accounting for 56.1 percent of the total number of enterprise nationwide.[4]

(3) Joint-Stock System
To realize the separation of ownership and management, China launched joint-stock system reform in 1984, which was a preliminary step in the reform of state-owned enterprise property rights. Statistics show that by 1991 there were 3,220 joint-stock system experimental enterprises nationwide (excluding joint-stock cooperative enterprise, jointly operated enterprise, and Sino-foreign joint ventures).[5]

3. *The Stage of Reform Based on Establishing the Modern Enterprise System and Carry Out Strategic Reorganization*
In November 1998, the Third Plenary Session of the Fourteenth CPC Central Committee expressly required the establishment of a modern enterprise system. In September 1995, the Fifth Plenary Session of the Fourteenth CPC Central Committee officially required readjusting the state-owned economic pattern, which caused China's state-owned enterprise reform to enter a stage of reform aimed at setting up the modern enterprise system and carrying out strategic reorganization.

---

[3] Zhou Shulian, "A Theoretical Analysis of 20 Years of State-owned Enterprise Reform in China," 2000.

[4] Wang Haibo 王海波. "Zhongguo guoyouqiye gaige deshijian jincheng (1979–2003nian) 中国国有企业改革的实践进程 (1979–2003 年) [The Practices and Progresses of China's State-Owned Enterprise Reform (1979–2003)]," 2005.

[5] Zhang Wenkui 张文魁. *Zhongguo guoyouqiye chanquan gaige yu gongsi zhili zhuanxing* 中国国有企业产权改革与公司治理转型 [*China's State-Owned Enterprise Property Rights Reform and Corporate Governance Transition*], 2007.

(1) Establishing a Modern Enterprise System

According to the *Decisions on Several Issues in Setting up the Socialist Market Economy* (关于建立社会主义市场经济若干问题的决定) ratified at the Third Plenary Session of the Fourteenth CPC Central Committee, state-owned enterprise reform was to establish a modern enterprise system characterized by "well-defined property rights, clear-cut responsibilities, separation of government and business, and scientific management." To carry out this ruling, the state selected 100 state-owned large- and medium-sized enterprises from different categories to set up the modern enterprise system on a trial basis and then disseminate it on a broader basis. A tracking statistical survey conducted by the National Bureau of Statistics found that by the end of 2001, 3,322 (or 76 percent) of the 4,371 enterprise surveyed (most of them were state-owned enterprise)[6] had been reorganized in accordance with the modern corporate system.[7]

(2) Strategic Reorganization of State-Owned Enterprise

In 1995, the underlying philosophy of China's state-owned enterprise reform changed from "invigorating individual enterprise" to "invigorating all enterprise as a whole." Under this philosophy, the Fifth Plenary Session of the Fourteenth CPC Central Committee in 1995 required "invigorating large enterprise while relaxing control over small ones" in a bid to rejuvenate the entire state-owned economy. As a result of consolidation, mergers and reorganization, state-owned enterprise gradually concentrated in the key industries and sectors that constitute the lifeline of the national economy. In 1998, there were 238,000 state-owned industrial and commercial enterprises in China. In 2006, the number of state-owned enterprise was reduced to 119,000. Since the State-owned Assets Supervision and Administration Commission of the State Council (SASAC) was established in 2003, the number of central government controlled enterprise decreased from 196 to 153 (by the end of November 2007) and 82.8 percent of their assets were

[6] Including 514 key state enterprise, 181 central government controlled state-owned backbone enterprise, 93 enterprise selected by the State Council to set up the modern enterprise system on a piloting basis, 121 enterprise groups (parent companies) selected by the State Council to operate on a piloting basis, and over 3000 key provincial enterprise and piloting enterprise.

[7] Zhang Zhuoyuan 张卓元. "Shenhua guoqi gaige fazhan hunhe suoyouzhi 深化国企改革发展混合所有制 [Deepening State-Owned Enterprise Reform and Developing Mixed Ownership]," 2003.

concentrated in the areas of petroleum and petrochemical, electricity, defense, communications, transportation, mining, and metallurgy.

B. *Development of Non-State-Owned Enterprise*

Over the thirty years of reform and opening, China saw the emergence and development of a non-state-owned economy. It has now become an important part of China's economy. At present, the private economy accounts for 65 percent of GDP, employs 77.3 percent of the urban workforce and contributes 78.6 percent of national tax revenue.[8] Thus, it has become an extremely important force in China's economic development.

1. *Private Enterprise Development*

Over the thirty years of reform and opening, along with the gradual relaxation of legal restrictions and the continuous improvement in the legal status of private enterprise, many private enterprises have developed. In general, the private enterprise development process can be divided into three stages: Stage 1 (December 1978–March 1988) was the "embryonic" stage; Stage 2 (April 1988–September 1992) was the stage of initial development; and Stage 3 (October 1992-present) has been the stage of rapid development.

(1) The Embryonic Stage of the Development of Private Enterprise

In the 1980s, individual industrial and commercial households underwent rapid development, while "sole proprietorships" also emerged, thereby laying the groundwork for "sole proprietorships" to evolve later on into private enterprise. Due to policy constraints at the time, these "production organizations" of a private nature were only allowed to exist in the form of "individual industrial and commercial households," "cooperative operation enterprise," or "collective enterprise." It was not until 1988, when the legitimacy of private enterprise was established in law, that enterprises were finally able to legally call themselves "private enterprise," (see Figure 2.2).

---

[8] The data used here according to a broad understanding of non-state-owned economy, taking that anything other than the state-owned economy is part of the private economy.

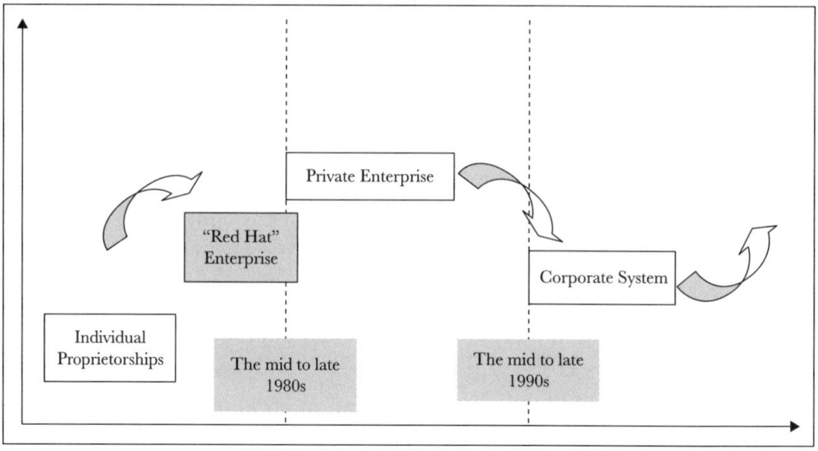

Figure 2.2. The Evolution of the Organizational Form for Private Enterprise.

These changes in external policy and the legal environment both indicated a relaxation in the legal restrictions regarding private enterprise. Specifically, the policy and legal environment has undergone an evolution from "allowing the individual economy to develop under the auspices of strengthening management" to "allowing the expansion of the individual economy." In 1982, the Constitution clearly established the legitimacy of the individual economy. In 1983, in a government document entitled *Several Issues relating to Current Rural Economy Policy* (当前农村经济政策的若干问题), a tolerant attitude was adopted towards the development of private enterprise. In 1987, the CPC Central Committee issued the *Decisions on Deepening Rural Reform* (关于把农村改革引向深入的决定) and provided "policy space" for the further development of private enterprise.

(2) The Initial Development Stage of Private Enterprise

It was during this stage that the legal status of private enterprise was established. In April 1988, an Amendment to the Constitution of China affirmed, for the first time, the legal status of the legitimate rights and interests of the private economy and its rights to lawful development. In June 1988, the State Council promulgated the *Interim Regulations on Private Enterprise* (私营企业暂行条例) as a comprehensive statute governing private enterprise. In addition, the *Provisional Regulations on Private Enterprise Income Tax* (私营企业所得税暂行条例) and the *State Council Regulations Governing the Levy of Individual Income Adjustment Tax on*

Private Enterprise Investors (国务院关于征收私营企业投资者个人收入调节税的规定) were promulgated shortly thereafter.

(3) The Stage of Rapid Development for Private Enterprise
When the Fourteenth CPC Congress and the Third Plenary Session of the Fourteenth CPC Central Committee was convened, policymakers further steered the course of reform to the establishment of a socialist market economic system and established the guidelines of keeping public ownership as the mainstay of the economy and allowing diverse forms of ownership to develop side by side. After the *Company Law* (公司法) was enacted, in the mid to late 1990s, the corporate form of organization began to be widely adopted.

As the legal status of private enterprise was further ensured and the protection for private property rights was strengthened, a large number of "red hat" enterprises were transformed into private companies. As state-owned enterprise reform deepened, under the guidance of an "advance and retreat" reform policy of "invigorating large enterprise while relaxing control over small ones," a considerable number of state-owned enterprise were restructured into corporate enterprise controlled by "non-state-owned" entities and operated under the "private mechanism."

2. *Development of Foreign-Funded Enterprise*

In 1980, the Chinese government approved the establishment of the first Sino-foreign joint venture, the Beijing Aviation Food Co. Ltd. Since then, foreign-funded enterprise has evolved for nearly thirty years. In general, foreign-invested enterprise has undergone three development stages: Stage 1 (December 1978–September 1992) was the exploratory stage; Stage 2 (October 1992–September 2002) was the stage of rapid development; and Stage 3 (October 2002-present) has been the stage of stable development.

During Stage 1, at the Third Plenary Session of the Eleventh CPC Central Committee, China officially pledged to open to the outside world. However, legislation and infrastructure had yet to be improved and foreign investors still had serious misgivings about investing in China. At this stage, foreign investors were mainly engaged in investigation of investment possibilities. During the period from 1979 to 1991, China approved and established 42,503 foreign direct investment (FDI) enterprises in total, an average of 3,269 enterprises a year.

After the Thirteenth CPC National Congress was convened, China clearly set the course of reform to the establishment of a socialist market economy. As more regions and sectors were opened, the development foreign-funded enterprise entered Stage 2. During this stage, the attitude of foreign-funded enterprise changed from being tentative to proactive. The number of foreign-funded enterprise continued to grow and the scale of their operation also continued to expand. Moreover, foreign-funded enterprise entered into more areas. From 1992 to 2001, China approved and established 347,522 FDI enterprises in total, or an average of 34,752 enterprises a year, representing a 10.6-fold increase over Stage 1.

Subsequent to China's accession into the World Trade Organization (WTO) and the convening of the Sixteenth CPC National Congress, foreign-funded enterprise entered the stable development stage. During this stage, foreign-funded enterprise development has had the following characteristics: (1) foreign-funded enterprise increased capital and technology-intensiveness and became increasingly concentrated in high-tech and equipment manufacturing industries; (2) the merger and acquisition of Chinese enterprise by multinational firms became a new trend; and (3) foreign-funded enterprise gradually transferred their investment into tertiary industry. From 2002 to 2006, China approved and established 204,402 FDI enterprises in total, or an average of 40,880 enterprises a year.

C. *Change in Industry Ownership Structure*

Through thirty years of reform, China has made substantial progress to the ownership structure of industrial enterprise. On one hand, state-owned enterprise has strengthened their role in the national economy; on the other hand, private and foreign-funded industrial enterprise now account for an increasingly large proportion of the national economy. They have now become an essential part of the national economy. In general, we can divide the changes in China's industrial ownership structure into three stages: Stage 1 (December 1978–1992) was the "monolithic" stage of state-owned enterprise; Stage 2 (October 1993–2002) was the stage during which private and foreign-funded enterprise rapidly gained market share; Stage 3 (2003–present) has been the stage of balanced influence among state-owned, private, and foreign-funded enterprise (see Table 2.1).

Table 2.1. Changes in Industry Ownership from 1978 to 2006 (per Gross Industrial Output Value) Unit: RMB 100 million

Year	State-owned and state-controlled industrial enterprise		"Private" industrial enterprise		"Foreign funded" industrial enterprise		State-owned enterprise and non-state-owned industrial enterprise above moderate scale
	Industry output value	Share (%)	Industry output value	Share (%)	Industrial output value	Share (%)	Gross industrial output value
1978	3289	77.6	948	22.4	–	–	4237
1992	17824	51.5	16775	48.5	–	–	34599
2002	45179	40.8	33138	29.9	32459	29.3	110776
2006	98910	31.2	117602	37.2	100077	31.6	316589

Note: (1) "Foreign-funded" enterprise data are the sum of foreign funded enterprise as well as investment from Hong Kong, Macau, and Taiwan; (2) "Private" industrial enterprise data refer to: the data of "collective enterprise" in 1978; the sum of collective, individual, and other enterprise in 1992; and in 2002 and 2006, the gross industrial output value minus the gross output value of state-owned and state-controlled industrial enterprise and the gross output value of "foreign-funded" industrial enterprise; (3) state-owned enterprise data in 1978 and 1997 are based on the statistics on the state-owned industry but in 1998 we began to use statistics on state-owned and state-controlled enterprise; (4) As the statistics of the National Bureau of Statistics are complied on a different basis, we use the data of all industrial enterprise prior to 1998 and the data of state-owned enterprise and non-state-owned industrial enterprise above moderate scale after 1998.
Source: National Bureau of Statistics. *Zhongguo tongji nianjian* 中国统计年鉴 [*China Statistical Yearbook*], multiple years.

During Stage 1, state-owned enterprise conducted a series of reforms such as power-delegating and profit-sharing, transformation of their operational mechanisms, and the separation of ownership and management, while private and foreign-funded enterprise were still in the exploratory or startup stage. Among all industrial enterprise, the share of state-owned enterprise declined but was still over 50 percent, thereby producing the "monolithic" patterned economy. For example, the industrial output value in 1978 totaled RMB 423.7 billion, of which state-owned industrial enterprise accounted for 77.6 percent and collective enterprise accounted for 22.4 percent; the gross industrial output value in 1992 reached RMB 3,459.9 billion, of which state-owned industrial enterprise accounted for 51.5 percent and non-state-owned industrial enterprise (including collective, individual and other enterprise) accounted for 48.5 percent.

During Stage 2, as reform of state-owned enterprise deepened and private and foreign-funded enterprise grew more rapidly, state-owned industrial enterprise continued to lose share in the economy while private and foreign-funded industrial enterprise' share increased, thereby resulting in a "4:3:3" pattern in the industry ownership structure. In 2002, the gross industrial output value reached RMB 11.1 trillion, of which state-owned industrial enterprise accounted for 40.8 percent, private enterprise accounted for 29.9 percent and foreign-funded enterprise accounted for 29.3 percent.

During Stage 3, China's reform entered a new stage of improving the socialist market economic system. After China's accession into the WTO, the plan of transforming the state-owned economy was effectively implemented and the space for development of the private economy was further expanded. In terms of structure, there was a balance between the three ownership models. In 2006, gross industrial output reached RMB 31.6 trillion, of which state-owned industrial enterprise accounted for 31.2 percent, private enterprise 37.2 percent, and foreign-funded enterprise 31.6 percent.

Enterprise reform has been the central component of reforming China's whole economy, unleashing the vitality of state-owned, private, and foreign-funded enterprise. It has not only pushed forward the establishment and refinement of the socialist market economy on the micro dimension, but also leveraged the vitality, control, and influence of the state-owned economy. As a result, it has ensured the stable operation of the national economy and boosted the overall international competitiveness of the Chinese economy.

II. *The Opening of China's Industrial Economy*

In looking at the thirty-year opening process of China's industrial economy, it is apparent that opening to the outside world has not only pushed forward economic reform and enhanced the development vitality and strength of China's economy, but also accelerated the merging of China's industry into the international division of labor system. The industrial sector of China's economy has become the area with the highest degree of openness. Meanwhile, it is the sector where external resources are utilized in the most concentrated way. The opening of China's industrial economy itself has been a two-way process, which can be understood from the perspectives of "bringing in" and "going out."

A. *The Foreign Investment Utilization Process of Chinese Industry*

Similar to the gradualist approach in reforming China's industrial sector, the process of utilizing foreign investment has also been a piecemeal process growing from small to big, from single points to surface, and from local to global. We can divide this process into three stages: Stage 1 (December 1978–1991) was the stage of exploration, during which people pushed for reform; Stage 2 (1992–2001) was the stage of rapid development; Stage 3 (2002–present) has been the stage of innovative development (see Table 2.2).

1. *The Stage Exploration and Pushing for Foreign Investment in Chinese Industry*

During this stage, foreign investment utilization in China's industry was "exploratory" in the sense that opening-up policies and laws were established from scratch and opened areas were gradually expanded. From 1979 to 1991, the amount of foreign investment as according to signed agreements and contracts totaled USD 52.59 billion (USD 4.05 billion a year); the actual amount of foreign investment totaled US 25.06 billion (or USD 1.93 billion a year). For details, see Tables 2.3 and 2.4. At this stage, most foreign direct investment in China was focused around cooperatively managed enterprise. In 1988, foreign investors began to concentrate their investment in joint-venture (JV) operations. Geographically, FDI was concentrated in special economic zones and opened coastal cities. The sectors of investment were mainly labor-intensive export processing projects. It is worth noting that capital from overseas Chinese was a major source of FDI at this stage.

Table 2.2. Foreign Investment Utilization Policy and Legal Environment Change of the Chinese Industry

Stage	Year	Content	Remarks
Exploration and push stage	1978	The Third Plenary Session of the Eleventh CPC Central Committee required proactively pursuing economic cooperation with all countries worldwide and vigorously importing advanced technology and equipment under the principle of self-reliance	China's export-oriented economic development strategy was established
	1979	The *Law of the People's Republic of China on Sino-Foreign Equity Joint Venture Enterprise*[9] was passed at the Second Session of the Tenth National People's Congress	
	1980	The Fifth Meeting of the Fifth NPC Standing Committee officially approved the establishment of four special economic zones (Shenzhen, Zhuhai, Shantou, and Xiamen)	
	1984	China decided to further open fourteen coastal port cities, including Shanghai, Tianjin, Dalian, Qinhuangdao, Yantai and Qindao	
	1985	Established coastal open economic zones in the Yangtze River Delta and Pearl River Delta as well as Xiamen, Zhangzhou and Quanzhou Delta regions	Formed the foreland for opening to the outside world
	1986	The *Law of the People's Republic of China on Foreign-funded Enterprise*[10] was ratified at the Fourth Session of the Sixth National People's Congress The State Council set up a leading group for foreign investment and published the *Regulations of The State Council on Encouraging Foreign Direct Investment*[11] (also known as "22 Articles")	Foreign investment utilization was codified into law
	1987	Set up the Foreign Investors Association of China	
	1988	The First Session of the Seventh National People's Congress approved building Hainan into the largest special economic zone	
	1989	The State Council approved and established Taiwan Businessman Investment Zones in Fuzhou, Haicang and Xinglin	
	1990	China implemented the Pudong development strategy	

9 中华人民共和国中外合资经营企业法
10 外资企业法
11 国务院关于鼓励外商投资的规定

Table 2.2 (*cont.*)

Stage	Year	Content	Remarks
Fast development stage	1992	China opened the inland regions (along the borders, rivers, inland province capitals and roads)	
	1995	The state promulgated and implemented the *Catalogue for the Guidance of Foreign Investment Industries*[12] and the *Provisional Regulations Guiding the Direction of Foreign Investment*[13]	This is the first time foreign investment utilization policy and industry policy were combined
	1997	The *Catalogue for the Guidance of Foreign Investment Industries*[14] was adjusted	Further expanded the areas of investment, with few forbidden zones left for foreign investment except for a few sectors involving the national security
	2001	Amendment to the Law of the People's Republic of China on Sino-Foreign Cooperative Enterprise and *Law of the People's Republic of China on Foreign-funded Enterprise* was passed at the Fifth Meeting of the Ninth National People's Congress	

12 外商投资产业指导目录
13 指导外商投资方向暂行规定
14 外商投资产业指导目录

Table 2.2 (*cont.*)

Stage	Year	Content	Remarks
Innovative development stage	2002	The Sixteenth CPC National Congress required boosting the quality and level of foreign investment utilization in China	Foreign investment utilization entered a new stage
	2002	The state promulgated *Interim Provisions on the Utilization of Foreign Investment to Restructure State-Owned Enterprise*[15]	Further detailed the operational procedures and rules for foreign investors to acquire or take over state-owned enterprise
	2003	The state promulgated *Interim Provisions on Mergers and Acquisitions of Domestic Enterprise by Foreign Investors*[16]	
	2007	The *Enterprise Income Tax Law*[17] was ratified at the Fifth Session of the Tenth National People's Congress	Passage of this law marked the transition of foreign investment utilization policy means from offering preferential measures into fostering a fair and equitable environment

Source: Compiled by the authors.

15 利用外资改组国有企业暂行规定
16 外国投资者并购境内企业暂行条例
17 企业所得税法

Table 2.3. Three Forms of Foreign Investment Commitment per Contract in 1984–2006 Unit: USD 100 million

Year	JV operation	Cooperative operation	Wholly owned operation	Year	JV operation	Cooperative operation	Wholly owned operation
1984	10.67	14.84	0	1996	318.76	142.97	268.10
1985	20.30	34.96	0.46	1997	207.26	120.66	176.58
1986	13.75	13.58	0.20	1998	172.86	116.56	217.53
1987	19.50	32.33	4.71	1999	135.15	68.03	207.06
1988	31.34	16.29	4.81	2000	196.48	81.17	343.09
1989	26.59	10.83	16.54	2001	175.36	83.00	429.99
1990	27.04	2.54	24.44	2002	185.02	62.17	572.55
1991	60.80	21.38	36.67	2003	255.06	74.79	816.09
1992	291.23	132.55	156.90	2004	276.41	77.88	1172.75
1993	557.74	354.10	304.57	2005	324.42	86.91	1459.09
1994	401.94	203.07	219.50	2006	329.37	80.74	1515.57
1995	397.41	178.25	336.58	1984–2006	4334.48	2009.60	8283.77

Source: National Bureau of Statistics: *China Statistical Yearbook*, 1985–2007.

Table 2.4. China's Actual Foreign Investment Utilization in 1978–2006

Year	Number of projects	Amount of foreign investment utilized (US$ 100 millions)	Year	Number of projects	Amount of foreign investment utilized (US$ 100 millions)
1979–1984	3724	41.04	1996	24556	417.26
1985	3073	19.56	1997	21001	452.57
1986	1498	22.44	1998	19799	454.63
1987	2233	23.14	1999	16918	403.19
1988	5945	31.94	2000	22347	407.15
1989	5779	33.93	2001	26140	468.78
1990	7273	34.87	2002	34171	527.43
1991	12978	43.66	2003	41081	535.05
1992	48764	110.08	2004	43664	606.30
1993	83437	275.15	2005	44001	603.25
1994	47549	337.67	2006	41485	694.68
1995	37011	375.21	1979–2006	594427	6918.97

Source: National Bureau of Statistics, *China Statistical Yearbook*, 2007.

2. *The Rapid Development Stage of FDI in Chinese Industry*
After the establishment of the socialist market economy was set as the direction of reform in China, more areas were opened under the principle of "swapping technology for market access." The *Catalogue for the Guidance of Foreign Investment Industries* was promulgated and amended in 1995 and 1998 respectively. During this stage, foreign investors began to swiftly, and on a large scale, enter China's light and electromechanical industries. From 1998, the principal form of foreign investment in China shifted from JV operations to wholly-owned operations. From 1992 to 2001, the amount of foreign investment commitment according to signed agreements and contracts reached a total of USD 692.70 billion, or USD 69.27 billion a year, representing a 17.1-fold increase over the amount at Stage 1; the amount of foreign investment actually utilized reached USD 370.17 billion in total or USD 37.02 a year, representing a 19.2-fold increase over the amount Stage 1.

3. *The Stage of Innovative Development for FDI in Chinese Industry*
After accession into the WTO, China's economic opening to the outside world changed from the traditional gradual approach to an all-out push towards engagement with the world. In 2002, the Sixteenth CPC National Congress required boosting the quality and level of foreign investment in China, pushing China's FDI enterprise into the innovative development stage. At this stage, China shifted the focus of FDI from quantity to quality and underscored the importance of using foreign investment to advance and upgrade industrial structure and promote regional development. In response to the new trend of multinational mergers and acquisitions occurring in China, the government enacted relevant laws and regulations such as *Interim Provisions on the Utilization of Foreign Investment to Restructure State-Owned Enterprise* (利用外资改组国有企业暂行规定) and *Interim Provisions on Mergers and Acquisitions of Domestic Enterprise by Foreign Investors* (外国投资者并购境内企业暂行条例). This legislation aimed to further regulate the multinational firms' merger and acquisition activity in the Chinese market and promote the diversification of foreign investment in China. During the 2002–2006 period, the amount of foreign investment commitment according to signed agreements and contracts reached a total of USD 740.56 billion, or USD 148.11 billion a year, representing a 2.4-fold increase over the amount at Stage 2; the amount of foreign investment

actually utilized reached USD 296.67 billion or USD 59.33 billion a year, representing a 1.6-fold increase over the amount at Stage 2.

B. *The Internationalization of Chinese Industry*

Since the launching of the reform and opening policy, Chinese industrial enterprise have gradually embarked upon a journey of internationalization and become important participants in the international market. China's industrial internationalization process can be divided into three stages: Stage 1 (1978–1991) was the stage of exploratory development; Stage 2 (1992–2000) was the stage of initial development; Stage 3 (2001–present) has been the stage of rapid development.

During Stage 1, China's industrial internationalization was basically in a state of exploratory development. After China's export-oriented economic development strategy was established at the Third Plenary Session of the Eleventh CPC Central Committee, the government gradually relaxed control over international operations and activities. As state-owned enterprise reform deepened, some large- and medium-sized state-owned enterprise gradually received permits to operate overseas and began to make forays into overseas markets. China's industrial enterprise started their internationalization endeavor with trade and gradually moved to overseas production with a focus on developing resources that were in short supply and conducting small-scale production activity. According to sector, the investment was mainly concentrated in mineral and aluminum production. Geographically, such investment was made mostly in developing countries and only a few investment projects were located in developed countries, including projects in the United States, United Kingdom, and Germany. From 1979 to 1991, China set up 911 non-trading enterprise overseas amounting to a total investment of USD 2.48 billion. Chinese investors contributed USD 1.06 billion to these enterprises, accounting for 42.79 percent of total investment. Approximately 60–70 percent of Chinese investment was made in the form of technology and equipment.[18]

During Stage 2, along with increased opening to the outside world, a group of industry-leading enterprise began to explore possibilities in international development. During the period from 1992 to 2000,

[18] Liu Yan 刘研. *Kuaguo gongsi yu zhongguo qiye guojihua* 跨国公司与中国企业国际化 [*Multinational Firms and Chinese Enterprise Internationalization*], 1992.

there was a fundamental change in China's industrial internationalization entities and a number of strong and capable industrial enterprises went global. For example, Baogang, Haier, and TCL set up enterprise overseas and actively pursued a strategy of multinational operation. Geographically, investment was based in over 160 countries and regions worldwide. By the end of 2000, there were 2,859 enterprises (non-finance and non-trade enterprise) approved by or registered with the former Ministry of Foreign Trade and International Cooperation; the cumulative overseas investment by Chinese investors reached US$ 3.73 billion.[19]

During Stage 3, Chinese industrial internationalization began to progress rapidly. In 2000, "going out" or "going global" was officially established as a new strategy for a new era. In 2001, after China joined the WTO, China's industrial enterprise showed strong enthusiasm for participating in international operations. After the going-global strategy was laid down in the Tenth Five-Year Plan in 2001, the state enacted a series of policies aimed at encouraging overseas investment, including policies and regulations governing the annual review of foreign investment enterprise and the establishment of chambers of commerce overseas. Industries and local governments also promulgated their own policy measures for encouraging the development of overseas enterprise. Supported by this series of policy initiatives, China has sustained rapid FDI growth in recent years. In 2007, China's (non-finance) investment overseas reached USD 18.72 billion (see Figure 2.3). Geographically, Asia and Latin America are the most important destinations for China's FDI. In regard to investment paths, the ways by which China's industrial enterprise make overseas investment have been increasingly diversified. In 2006, overseas mergers and acquisitions accounted for 53 percent of China's foreign investment flow.

Since launching of the reform and opening policy, China's industrial internationalization has followed a gradualist or piecemeal development approach. In addition, the investment approach has evolved from investment by cash, technology, and management at the outset into green-field investment and cross-border mergers and acquisitions. In terms of sector, China's textile and garment, home appliance, and communications equipment manufacturing industries with

[19] Lu Tong 鲁桐. Zhongguo qiye de guojihua zhanlüe 中国企业的国际化战略 [*The Internationalization Strategy of Chinese Enterprise*], 2003.

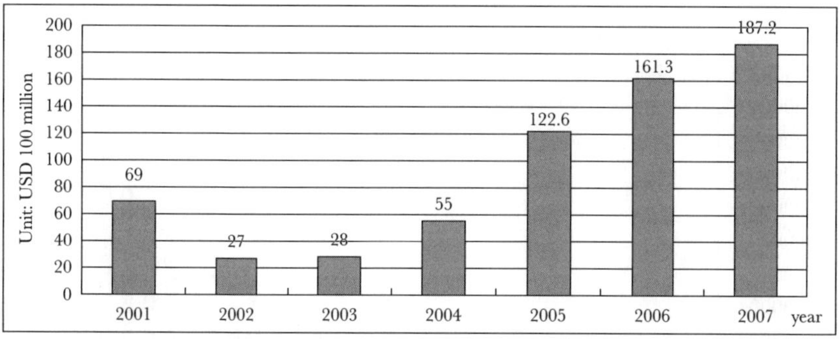

Source: Statistical Bulletins of China's Outward Foreign Direct Investment (Non-Finance Part).

Figure 2.3. China's Foreign Direct Investment (Non-Finance) in 2001–2007.

international competitiveness have done the most to expand overseas through investment projects and international outsourcing. Geographically, China's overseas investment has expanded from a limited number of developing countries to countries worldwide.

Generally speaking, China has handled the relationship between "bringing in" and "going out" quite well, it has opened its industries to investment and embraced an opening-up approach characterized by pragmatism as well as "gradualism and collaboration." At the initial stage of opening-up, China's industry adopted for the "bringing in" approach and enhanced its strength by welcoming foreign capital, technology, and equipment. And, to better leverage the strengths of domestic and international markets and resources and to better participate in the international system, China's industry launched the "going out" or "going global" strategy at the right time, achieving rapid international development.

III. *China's Industrial Economic Development*

Thirty years of reform and opening has been thirty years of rapid growth of China's industry. China is not at the forefront of global industrial growth but nonetheless occupies an increasingly important position in terms of global industry. In terms of the value of its industrial output, the products of its industry, its FDI utilization, and the import and export of industrial products, China has become a *de facto* industrial country. It is worth noting that China has yet to become

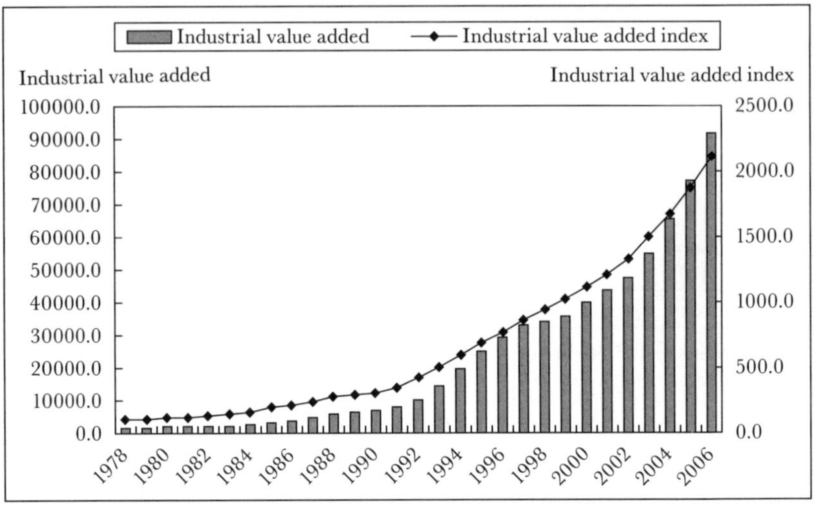

Source: National Bureau of Statistics, *China Statistical Yearbook*, 2007.

Figure 2.4. China's Industrial Value Added in 1978–2006.

one of the world's industrial powerhouses; the international status of China's industry is mainly a result of its scale and its international competitive advantages are mainly based on low cost.

A. *The Rapid Growth of China's Industry*

For thirty years, China's industry has sustained rapid growth, with an average growth rate exceeding 10 percent per year, which is one of the fastest worldwide. In nominal terms, China's industrial value added surged from RMB 160.70 billion in 1978 to RMB 9.13 trillion in 2006; based on comparable prices, the industrial value-added index was 100 in 1978 and 2116.1 in 2006. In other words, between 1978 and 2006, the industrial value added increased 21.16-fold and the average annual growth rate reached 11.52 percent, which was 1.82 percent higher than the average annual growth rate of GDP (see Figure 2.4).

China's industrial production capability has also grown rapidly in thirty years of development. China has built up enormous production capacity in the industries of metallurgy, chemicals, machinery, electronic communications equipment, and transportation equipment. China's production of air conditioners, color televisions, washing machines, and refrigerators started from scratch in 1978, but thereafter grew rapidly over the next three decades; chemical fiber, ethylene, steel, and automobile production increased dozens-fold; cement and soda ash production also expanded over ten-fold. The output of key industrial products has ranked at the forefront worldwide. Every year since 2003, China's output of crude steel, coal, cement, fertilizer, and cotton has ranked first and electricity output ranked second globally (see Table 2.5).

Table 2.5. China's Output of Key Industrial Products (1978–2006)

	1978	1990	2000	2006	2006/ 1978[1]
Raw coal (100 million tons)	6.18 (3) [2]	10.80 (1)	12.99 (1)	23.73 (1)	3.84
Crude oil (10,000 tons)	10405.00 (8)	13831.00 (5)	16300.00 (5)	18476.57 (6)	1.78
Electricity (100 million kWh)	2566.00 (7)	6212.00 (4)	13556.00 (2)	28657.26 (2)	11.17
Sugar (10,000 tons)	227.00 (8)	582.00 (6)	700.00 (4)	949.07 (3)	4.18
Chemical fiber (10,000 tons)	28.46 (7)	165.42 (2)	694.00 (2)	2073.18	72.85
Cloth (100 million m^2)	110.30	188.80	277.00	598.55	5.43
Ethylene (10,000 tons)	38.00	157.20	470.00	940.51	24.75
Soda ash (10,000 tons)	132.90	379.50	834.00	1560.03	11.74
Steel (10,000 tons)	2208.00 (5)	5153.00 (4)	13146.00 (1)	46893.36 (1)	21.24
Cement (10,000 tons)	6524.00 (4)	20971.00 (1)	59700.00 (1)	123676.48 (1)	18.96
Metal cutting machines (10,000 sets)	18.3	13.5	17.7	57.3	3.13
Cars (10,000 cars)	14.91	51.40	207.00	727.89	48.82
Washing machines (10,000 units)	0.04	662.68	1442.98	3560.50	89012.50
Household refrigerators (10,000 units)	2.80	463.06	1279.00	3530.89	1261.03
Room air conditioners (10,000 units)	0.02	24.07	1826.67	6849.42	342471.00
Color televisions (10,000 sets)	0.38	1033.04	3936.00	8375.40	22040.53

Note: [1]Refers to the ratio of the product's output in 2006 to its output in 1978; [2]Figures in brackets refer to the product's global rankings in terms of output in the related years.
Source: National Bureau of Statistics, *China Statistical Yearbook*, 2007.

B. *The Progress in Structure Adjustment and Upgrading Chinese Industry*

The modification and upgrading of China's industrial structure is a topic in national economic development that merits special attention. During the thirty years of reform and opening, the modification and upgrade of China's industrial structure has gone through three stages, achieving remarkable accomplishments. Stage 1 (1979–1984) was the stage during which the ratio of light to heavy industry was modified; Stage 2 (1985–1998) was the stage during which there was coordinated development of light and heavy industries; Stage 3 (1999–present) has been the stage of heavy industrialization (see Figure 2.5).

During Stage 1, in light of the structural contradiction involved in giving priority to the development of heavy industry, China began to make a drastic readjustment to its industrialization strategy. As a result, the strategy of prioritizing heavy industry was replaced by a strategy aiming for balanced development of light and heavy industries. Through this transition, policymakers gave up on the idea of purely prioritizing heavy industry. Based on a preliminary adjustments made from 1979 to 1980, China made further modifications in 1981 and continued to readjust in from 1982 to 1984. In the end, the structure of light and heavy industry was modified to an extent large enough to ensure reasonable development. During the period from 1979 to 1984, the average annual output value of light and heavy industry grew by 12.3 percent and 7.2 percent respectively; the ratio of light and heavy industry in the gross industrial output value changed from 43.1:56.9 in 1978 to 47.4:52.6 in 1984 (see Figure 2.5). Through this modification proccss, light industry began to evolve towards an advanced structure. In particular, light industry underwent two periods of development. In the first period, the development of light industry was focused primarily on agricultural products; in the second period, development focused on non-agricultural products.[20]

In fact, this stage's development of light and heavy industry proceeded amid an adjustment of the developmental relationship between the processing industry and basic industry. China experienced macroeconomic overheating three times in the first half of 1985, in 1988, and in the first half of 1993 respectively. While the processing industry

[20] Wang Yueping 王岳平. *Kaifang tiaojianxia de gongye jiegou shengji* 开放条件下的工业结构升级 [*Upgrading Industrial Structure under Open Conditions*], 2004.

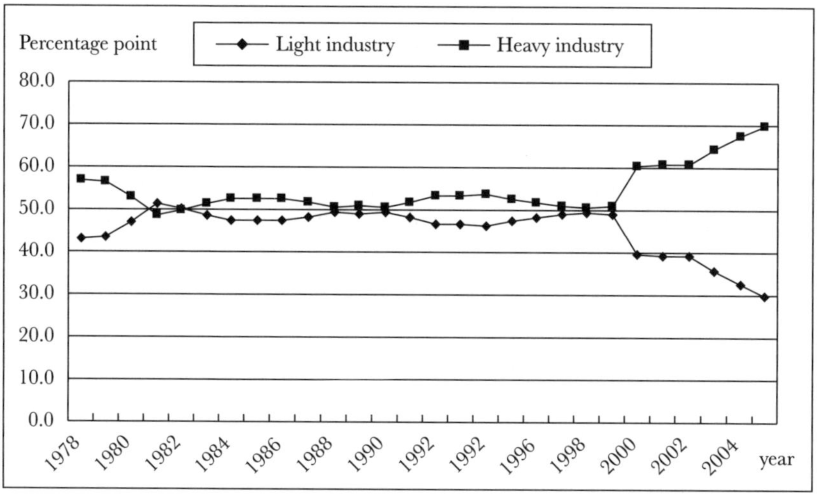

Sources: Department of Industry and Transportation of the National Bureau of Statistics, *China's Industrial Economy Statistical Yearbook*, 2004: 24; National Bureau of Statistics, China Statistical Yearbook, 2004: 505; National Bureau of Statistics, *China Statistical Yearbook*, 2007: 501.

Figure 2.5. Light and Heavy Industry Output Value as a Percentage of Total Industrial Output Value in 1978–2006.

grew too rapidly, basic industry (energy and raw materials) had acute constraints. To resolve this, China boosted investment in basic industry and leveraged the regulating role of market prices. By the mid-1990s, China had basically alleviated the constraints of basic industry. During this stage, there was also substantial progress in upgrading China's industrial structure as well as growth in some highly technologically dependent industries (e.g. the home appliance and electronic communications industries). In addition, there were also some changes in the structure of industrial products, increasing the amount of good quality products with high technological content.

During Stage 3, heavy industry grew quickly and began to again dominate China's industry.[21] In terms of the value added growth rate, after 1999, heavy industry far outgrew light industry, with the ratio between the output value and value added growth of heavy and light

[21] Chen Jiagui 陈佳贵 et al. *Zhongguo gongyehua jincheng baogao* 中国工业化进程报告 [*China Industrialization Progress Report*], 2007.

industry widening in favor of heavy industry. As can be seen below, this trend towards heavy industry became very pronounced (see Figure 2.6). In 1999, heavy industry accounted for 50.8 percent of the aggregate industrial value added. In 2006, it accounted for 69.5 percent of the aggregated industrial value added. However, the growth mechanism of heavy industry at this time was qualitatively different from its growth mechanism before the reform and opening. This time, heavy industry growth was driven by changes in the consumption structure, the accelerated pace of urbanization, and increased investment in transportation and infrastructure. In fact, this trend towards heavy industry can be seen as an inevitable outcome of reform and opening and economic development. It was in line with the transition from labor-intensive industry to capital- and technology-intensive heavy industry. This transition conformed to the general laws of economic evolution. In addition, in the face of limited resource and environmental pressure, the Chinese government in 2002 lost no time in promoting the idea of "new industrialization" and took a series of measures promoting the intensive development of China's industry.

Generally speaking, during the thirty years of reform and opening, the changes to China's industrial structure have not only abided by the principles of the market economy but also followed the general rules of industrial structure evolution. At the same time, China has pursued "domestic and international" development and aroused the enthusiasm of all parties to boost industrial development, thereby enabling China's industry to grow on a sustainable basis.[22] More importantly, while pushing forward industrial development, the Chinese government was able to craft a series of development strategies for different stages of industrial growth, strategies which have been based on actual circumstances, and not just textbook examples. According to what has been necessary at the time, the government has launched initiatives giving priority to the development of light industry, followed by those aimed at vigorously developing basic industry, and finally those aimed at promoting "new industrialization."

[22] Chen Jiagui et al., *China Industrialization Progress Report*, 2007: 14–18.

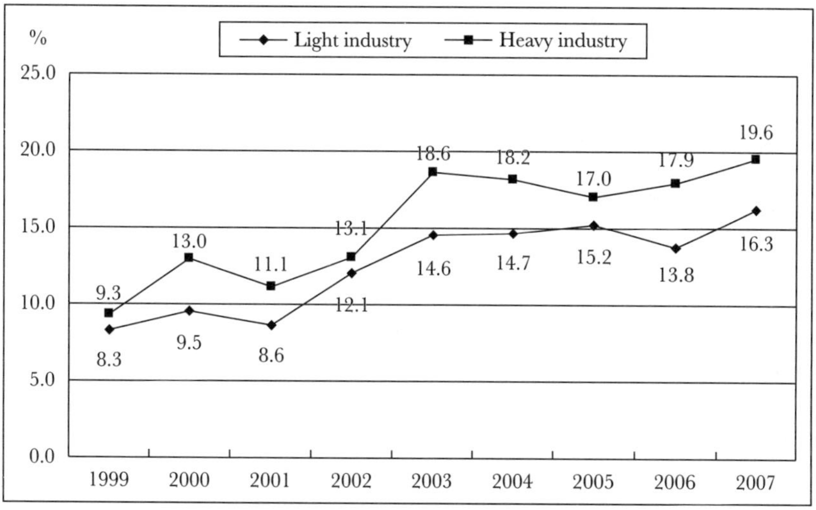

Source: Statistical Communiqué of the People's Republic of China on the National Economic and Social Development (1998–2007) (electronic version).

Figure 2.6. A Comparison of Light and Heavy Industry Value Added Growth Rates during 1999–2007.

C. *China's Progress towards Industrialization*

Through thirty years of rapid industrialization, China has been transformed from an agricultural economy into an industrial economy. If we divide the industrialization process into three stages (i.e., the initial stage, middle stage, and late stage of industrialization) and each stage is subdivided into the first half and the second half, then China as a whole has entered into the second half of the middle stage of industrialization (see Figure 2.7).[23]

By conducting econometric analysis of the level of development, industrial structure, employment structure, and spatial structure of the Chinese economy, we built a model to evaluate China's industrialization, using the model to perform an evaluation of China's industrialization.[24] The results of this evaluation indicate that the composite

[23] Chen Jiagui et al., China Industrialization *Progress Report*, 2007: 14–18.

[24] For the specific evaluation method of China's industrialization level and the basis of stage classification, see Chen Jiagui et al, China Industrialization *Progress Report*, 2007: 19–36.

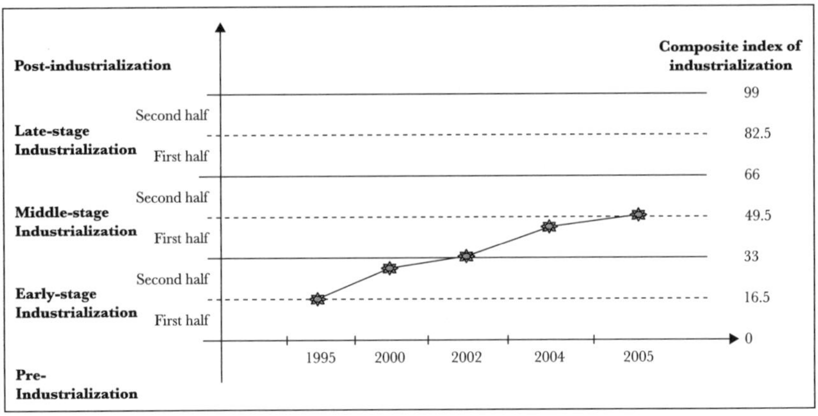

Source: Chen Jiagui et al., *China Industrialization Progress Report*, 2007: 47.

Figure 2.7. China's Industrialization.

index of China's industrialization level was 18 in 1995, 26 in 2000 and 50 in 2005, suggesting that China as a whole entered into the second half of the middle stage of industrialization in 2005.

During the period 1995–2005, China underwent rapid industrialization. Compared with the Ninth Five-Year Plan period, the Tenth Five-Year Plan period was a time in which the pace of industrialization was drastically accelerated. During the period from 1995 to 2000, the composite index of China's industrialization level increased 1.6 a year; during the 2000–2005 period, the composite index increased 4.8 a year. In 1995, China was still in the second half of the initial industrialization stage and remained at this stage until the Tenth Five-Year Plan period. In 2002, China entered from the initial industrialization stage to the middle industrialization stage. China has now entered into the second half of the middle industrialization stage.

During the period from 1995–2005, the drivers of China's industrialization process changed. During the Ninth Five-Year Plan period, structural upgrading of tertiary industry was the key factor driving China's industrialization process. During the Tenth Five-Year Plan period, however, industrial structure upgrading replaced industrial structure adjustment to become the key driver of China's industrialization process. This is indicative of a gradual shift of focus in China's industrialization process from quantitative expansion to quality improvement.

In China's industrialization process, we notice that the starting point of industrial development varies from region to region, as does the resource endowment and development policy among regions. An upshot of these factors working together is that different regions are at different stages of industrialization while they are advancing towards the advanced stage of industrialization. For example, Beijing and Shanghai are two cities with the highest degree of industrialization in China. They have now entered into the post-industrialization stage. By contrast, Tibet is a region with the lowest degree of industrialization, being still at the pre-industrialization stage. Other regions are at the different stages of pre-industrialization, mid-industrialization and late-industrialization (see Table 2.6).

D. *China's Industrial Competitiveness*

Along with the growth of China's industry, its industrial-product exports have also grown over time. Now China plays an increasingly important role in the world market. WTO statistics show that China's finished-product exports totaled USD 8.71 billion in 1980, accounting for 0.8 percent of the world's finished product exports and USD 895.43 billion in 2006, accounting for 10.84 percent of the world's total. From 1980 to 2006, China's finished industrial-product exports grew at an average annual rate of 19.5 percent, while the annual growth rate for world at large was 8.09 percent (see Figure 2.8). In 2006, the value of China's imports and exports ranked third globally, ranking behind the United States and Germany.[25]

With this rabid growth in exports, China has optimized its export system. In terms of the diversity of products that China's exports, the proportion of finished industrial products has been on the rise, while the share of primary products has been in decline. Statistics show that in 2007, exports of primary products accounted for only 5.1 percent of China's total exports; in 1980, the number was 50.3 percent. In terms of the makeup of these finished product exports, the export of electromechanical products as a percentage of China's total export has been increasing. In line with this trend, Chinese electromechanical

[25] WTO, *International Trade Statistics* (electronic version), 2007:12.

Table 2.6. A Comparison of China's Industrialization Stages by Regions (2005)

Stage \ Region		National	4 economic blocks	7 major economic regions	31 provinces, autonomous regions and municipalities
Post-industrialization stage					Shanghai (100), Beijing (100)
Late stage of industrialization	Second half of the stage			Yangtze River Delta (85) Pearl River Delta (80)	Tianjin (96), Guangdong (83)
	First half of the stage		East (78)	Bohai Bay (70)	Zhejiang (79), Jiangsu (78), Shandong (66)
Middle stage of industrialization	Second half of the stage	National (50)			Liaoning (63), Fujian (56)
	First half of the stage		Northeast (45)	Northeast (45)	Shanxi (45), Jilin (39), Inner Mongolia (39), Hubei (38), Hebei (38), Heilongjiang (37), Ningxia (34), Chongqing (34)
Initial stage of industrialization	Second half of the stage		Middle (30) East (25)	Six provinces in central China (30) Great Northwest (26) Great Southwest (24)	Shaanxi (30), Qinghai (30), Hunan (28), Henan (28), Xinjiang (26), Anhui (26), Jiangxi (26), Sichuan (25), Gansu (21), Yunnan (21), Guangxi (19), Hainan (17)
	First half of the stage				Guizhou (13)
Pre-industrialization stage					Tibet (0)

Note: Figures in brackets refer to the composite index of industrialization.
Source: Chen Jiagui et al., *China Industrialization Progress Report*, 2007: 41.

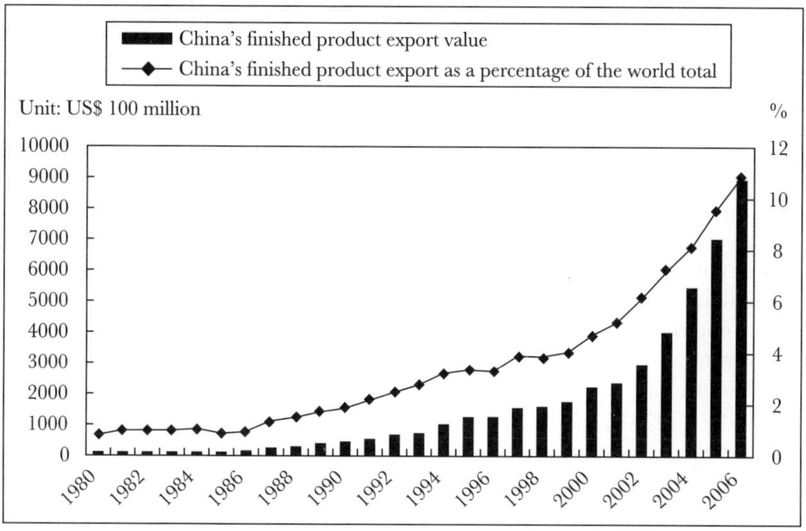

Source: WTO, *International Trade Statistics.*

Figure 2.8. China's Finished Industrial Product Exports in 1980–2006.

products have begun to account for an increasingly large share of the world's electromechanical product market. In 1995, electromechanical products overtook textile products to become China's single largest export, indicating a dramatic change in China's export market. Statistics from China's Customs office show that exports of electromechanical products totaled USD 701.17 billion in 2007, accounting for 57.6 percent of China's total exports. As a portion of global total exports, China's electromechanical product exports are also on the rise, beginning to occupy an important position therein. In 2006, China's exports of office and communications equipment accounted for 19.80 percent of the world total. Specifically, exports of electronic data processing and office equipment, communications equipment, and machinery and transportation equipment accounted for 26.13 percent, 22.71 percent, and 10.46 percent of the global total respectively (see Table 2.7).

Table 2.7. China's Electromechanical Product Exports in 1980–2006 Unit: US$100 million

	1980	1985	1990	1995	2000	2006
Machinery and transportation equipment	8.43 (0.16)	–	108.33 (0.89)	314.07 (1.62)	826.00 (3.14)	4563.43 (10.46)
Office and communications equipment	0.68 (0.08)	0.97 (0.07)	31.26 (1.05)	145.06 (2.40)	434.98 (4.50)	2873.31 (19.80)
Electronic data processing and office equipment	–	–	–	–	186.38 (5.02)	1345.07 (26.13)
Communications equipment	–	–	–	–	195.08 (6.78)	1236.15 (22.71)
Integrated circuit and electronic components	–	–	–	–	53.52 (1.74)	292.09 (7.44)
Automobile products	0.63 (0.05)	–	2.58 (0.08)	6.21 (0.14)	15.81 (0.27)	144.11 (1.42)

Note: Figures in parenthesis refer to the percentage of each product in the world's total export value.
Source: WTO, *International Trade Statistics.*

Generally speaking, the international competitiveness of China's industry has been on the rise. Changes in the trade competition index (net export index) and Revealed Comparative Advantage Index (RCA) both indicate that the international competitiveness of China's industry has continued to rise over the thirty years since reform and opening (see Figure 2.9).

E. *China's Industrial Management System*

During the thirty years of reform and opening, China has accomplished the transition of its industry management system from a one based on planned economic management to one based on the socialist market economy. Market mechanisms have become important means of economic management. Meanwhile, industry management departments, management targets, and management methods have changed significantly. In general, changes in China's industry management system since reform and opening can be divided into two major stages: Stage 1 (1978–1992) was a stage of adjusting of the industry management system in a transitionary period; Stage 2 (1993–present) has been

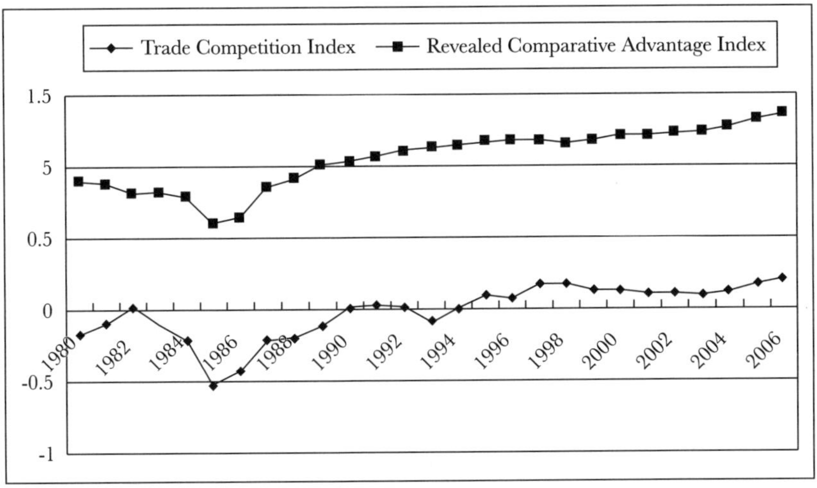

Source: WTO, *International Trade Statistics.*

Figure 2.9. The International Competitiveness Index of China's Finished Industrial Products in 1980–2006.

a stage of establishing and refining the industry management of the socialist market economy.

During Stage 1, reforms of China's industrial management system focused on enhancing the vitality of microeconomic entities and enterprise, adjusting the relationship between the government and enterprise, and enabling enterprise to become real economic entities in the legal sense.

Reform of China's industrial management system started in 1979 with the introduction of the power-delegating and profit-sharing scheme and the breakup of the highly centralized command and control management system. At the same time, government organizational reform also proceeded on a steady course. In 1982, during the first round of organizational reforms, the China Shipbuilding Industry Corporation and the China Automotive Industry Corporation were established through the merger and reorganization of industries to break sector and regional boundaries. In fact, launching reforms of the economic management system and replacing administrative organs with economic entities amounted to a major breakthrough for China. In 1988, during the second round of organizational reform, the State Council made progress in adjusting and reducing the number of industry management departments and authorities. For example, the State Council abolished the Ministry of the Coal Industry, the Ministry of the Petroleum Industry, and the Ministry of the Nuclear Industry; it also reorganized the Ministry of Energy, abolished the State Machine-Building Industry Commission and the Ministry of Electronic Industry, and established the Ministry of Machinery and Electronic Industry; it abolished the Ministry of Aeronautics Industry and the Ministry of Astronautics Industry and established the Ministry of Aeronautics and Astronautics Industry. Meanwhile, the China National Petroleum Corporation, China Weaponry Industry Corporation, and China National Nuclear Industry Corporation were also established in place of the former ministries.

During Stage 2, management system reform focused on gradually implementing the separation of government and business and leveraging the market in allocating resources.

In 1993, during the third round of organizational reform, the separation of government and business was furthered. The State Council abolished the Ministry of Aeronautics and Astronautics Industry and established China Aviation Industry Corporation and China Aerospace Industry Corporation to replace it. After abolishing the Ministry of Light Industry and the Ministry of Textile Industry, the State Council established China National Light Industry Council and China National Textile Council (which were not a part of the list of ministries and commissions). These reforms made progress in delegating the responsibilities of these former ministries to industry associations. Some of their regulatory functions were also transferred into the respective industry bureaus affiliated with the State Economic and Trade Commission. In 1998, during the fourth round of organizational reform, the state surrendered its strategy of directly managing enterprise. As a result, the six ministries in charge of the electricity, metallurgy, coal, chemical, machinery, and electronics industries were abolished and reorganized into six bureaus affiliated with the State Economic and Trade Commission. Meanwhile, all the responsibility for managing profit-oriented enterprise run by the military and armed police forces as well as the people's courts, the people's procuratorates, and the public security organs were transferred to local governments. At the same time, the central party and government departments also severed ties with their affiliated economic entities and enterprise. This laid the groundwork for the eventual separation of government and business functions and the transformation of government functions. In 2003, during the fifth round of organizational reform, the legal separation of government and business was finally realized. The state also abolished the State Economic and Trade Commission and established the *State-owned Assets* Supervision and Administration Commission of the State Council. Since then, the central and local governments have established respective authorities for the management of state-owned assets. In 2007, during the sixth round of organizational reform, the state launched the "super-ministry system" reform, aimed at better leveraging collaboration between different ministries in managing the economy.

IV. *Summary*

Behind the hubbub surrounding the "Chinese model," the "China experience," and the "China miracle" lies the undisputable truth that China's industrial economy has made an enormously important contribution to development of the national economy. Why has the reform and opening of China's industry made such remarkable accomplishments? In brief, its success can be attributed to the following seven factors.

A. *China's Industrial Reform Has Been Consistently Market-Oriented*

Whether it has been reform of state-owned enterprise, encouraging the development of private enterprise, or reform of the industry management system, China has continued to move in the direction of market-oriented reform. State-owned enterprise reform has involved introducing the power-delegating and profit-sharing scheme, implementing the contract management responsibility system, establishing the modern enterprise system, restructuring state-owned enterprise into modern corporate organization, and conducting a strategic reorganization of the state-owned economy. In essence, China has steered an unwavering course towards market-oriented reform; in doing so, it has adjusted the relationship between government and enterprise, expanded business management autonomy, and enabled enterprise to become market and legal entities capable of operating independently and autonomously. As for the development of private enterprise, China has also steered a course toward market-oriented reform. In the beginning, China allowed the individual economy to develop as a new economic sector. In 1982, the Constitution officially established the legitimacy of the individual economy. China then gave the green light for private enterprise to develop as new economic entities. Then in 1988, the Constitution officially established the legitimacy of private enterprise. Originally, private enterprise was only allowed to develop in a few industries. But in 2005, the State Council issued the *Several Opinions of the State Council on Encouraging, Supporting and Guiding the Development of Non-Public (Individual and Private) Economy* (国务院关于鼓励支持和引导个体私营等非公有制经济发展的若干意见), laying down the guiding philosophy of allowing private enterprise to develop in any industry "unless expressly prohibited." The reform of China's industrial enterprise has consistently emphasized cultivating and developing market entities, fostering a fair and equitable environment for market competition, and establishing and refining the legal environment.

In addition, the system for managing industries has also evolved from being managed according to the planned to being managed in a market-economy style. The reforms of the industry management system during the period from 1978 to 1992 had clear "transformational" character, apparent in the decline of command-oriented economic planning and rise of guidance-oriented economic planning; it was also apparent in the elimination of a wide variety of administrative organs and their replacement by economic organizations who assumed the responsibilities of managing economic entities. Since 1993, the separation of government and business has been gradually furthered. As a result, the government agencies in charge of the industrial economy have been reduced in number year over year, either by being abolished or reorganized into industry associations. In general, the state no longer assumes the functions of or has the power to directly manage enterprise. Meanwhile, the establishment of the State-owned Assets Supervision and Administration Committee (SASAC) has also furthered the separation of government and business.

B. *The Reform, Opening, and Development of China's Industry Has Been Jointly Pushed by State-Owned Enterprises and Non-State-Owned Enterprises*

Through thirty years of reform and opening, the ownership structure of China's industrial economy has gradually evolved from a "monolithic" economy of state-owned enterprise into the current "balance of power" among state-owned, private, and foreign-funded enterprise. In fact, from the micro perspective, both state-owned and non-state-owned enterprise has pushed forward reform, opening, and development both horizontally and vertically.

Vertically, the reform state-owned enterprise has been deepened through the introduction of the power-delegating and profit-sharing mechanisms as well as through property rights reform aimed at unleashing the productive power of enterprise. Along with the gradual implementation of market-oriented reform and the continuous improvement of the policy and legal environment, private and foreign-funded enterprise have moved from the exploratory and startup stage into the accelerated development stage. As a result, over time, they have grown big and strong. Horizontally, under the "advance and retreat" guideline of "invigorating large enterprise while relaxing control over small ones," state-owned enterprise have undergone strategic reorganization and retreated from the economy on some fronts. Specifically, they have withdrawn entirely from some competitive areas and further concentrated their operation in the key industries and sectors that have a direct bearing on national security and the national economy. As state-owned enterprise has retreated, private and foreign-funded enterprise has stepped into these competitive areas, increasing in size and strength.

Generally speaking, state-owned and non-state-owned enterprise have jointly pushed forward industrial reform, opening, and development by proceeding with "gradual deepening" of reform on the vertical dimension and "combining advance with retreat" and "pursuing collaborative development" on the horizontal dimension. The success of this approach is evident in the compatibility of the aptly timed adjustment of industry ownership structure and reform of the industrial economy.

C. *China's Industrial Reform Is Based on Invigorating Enterprises*

The Third Plenary Session of the Eleventh CPC Central Committee was preceded and followed by a fierce debate on how to further economic reform. The most representative and creative thought in this debate was an "enterprise-based theory" (企业本位论) put forward by Jiang Yiwei. In his opinion, reform should be tied neither to "state-centered theory" (国家本位论) nor move toward adopting "localized theory" (地方本位论). Instead, reform should embrace "enterprise-based theory" as the guiding philosophy. The "enterprise-based theory" stresses that enterprises should be the basic unit of the modern economy, acting as an active economic organism with independent interests. The theory holds that under the socialist system, the relationship between the state and enterprise should exhibit the clear separation of government and business.[26] Under the guiding philosophy of the "enterprise-based theory," invigorating enterprise became a central part of China's economic reform.

For state-owned enterprise, the era of power-delegating and profit-sharing reforms focused on restructuring the highly centralized planned economy and enhancing the vitality of enterprise by increasing their management independence; the contract management stage of reform emphasized the goal of separating government from business and ownership from management as well as promoting the vitality of enterprise by transforming their operational mechanisms; the stage of reform that established the modern enterprise system underscored the need for enterprise to adapt to the market economy through innovation and to become independent market competitors that assume sole responsibility for their profits and losses, pursue self-development, and exercise self-constraint. At the same time, the reform initiative of "invigorating large enterprise while relaxing control over small ones" emphasizes the transition from "invigorating individual enterprise" to "invigorating all enterprise as a whole" and making adjustments in a bid to put the national economy on the market-oriented track. Similarly, reform initiatives concerned with the development of private and foreign-funded enterprise have also focused on invigorating enterprise and enhancing the vitality of enterprise by bettering the economic environment.

Enterprises are the principal economic actors and the sources of productivity. It was only by focusing on invigorating enterprise that economic reform has found a target and a method by which to measure success. Based on the actual circumstances as observed on the ground, China can push forward reform, unleash enterprise productivity to the maximum extent possible, and promote the development of the industrial economy.

---

[26] Jiang Yiwei 蒋一伟. "Qiye benweilun 企业本位论 [Enterprise Based Theory]," 1980.

D. *China Has Followed a Gradualist Approach of "Piloting, Then Diffusing" in throughout the Reform and Opening Process*

Not all reform and opening initiatives were simultaneously implemented nationwide when they were launched. Instead, they were first adopted within a smaller scope on a pilot basis and, based on the results and experiences of trials, expanded to a larger scope.

In reforming state-owned enterprise, China has followed a path of local experimentation followed by national diffusion. This strategy has been applied for all kinds of reform, whether it be introducing the power-delegating and profit-sharing scheme, the economic responsibility system, undertaking tax-for-profit reforms, introducing the contract management responsibility system, or setting up the modern enterprise system (see Table 2.8).

The gradual "trial first, diffusion after" strategy is also an accurate description of China's opening process in general. In 1980, China started by setting up four special economic zones; in 1984, it opened fourteen coastal cities; in 1985, it set up three more open economic zones on the coast; in 1992, it opened inland areas along the borders, rivers, inland provincial capitals and roads. The sequence of reform was first to conduct experiments in special economic zones, then to expand them to coastal areas and open cities, and finally radiate them nationwide. In terms of industrial sector, it was also a process in which the scope of investment was gradually relaxed in one industry after the other. In addition, the principal form of FDI utilization proceeded from cooperative operation to JV operation and then to wholly owned operation.

E. *China Has Leveraged the Role of Local Governments in the Industrial Reform and Development Process*

China's economic reform has been a process in which the central government delegates power to and shares profit not only with enterprise but also with local governments. Under the planned economic system, local governments were merely puppet organs that were installed to carry out orders of the central government and enjoyed little autonomy. It is fair to say that at that time local government enthusiasm and creativity was largely stifled. During the industrial reform process, the central government began to delegate power to local government

Table 2.8. The "Piloting, then Diffusion" Path of China's State-Owned Enterprise Reform

Reform initiatives	Piloting	Diffusion	Policy or system formation
Power-delegating and profit-sharing	In October 1978, six state-run industrial enterprise, including Chongqing Iron and Steel Corporation, took the lead in the trial program; In May 1979, the state selected eight enterprise, including Shougang Group Corporation, to join the trial program	In 1981, state-run enterprise began to implement the regulation calling for the expansion enterprise autonomy.	In July 1979, the State Council issued the *Regulations on Expanding Operation and Management Autonomy of State-Run Industrial Enterprise*[27]
Contract management responsibility system	In 1982, the State Council approved eight large and medium-sized state-owned enterprise, including Shougang and the Second Auto Works (now known as Dong Feng Motor Corporation), to implement the contract management responsibility system on a trial basis.	In 1987, the state decided to implement the contract responsibility system nationwide starting in the second half of the same year.	In February 1988, the State Council promulgated *Provisional Regulations on the Contract Management Responsibility System of Industrial Enterprise Owned by the Whole People*[28]
Reform of the Joint-stock system	In July 1984, Beijing Tianqiao Department Store Co., Ltd. was officially established; in November 1984, Shanghai Feilo Acoustics Co., Ltd. floated its IPO; subsequently, a few enterprise based in Guangzhou began to implement the joint-stock system on a trial basis; in the late 1980s, the state gave green light for experimenting with the joint-stock system within on a moderate scale.	Widely promoted and implemented after the Third Plenary Session of the Fourteenth CPC Central Committee	At the end of 1988, the State Council issued *The Guiding Opinions on Actively and Steadily Pushing Forward the Joint-Stock System Reform of State-Owned Enterprise;*[29] in 1992, the *Opinions on Standardizing Limited Joint-Stock Companies*[30] was issued; in 1993, the *Company Law* was enacted.

[27] 关于扩大国营工业企业经营管理自主权的若干规定
[28] 全民所有制工业企业承包经营责任制暂行条例
[29] 关于积极稳妥地推进国有企业股份制改革的指导意见
[30] 股份有限公司规范意见

Table 2.8 (*cont.*)

Reform initiatives	Piloting	Diffusion	Policy or system formation
Setting up the modern enterprise system	In 1994, the state selected 100 state-owned large and medium-sized enterprises from different sectors to set up the modern enterprise system on a piloting basis. Meanwhile, a number of enterprises were also selected in each region and sector to join the piloting program.	The Tenth Five-Year Plan required that "the vast majority of state-owned large and medium-sized enterprise preliminarily set up the modern enterprise system by the end of the 20th century"	In 2000, the State Council issued *The Basic Regulations for State-Owned Large and Medium-Sized Enterprise to Set Up the Modern Enterprise System and Strengthen Management (Trial)*[31]

Source: Compiled by the authors.

and adjusted the revenue-sharing relationship between the central and local governments. As a result, local governments have established independent objectives and systems. Therefore, they have an incentive to invigorate local enterprise and promote the growth of the local economy.

In terms of reforming state-owned enterprise, due to the fact that the growth of local economy is closely related to the development of local state-owned enterprise, it is inevitably in the interest of local governments to create systems that promote the development of and creativity in state-owned enterprise; thus local governments become promoters of reform. After the central government has set the direction of reform, local governments then push forward reform forward based on their local circumstances. In particular, local governments have experimented with new ideas for reform and disseminated them if they prove successful upon approval from the central government. For example, the power-delegating and profit-sharing scheme was first tried by six enterprises in Sichuan; the reorganization of the joint-stock system in small and medium-sized state-owned enterprise was based on the "Zhucheng experience." Such innovations have provided successful examples that push forward China's reform. In addition, local governments have used every possible method to try and woo

[31] 国有大中型企业建立现代企业制度和加强管理基本规范 (试行)

outside investors, encouraging them to start businesses and invest in their jurisdictions; this has also enhanced the development of private and foreign-funded enterprise.

In our opinion, China's industrial reform has been a "top down" process in which the central government sets the direction and the local government carries it out. Meanwhile, however, it has also been a "bottom up" process in which the local government experiments based on the unique local conditions and promotes such successful examples nationwide after receiving approval from the central government. In this "top-down" interactive process, local governments have played an important role in pushing forward China's reform.

F. *China Has Consistently Integrated the Reform of the Industrial Economy with the Process of Accelerating Industrialization*

During the thirty years of reform and opening, China has undertaken an industrialization process which has been the largest in human history. As a result, China has moved from the initial stage of industrialization to the second half of the middle stage and also entered an period of accelerated development for heavy industry. This industrialization process has, in fact, also been a process of adapting the potentials of production with actual production.

At the beginning of its industrialization process, China shifted its development strategy from giving priority to the development of heavy industry to optimizing the development of light industry, correcting the unbalanced industrial structure. The drive for making this change came from the reform of China's industrial economy. For state-owned enterprise, reform awakened their ambition and unleashed their productivity. For private enterprise, including proprietorships, "red-hat" enterprise, private enterprises, and corporate enterprises, reform of the industrial economy accelerated their development and enabled them to become an important driving force in China's industrialization process. For foreign-funded enterprise, reform also promoted their development. At the same time, these foreign-funded enterprises also provided capital and technical support which further pushed forward China's industrialization. All in all, reform of the industrial economy unleashed the productivity of state-owned, private, and foreign-funded enterprise, and pushed forward China's industrialization from the initial stage of industrialization to current state, in the second half of the middle stage.

Since 1999, amid the accelerated growth of heavy industry, how to take a "new approach" to industrialization has became an important question for China. In truth, finding a way to move industrialization forward was a requirement put forth by the stage of development. This "new approach" has emphasized integrating industrialization and informatization, paying utmost attention to the environment, reducing resource consumption, leveraging the strengths of human resources, and increasing the use of technology. In working to achieve these goals, in addition to the endeavors by enterprise, guidance and stimulus by the government has also played an important role. In 2007, China launched the sixth round of organizational reform and established the Ministry of Industry and Information Technology, the Ministry of Environmental Protection and the Ministry of Human Resources and Social Security, as well as the National Energy Bureau. The chief objective of this round of reform was to bring the government into a position of being better able to serve the needs of this new type of industrialization.

Regardless whether one looks at China's industrialization in terms of its progress to the second half of the middle stage of industrialization or in the way it has faced the need to develop a new kind of industrialization development, China has always integrated reform of the industrial economy with the process of industrialization, adapting its production to developments in productive capacity.

G. *China Has Always Integrated the Processes of Industrial Reform and Industrial Opening*

Since 1978, China has closely integrated the process of reforming industry opening industry; China has also continued its commitment to the developing both domestically and internationally, leveraging domestic and foreign factors to jointly push forward the development of China's industrial economy.

Reform has promoted the opening of China's industry. China's industrial reform has not only enabled enterprise to gradually turn into market economy entities but also brought about an important change in the way the government manages the economy; the market has become the most important channel for allocating resources. Due to the increasing productivity of business entities and the continuous improvement of the market's competition environment, China has attracted an enormous amount of foreign capital. Meanwhile, China's industrial product exports have also grown rapidly. Some enterprises have also expanded globally by way of M&A and natural expansion. Also, ass industrial reform has deepened, China has paid more attention to the quality of foreign investment, implying that China has opened to the outside world at a higher level.

Meanwhile, China has achieved its goal of promoting reform through opening to the outside world. Economic opening has not only attracted the capital, technology, and management expertise needed for China's industrial development but also pushed forward the progress of industrial reform. In addition, opening to the outside world has furthered reform at the systemic level. China's accession into the WTO was a milestone event in the sense that it signified China's acknowledgement of the rules for international competition; it is also significant because accession has required that China restructure the systems and mechanisms of its industrial economy to bring them into line with international rules.

After thirty years of reform and opening, China has become a major industrial country. The international competitiveness of China's industry has increased but China has yet to become an industrial powerhouse. China is still in the second half of the middle industrialization stage and at the lower end of the global division of labor. In the future, China's industrial development will face the constraints of limited resources and environment concerns as well as pressure from trade disagreements. Therefore, only by walking the path of scientific development, pursuing a new kind of industrialization, and boosting its ability to independently innovate, can China transform itself from a major industrial country into an industrial powerhouse, and eventually realize the ambitious goal of industrial modernization.

Bibliography

Chen Jiagui 陈佳贵 et al. *Zhongguo gongyehua jincheng baogao* 中国工业化进程报告 [*China Industrialization Progress Report*]. Social Sciences Academic Press, 2007.

Department of Industry and Transportation of the National Bureau of Statistics. *Zhongguo gongye jingji tongji nianjian* 中国工业经济统计年鉴 [*China's industrial Economy Statistical Yearbook (2004)*]. China Statistics Press, 2004.

Jiang Yiwei 蒋一伟. "Qiye benweilun 企业本位论 [Enterprise Based Theory]." *Zhongguo Shehui Kexue* 中国社会科学 [*China Social Sciences*] No. 1 (1980).

Liu Yan 刘研. *Kuaguo gongsi yu zhongguo qiye guojihua* 跨国公司与中国企业国际化 [*Multinational Firms and Chinese Enterprise Internationalization*]. China Citic Press, 1992.

Lu Tong 鲁桐. *Zhongguo qiye de guojihua zhanlüe* 中国企业的国际化战略 [*The Internationalization Strategy of Chinese Enterprise*]. Economic Management Press, 2003.

National Bureau of Statistics. *Zhongguo tongji nianjian* 中国统计年鉴 [*China Statistical Yearbooks*]. China Statistics Press, Various Years.

Wang Yueping 王岳平. *Kaifang tiaojianxia de gongye jiegou shengji* 开放条件下的工业结构升级 [*Upgrading Industrial Structure under Open Conditions*]. Economic Management Press, 2004.

WTO, *International Trade Statistics (2007)*: p12 (Website: http://stat.wto.org/).

Zhang Dicheng 张迪诚. *Zhongguo guoyouqiye gaige biannianshi* 中国国有企业改革编年史 (1978–2005) [*The Annals of China's State-Owned Enterprise Reform (1978–2005)*]. Chinese Workers Press, 2006.

Zhang Wenkui 张文魁. *Zhongguo guoyouqiye chanquan gaige yu gongsi zhili zhuanxing* 中国国有企业产权改革与公司治理转型 [*China's State-Owned Enterprise Property Rights Reform and Corporate Governance Transition*]. China Development Press, 2007.

Zhang Zhuoyuan 张卓元. "Shenhua guoqi gaige fazhan hunhe suoyouzhi 深化国企改革发展混合所有制 [Deepening State-Owned Enterprise Reform and Developing Mixed Ownership]." *Zhongguo keji chanye* 中国科技产业 [*China Science & Technology Industry*] No. 12 (2003).

Zhou Shulian 周叔莲. "20nian zhongguo guoyouqiye gaige jingyan de lilunfenxi 20 年中国国有企业改革经验的理论分析 [A Theoretical Analysis of 20 Years of State-owned Enterprise Reform in China]." *Journal of CASS Graduate School* No. 3 (2000).

Zhu Haibo 汪海波. "Zhongguo guoyouqiye gaige deshijian jincheng (1979–2003nian) 中国国有企业改革的实践进程 (1979–2003年) [The Practices and Progresses of China's State-Owned Enterprise Reform (1979–2003)]." *Zhongguo jingjishi yanjiu* 中国经济史研究 [*Researches in Chinese Economic History*] No. 3 (2005).

CHAPTER THREE

LABOR MARKET DEVELOPMENT AND EXPANSION OF RURAL AND URBAN EMPLOYMENT

Cai Fang

I. *Introduction*

Economic reform in China can be described as the transition from a planned economy to a market economy through the process of dualistic economic development, as first proposed by Arthur Lewis.[1] Centrally planned economies usually reject the labor allocation mechanisms of the market and instead use the planning system to allocate labor; the economic policies adopted by these countries tend to provide for an accumulation of resources for industrialization, achieved by separating urban and rural factors markets, thereby giving agricultural and rural areas unequal access to resources and ensuring a higher standard of living for urban residents.[2] China's own planned economy was no exception to these trends. China's long-standing divide between urban and rural areas is the result of adopting a development strategy emphasizing the development of heavy industry and utilizing a system of planned labor allocation and employment. The employment system under a planned economy consisted of two key elements.

First was the exclusive policy of comprehensive urban employment. The pursuit of capital-intensive industrialization in the capital-scarce economy resulted in limited employment absorption capacity in the urban sector.[3] It was thus thought that an absence of government intervention in allocating labor force would lead to a high unemployment rate in urban areas and endanger political stability. To secure stable

[1] Lewis, Arthur. "Reflections on Unlimited Labour," 1972.

[2] Knight Knight, John and Lina Song. *The Rural-urban Divide: Economic Disparities and Interactions in China*, 2005.

Anderson, K. "Lobbying Incentives and the Pattern of Protection in Rich and Poor Countries," 1995.

[3] Feng Lanrui 冯兰瑞 and Zhao Lukuan 赵履宽. *Zhongguo chengzhen de jiuye he gongzi* 中国城镇的就业和工资 [*The Employment and Wages in China's Urban Areas*], 1982.

and life-long employment for urban workers, the government departments of labor and personnel made job allocation part of the overall economic plan. At that time, the only two absorbers of labor force were state-owned enterprises and urban collectives. Once a worker was assigned to a post, there was basically no opportunity to change jobs, and also no fear of them being dismissed or unemployed.

The second component was the household registration system (the *hukou* system), which separated the population and labor markets of rural and urban areas, preventing the emergence of an integrated labor market. Since labor mobility was restricted between rural and urban areas and also between regions, (consistent with the policy goal of guaranteeing that the state and urban residents would be able to obtain agricultural products at low prices and preventing rural factors of production from flowing out of the agricultural sector), much less surplus rural labor than expected was absorbed by the growth of heavy industry when compared to traditional development economics. But the Chinese *hukou* system was not only a population registration system, it was also tied to a host of welfare policies, including the rationing of basic necessities, social security for urban residents, and other public service provisions, which, in addition to *hukou* system, effectively deterred labor mobility and prevented equal treatment of residents of rural and urban areas.

Such institutional arrangements slowed down China's economic growth and social development during the planning period. First, as the economy grew, the labor policies hampered employment expansion. Because of excessively concentrated investment in heavy industry, which was incapable of absorbing massive amounts of excess labor, surplus laborers were not able to flow out of agriculture. Simulation has shown that a total of forty percent of employment opportunities were lost in the period from 1952 to 1980.[4] This uneven distribution between rural and urban sectors resulted in inefficient resource allocation. In 1978, there were 74.5 million employees in the urban state-owned sector, in possession of fixed assets worth 448.8 billion yuan; and in agriculture, there were 283 million laborers, in possession of fixed assets worth less than 95 billion yuan. That is, the value of fixed

[4] Cai Fang, Lin, Justin Yifu, and Yong Cao. *The Chinese Economy: Reform and Development*, 2009.

assets per worker was 6024.2 yuan in the state non-agricultural sector and 335.7 yuan in agriculture.

Second, enterprises' lack of autonomy in hiring and firing workers and the government's restriction of labor mobility between rural and urban areas and between industry sectors lessened the incentive to micro-manage, leading to technical inefficiency. Most economists agree that during the planning period, the overall contribution of total factor productivity to economic growth was negative.[5] The lack of technical efficiency as well as inefficiency in allocation not only postponed the progress of economic development, but also created a large gap in the income of rural and urban areas.[6]

The market-oriented reform of labor policy has been a process of institutional transition, but at the same time, it has been dependent on reforms in other areas of the economic system. As the result of these reforms, the labor market is maturing and an increasing portion of the workforce is allocated according to market forces, evident in the increased labor mobility, market-oriented method of determining labor compensation, returns on human capital, mechanisms incentivizing hard work, and employment expansion. In regard to the reform of China's labor system and the results of these reforms, there are three noteworthy features. First was the pre-reform separation of urban and rural labor markets by formal institutional arrangement–through the household registration or *hukou* system. Second is that through reform, development, and the formation of a new system, China has basically completed the process of unifying its segmented labor market. Third is that during the transition and reform of the labor market, China has, at the same time, continued to move forward in transitioning towards dualistic development. These facts make China a good example of how institutional change can promote the healthy development of the economy.

The economic reforms began in the late 1970s and the resulting effects on economic growth have been widely acknowledged around the world and have aroused high levels of interest in other countries,

---

[5] Perkins, Dwight. "China's Economic Growth in Historical and International Perspective," 2005.
Yang Jianbai 杨坚白. "Sudu, jiegou, xiaolü 速度, 结构, 效率 [Speed, Structure and Efficiency]," 1991; World Bank. *China 2020: Development Challenges in the New Century*, 1997.

[6] Yang, Dennis and Cai Fang. "The Political Economy of China's Rural-Urban Divide," 2003.

especially developing countries with starting points similar to that of China. Reform of China's policy regarding labor mobility has not, as some scholars have asserted,[7] lagged behind the progress of other areas of reform; in contrast, as an important component of economic reform in general, reform of labor mobility policy has stayed in touch with rhythm and mode of, and shares the typical features of, China's other reforms. A review of the formation and reform process of China's labor policies, with analysis of the political economy at the time of their creation and reasons behind them, can be instructive for scholars and policy makers in other countries. At the same time, the theoretical and empirical analysis of China's reform can also contribute to the advancement of transitional and developmental economics.

II. *Release and Reallocation of Rural Labor*

The core of the household registration, or *hukou*, system was the restriction of both the movement of the population and the economic mobility of agricultural labor, the exclusion of the rural population from urban welfare systems, and the restriction of rural workers from non-agricultural jobs. Later on, Lewis[8] showed that in developing countries, a dualistic economic structure prevailed, formed under conditions similar to the divided labor market produced by the *hukou* system in China. The results were that, on one hand, the widening price gap between agricultural and industrial products caused an income gap between urban and rural areas; on the other hand, the household registration system also led to urban and rural residents having unequal access to the fruits of industrialization. At the same time, it led to tremendous losses in the efficiency of resource allocation. Under this institutional arrangement, the agricultural policy system strictly controlled all factors of production, restricted farmers' activities to a designated sector and area, and deterred migration of labor force in terms of geography and economic sector. This policy seriously impacted both technical and resource allocation efficiency.

The introduction of household responsibility system (HRS) became the first step of the Chinese economic reform. First initiated in the

[7] e.g. Lardy, Nicholas R. *China in the World Economy*, 1994.
[8] Lewis, W.A. "Economic Development with Unlimited Supplies of Labour," 1972.

early 1980s, HRS rapidly spread throughout the country. In early 1980 only 1.1 percent of production units utilized the system, but usage reached 20 percent by the end of that year. By the end of 1984, it was 100 percent of production units and 97.9 percent of farmers. According to one scholarly study, about 46.9 percent of increases in agricultural output between 1978 and 1984 can be attributed to the national adoption of this system.[9]

With the manifold increase in work effort that the system resulted in, there was a significant decline in the labor needed for agriculture and a surplus emerged. In order to absorb it, peasant households, which now had operational autonomy, initially expanded their work from being used solely for production of grains into other agricultural sectors. From that point, their work continued to expand from cultivation to the comprehensive development of market-directed agriculture, forestry, animal husbandry, fisheries, and household sideline production, greatly changing the agricultural production structure, and improving labor utilization and income levels. With these improvements in agricultural productivity, the capacity of both traditional cultivation and "big agriculture" (including farming, forestry, animal husbandry, sideline production, and fisheries) to absorb labor was ultimately limited.

However, in the early 1980s, the government did still not encourage labor to leave the countryside. However, realizing the inevitability of laborers transferring out of agriculture, and noting the potential for the development of small industries located in the countryside, the government promoted a form of agricultural labor transfer called "leaving the land but not the hometown." i.e., encouraging peasants to shift out of agricultural production to employment in township and village enterprises (TVEs). In 1978, the labor force employed in commune and brigade enterprises (analogous to the later-used term, TVEs) numbered 28.27 million, rising sharply to 69.79 million by 1985. However, in 1985 the rural people who had transferred to jobs in TVEs accounted for only 18.8 percent of total 370 million rural laborers; some 300 million workers remained in agriculture. According to the prevailing estimates, 30–40 percent of the agricultural workforce—in absolute terms, 100 million to 150 million people—was surplus.[10]

---

[9] Lin, Justin Yifu 林毅夫. "Rural Reforms and Agricultural Productivity Growth in China," 1992.

[10] Taylor, J.R. "Rural Employment Trends and the Legacy of Surplus Labor, 1978–1989," 1993: Chapter 8.

Faced with competition from other job seekers, the stagnation of TVEs, and the acceleration of urban reforms in the mid-1980s, rural residents began to transfer to large, medium, and small cities in search of non-agricultural jobs.

Gradual abolition of institutional obstacles has been the key to increased labor mobility since the 1980s. Observing the narrowing capacity of rural sectors to absorb surplus labor, in 1983, the government began to allow farmers to engage in long distance transport and marketing of their products beyond local market places. This was the first time that Chinese farmers had obtained legitimate rights to do business outside their hometowns. In 1984, regulations were further relaxed, and farmers were encouraged by the state to work in nearby small towns. A major policy reform took place in 1988, when the central government allowed farmers to work in enterprises or run their own business in cities on the condition that they were self-sufficient.[11]

In the 1990s, the central government and local governments took a series of measures that relaxed policies restricting migration and achieved a certain degree of reform of the household registration system as well. In this period, policies towards labor mobility in different regions diverged. The divergence could be first seen between central and local governments. Concerning employment, income, and social security of the country as a whole, the central government encouraged the migration of laborers between rural and urban areas and across provincial borders, while local governments' attitudes towards migration tended to differ depending on whether regions were sending or receiving migrants. In relatively poor regions, whose numbers of surplus laborers and economic share of agriculture were high, policies towards labor migration tended to be encouraging and supportive, with the governments taking measures to help farmers move out to seek better jobs and pay. In more advanced regions, however, governments were more concerned with the security of local employment, and welcomed migrant workers only when local economies needed extra labor. In those regions, policies towards the inflow of migrants changed cyclically, depending on the changing pressures for local governments

[11] At the time, rationing system of food and necessities had not been abolished and people without local *hukou* were not entitled to coupons for buying food and other necessities on the local market.

over time—that is, whenever local unemployment become severe, they tend to take measures to supplant migrant workers.[12]

By the 21st century, the decision-making power for reform of the household registration system had actually fallen to local—in particular urban—governments. At the time, the policy orientations of migrant-receiving regions began to diverge as well. While the legitimacy of policies concerning migration are based on the *hukou* system, in reality, the institutional factors restricting the flow of labor are not found only in the *hukou* system itself. The real issue is the costs related to the provision of social security, social welfare, and other public services behind the *hukou* system. As such, two kinds of local governments have changed from their former negative attitudes towards migration. The first are those fast-growing cities that have significantly benefited from the ample supply of migrant workers. The second are those who already have financial problems, and are as a result already unable to provide services to their citizens, and thus do not face any negative consequences by welcoming in more outside laborers.

However, in large and super-sized cities, where a variety of social welfare provisions are still related to, and based on, whether or not the recipients have local *hukou* identity, the governments are reluctant to adopt substantive reform of *hukou* system because they expect overwhelming demands for local welfare. Even now, the active role played by labor mobility in promoting the development of the labor market is inarguable, even in regions receiving migrant workers. Although there have been different orientations and cyclical swings in policy towards migration, during the entire reform period, both central and local governments have taken a host of policy measures to ease somewhat the strict restrictions on migration—specifically, this has resulted in the gradual repeal of the *hukou* system.[13] This process can be best seen through the following institutional adjustments.

---

[12] Cai Fang 蔡昉, Du Yang 都阳, and Wang Meiyan 王美艳. "Huji zhidu yu laodongli shichang baohu 户籍制度与劳动力市场保护 [The *Hukou* System and Protecting the Labor Market]," 2001.

[13] Closely examining the whole picture of reforms of the *hukou* system and related institutions, especially in noticing the demand for migrant workers in urban sectors, one cannot conclude that there has been a stagnation of the reform process. Lacking such a broad perspective on China's economic development, Chan and Buckingham (2008) suggested that the cumulative effect of the new round of *hukou* reform has nothing to do with abolition of the *hukou*, but instead makes migration harder than before.

As stated, in the 21st century, the decision-making power for reform of the household registration system was delegated to local governments. This began with the *hukou* reforms in small towns in 2000. This was characterized by "minimum conditions and comprehensive liberalization." In more than 20,000 small towns nationwide, the conditions for registration were reduced to just "having stable sources of life and legal domicile in the city;" any individuals or families meeting these conditions could apply to obtain an urban *hukou*. The governments in many medium-sized cities and even some provincial capitals also made major efforts to reform their *hukou* systems, which was characterized by "abolishing quotas, granting conditional access." Their approach was to relax the eligibility criteria, substantially lowering the threshold for settling in their cities. Policies towards migrants in super-sized cities like Beijing and Shanghai, whose reforms were characterized by "building a high threshold and opening city gates," gave a green light for the introduction of migrants with special skills, in effect raising the entry threshold for ordinary workers.

Urban welfare reforms thus created an institutional basis for the flow of rural workers into cities. The urban economic reforms that came into force gradually in the late 1980s, such as the development of the non-state-owned economy, which spurred a great demand for workers, as well as reforms of the food rationing, housing distribution, health care, and employment systems, have all reduced the costs for rural workers of moving to the city, settling down, and finding work. Also, with several important incidents and the resolution of several problems as a turning point, and the working and living conditions of migrant workers improved significantly.[14]

The follow-up to the "Sun Zhigang incident," which happened in the coastal city Guangzhou in 2003, clearly marked a major change in policy orientation. Sun Zhigang, a 27-year-old university graduate, was employed in a garment company in Guangzhou. Due to the lack of a local *hukou* or temporary resident permit, he was detained by the police and beaten to death. This incident attracted widespread public criticism, targeted directly at the unreasonable institutions behind the criminal acts of the law enforcement officers. Even as the perpetrators were brought to justice, the event set off strong criticism of the *hukou* system and temporary residence permits. The central government

[14] Wang Meiyan 王美艳. "Wage Arrears and Discrimination against Migrant Workers in China's Urban Labor Market," 2009.

also attached great importance to this, evidently becoming aware of the inconsistencies between the system and the laws of economic development and requirements for a harmonious society. Thus, the fastest adaptive reform of an institution that had been seen in history subsequently took place. Only three months after the incident, the Sate Council abolished the *Measures for the Custody and Repatriation of Vagrants and Beggars* (城市流浪乞讨人员收容遣送办法), which had been in force for over twenty years. Along with this, the State Council also promulgated the *Measures for Assisting Vagrants and Beggars with No Means of Support in Cities* (城市生活无着的流浪乞讨人员救助管理办法), fundamentally changing the orientation of policy for urban vagrants from detention to aid, and abolishing the legal basis for law enforcement officers' intervention in population movement.

As a result of these institutional changes and policy adjustments, the scale of rural labor mobility has grown, developing into a "migrant workers tide" which has caught the attention of the world. There has never been a consistent official figure regarding the migration of rural workers, and scholars often roughly estimate on the basis of partial surveys. Using inductions that have been made before, the space below offers a broad account of the numerical changes in labor mobility beyond township boundaries prior to 2000.[15] In 1983 there were only 2 million migrant workers, increasing to 30 million by 1989, 62 million in 1993, and 75.5 million in 2000. After 2000, the National Bureau of Statistics annual survey has estimates, which are shown in Table 3.1. This migration, which is the world's largest in terms of scale and scope, has in the end led to substantial reduction of surplus labor in rural China and has been bringing China closer to the first Lewis turning point.[16]

---

[15] Ministry of Agriculture Task Force. "Zhongguo nongcun renkou bianhua he tudi zhidu gaige 中国农村人口变化和土地制度改革 [Demographic Change and Reform of the Land System in Rural China]," 2001.

[16] See Cai Fang 蔡昉 and Wang Dewen 王德文. "Zhongguo jingji zengzhang kechixuxing yu laodong gongxian 中国经济增长可持续性与劳动贡献 [The Sustainability of Economic Growth and the Labor Contribution]," 1999 for the latest estimation of rural surplus labor force, and Cai Fang 蔡昉. "Approaching a Triumphal Span: How Far Is China Towards its Lewis Turning Point?" 2008 As for "first Lewis turning point", a point differentiated from the point where marginal productivities of labor in agricultural and modern sectors become equal, it is referred to the period of time, which was no longer characterized by unlimited supply of labor, while the dual economy feature still exists—that is, without an increase in wage rate in modern sector, labor supply can be embarrassed (Lewis, "Reflections on Unlimited Labour.").

Table 3.1. Migrant Workers and Urban Employment

Year	Migrant Workers (million)	Urban Employment (million)	Ratio (1/2, %)
2000	78.49	212.74	36.9
2001	83.99	239.4	35.1
2002	104.7	247.8	42.3
2003	113.9	256.39	44.4
2004	118.23	264.76	44.7
2005	125.78	273.31	46.0
2006	132.12	283.10	46.7
2007	136.49	293.50	46.5
2008	140.41	302.10	46.5

Source: National Bureau of Statistics (NBS), *China Statistical Yearbook*, various years; NBS, *China Yearbook of Rural Households Survey*, various years.

III. *Urban Employment Shock and Labor Market Development*

The reform of urban employment system has been characterized by incremental adjustment beginning as early as the 1980s, with the first break from planned allocation of the labor force in 1980. In order to solve the employment issues of the youth who had been sent to the countryside and returned to cities as well as new graduates, the government first introduced the triple-channel model of employment, a model that directed the youth toward government-intermediated employment, self-organized employment, or self-employment. Though it was just a minor change in urban employment policy, carried out in a marginal manner, it was the first to allocate labor outside the planned system. Therefore, this policy can be considered to be first step of urban employment policy reform.

The reform program known as "vitalizing the system of permanent employment," initiated in 1987, made changes to the core system of the "iron rice bowl" and began revising the traditional labor policies of the planning system. State-owned enterprises began to be required to recruit new workers based on a voluntary contract with them. Under the new labor management system, workers currently working at an enterprise were to be re-chosen and contracted based on their performance and efforts at work. With this reform, enterprise workers began to become aware of the risk of unemployment due to overstaffing, shrinking business, or misbehavior; however, at the time, the state required enterprises not to completely dismiss their workers.

The reform of China's state-owned enterprises (SOE) started in early 1980s and was characterized by a decentralization of power and allowing enterprises to take partial profits. Each step of the reform has delegated more rights to SOEs, allowing them to make decisions on labor employment; as the state has gradually granted autonomy to enterprises, managers of SOEs have gained the authority to select and dismiss workers, and to determine and adjust compensation in accordance with the enterprise's profitability and workers' performance. With this change in the institutional environment and with increasing pressure on enterprises to compete, employment became more and more market-oriented and the "iron rice bowl" system was gradually broken up.

During the early stage of labor policy reform, the relaxation of labor regulations and the delegation of employment autonomy to enterprises were motivated chiefly by the need to solve the problems presented by the massive increase in the size of the urban labor force—youth returned from the countryside and new graduates—and to improve the system of incentives for enterprise workers. However, since urban enterprises had only soft-budget constraints, their managers lacked sufficient motivation to utilize the labor market as a distributor of resources. Only when SOEs began to face stronger outside competition in 1990s did the relaxed state regulations of labor allocation and autonomy of employment become stimuli for development of the labor market.

Due to the economic downturn and rapid industrial structural change that accompanied the East Asian financial crisis, in the late 1990s, many SOEs, which lost their comparative advantage and competitiveness, were unable to fully utilize their production capacity. To respond to this pressure, SOEs managers were forced to exercise their right to employment autonomy by disposing of workers; hundreds of thousands urban workers were forced to leave their posts. By utilizing official statistics published by the National Bureau of Statistics (NBS), we estimated the surveyed unemployment rate of urban residents according to standard definition of the International Labor Organization (ILO). These are compared with the officially reported figures of registered unemployment in urban areas. The results are shown in Table 3.2. As is shown in the table, the unemployment rate began increasing in 1997 and reached its peak in 2000. The severity of the unemployment during this time posed a challenge to the Chinese government, which coped with the shock to the labor market by helping the unemployed get reemployed or covered by the safety net.

Table 3.2. Urban Labor Market Indicators (%)

	Surveyed unemployment rate	Registered unemployment rate	Labor force participation rate
1995	4.0	2.9	75.9
1996	3.9	3.0	72.9
1997	4.5	3.1	72.1
1998	6.3	3.1	71.2
1999	5.9	3.1	72.9
2000	7.6	3.1	66.1
2001	5.6	3.6	67.3
2002	6.1	4.0	66.5
2003	6.0	4.3	63.4
2004	5.8	4.2	64.0
2005	5.2	4.2	64.6

Source: NBS, *China Population Statistical Yearbook*, various years; NBS and MOLSS, *China Labor Statistical Yearbook*, various years; NBS, *China Statistical Yearbook*, various years.

In the late 1990s, a large number of urban workers were laid off by their employers and, as a result, the urban unemployment rate climbed for a few years. To address the situation, the government implemented a series of policies and measures aimed at easing labor market pressure which involved different parties, including governments at various levels as well as communities, enterprises, and laborers. In May 1998 and again in September 2002, the CCP Central Committee and the State Council held conferences focused on the guaranteed basic living standard and reemployment for laid-off workers of SOEs, where arrangements were made for the implementation of a proactive employment policy with reemployment as main goal. The essential parts of this policy can be summarized as (1) macroeconomic policy aimed at boosting employment through sustained economic growth, (2) support policy that focused on promoting reemployment for laid-off and unemployed workers, (3) labor market policy that aimed to match the labor force to employment needs, (4) macroeconomic regulations that aimed to reduce unemployment, and (5) social security policy that aimed to guarantee the basic livelihood of laid-off and unemployed workers and actively promote reemployment.

Under this employment policy, the central and local governments both played an important role in helping the unemployed get reemployed through a variety of measures, including exemption from taxes, fiscal inputs, micro finance, social security subsidies, employment assistance, and even the creation of community work programs. In addition, the governments also made efforts to encourage the development of the non-public, service, and informal sectors of the economy, as well as the development of small and medium-sized enterprises, which were thought to be, and in fact were, enormous absorbers of unemployed labor. In using such a diverse array of policy measures to expand employment, the government gradually set forth a principle of formulating and implementing policy that prioritized employment. In comparison to the previous methods of policy formulation, a significant difference is that this new principle causes government functions to abide by market forces. This is to say that, in the final analysis, employment expansion relies on the labor market and not the government. Through the process of coping with the shock to the labor market, which involved removing institutional obstacles segregating the labor markets of rural and urban areas, different regions, and forms of ownership, as well as allowing the market to determine the prices of production factors, most of the policy measures taken to promote employment and reemployment have operated through mechanisms of the labor market.

Since the reforms initiated in the late 1970s, strong economic growth has spurred a rapid increase in urban employment, and even after the severe shock to the labor market, this trend has not diminished. In the period from 1997 to 2007, even without counting rural-to-urban migrants, urban employment levels grew by 41.2 percent, or 3.7 percent growth per year. In the same period, the composition of and the factors driving the expansion of urban employment have changed dramatically: of total urban employment, while in state sector employment dropped by 41.8 percent and 75.1 percent in collective sector, in share-holding cooperatives and joint ownership units employment increased by four fold, 5.1 times in corporations, nearly two times in the private and individual sectors, 1.7 time in joint-ventures, and 2.1 times in the informal sector that official statistic system cannot cover and thus takes the form of statistic residual (Figure 3.1).[17]

[17] We view the difference between actual numbers of urban employment based on household survey and numbers of reported work-unit employment as informal employment. In 2007, this informal part of urban employment was 96.6 million, accounting for 33 percent of the urban total. See Cai Fang 蔡昉. "Zhongguo jiuye tongji de yizhixing: Shishi he zhengce hanyi 中国就业统计的一致性: 事实和政策涵义 [The Consistency of China's Statistics on Employment: Facts and Implications for Public Policy]," 2004 for explanations on the data sources and method of calculation.

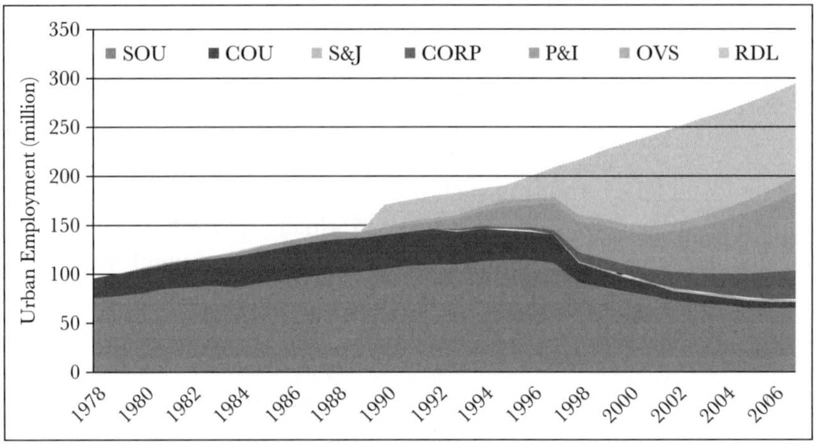

Note: SOU—State-owned Units, COU—Collective-owned Units, S&J—Shareholding Cooperative Units and Joint Ownership Units, CORP—Limited Liability Corporations and Share Holding Corporations, Ltd., P&I—Private Enterprises and Self-employed Individuals, OVS—Units with Funds from Hong Kong, Macao and Taiwan, and Foreign Funded Units, RDL—Residual.
Source: NBS (various years)

Figure 3.1. Changes in Employment Structure since the Reform.

As is shown in Figure 3.1, the major driver of urban employment expansion has been the so-called "residual" sector, which is the difference between total number of urban employment from household based survey and the work-unit employment number of urban employment from work-unit-based reporting statistics.[18] Before 1997, the share of residual employment was only about 10 percent, but it increased to 33 percent in 2007, a total increase of 41.2 percent in the ten year period. There are two factors that cause underreporting in the work-unit-based reporting system. The first factor is that as a result of diversification and informalization of the economy, some work units were never included in the system, which causes the error of "missing units." The second factor is that units have a motivation to deliberately underreport the numbers of employees, or even to not report altogether, in order to reduce their burdens (the number of employees in a work unit is tied to some responsibilities such as paying premiums for social security programs). More practically, many workers are now employed through agents and not counted as employees of their own,

[18] The detailed explanation about the two statistical programs of urban employment can be seen in Cai, "The Consistency of China's Statistics on Employment," 2004.

which also leads to underreporting. Also, the reemployed and migrant workers are rarely reported by their employers.

Before employment reforms for SOEs were initiated to break the "iron-rice-bowl" in the late 1990s, the non-publicly-owned sectors had only employed only a few turned-over workers, in addition to absorbing migrant workers. It was only after the reform of urban employment system was accomplished and the "iron-rice-bowl" was, for the most part, broken that labor allocation became market-based. During this time, the government implemented a subsidy program for laid-off workers, built up an unemployment insurance system, a basic pension scheme, and a minimum living standard program to protect urban workers; at the same time, it liberalized labor market regulations to encourage labor mobility. As a result, the following growth of the urban employment and diversification of the employment structure both occurred through labor market mechanisms.

Concerning the changes in labor market indicators presented in Table 3.2, we can see clearly three facts. First, since reform of the employment system began in the late 1990s, urban unemployment rate has not risen steadily; in fact, after reaching the peak of 7.6 percent in 2000, it actually tended to decline with some fluctuations. Secondly, at the time when unemployment first appeared in the late 1990s, there was not an unemployment insurance system available for laid-off workers. To avoid a possible social shock, a unique form of unemployment insurance was arranged by the Center for Reemployment Services, which operates at the enterprise level and provides laid-off workers with a basic living allowance and reemployment services. Since 2001, with the development of the unemployment insurance system, the government has encouraged the transformation from laid-off workers being protected by the service center to being covered by unemployment insurance. As a consequence, while the numbers of laid-off workers have decreased, the numbers of registered unemployed have increased, which doesn't necessarily indicate a problem with actual unemployment. Finally, the decline in the labor force participation rate can be attributed to the effect of discouraged workers—those who are chronically unemployed, willing to work but are unable to find a job, or those who have remove themselves from the labor force.[19]

[19] Cai Fang 蔡昉 and Wang Meiyan 王美艳. "Nongcun laodong li shengyu jiqi xiangguan shishi de chongxin kaolü—yige fansheshishifa de yingyong农村劳动力剩余及其相关事实的重新考虑一个反设事实法的应用 [Reanalyzing Surplus Labor and Related Facts in China—A Counterfactual Analysis]," 2007.

As the employment environment has improved, the labor force participation rate has tended to increase, even after adjustment for the fact that higher education enrollment grew substantially during the time.

In short, if we incorporate various sources of statistics into our analysis, it can be concluded that the effect of economic growth on employment expansion during the reform period is positive and that it has been generated mainly by the development of the non-publicly-owned and informal sectors. By deconstructing by sector the changes in employment dynamic in the ten-year period between 1997 and 2007, one can observe that during the first few years, there was a structural adjustment, indicated by the absolute decline in employment in traditional sectors and rise in newly emerged sectors, while the second half saw a normalization of employment expansion—that is, employment in formal sectors grew on a stable track and tended to contract in informal sectors, as represented by the changes in "residual" employment.

IV. *China's Experience of Labor Market Development and Transition*

When analyzing the future possibilities for Chinese reform and development, most observers list the huge population and the resultant employment pressure as the top challenges. Since the late 1990s, people have turned their eyes to the grave situation of urban lay-offs and unemployment as well as underemployment in rural areas, as reflected by the large-scale flow of rural laborers into cities. A skin-deep analysis of China's labor market after the financial crisis in late 1990s often leads people to conclude that the crisis' impact on the labor market at the time was adverse to the expansion of employment and that the reform of the SOEs employment system carried out in the midst of the financial crisis to reduce staff and improve efficiency just "added fuel to the fire." In fact, however, the *de facto* expansion and structural change of urban and rural employment described above shows that since the 1990s, in the reaction to the crisis, enormous breakthroughs have been made in the reform of China's employment system and the development of its labor market, so that a fundamental change has occurred, bringing the market-led allocation of labor force resources from merely a marginal role to a comprehensive one. This process has demonstrated several significant features of the labor market's transition and development in China.

A. *Combination of Labor Market Transition and Employment Expansion*

One of the characteristics of Chinese economic reform commonly recognized by scholars is the close relationship between reform and development—namely, further development has been set as the objective of conducting reform and the criteria by which the success of reform is evaluated.[20] The process of labor market development and transition in China has also exposed such characteristics. Because of its huge reserve of surplus labor in agriculture, the institutional segmentation of the labor markets of rural and urban sectors, and the resulting low and long-deflated wage of rural-to-urban migrant workers, the economic development in China can be characterized as a case of Lewisian dualistic economic development.[21] Compared to the Lewis model, however, China's dualistic development has its own distinct features, embodied in the pre-reform central planning system and the economic transition during the reform period. Nonetheless, the criteria by which to evaluate the success of reform is whether the transition of rural laborers out of agricultural and their migration to urban areas does or does not result in the expansion of employment.

In what follows, we shall analyze China's dualistic economic development through summarizing the effects of the reform and opening policy on labor market development and employment expansion.

During the reform period, economic growth in China has fully utilized the reallocation of its abundant labor force. The successful reform over the past decades has not only enhanced technical efficiency by improving the incentive mechanisms at the micro level, but also made gains in efficient resource allocation by developing markets for production factors, especially by promoting labor mobility. In their deconstructive analysis of China's GDP growth from 1978 to 1998, Cai and Wang[22] found that the labor mobility from agriculture to nonagricultural sectors contributed 21 percent to overall growth, while the unexplained growth was only 3 percent. This shows clearly that there were gains in productivity during the dualistic economic development characterized by unlimited labor supply.

---

[20] For examples, see: Naughton, Barry. *The Chinese Economy: Transitions and Growth*, 2006: Chapter 4; and Lin, Justin, Cai Fang, and Li Zhou. *The China Miracle: Development Strategy and Economic Reform* (revised edition), 2003: Chapter 9.

[21] Cai, "Approaching a Triumphal Span," 2008.

[22] Cai and Wang, "The Sustainability of Economic Growth and the Labor Contribution," 1999.

B. *Combining Incremental and Wide-Sweeping Reform*

It is commonly recognized that Chinese reform has taken a gradual approach while making incremental adjustments. The transition and development of the labor market, however, have employed both gradual and radical approaches, combining incremental with wide-sweeping reforms. Prior to the severe labor market shock of the late 1990s, the non-public economy had already been established through policy changes and had expanded as a significant sector of the Chinese economy, which laid a foundation for supporting the reemployment of laid-off workers and absorption of new entrants into labor market during the shock period. For example, the 1988 amendment to the Constitution endowed non-public economic entities with legal status, which insured steady and fast development of the private and individual sectors of the economy. As a result, the employment share of state- and collective-owned enterprises declined from 99.8 percent in 1978 to 71.6 percent in 1996. That is, the non-public sector expanded enough to absorb the unemployed and laid-off workers resulting from the labor market shock.

Similarly, as reform of employment policies took off and the labor market developed, the newly developed urban workforce began to be allocated by the labor market, which used market mechanisms to absorb the surplus labor force. In this way, economic growth has simultaneously created formal and informal employment opportunities—that is, through mitigating damages of the severe employment shock, the labor market matured to a higher level of development.

C. *Combining Quantitative Adjustment and Wage Adjustment*

In other transitional countries radical reform has resulted in economic contraction; when labor market transition has taken the form of quantitative adjustment, it has usually led to massive unemployment and therefore social instability. On the other hand, when transition of the labor market has taken the form of wage adjustment—namely the reduction of wage level, it has led to severe poverty, which also causes social unrest.[23] However, throughout the entire process, and at each step, of labor market reform in China, these two approaches have

[23] Knight and Song, *Towards a Labour Market in China*, 2005: 6–7.

been jointly employed so that the positive effects of reform have been maximized while negative effects minimized.

Two difficulties facing labor market reform were the rigid institutional determination of wage and overstaffing in state- and collectively-owned enterprises. In the early stages of labor market reform, marginal reform of the wage determination mechanism was undertaken by accepting rural migrant workers in urban labor markets and recruiting new employees through the newly developed market channel. Since then, by way of incremental adjustments to the wage system, the rigid mechanism for wage determination has been gradually liberalized. As the number of new laborers—namely migrant workers and new entrants—has grown, the wage rates have tended to move towards equilibrium. During the shock to the labor market in the late 1990s, quantitative adjustment was carried out at expense of massive unemployment and lay-offs; afterwards, when the unemployed got reemployed, they began to accept market determined wages. This transformation of wage determination mechanism expanded role of the market in allocating labor and promoting employment, which helped mitigate the negative effects of quantitative and wage adjustments both required for labor market reform.

D. *Incorporating Liberalization with Regulation*

The transition from planned to market allocation of labor has required thorough reform of employment institutions and loosening of regulations concerning the labor market, namely by process of deregulation. Throughout the entire process of China's economic reform, progress has been accompanied by policy rectification aiming at eliminating restrictions on labor mobility, breaking down the "iron-rice-bowl" system of urban employment, and integrating the labor markets of rural and urban sectors as well as among different forms of ownership. This deregulation has helped China achieve its international comparative advantage in labor-intensive industry by allowing full use of its abundant labor force. The flexibility of the labor market that emerged through these reforms has been the envy of other developing and transitional countries, such as India.[24]

[24] See Ministry of Finance of India, *Economic Survey, 2005–06*, 2006: 209.

What is worth noting, however, is that these processes (creating new legislation and regulations while eliminating old ones), required for the construction of a market economy, have never stopped. As early as 1994, the Standing Committee of the National People's Congress passed the *Labor Law* (劳动法), formulating the legal framework for employment promotion, individual and collective contracts, working and resting hours, labor compensation, workplace safety and hygiene, special protection for female and underage employees, occupational training, social insurance and benefits, labor dispute resolution, labor inspections, legal liability, etc. After the labor market encountered the severe shock in the late 1990s, the central government serially issued a host of labor regulations up to the end of 1994. Together with the 1994 *Labor Law*, they provide stipulations on almost all aspects of employment. Although in a certain period, particularly during the severe employment shock, some items of the *Labor Law* and related regulations were not strictly enforced due to concerns regarding the flexibility of labor market, they still formed a protective umbrella of rules to follow in labor relations.

With the changes circumstances of the labor market over time, in the new century, the legislative process has been accelerated. In 2007 alone, three laws related to labor relations were promulgated. First was the *Employment Contract Law* (劳动合同法), which was formulated to improve the employment contract system, specify the rights and obligations of the parties to an employment contract, protect the lawful rights and interests of employees, and build and develop harmonious and stable employment relationships. A second was the *Employment Promotion Law* (就业促进法), which was supposed to serve as a legal tool for implementing active employment policies by promoting employment and coordinating economic development and increased employment. The third was the *Law on Labor Disputes Mediation and Arbitration* (劳动争议调解仲裁法), a law that established a system for settling labor disputes and providing lawful assistance to the parties of labor disputes, especially protecting the rights and interests of workers.

E. *Simultaneously Undertaking Both Bottom-Up and Top-Down Reform*

One of the characteristics of China's employment policy reform has been the compatibility of its goals; by expanding employment, the goal of labors to increase their wages and the goal of the government to improve the standard of living and reduce the income gap can be simultaneously achieved. Throughout the entire process of the labor market's transition and development, workers in both rural and urban areas have broken through institutional barriers by spontaneously crossing regional, sectoral, and ownership boundaries to seek better pay and jobs, pushing forward the bottom-up development of the labor market. At the same time, the government, responding to enhanced labor mobility and newly created demand, has methodically removed institutional restrictions on the labor market and reformed traditional employment policies. When China's labor market was shocked with high unemployment and poverty at the turn of century, the government not only sped up the process of establishing a social security system to protect the jobless, but also implemented proactive employment policies to help them get reemployed. This mutually compatible system, combining bottom-up and top-down labor market reforms, has guaranteed that market-oriented reform is consistent with the goal of improving peoples' livelihood.

V. *Conclusions and Prospects: The Unfinished Task of Reform*

In assessing the degree of development in the labor market and effects of employment expansion in rural and urban areas, one can confidently assert that China's reform of the employment system has never lagged behind the reforms of other areas in terms of progress, depth, or successfulness. However, a well functioning and mature labor market cannot be formed overnight; also, labor market institutions, with their host of different functions, are not without variation. Therefore, the labor market everywhere is always in a state of reshaping, transition, and growth. Given the pair of transformational tasks facing China—namely the transformation from a dualistic economy to an integrated economy and the transformation from planned economy to market economy—there exist many unfinished tasks for labor market reform. What follows is a summary of some priority areas for further reform of the labor market.

A. *Reforms of the* Hukou *System and Related Institutions*

As long as the *hukou* system continues to serve as a policy tool for dividing rural and urban labor markets, the institutional obstacles to labor mobility and population migration will remain. This can be clearly understood by examining the unique process of urbanization in China. The share of urban residents of the total population has increased from 17.9 percent in 1978, 23.7 percent in 1985, 26.4 percent in 1990, 36.2 percent in 2000, to as high as 44.9 percent in 2007. While these figures do reflect the progress of urbanization over the past three decades, the changes can mostly be attributed to changes in the statistically defined inclusion of population groups. Based on the 2000 census and a 2005 sampling survey of one percent of the population, the urban share of the population has increased from 36.6 percent in 2000 to 44.7 percent in 2005, but a large proportion of urban population still holds an agricultural *hukou*. During this same period, the proportion of urban residents who hold agricultural *hukou* has increased from 40.3 percent to 46.8 percent. This means that the urbanization during this period can be attributed, to a large extent, to the phenomenon of rural residents changing their residency without changing their *hukou*. The increase in number and proportion of people living in urban areas with agricultural *hukou* is mainly the consequence of two phenomena, which are characteristic of Chinese-style urbanization during the process of development and reform.

First of all, the change of the boundary lines between rural and urban areas has contributed to the increase in the number of urban residents. There are three reasons that statistics may show an increase in the urban population and decrease in the rural population. When a county, by fulfilling certain criteria, is re-categorized as a city, or a township is administrative changed into a town, their village committees are turned to residence committees, and the residents become categorized as urban population, though their *hukou* identify may still remain agricultural. In another case, when a county outside a municipality is re-categorized as a district of the municipality, the population of the new district is counted as urban, even while the identities of the village communities and their agricultural *hukou* may remain unchanged. Through such administrative changes, the urbanization level according to statistics is increased. During the reform period, especially since the 1990s, such administrative changes have been carried out frequently and have contributed a great deal to urbanization.

Secondly, rural-to-urban migration is a major contributor to urbanization in China. As the policies of urban areas toward labor mobility have been relaxed—specifically, as urban regulations on access to residency, employment, compulsory education, and relevant public services have become more tolerant to outsiders without local *hukou*—rural migrant workers and their dependents have tended to work and stay longer in cities and towns. And, by the administrative definition, once migrants stay in cities and towns more than six months, they are counted as permanent urban residents, and thus contribute to the statistical term on urbanization.

China's economic transition has gradually removed many institutional barriers deterring labor mobility, advancing urbanization and making up for the structural lag accumulated during the pre-reform period. On the other hand, the unique process of urbanization in China, which has been characterized by the expansion in the number of temporary job seekers in urban areas but not an increase in the number residents with urban *hukou*, also has its downside. Put simply, the separation between work place and residence leads to some problems.

First, it distorts the demographic structure of rural areas. Under the present institutional arrangement, rural-to-urban migration increases the labor force of the urban sector, and leaves rural population less productive. Because of the *hukou* system, migrant workers do not expect to live in cities permanently, in most cases their spouses, parents, and children are left behind in their home villages. But the large proportion of women, children, and elderly in rural areas makes rural populations more dependent, weakening their ability to socially and economically develop.

Second, the *hukou* system distorts labor market data and delays the response time between the supply and demand of labor. In a normal labor market, where potential workers and jobs exist in the same locality, any quantitative or structural changes in demand for labor force can be adjusted for by changes in employment, wage rates, and relocation of labor among sectors. But because the *hukou* system separates labor demand (in coastal and urban areas) and labor supply (in inland and rural areas), labor supply responds to change in labor demand in a much slower way, which often causes irrational booms and busts in labor migration at particular times and places. More fundamentally, urban policies discriminating against migrants, while being modified on many aspects as the reform progresses, may still be used as long as the basis for their legitimacy—the *hukou* system—exists.

Third, it prevents migrant workers and their families from being able to receive the housing, health care, and education at reasonable prices. The current phase of development in China's dualistic economy has been characterized by the emergence of a third category of population, migrant workers and their accompanying dependents, which exist apart from permanently registered rural and urban residents. The exclusion of migrants from the basic social security system is inconsistent with the overall goals set by the central government to equalize social welfare and public services between rural and urban residents. Without reform of the *hukou* system, migrants are very likely to be left behind as the social security system in rural and urban areas progresses.

In the new century, local governments have made much greater efforts to reform the *hukou* system. In recent years, one common practice in this reform area has been to attempt to establish a unified *hukou* regime integrating rural and urban population registration by abolishing the distinction between agricultural and non-agricultural *hukou* identities and integrating them into a unified residential *hukou* system. As of 2007, there were twelve provinces that had carried out reforms of this kind. In addition, many cities have further loosened the criteria for applying for local registration for families being reuniting, the elderly joining adult children, youth joining parents, investors, individuals with special skills, and those purchasing property locally.

However, such reform has encountered some difficulties. One notable challenge facing local governments is that the *hukou* is not simply a population registration system, but also one of the welfare benefits contained in it. An attraction of an urban *hukou* is that it entitles the holder to social security and other public services whose provision is affiliated with *hukou* status and differentiated between rural and urban areas. Even if a city announces an unified population registration system, or loosens criteria for migrants to apply for local *hukou*, if its financial situation is such that it is unable to provide universal public services to all residents regardless of their origin—that is, residents traditionally categorized as rural residents have equal access to social welfare and public services—changing the population registration system is meaningless. In fact, many reforms of the *hukou* system announced by cities have been languishing because fiscal restraints have made it impossible to keep it accompanied with the related entitlements.

However, reform of the *hukou* system has never stopped. Quite the opposite, through these trial-and-error experiences, the goal of *hukou* system reform has become clearer—to form an integrated labor market and unified social welfare system between rural and urban areas. On the surface, there seems to be a paradox: the more value a *hukou* identity contains, the more difficult it is to push reform forward, but without *hukou* reform there is no way to alter the value of the attached social services. However, if the reform in this area takes an indirect approach—by removing the welfare provisioning functions from *hukou* status instead of changing *hukou* identity for a certain group of people. Once the *hukou* no longer serves as an identifier used determine whether or not a person should be provided with certain public services, this dilemma can be resolved.

Since the beginning of this century, a host of reforms of the welfare regimes affiliated with *hukou*, which include social security, social protection, compulsory education, and other public services, have been under way. Not only has the central government set the goal of narrowing the gap in public services between rural and urban areas, but local governments have also recognized the key role that such reforms should play. All in all, linking *hukou* reform to the unification of the social welfare system will help to advance reform in this field.

B. *Construction of Labor Market Institutions*

Olson[25] and Anderson[26] have both individually examined why governments in poor countries tend to implement policies favoring urban areas while governments in rich countries tend to do the opposite; they concluded that it was in order to protect agricultural. The same analytical tools can also be applied to investigate a similar change in labor relations, which abides by the "law of supply and demand;" the long-term demand and supply relationship determines the relative bargaining power of workers and employers and the relative influence of different social classes on government policies. Putting aside the question of whether the government's or entrepreneurs' treatment of workers is inherently unfair, once the labor shortage period comes, there will be significant changes, such as new legislation to protect the rights of workers, a larger role for trade unions in employment relations and determination of wage, employers improving working conditions according to law in order to ensure a stable supply of labor,

---

[25] 1985.

[26] Anderson, "Lobbying Incentives and the Pattern of Protection in Rich and Poor Countries," 1995.

and more and more freedom for workers to choose where they want to work. Therefore, China's Lewis point will be an opportunity to further establish labor market institutions.

However, this does not imply that the improvement of labor relations is something spontaneous or automatic. While the changes in labor demand relative to supply will help trade unions gain bargaining powers, the specifics will differ from firm to firm. While workers in large firms will be the first to gain bargaining power against their employers due to the better market forces in such firms, workers in small and medium enterprises will have difficulty acquiring this power due to the lack of strong market forces and low profits of small and medium-size enterprises, which are unable to share the fruits of growth.[27] Facing such a dilemma, the role of the governmental in regulating the labor market will become indispensable. International experiences suggest that if governments are incapable of making sound policy to meet to the requirements of the coming stage of development, the institutional discrimination against ordinary workers formed under dualistic economy would continue, leading to dissatisfaction of the working class and possibly even fierce social conflict.

The fast economic growth in China has been achieved under a Chinese-style pattern of dualistic economic development. The favorable factors impacting economic growth have managed to remain mobilized throughout these three decades of fast growth. However, economic growth has not been able to solve the social problems that have emerged as a result of this dualistic economic development. Now, as a result of huge demographic transition, China's economic development is approaching its Lewis turning point and witnessing the disappearance of its unlimited labor supply. Since the dualistic structure of the economy is not only a divide between traditional and modern economic sectors but also evidenced in the segregation of the labor market, the approaching turning point implies an urgent demand for institutional changes. That is, the conditions are ripe for solving a

[27] In "Countervailing Power," (In *The Essential Galbraith*, by K. John Galbraith, 2001) Galbraith discusses the concept of countervailing power and how it influences intensity of incentives. He mentions in particular how countervailing power can be clearly observed in labor market. To understand similar debates, also see discussion about enterprises' viability (Lin, Justin Yifu 林毅夫."Zisheng nengli, jingji fazhan yu zhuanxing: lilun yu shizheng 自生能力、经济发展与转型: 理论与实证 [*Viability, Economic Development, and Transition: Theories and Empirics*], 2004).

host of problems, including migration of rural labor force, income inequality and poverty, and insufficient guarantees for workers' rights. It is critical for the Chinese government to accurately understand the changing nature of this development stage, and to respond according to these changes, in order that it may adjust policy orientation and resolve these long-standing problems so that the economic growth can be sustained and societal harmony maintained.

C. *The Establishment and Perfection of Social Security System*

In 1997, China's State Council officially announced that it would set up a unified urban employee pension system that would combine a social pooling system with individual retirement accounts. After a decade of reform in this direction, China has achieved initial successes, thanks in part to its setting of clear goals. Reform of the pension system, like other social security systems, is not only an inevitable result of China's overall economic reform, but also a requirement for labor market reform. It has played the distinctive role of safeguarding the reform climate. However, reform of the urban basic pension system is far from completed, as evidenced in the following respects.

First, the coverage of this system is still very low. Data from *The China Labor Statistical Yearbook* show that the number of the participants in urban basic pension insurance scheme reached 131 million by the end of 2005, accounting for only 17 percent of total employed population and 48 percent of the employed urban population. Such low coverage rates are mainly because of the absence of a universal rural pension program and the increasingly expanding proportion of informal employment in urban areas, workers of which are excluded from the urban pension scheme. In particular, informal employment comprising of reemployed laid-off workers, farmers who have relocated after their land was requisitioned, and the vast majority of migrant workers, are all not covered by any pension security system.

Second, the amount of socially pooled funds under this system is still insufficient. As early as 1998, the State Council set out the reform objective of unifying the pension system at the provincial level. A decade later, however, there are still 19 provinces that have not cemented their overall structure or began pooling at the provincial level. In this area, reform is not only failing to reach the set objective but also disconnected from the market system. The low level of pooled capital has reduced the portability of pension insurance. This means that even in the midst of an increasingly mobile workforce, those who change employment locations are unable to carry social security plans with them.

Finally, the individual retirement accounts, a pillar of this system, are both empty and narrow in scope. In 2001, China initiated pension reform on a piloting basis to establish individual retirement accounts, first in Liaoning Province and subsequently in Jilin and Heilongjiang. Thereafter, another eight provinces, municipalities, and autonomous regions were selected to pursue piloting operations, but the vast majority of the provinces never started the operations. Meanwhile, in trying to enrich the empty accounts in the piloting provinces, the contribution rates to individual accounts declined. In Liaoning, for instance, the contribution rate to individual accounts was reduced from 11 percent to 8 percent of gross payroll and funded solely by personal contribution. The employer's matching contribution was no longer transferred into individual accounts and instead diverted into pooled social insurance funds. When the piloting reform was expanded to Jilin and Heilongjiang provinces, the contribution rate to individual accounts was further reduced to 5 percent. In subsequent piloting operations in another eight provinces, the percentage was further dropped to 3 percent of gross payroll. In areas where no piloting reform was conducted, the pooled account and individual accounts were still mixed to supplement each other. As a result, the huge deficit on individual retirement accounts continues to swell.

Whereas some may argue that the imperfect pension system and its lagging reform are part of the gradual reform approach adopted in China, they are in fact due to the lack of a clear blueprint for reform in the first place. Although the goals of pension system reform were set as early as in the late 1990s, it would be better to formulate its reform step-by-step, taking into account a plethora of newly emerging factors such as the characteristics of demographic transition, the types of economic systems, the nature of public finance, and the extent of labor market development, and then incorporating them into the institutional design.

Bibliography

Anderson, K. "Lobbying Incentives and the Pattern of Protection in Rich and Poor Countries." *Economic Development and Cultural Change* Vol. 43, No. 2 (1995): 401–423.

Cai Fang 蔡昉. "Zhongguo jiuye tongji de yizhixing: Shishi he zhengce hanyi 中国就业统计的一致性：事实和政策涵义 [The Consistency of China's Statistics on Employment: Facts and Implications for Public Policy]." *Zhongguo renkou kexue* 中国人口科学 [*China Population Studies*] No. 5 (2004).

Cai Fang 蔡昉. "Approaching a Triumphal Span: How Far Is China Towards its Lewis Turning Point?" *UNU-WIDER Research Paper* No. 9 (2008).

Cai Fang 蔡昉, Du Yang 都阳, and Wang Meiyan 王美艳. "Huji zhidu yu laodongli shichang baohu 户籍制度与劳动力市场保护 [The *Hukou* System and Protecting the Labor Market]." *Jingji Yanjiu* 经济研究 [*Economic Research Journal*] No. 12 (2001).

Cai Fang 蔡昉 and Wang Meiyan. "Nongcun laodong li shengyu jiqi xiangguan shishi de chongxin kaolü—yige fansheshishifa de yingyong 农村劳动力剩余及其相关事实的重新考虑一个反设事实法的应用 [Reanalyzing Surplus Labor and Related Facts in China—A Counterfactual Analysis]." Zhongguo nongcun jingji 中国农村经济 [*China's Rural Economy*] No. 10 (2007): 51–65.

Cai Fang 蔡昉 and Wang Dewen 王德文. "Zhongguo jingji zengzhang kechixuxing yu laodong gongxian 中国经济增长可持续性与劳动贡献 [The Sustainability of Economic Growth and the Labor Contribution]." *Jingji Yanjiu* 经济研究 [*Economic Research Journal*] No.10 (1999).

Cai Fang, Lin, Justin Linfu, and Yong Cao. *The Chinese Economy: Reform and Development*. McGraw-Hill, 2009.

Feng Lanrui 冯兰瑞 and Zhao Lükuan 赵履宽. *Zhongguo chengzhen de jiuye he gongzi* 中国城镇的就业和工资 [*The Employment and Wages in China's Urban Areas*]. The People's Press: 1982.

Fields, Gary. "Dualism in the Labor Market: a Perspective on the Lewis Model after Half a Century." *The Manchester School* Vol. 72, No. 6 (2004): 724–735.

Galbraith, K. John. "Countervailing Power." In *The Essential Galbraith*, by, K. John Galbraith. Mariner Books: 2001.

Knight, John and Lina Song. *The Rural-urban Divide: Economic Disparities and Interactions in China*. New York: Oxford University Press, 1999.

——. *Towards a Labour Market in China*. New York: Oxford University Press, 2005.

Lardy, Nicholas R. *China in the World Economy*. Washington, D.C.: Institute for International Studies, 1994.

Lewis, Arthur. "Reflections on Unlimited Labour." In *International Economics and Development*, editeby by L. Di Marco. New York: Academic Press, 1972: 75–96.

Lewis, W.A. "Economic Development with Unlimited Supplies of Labour." In *The Economics of Underdevelopment*, edited by A.N. Agarwala and S.P. Singh. Bombay: Oxford University Press, 1958. Originally published in *The Manchester School of Economic and Social Studies* No. 22 (1954): 139–191.

Lin, Justin Yifu 林毅夫. "Rural Reforms and Agricultural Productivity Growth in China." *American Economic Review* No. 82 (1992): 34–51.

——. "Zisheng nengli, jingji fazhan yu zhuanxing: lilun yu shizheng自生能力、经济发展与转型: 理论与实证 [*Viability, Economic Development, and Transition: Theories and Empirics*]. Beijing University Press: 2004.

Lin, Justin, Cai Fang, and Li Zhou. *The China Miracle: Development Strategy and Economic Reform* (revised edition). Hong Kong: Chinese University Press, 2003.

Ministry of Agriculture Task Force. "Zhongguo nongcun renkou bianhua he tudi zhidu gaige 中国农村人口变化和土地制度改革 [Demographic Change and Reform of the Land System in Rural China]." Topic Report. Beijing, 2001.

Ministry of Finance of India, *Economic Survey, 2005–06*. New Delhi: Ministry of Finance, 2006.

National Bureau of Statistics. *Zhongguo Tongji Nianjian* 中国统计年鉴 [*China Statistical Yearbook*],.Various Years.

Naughton, Barry. *The Chinese Economy: Transitions and Growth*. Cambridge, Massachusetts & London, England: The MIT Press, 2006.

Perkins, Dwight. "China's Economic Growth in Historical and International Perspective" (translated into Chinese). *China Economic Quarterly* Vol. 4, No. 4 (2005): 891–912.

Qian Fenyong 千奋勇. "Zai qunzhongxing de weida shijian zhong tanxun zhenli zhilu—cong yikezhao meng baochan daohu he sucao shuangbao kan jiefangsixiang yu shishi yaoqiu shi 在群众性的伟大实践中探寻真理之路—从伊克昭盟包产到戶和畜草双承包看解放思想与实事求是 [Searching for the Truth through Practice: Understanding Reform through Household Responsibility System in Inner Mongolia]." In *E'erduosi jingji xianxiang yanjiu chenghuo huicui* 鄂尔多斯经济现象研究成果荟萃*Selected Essays on Erdos Economic Phenomena*, edited by Xia Ri 夏日. Huhhot: Inner Mongolia People's Press, 2001.

Taylor, J.R. "Rural Employment Trends and the Legacy of Surplus Labor, 1978–1989." In *Economic Trends in Chinese Agriculture: The Impact of Post-Mao Reforms*, edited by Kueh, Y.Y. and R.F. Ash. New York: Oxford University Press, 1993.

Todaro, M. "A Model of Labour Migration and Urban Unemployment in Less Developed Countries." *American Economic Review*, March (1969): 138–148.

Wang Meiyan 王美艳. "Wage Arrears and Discrimination against Migrant Workers in China's Urban Labor Market." In *The China Population and Labor Yearbook, Volume 1—The Approaching Lewis Turning Point and Its Policy Implications*, edited by Cai Fang 蔡昉. Leiden, Boston: Koninklijke Brill, 2009.

World Bank. *China 2020: Development Challenges in the New Century*, Washington D.C.: 1997.

Yang, Dennis and Cai Fang. "The Political Economy of China's Rural-Urban Divide." In *How Far Across the River: Chinese Policy Reform at the Millennium*, edited by Nicholas C. Hope, Dennis Tao Yang and Mu Yang Li. Stanford: Stanford University Press, 2003.

Yang Jianbai 杨坚白. "Sudu, jiegou, xiaolü 速度. 结构. 效率 [Speed, Structure and Efficiency]." *Jingji Yanjiu* 经济研究 [*Economic Research Journal*] No. 9 (1991).

Yu Guangyuan 于光远. *1978:Wo qinli de naci lishi dazhuanzhe: shiyijisanzhongquanhui de taiqian muhou* 1978: 我亲历的那次历史大转折:十一届三中全会的台前幕后 [*The Historical Turn I Personally Experienced in 1978: The Third Plenary Session of the Eleventh Central Committee*]. Beijing: Central Compilation and Translation Press, 2008.

CHAPTER FOUR

THE INTRINSIC LOGIC OF CHINA'S BANKING INDUSTRY REFORM

Yi Gang[1]

The characteristics of a planned economy are as follows: ill-defined property rights, government functions mixed in with business functions, state affairs administered by command and control, and the presence of political incentive and internal supervision. The characteristics of a market economy include: well-defined property rights, government functions separated from business functions, state affairs administered by law, and the presence of economic incentive and social supervision. China's thirty years of reform and opening have been a process of transition from a planned economy to a socialist market economy and a process in which the characteristics of the planned economy have gradually faded, while those of the market economy have gradually emerged. What has been the course of the transition from a planned economy to the market economy? Simply put, it has been a course that has protected an increasingly clear-cut property rights system under which economic entities proliferate (from single to multiple entities), centralized decision-making power becomes decentralized, and the government delegates power to, and shares profit with, economic entities as well as enabling them to make decisions independently and assume responsibility for the consequences of their actions.

The reform of China's banking industry is a typical example of the above process. Prior to 1978, China's financial business was basically operated by a single entity—the People's Bank of China (accounting for more than 93 percent of total financial business). The process of reform has been a process of the partitioning of the People's Bank of China, forming the Industrial and Commercial Bank of China, the Agricultural Bank of China, the Bank of China and the China

[1] The author gratefully acknowledges the assistance of Ji Min 纪敏 in this research.

Construction Bank and ten other share-holding banks, the emergence of independent legal entities such as urban commercial banks and rural credit cooperatives, and the gradual entry of foreign-funded banks after the financial sector was opened to foreign investors. During this process, the securities industry and insurance industry that had previously been under the administration of the People's Bank of China were delegated to other institutions. The China Securities Regulatory Commission and China Insurance Regulatory Commission were established in 1992 and 1998 respectively to take over the regulatory functions for the securities and insurance sectors.

During this one-to-many process, market economy characteristics have gradually become very pronounced. China first needed to define property rights. The market requires the right to equal exchange and the precondition of such exchange is to define property rights. As a result, in this process, China has "broken up the family" of banks multiple times. In particular, the Bank of China, the Agricultural Bank of China, and the Industrial and Commercial Bank of China were spun off from the People's Bank of China; the China Construction Bank was separated from the Ministry of Finance; and rural credit cooperatives were decoupled from the Agricultural Bank of China. The purpose of this breakup was to clearly define the property rights of different entities and enable them to assume responsibility for their actions.

Secondly, China needed to separate government and business functions. In a planned economy, both elements are mixed and government serves as the command center. Government decides what to produce, how much to produce, and for whom to produce. Government also determines circulation, distribution, and price. In a market economy, the market plays the fundamental role in allocating resources and the economic decision-making process is decentralized. Economic decisions are selected and made mainly by enterprises and households. Under this system, the separation of government and business becomes inevitable.

Thirdly, China should be governed by law. When property rights are clearly defined and decision-making decentralized, unless initial rules are set, China may fall into chaos. To avoid this requires governing the country by law. The state has enacted macroeconomic policy and exercised macro-control over the economy but the power of government should be defined so that it administers in accordance with law. In addition, government should abide by business and individual property rights and refrain from willfully intervening in the economic activities of individual enterprises.

Fourthly, incentives should be compatible and mutually reinforcing. Why is the market economy effective? Because it can better resolve the incentive issue and boost people's enthusiasm and creativity to the maximum extent possible; this is done by linking the effort of an individual person to his or her income and tying the effort of an enterprise to its profit. Under the rule-of-law framework, the effort and creativity of an economic entity are linked to its material interests. Compared with the systems of "eating from the same communal bowl" and egalitarianism of the planned economy, economic incentives of the market economy are the source of efficiency.

Fifthly, China should create a system for social supervision. The market economy is in essence a law-governed economy. Such an economy requires transparency and, as a result, entails setting standards for accounting and establishing a system for public disclosure. Economic entities and the public have the right to know and exercise social supervision over the operations of the market and ensure its equity and justice. Social supervision does not exclude internal supervision. The ruling party's supervision, the government's system of internal auditing, and enterprises' internal control mechanisms are all important, but a market economy requires supervision by civil society.

This paper will summarize the intrinsic reasoning of banking industry reform by conducting a review of the three-decade market-oriented reform process of China's banking industry. Banking industry reform is an important part of China's transitional process from a planned economy to a market economy. Conducting a thorough analysis of banking industry reform will aid in understanding the intrinsic reasoning behind all of China's economic transition.

I. *The Starting Point of Reform: Replacing Government Funds for Enterprises with Bank Loans to Enterprises and Establishing Commercial Banks*

If bank reform is the starting point of reforming the entire financial system, then replacing government funds for enterprises with bank loans to enterprises is the starting point of bank reform.

A. *The Conditions for Replacing Government Funds for Enterprises with Bank Loans to Enterprises: A High Degree of Economic Monetization*

Before reform was initiated in 1978, under the highly centralized planned economy system, funds were allocated through fiscal channels set by the state plan. Under such a system, the sources of enterprise funds had the following characteristics: long-term funds were provided by the treasury and short-term funds were provided by banks; interest-free funds were provided by the treasury and interest-bearing funds were provided by banks; normal funds were provided by the treasury and abnormal funds were provided by banks. This system lasted until 1978.

The Third Plenary Session of the Eleventh Central Committee, held in 1978, was the prelude to economic reform. As rural China introduced the household contract responsibility system with remuneration linked to output and developed township enterprises, urban economic entities reinstated enterprise bonus and profit retention measures. The public finance system implemented a system where each level of authority took full responsibility for its budget. As a result, the national income distribution pattern was drastically changed, with the share of public finance in funds allocation dropping swiftly and the proportion of business and individual income rising sharply. Business and individual income flew into banks through credit channels. During the 1978–1992 period, residential savings and deposits as a percentage of GNP rose from 5.9 percent in 1978 to 48 percent in 1992, while fiscal revenue as a percentage of GNP fell from 31 percent to 13 percent. As a result of this huge readjustment of the country's income distribution pattern, the degree of economic monetization increased significantly. During the 1978–1992 period, income rose approximately 19-fold, whereas the GNP, adjusted according to the official price index,[2] increased by only 231 percent. Meanwhile, the official price index and free market price index[3] increased by merely 125 percent and 141 percent respectively, thus causing the income/real GNP ratio to increase steadily from 0.32 to above 1.0.[4] This reflected the

[2] Official prices refer to the prices of consumer goods and capital goods within the state plan under the dual-track price system.

[3] Free market prices refer to the prices of consumer goods and capital goods outside of the state plan under the dual-track price system.

[4] An international comparison shows that this ratio was 0.37 in India as of 1978 (virtually on par with China's level) and rose only to 0.47 in 1990, compared with 0.67 in the United States and 0.57 in Korea.

monetization effects of systematic reform. The increase in the degree of monetization resulted in relatively ample bank funds and the decrease in fiscal expenditure as a percentage of GDP, thereby creating favorable conditions for replacing government funds for enterprises with bank loans to enterprises.

B. *The Implementation and Significance of Replacing Government Funds for Enterprises with Bank Loans to Enterprises*

In 1979, the state began to conduct a pilot program replacing government funds for enterprises with bank loans to enterprises in the area of fixed asset investment. In 1985, the pilot program was implemented nationwide. By replacing government funds for enterprises with bank loans to enterprises, bank loans contributed an increasingly larger share to economic construction funds. During 1981–1992, state budget funds as a percentage of social fixed asset investment sources fell from 28 percent to 4.3 percent, whereas the share of domestic loans surged from 12.69 percent to 27.4 percent.

As discussed theoretically by Hungarian Economist *János Kornai* in *Economics of Shortage*, a typical characteristic under the planned economic system is soft-constraints of corporate budgets. Under the original government-funded investment system, the funds recipients did not need to repay principals or pay interest; the demand for government funds (appropriations) became infinitely great; projects cannot be effectively ranked in terms of rate of return because it could not be identified for each project; this was a disservice to the creation of legal-entity enterprises, producing a system where there always existed a hunger for investment and each locality and industry tried every means to acquire it. Analysis shows that by the end of 1995 the majority of principals and interest of banks loans used to replace government funds for enterprises had been converted into state share capital. The debt-for-equity swap initiated in 1998 also included a portion of state-held shares converted from debt arising when bank loans were used to replace government funds for enterprises, which suggests that the vast majority of fiscal appropriations replaced with bank loans were subsequently converted into state share capital because they could not be repaid or swapped for equity under the debt-for-equity swap scheme. Nevertheless, replacing government funds for enterprises with bank loans to enterprises was still of great historical significance. First of all, after the switch, enterprises needed to balance their books and compare bank loan interest rates and project rate of return; secondly, it suppressed to some extent the thirst for investment; and thirdly, it was conducive to setting forth the responsibility of legal business entities as the loan repayment entity. As a result, enterprises began to have a sense of responsibility for protecting property rights.

Replacing government funds for enterprises with bank loans to enterprises was the starting point of three-decades of financial reform. It was also the logical starting point of the thirty-year financial reform. Beginning then, state-owned enterprises began to shift from operating according to political incentives to economic incentives. Correspondingly, banks also began to transform themselves from executors of the state plan and state finance cashiers into specialized banks. At that time, when all enterprises were publically owned and the planned economic system was highly centralized, it was relatively easy to enhance economic incentives and budget constraints of enterprises through appropriate means because there were few areas involved in doing so and it complied with the requirement of gradual reform. In regard to the reasoning behind comprehensive bank reform, replacing government funds for enterprises with bank loans to enterprises increased the dependence of enterprises on bank loans, while boosting their budget constraints, thereby making banks' transition to being commercialization-oriented inevitable.

C. *The Creation of Commercial Banks*

The next step was for banks was for banks to become real (de facto) banks, thus came the demand for the creation of commercial banks. Along with the substitution of bank loans for government appropriations and the furtherance of the reform of the entire economic system, there was an increasing urgency for further financial reform. Investment projects (enterprises) need owners (legal persons), and banks need incentives to encourage enterprises to repay their loans when they are due. The macro-unified bank system was no longer appropriate and as a result the central government put on its agenda the transformation of planned-economy banks into real banks. As early as October 4, 1979, Deng Xiaoping pointed out at a seminar for high-ranking government officials that "banks should focus on economics. Now they are only bookkeepers and accountants and fail to play the banking role." At a seminar attended by the party chiefs of provinces, municipalities and autonomous regions, he added "Banks should become a lever for economic development and technological innovation. We should turn banks into real banks." Under this guiding philosophy, China began to proceed, step by step, with reform of the financial system.

It started by separating specialized state-owned banks from the central bank. The Agricultural Bank of China was reestablished in January 1979, while the Bank of China and State Administration of Foreign Exchange were set up in March 1979. Subsequently, the People's Insurance Company of China was reestablished and trust and investment companies were created in regions across the nation, thereby resulting in an early diversification of financial institutions and businesses.

On January 1, 1984, the State Council decided that, from that date, the People's Bank of China should officially take on the functions of a central bank and concentrate efforts on researching and implementing national financial macro-management strategies and financial regulations as well as strengthening credit quantity control and funds reconciliation between financial institutions to maintain monetary stability. Meanwhile, the Industrial and Commercial Bank of China was established to take over the industrial and commercial credit and savings business that had previously been conducted by the People's Bank of China.

D. *Separating Policy Banks and Specialized State-Owned Banks*

After the People's Bank of China became the central bank in 1984, the Industrial and Commercial Bank of China, the Agricultural Bank of China, the Bank of China and the China Construction Bank became state-owned commercial banks (originally known as the "big-four" specialized banks) but there was a problem that remained unsolved at that time. The problem was that the state needed commercial banks to support some industries and enterprises and sometimes asked them to carry out political tasks such as agricultural product purchase, "dumpling loans"[5] and "stability and solidarity loans." When commercial loans and policy loans coexisted, commercial banks would be exposed to the moral hazard of classifying all losses due to misconduct and favoritism as policy loan losses.

[5] Editor's note: Emergency loans issued right before the Spring Festival holiday, the traditional food of which is dumplings.

At the Third Plenary Session of the Fourteenth Central Committee, held in 1993, the *Decisions of the CPC Central Committee on Several Issues in Establishing the Socialist Market Economy System* (中共中央关于建立社会主义市场经济体制若干问题的决定) were issued, formally establishing the objective of economic reform: establishing the socialist market economy and letting the market play the fundamental role in resource allocation under state macro-control. Under the guidance of this objective, during 1993–1994, China launched reform in the five major systems of finance, taxation, investment, foreign trade, and foreign exchange. The *Decisions of the State Council on Financial System Reform* (国务院关于金融体制改革的决定) required the establishment of policy banks, ending the situation where policy financial business and commercial business were mixed. In 1994, China set up three policy banks: the State Development Bank, the Agricultural Development Bank of China and the Export-Import Bank of China, which were mandated to conduct policy financial businesses in the respective areas of infrastructure development, key agricultural products purchase, and import and export. Policy banks were expressly required to strengthen business management and act in accordance with the principle of assuming their own risk exposure, pursuing breakeven operation and refraining from competition with commercial financial institutions.

E. *The Significance of Creating Policy Banks*

The establishment of policy banks was another symbolic accomplishment after the first such accomplishment of replacing government funds for enterprises with bank loans for enterprises. The path of market-oriented bank reform has shown that state-owned enterprise reform is the basis of state-owned bank reform, and that soft-constraints on the budgets of state-owned enterprises were the heart of the problem in the old system. Replacing government funds for enterprises with bank loans to enterprises was the starting point in resolving this issue, but whether it could be successful or not was to a large extent dependent on the behaviors of funds providers (*i.e.* state-owned banks). If policy business and commercial business were not separated, bank behavior would be distorted. On the one hand, they may use policy goals as a pretext for relaxing loan repayment constraints for enterprises; on the other hand, they may also seek central bank refinancing and fiscal subsidies to the maximum extent possible and they are thus under no pressure to embrace commercialization-oriented reform. Take infrastructure development as an example. During the period from 1979, when pilot projects for the substitution of bank loans for government funds for enterprises were launched, to 1994, when the State Development Bank was established, state investment in infrastructure development (including central bank refinancing and fiscal subsidies) increased significantly, but many projects still lacked both working capital and statutory capital. These projects were built and operated using only bank loans. They were unable to repay principals or pay interest and unlikely to remain commercially sustainable. This example shows that even though fiscal appropriations were in form replaced by bank loans, if policy financial business was not systematically separated from commercial financial business, the corresponding financial constraints could still not be established and credit funds would in essence remain fiscal funds. So there was no way to proceed with bank commercialization.

Setting up policy banks was a logically sound approach. In retrospect, China's path was somewhat simple minded both at the beginning and after policy banks were established; commercial banks still had a great deal of policy business that needed to be handled by the state. However, it was during this process that China gained further knowledge of the transition process. The problems facing us were more complicated and profound than they appeared to be. When enterprises failed to carry out property rights reform as desired and they assumed numerous social responsibilities, it was very difficult for banks to impose hard budget constraints on them. In this case, turning banks into de facto banks remained wishful thinking.

With the deepening of market-oriented reform and changes in the economic environment, after enterprises have carried out property rights reform, policy banks can also be transformed into self-sustained commercial banks. Even though it is still premature to draw any conclusions about the State Development Bank's lower rate of non-performing loans when compared to commercial banks, if the reform of lending mechanisms can effectively mitigate local government's moral hazard, the current low non-performing loan rate of State Development Bank will be sustainable. Not only can policy banks be restructured, policy businesses can also be conducted by way of bidding. After the state sets subsidy rates, it can invite bids from banks and make subsidized policy business to be commercially sustainable. As an example, student loans are a success story of market-oriented bidding.

Therefore, under the market economy, it has become increasingly unnecessary for policy banks to exist except in very few areas. This point is well supported by the transformation of the State Development Bank into a commercial bank since 2008.

II. *Preventing and Mitigating Financial Risk*

On July 2, 1997, the Thai central bank announced devaluation of Thai Baht against the U.S. dollar and adopted the managed-floating exchange rate regime. This series of devaluations marked the beginning of the Asian financial crisis. In spring of 1997, the Chinese government began to prepare for the National Financial Working Conference, demonstrating foresight in predicting likely financial problems. The breakout of the Asian financial crisis heightened the necessity of convening the conference.

In the fourth quarter of 1997, China held the National Financial Working Conference and published a press release themed around the deepening financial reform, rectifying the financial order, and mitigating financial risk. At that time, China faced serious financial problems: (1) the high non-performing asset ratio and capital inadequacy of state-owned banks; (2) the higher non-performing asset ratio of non-bank financial institutions, some of which failed to repay debt (including foreign debt); (3) some localities and sectors set up numerous financial institutions without authorization, with payment crisis and runs on banks possible at any time; (4) a substantial amount of illicit behaviors or violations on the equity and futures markets; and (5) an increasing number of serious cases involving fraudulent and collusive activity by financial practitioners.

The key causes for these problems included: (1) the transition from planned economy to market economy. A large number of financial institutions were incorporated in the form of legal entities at a time when property rights were ill-defined and the rule of law was not well-established. The senior executives of these institution lacked strong legal awareness and had perilous ideas about credit, taking for granted that everything belongs to the state and risks should be taken by the state. As a result, blind expansion was pursued under budgets with soft constraints and there existed almost no corporate governance structure; (2) the explosive economic cycle that began in 1992. During this economic cycle, local governments across the country blindly built projects and rashly put up establishments. By 1993–1994, overheating of the economy and bubbles were in the making; by 1997, significant risks emerged and non-performing loans surged. China's GDP growth rate fell year over year for seven consecutive years, beginning in 1992 and reaching its lowest in 1999. The most difficult period of this cycle was 1997–1999. This pattern also holds true in terms of the effective interest rate cycle. The effective interest rate was very high during 1995–1997 because the inflation rate plunged during the three years and the consumer price index (CPI) even fell into negative territory in 1998 and 1999. Since the nominal interest rate's downward adjustment was behind the curve, the effective interest rate became excessively high. The excessively high effective interest rate tilted national income in favor of residents but in disfavor of enterprises, exacerbating the difficulties of state-owned enterprises. Meanwhile, the narrow spread between bank deposit and loan interest rates, plus the low loan collection rate, caused banks to suffer losses; (3) ill-defined responsibility and moral hazard. Governments and authorities at all levels wanted to benefit from the financial resources of financial institutions and set up a large number of financial institutions without authorization to provide financial resources for all-out construction. When the payment crisis broke out, many local governments left things to luck in anticipation of being rescued by the central government. In the newly established and expanded financial institutions, a considerable number of senior executives and practitioners were poorly qualified and connected one way or the other to the regulatory authorities. They operated in violation of laws and regulations through concealed accounts and improper competition and by abusing power for personal gain and committing financial fraud. Under such unhealthy market conditions, it was inevitable that problems would emerge.

The Chinese government decided to improve and rectify the financial order mainly by: (1) pushing forward reform and solving problems of the financial system, mechanisms, and institutions reform; (2) enhancing financial legislation and strengthening regulation; (3) proactively protecting depositors' interests and maintaining social stability; and (4) defining responsibilities and combining basic centralization with decentralization to leverage economic fervor at both the central and local levels.

In handling financial risk and problematic financial institutions, the principle was to protect the interests of depositors and enable their deposits to be repaid. The difficulty was deciding who paid the bill.

This was the most painful decision. In the end, the State Council decided to pinpoint the sources of funds under the principle of "whoever sets up such financial institutions assumes responsibility for handling these risks"—that is, "whoever fathered the child carries him or her home." What criteria should be used to identify the "biological fathers"? Some looked to shareholders. However, shareholders assume only limited liability. After share capital is lost, it is very difficult for them to contribute more capital. By contrast, the central government and local government assume unlimited liability. For the repayment of deposits to depositors, unlimited liability is distinguished by the criterion of whether shareholders are affiliated with central government or local government. In the event that such liability cannot be distinguished pursuant to the above criterion, the liability was basically assumed by the central government. Of course, many local governments cried loudly about their grievances. To slice through a knot with a sharp knife, the central government acted resolutely and ruthlessly according to the above principle. And, looking back, it is fair to say that the entangled net of liability was basically sorted out according to this principle.

In June 1998, the Hainan Development Bank, which operated as a share-holding bank, was closed by the People's Bank of China with approval by the State Council. The central government footed the bill for its bankruptcy and liquidation costs. In November 2001, the People's Bank of China ordered five Hainan-based companies (Hainan SEG International Trust & Investment Company, Hainan Huayin International Trust & Investment Company, Hainan Huitong International Trust & Investment Company, Hainan International Leasing Company Ltd. and Sanya Zhongya International Trust & Investment Company) to cease operation for internal rectification. As these five companies were share-holding corporations whose shareholders came from various sectors as well as local and private capital markets, the central government also footed the bill for their bankruptcy and liquidation costs. Some trust and investment companies (*e.g.* Guangdong international Trust & Investment Company) were local firms that were operated locally by local shareholders. The local government assumed responsibility and footed the bill for the bankruptcy and liquidation of these companies. Local governments were primarily responsible for liquidating and footing the bill for the rural cooperative funds, the stock service departments of supply and marketing cooperatives, and the "triple financial irregularities" in urban areas. This cleanup and rectification was carried out under the guidance of central government policy in accordance with the law.

In handling financial risks, if the local governments have difficulty raising debt service funds, they can seek special loans from the central government and use the proceeds to pay back individual liabilities and lawful foreign debts owed by the closed local financial institutions. In 2000, with the approval of the State Council, the People's Bank of China and the Ministry of Finance jointly issued the *Administrative Regulations on Special Loans Granted by Central Government to Local Government* (地方政府向中央专项借款管理规定), emphasizing that the people's government at the provincial level should submit applications for special loans to the State Council for approval on a case-by-case basis; special loans should be borrowed and repaid in a unified way by the people's government at the provincial level. The amount of principal and interest payment should be included in the provincial budget. The people's government at the provincial level should issue to the Ministry of Finance a letter of undertaking on debt repayment in due course and the letter of undertaking shall be duly approved by the Ministry of Finance. Based on the letter of undertaking, the People's Bank of China can authorize the relevant branch to enter into a special loan agreement with the people's government at the provincial level. The administrative regulations prescribe that in the event of a local government failing to make payment as per the schedule set forth in the loan agreement, the Ministry of Finance will deduct the amount overdue from the transfer payment and tax rebate funds disbursed from the central government to the local government based on the deduction notice issued by the People's Bank of China. At present, debt service has proceeded in an orderly fashion and the system of debt repayment responsibility for local government has basically been put in place.

In special circumstances for which China has yet to set up its deposit insurance system, the State Council decided to use special loans to help local governments mitigate financial risks. Experience has since shown that this approach is absolutely correct. The formulation and implementation of the special loan policy played an important role in effectively resolving the shortage of funds used to repay the debts of financial institutions shut down for reorganization as well as mitigating moral hazards, defining responsibilities and boosting public confidence in government, especially in effectively preventing and mitigating local financial risks and maintaining financial and social stability. Along with the rapid economic and financial development, China will also gradually set up a mitigation mechanism for long-term financial risks. The special loans arranged as a contingency risk control measure have significantly diminished over time.

By improving and correcting the financial order, China made a preliminary attempt to define financial risk mitigation responsibilities according to property rights. It can be imagined that this was a very painstaking process because capital contributors (especially local governments at all levels) had never thought of taking up such an enormous responsibility. By handling financial risks under the clear-cut responsibility of "whoever fathered the child carries him or her away," China has significantly raised the local government's awareness of financial risks and reduced the enthusiasm of local governments to pursue financial operations. Local governments have realized that undertaking financial operations can mobilize financial resources but may also have risks. If financial operations are not well managed, local governments may throw good money after bad money. This has played a positive role in reducing administrative interference in financial operations. Meanwhile, upholding the shareholder responsibility principle is in line with the principles of the market economy.

During the transition period, the non-performing assets of commercial banks surged due to the restriction of property rights and the lack of corporate governance as well as the cyclical factors such as economic overheating. The non-performing assets suddenly erupted after the Asian financial crisis broke out, bringing the non-performing asset ratio to a level even higher than that of crisis-stricken countries. In accordance with the lower accounting standards in force at that time, the non-performing asset ratio of China's banking industry was approximately 30 percent in the late 1990s. Some economists have asserted that China's banking industry was technically insolvent at the time. To rebuild public confidence in the financial industry and launch state-owned bank reform, China was forced to fix the issue of non-performing assets.

A. *Issuing Special Government Bonds to Raise Money for Capital Infusion*

In 1997, in the midst of a drastic increase in non-performing bank assets, the central government convened the Central Financial Working Conference and set a three-year deadline for significantly improving the national financial order and reducing the non-performing asset ratio by 2–3 percent a year.

As required by the conference, the Ministry of Finance in November 1998 issued RMB 270 billion in special government bonds with a maturity of thirty years and an annual interest rate of 7.2 percent. The proceeds raised from bond issuance were specifically used to replenish the capital base of the four state-owned banks. In particular, the People's Bank of China lowered the statutory deposit reserve rate from 13 percent to 8 percent; the bank funds, thus increased, were used to buy the special government bonds issued by the Ministry of Finance; the Ministry of Finance used the bond proceeds to inject capital into state-owned commercial banks; the state-owned commercial banks used the funds received to pay back central bank refinancing loans. For commercial banks, on their assets side, deposit reserves decreased and government bond holdings increased; on their liabilities side, share capital increased but refinance borrowings from the central bank decreased. Even though the available funds (liquidity) did not increase, the capital adequacy ratio improved. As for monetary policy, the central bank lowered the required reserve rate and, at the same time, reduced refinance loans to commercial banks. The net effect on the four state-owned banks was basically neutral, whereas the impact on other banks was the easing of monetary policy. On the treasury side, the interest expenditures on special government bonds were roughly in line with the funds occupancy expenses on capital increase. As a result, there was no increase in financial burdens. By 2004, when Huijin Investment Company acted on behalf of the state to make a new round of capital infusion into state-owned commercial banks, the special government bond interest rate payable by the Ministry of Finance to the four state-owned commercial banks fell to 2.25 percent per year. Meanwhile, the Ministry of Finance began to pay interests to bondholders (the state-owned commercial banks).

B. *Setting Up Financial Asset Management Companies*

As calculated according to the accounting standards then in force, the four state-owned commercial banks had an average capital adequacy ratio of more than 8 percent after receiving capital injections via special government bond issuance. As calculated according to the new, more prudent *Method for the Management of Capital Adequacy Ratios of Commercial Banks* (资本充足率管理办法), however, the capital adequacy ratio of the four state-owned commercial banks after deducting their total loan losses was only 2.29 percent, suggesting that they were insolvent.[6] Against this backdrop, it was very difficult to mitigate the credit risks built up over time by relying solely on the force of the four state-owned commercial banks. In 1999, the state decided to set up four financial asset management companies specifically responsible for receiving and disposing of approximately 1.4 trillion RMB of non-performing loans stripped from state-owned commercial banks. In 2000, after their non-performing loans were stripped, the non-performing loan rate of the state-owned commercial banks fell to 9.2 percent.

Financial asset management companies were set up at that time in consideration that if the commercial banks stripped off their non-performing assets internally to form "good banks, bad banks," then the central government would need to directly provide some preferential policies, such as tax exemption for the disposal of non-performing assets, to the state-owned commercial banks. The preferential policies were too broad. The issues associated with this were avoided by setting up financial asset management companies. Another consideration was whether to set up one or four asset management companies. To mitigate the moral hazard and facilitate the comparison of performance for disposing non-performing assets, the central government decided to set up four rather than one asset management company.

On the assets side of asset management companies, among the RMB 1.4 trillion of non-performing assets stripped, approximately RMB 100 billion came from the State Development Bank and the remaining was from the four state-owned commercial banks: the Industrial and Commercial Bank of China, the Agricultural Bank of China, the Bank of China, and the China Construction Bank. Approximately RMB 400 billion pertained to equity held by state-owned commercial banks under the debt-for-equity swap scheme, while approximately RMB 1 trillion fell under non-performing loans. On the liabilities side of asset management companies, approximately RMB 580 billion pertained to refinance loans from the People's Bank of China, while the remainder—RMB 820 billion—pertained to the bonds issued by the four state-owned banks with implicit guarantee by the treasury. The Ministry of Finance provided a solution for final losses, which was implemented after the approval of the State Council.

[6] Tang Shuangning 唐双宁. "Guanyu guoyou shangye yinhang gaige de jige wenti 关于国有商业银行改革的几个问题 [Several Issues with Reforming State-owned Commercial Banks]," March 25, 2005.

By the end of 2006, the four financial asset management companies basically reached the policy non-performing asset disposal and recovery objective set by the state. By then, they had carried out their historical mission in collecting and disposing of non-performing assets. The average recovery rate was slightly lower than 20 percent.

The significance of establishing asset management companies extends far beyond themselves. In as far as their form, China set up financial asset management companies by drawing on the experiences of the United States' Resolution *Trust* Corporation. On surface, it appears to be a technical design to dispose of non-performing assets. In actuality, however, the significance of doing so goes far beyond the use of market-oriented means to dispose of non-performing assets. Setting up financial asset management companies was an important step in the market-oriented reform process of banks and a meaningful step in the financial, and even the entire economic, reforms.

III. *Share-Holding Reform of State-Owned Commercial Banks*

Issuing RMB 270 billion of special government bonds to raise money for capital infusion and setting up asset management companies to strip off non-performing assets, although succeeded in making necessary preparations for state-owned commercial bank reform, was not enough. At the time, the four state-owned commercial banks still assumed heavy burdens and their capital adequacy ratios were still very low and even negative, partly due to accounting standard issues and partly due to left-over historical issues. The causes for non-performing assets were of course related to cyclical changes in the macroeconomic environment. However, they were a reflection of the state-owned bank disciplinary mechanism not being well established and the low level of market development. At that time, the state-owned commercial banks began to introduce some advanced management concepts and methods and gradually set up the operation performance and risk internal control mechanism. Generally speaking, however, the reform at this stage focused on streamlining the external relationship and introducing advanced management technology. Non-performing assets were handled on the surface without touching the state-owned commercial bank system and mechanism issues at a deeper level. To help state-owned enterprises get out of difficulty within three years and tackle key reform challenges, the central government used a host of measures such as debt-for-equity swap, technical renovation loan interest discount, and state-owned enterprise listing. As a result, the transitional costs of economic reform were concentrated in the financial sector, which was an important factor behind the drastic increase in the nonperforming assets of state-owned banks. Therefore, state-owned banks needed comprehensive and thorough reform.

A. *The New Stage of State-Owned Commercial Bank Reform*

The Huijin Investment Company was formed at the end of 2003 as a vehicle to inject capital into the Bank of China and the China Construction Bank. This marked a new stage of financial reform. The financial reform at this stage took place against a background with two major elements: (1) midway through the five-year transition period after China's accession into the WTO in November 2001, the financial industry experienced increasing pressure to open up to the outside world; and (2) since the second half of 2003, the Chinese economy has gradually moved away from deflation into a new round of growth cycle. So there was a macroeconomic environment for speeding up state-owned bank reform.

The *Decisions of the CPC Central Committee on Several Issues of Improving the Socialist Market Economy System* (中共中央关于完善社会主义市场经济体制若干问题的决定) was issued at the Third Plenary Session of the Sixteenth CPC Central Committee held in 2003. The ruling further laid down the objectives, tasks, and procedures for deepening financial enterprise reform and required commercial banks, securities firms, insurance companies, and trust and investment companies to become modern financial enterprises with adequate capital, rigorous internal control, secure operations, and superior service and profitability. Meanwhile, state-owned commercial banks were required to undergo share-holding restructuring, accelerate their disposal of nonperforming assets, reinforce their capital base, and create conditions for initial public offerings (IPOs). The new round of bank reform thus began.

B. *Setting up Huijin Investment Company and Conducting Financial Restructuring*

Financial restructuring was the prerequisite and basis for the shareholding reform of state-owned commercial banks. At the end of

2003, the CPC Central Committee and the State Council decided to select the Bank of China and the China Construction Bank to conduct share-holding reform on a piloting basis. At the same time, the Central Huijin Investment Company Limited[7] was established with a registered capital of US $45 billion (foreign exchange reserves) and it was hoped that such money could be used as capital infusion to fundamentally restructure the state-owned commercial bank system. In 2005, the Huijin Investment Company injected US $15 billion of capital to the Industrial and Commercial Bank of China. In the meantime, state-owned commercial banks once again stripped off a portion of non-performing loans. Since 2004, the Industrial and Commercial Bank of China, the China Construction Bank, the Bank of China, and the Bank of Communications have stripped off and sold approximately US $1 trillion of non-performing assets. From the perspective of state support, it is hoped that this financial restructuring is the "last supper" in the transition process. Subsequent to financial restructuring, the financial burden of state-owned commercial banks was significantly reduced and their asset quality improved noticeably. The capital adequacy ratios of state-owned commercial banks reached the 8 percent regulatory requirement, thereby providing favorable conditions for setting up share-holding companies and going public on the capital market. In addition to injecting capital to large-sized commercial banks, the Huijin Investment Company also injected capital into and restructured some securities firms and insurance companies. It has played an important role in mitigating financial risks and pushing forward reform of the financial system on all fronts.

Compared with the previous round of financial reform, this financial restructuring of state-owned commercial banks had two characteristics: (1) the market-oriented degree of non-performing asset disposal has increased. In 1999, non-performing loans were delegated to asset management companies at their book value and so this was a policy strip-off. Since 2004, non-performing assets have been sold to asset

[7] At the end of 2003, the Central Huijin Investment Company Limited was formed with a registered capital of US$ 45 billion. By nature, Huijin is a government investment corporation that acted on behalf of the state to inject US$ 60 billion of capital to the Bank of China, the China Construction Bank and the Industrial and Commercial Bank of China that underwent share-holding reorganization. In 2007, the state decided to set up the China Investment Corporation and the Central Huijin Investment Company Limited was reestablished as a wholly owned subsidiary of China Investment Corporation.

management companies via auction and as a result the central bank refinance loans can be recovered; and (2) setting up the Huijin Investment Company and using foreign exchange reserves rather than issuing treasury bonds to raise money for capital infusion. Before, to launch state-owned commercial bank reform, conduct financial restructuring, and encourage state-owned commercial banks to go public, the most preferred option was to issue treasury bonds and use the proceeds for capital infusion. This option, however, did not work. The nominal fiscal deficit and debt burden rate appeared to be very low at that time; but in consideration of the non-performing assets built up over time by financial institutions, including state-owned commercial banks and the huge gap in social security, the implicit financial burden was not low. Meanwhile, it was very urgent for state-owned commercial banks to carry out share-holding reform during the post-WTO transition period. Compared with the implicit burden of public finance and the huge expenditures required for the transition of public finance, the investment channels for state foreign exchange reserves at that time were quite narrow. Setting up the Huijin Investment Company using the state foreign exchange reserves as the registered capital has widened the investment channels for foreign exchange reserves and facilitate ownership diversification.

C. *Corporate Governance Reform*

Corporate governance reform is the current state-owned commercial bank reform's most salient feature. Previous reforms proceeded on the financial dimension and did not deal with many such profound issues as corporate governance. The purpose of these reforms is to establish a standard share-holding corporate governance structure. The reform focuses on mechanism transformation and involves adopting corporate governance structure, setting up an internal control mechanism, introducing strategic investors, using prudent accounting standards, and defining the role of intermediary institution. It is a more comprehensive and thorough reform.

D. *Capital Market Listing*

Further improving the equity structure and undergoing true market supervision and inspection by going public on domestic and foreign capital markets was the next step of share-holding reform for state-owned commercial banks. In June 2005, the Bank of Communications floated its IPO on the Hong Kong Exchange; in May 2007, it issued A-shares on the domestic market. In October 2005, the China Construction Bank floated its IPO in Hong Kong; in 2006, it issued A-shares on the domestic market. In June and July 2006, the Bank of China issued H-shares and A-shares respectively in Hong Kong and mainland China. In October 2006, the Industrial and Commercial Bank of China became the first financial enterprise that went public simultaneously in Hong Kong and Mainland China and floated the world's single largest IPO in history. Realistically speaking, the global ranking of capitalization does not mean anything. We should remember that the top rankings of Japanese commercial banks in the 1980s lasted only for a short while.

E. *Differences of This Reform*

Compared with past reform, these reforms had three pronounced differences: (1) the deepening of reform from pure financial restructuring to establishing a modern enterprise system. The purpose of issuing RMB 270 billion in special government bonds in 1998 to replenish capital for the four state-owned commercial banks and setting up financial asset management companies in 1999 to strip off RMB 1.4 trillion in non-performing loans was to mitigate risks for financial institutions. The purpose of these reforms is to restructure banks through capital infusion and establish a modern enterprise system. These reforms focused on the transformation of financial mechanisms and were, in general, more comprehensive and thorough; (2) introducing foreign strategic investors for the first time. This has had far-reaching influence on corporate governance, risk control, innovation, and competitiveness and laid the foundation for financial institutions to go global; and (3) the results of this round of reforms is much better than those of previous reforms. As a result of these reforms, China has established a standard share-holding corporate governance structure and risk internal control mechanism. Moreover, the capital adequacy ratios of state-owned commercial banks have increased significantly, their non-performing asset ratios have been in decline and their profitability has continued to rise over time. In retrospect, looking at the thirty years of financial reform, state-owned commercial banks undergoing share-holding reform and going public is the largest breakthrough and milestone in the entire financial industry transition process.

IV. *Reform of Rural Credit Cooperatives*

Other than state-owned commercial bank reform, reform of rural credit cooperatives is another reform that had a major breakthrough during this period. The overall strategy of this round of banking industry reform was "Grasping the two ends to bring along the middle." The "two ends" refer to the "big-four" state-owned commercial banks on one end and numerous rural credit cooperatives on the other.

The CPC Central Committee and the State Council have paid special attention to the reform and development of rural credit cooperatives. In 1996, the State Council decided to decouple rural credit cooperatives from the Agricultural Bank of China and to authorize the People's Bank of China to supervise and manage rural credit cooperatives. After the National Financial Working Conference was held in 2002, the State Council set up an ad hoc taskforce charged with deepening the rural financial and rural credit cooperatives reform. The taskforce came up with the *Method for Deepening Reform of Pilot Rural Credit Cooperatives*[8] (深化农村信用社改革试点方案). The scheme set out the overall requirements of "defining property right relations, strengthening the disciplinary mechanism, boosting service functionality, letting the state provide appropriate support and local government take responsibility" for the reform and development of rural credit cooperatives.

In June 2003, the central government selected eight provinces and municipalities, such as Jilin, to participate in pilot rural credit cooperatives reform. In August 2004, the State Council decided to add another 21 provinces, autonomous regions, and municipalities into the scope of these reforms and issued the *Opinions on Further Deepening Reform of Pilot Rural Credit Cooperatives* (关于进一步深化农村信用社改革试点的意见). All provinces, autonomous regions, and municipalities other than Hainan and Tibet (there are no rural credit cooperatives in Tibet) participated in this round of reform.

To support reform, the state offered strong policy support in the areas of finance, taxation, funds and interest rate. Under the mandate of Government Doc. No.15, the People's Bank of China and China

[8] Central Government of the PRC. "Tanhua nongcun xinyongshe gaige shidian fangan 深化农村信用社改革试点方案 [Methods for Deepening Reform of Pilot Rural Credit Cooperatives]," 2003.

Banking Regulatory Commission promptly formulated and released the funds support scheme when the reform trials started in eight provinces and municipalities. The People's Bank of China issued special central bank bills or special refinance loans to cover 50 percent of the insolvency amount (outstanding as of the end of 2002) of rural credit cooperatives in the piloting areas to help relieve them of their burden. The special central bank bills were used to replace the non-performing loans and operating losses of the rural credit cooperatives. A piloting province could select one option based on its actual situation or adopt "one province, two systems" provided that the total amount did not exceed 50 percent of the actual insolvency amount (as of 2002) of rural credit cooperatives.

The People's Bank of China helped relieve rural credit cooperatives of their burden by issuing special central bank bills and special refinance loans. The purpose of the funds support scheme was to enable the restructured rural credit cooperatives to clearly define their property rights, boost their financial position and improve their governance structure. The funds support scheme focused on relieving rural credit cooperatives of their burden, setting up a positive incentive mechanism, preventing rural credit cooperatives from further deterioration after reform, and mitigating moral hazard. Funds support was closely integrated with the rural credit cooperatives reform process in the design of special loan and special note issuance, payment conditions and evaluation procedures to maximize the policy effects of "buying the mechanism."

The special notes were cashed out to become the funds owned by credit cooperatives and were not required to be paid back. However, the special notes could be cashed out by credit cooperatives only after meeting a complete set of stringent requirements for capital increase, capital adequacy ratio increase, and non-performing asset decrease. Before cashing out the special notes, the credit cooperatives holding central bank bills should pay interest on a quarterly basis. The central bank bills were designed to provide a tremendously positive incentive mechanism for rural credit cooperative reform and local government and enable 99.9 percent of counties to choose the central bank note support method. By June 2008, the People's Bank of China had completed 18 special note issues, issuing RMB 165.6 billion of special notes to 2,387 rural credit cooperatives at the county (municipal) level, replaced RMB 135.3 billion of non-performing loans, and offset RMB 30.3 billion of operating losses. The central bank honored or cashed out RMB 120.6 billion of special notes for 1,771 rural credit cooperatives at the county (municipal) level, accounting for 74 percent and 72 percent of the number of counties (cities) opting for notes funds support and the amount of notes issued nationwide. In addition, the central bank granted RMB 1.2 billion of special loans to 44 counties (cities) in Xinjiang and Shanxi provinces. At present, the special note issuance and special loan disbursement has been carried out nationwide (except in Hainan), with more than 70 percent of special notes honored or cashed out. The smooth implementation of the funds support policy has played an important and positive role in relieving rural credit cooperatives of their burden, as well as supporting and pushing forward reform. Thus, the policy of "buying the mechanism" has yielded initial results.

Reform of rural credit cooperatives has been ongoing for nearly five years, since its initiation in 2003. Consensus holds that this round of reform is a major reform initiative in China's rural credit cooperative development process and even in the entire rural financial arena. It is a key reform that must succeed. Failure is not an option. This round of reform is of great significance for rural credit cooperatives to realize healthy and sustainable development, improve rural financial services, resolve the "tri-agrarian" issues and develop rural China. Due to reform, the rural credit cooperatives have gradually mitigated their heavy burden accumulated over time and put under effective control the systematic and regional payment risks that have long existed. The operating and financial conditions as well as asset quality of rural credit cooperatives have improved significantly, with agricultural credit such as household loans increasing sharply, service functions enhanced, and internal and external confidence in rural credit cooperative reform and development prospects greatly boosted. The reform has achieved significant progress and accomplishments. Under the four-level loan classification system, the non-performing loan rate of rural credit cooperatives was 9.3 percent at the end of 2007, representing a decrease of 28 percent since 2002, when the reform was launched; the capital adequacy ratio was 11.2 percent, representing a 20 percent gain over 2002. The rural credit cooperatives registered RMB 5.7 billion in losses in 2002 and RMB 45.3 billion in profits in 2007. The agricultural loans of rural credit cooperatives at the end of 2007 totaled RMB 1.43 trillion, accounting for 46 percent of their total loan portfolio and representing an increase of 6 percent over

2002. In addition, these loans accounted for 93 percent of agricultural loans granted nationwide, representing an increase of 12 percent since 2002.

Using central bank bills to support the reform of rural credit cooperatives was an extraordinary financial innovation. Central bank bills are liabilities for the central bank and risk-free assets for credit cooperatives. The central bank used the risk-free assets (central bank bills) to replace or offset the non-performing loans and cumulative losses of rural credit cooperatives at the country level. In particular, the ratio of non-performing loans replaced should not be less than 65 percent. In 2008, the U.S. Federal Reserve used the U.S. government bonds to swap toxic financial institution assets amid the subprime crisis. In light of this development, it is worth conducting further study and theoretical exploration of the practice of using central bank bills to support the reform of rural credit cooperatives in 2003.

V. *Thoughts on the Theoretical Aspect of Banking Industry Reform*

A. *Opening-Up is the Driving Force of Reform*

Looking back at China's thirty-year history of financial reform, we see that opening to the outside world has been constant through the entire reform process. Even at the outset of reform, Deng Xiaoping realized the importance of pursuing international cooperation and opening to the outside world. In 1979, China enacted the first *Law of the People's Republic of China on Chinese-foreign Equity Joint Ventures* (中外合资经营企业法). Meanwhile, China International Trust & Investment Company (CITIC) was established as an investment arm of the Chinese government to introduce foreign capital and conduct international economic and financial cooperation. CITIC successfully issued the first foreign debt. Some foreign-funded banks also began to set up representative offices and business entities in China. The Asian financial crisis of 1997 heightened the profound impact of economic and financial globalization on China. China joined the WTO in November 2001, which marked a new stage in China's economic and financial opening to the outside world. Under this background, the increased urgency of financial reform has pushed forward the share-holding reform of state-owned commercial banks.

The positive effects of opening to the outside world on reform are multifold. First of all, it enabled us to realize the existence of a gap with the outside world. Without opening to the outside world, there would be no information available and we might not have known what lagged behind. The restructured state-owned commercial banks might have received top global rankings in terms of market capitalization but lagged far behind in terms of profitability metrics such as per capita profit and return on capital. In respect to institutional functionality, market development, internal control mechanism and risk management expertise, it seems they were even further behind.[9]

Secondly, opening to the outside world has greatly promoted competition. In the planned economy, competition is demonized and denounced as duplicate construction. After years of reform, the principle of competition has been generally accepted in the manufacturing industry and the vast majority of the service industry. Today, industries that opened earlier and more directly to the outside world (*e.g.* the electronics industry) have collapsed. Instead, they have become the industries with global competitive advantages. In the financial area, however, people still remain skeptical about bringing in foreign investors to participate in competition. A typical question is whether it is necessary to invite foreign investors to participate in reform of state-owned banks. This issue should be understood from two perspectives: on the one hand, foreign investors can garner returns on investment; on the other hand, they can not only introduce technology and management but also bring in new competitive mechanisms. These are especially conducive to improving corporate governance and reducing external administrative interference. Moreover, it will also promote reform of intermediary services in accounting standards, transparency, and credit ratings. This is crucial for reinforcing the achievements of bank restructuring. Without offering foreign investor a certain proportion of equity, under the current system, the domestic shareholders may still find it difficult to extricate themselves from improper outside administrative interference even though the shareholders have been diversified through bank restructuring.

[9] Zhou Xiaochuan 周小川. "Zhongguo yinhangye gaige de changqixing, jianjuxing he fuzaxing 中国银行业改革的长期性、艰巨性和复杂性 [The Difficulty, Complexity, and Long-term nature of Reforming China's Banking Industry]," 2006.

A third issue in financial opening is financial security. An international comparison shows that foreign-funded banks have controlled more than 60 percent of the financial assets in the transitional countries of Eastern Europe and over 30 percent of the financial assets in the emerging market countries as a whole. In China, foreign-funded banks and foreign investors hold approximately 20 percent of equity interests in local commercial banks. The foreign equity holdings of Chinese commercial banks are therefore moderate. More importantly, the financial security of a country hinges on its macroeconomic robustness, legislative excellence, and the soundness of its financial system. In particular, it depends on whether the financial market infrastructure—such as trade, payment, clearance, depository trust, and information functionality—is well established. It is not dependent on the percentage of foreign equity holdings and not necessarily related to whether financial services are provided by domestic or foreign investors.

In regard to future trends, as globalization deepens, the financial markets of all countries worldwide will become more closely linked and the competition will become increasingly fierce. Due to this fact, China has no alternative but to steadfastly continue opening to the outside world. That China can narrow the gap between itself and industrialized countries through importation and boosting competitiveness via openness is a basic lesson of the thirty years of financial reform and the driving force for continued reform.

B. *About Separate Operation and Mixed Operation*

This issue will likely be debated for another 100 years. In the United States, the passage of the Glass-Steagall Act by Congress in 1933 separated commercial banking from investment banking. The principle of the Glass-Steagall Act was that mixed operations are exposed to excessive risks and therefore commercial banking and investment banking should be separated and regulated under different authorities. The two major reasons for separating commercial banking from investment banking are: (1) the sources of funds of commercial banks (on the liabilities side of the balance sheet) are business and consumer deposits and it is too risky to use such funds to conduct investment banking; and (2) unfair loan decisions may arise if commercial banks hold equity interests in enterprises because commercial banks are inclined to grant loans first to the enterprises in which they hold equity interests.

The Glass-Steagall Act drew upon the experiences and lessons from the 1929–1933 Great Depression in the United States.

Economists have continued to criticize the Glass-Steagall Act because they misread the history. The real cause of the Great Depression was the failure of the central bank (the Federal Reserve) to fulfill its role as a lender of last resort. Decision-makers were overconfident in the market's self-recuperation mechanism and failed to promptly provide the liquidity needed by the market to stop the self-reinforcing cycle of debt and deflation, which thus lead to the Great Depression. By the 1970s–80s, critics of the Glass-Steagall Act gained an upper hand; the separation of commercial banking from investment banking began to falter; a consensus was reached to repeal the Glass-Steagall Act. In 1999, the *Financial Services Modernization Act* was passed by the Congress and swiftly signed into law by President Clinton. The Glass-Steagall Act was thus eliminated, ending the 60-year separation between commercial and investment banking in the United States.

Chinese history is also worth examining. At the initial stage of reform and opening, China adopted the mixed operation model under which a commercial bank (the Bank of Communications) was allowed to operate brokerage and insurance businesses. In the midst of economic overheating and financial chaos at the end of June 1993, the Chinese government enacted 16 rectification measures, 13 of which were related to the financial sector. When reexamining the causes of financial chaos, policymakers held mixed operation partly to blame and decided to draw on the U.S. experience of separating commercial banking from investment banking. With the *Law of the People's Republic of China on the People's Bank of China* (中国人民银行法), the *Commercial Bank Law* (商业银行法) and the *Securities Law of the People's Republic of China* (证券法) enacted in 1995, China officially embarked on the path of separating commercial banking from investment banking and asked commercial banks to disconnect from their securities firms and insurance companies. As a scholar, I attended a seminar regarding separate operations and pointed out that the U.S. practice of operating commercial banking from investment banking was near an end and it was only a matter of time until the Glass-Steagall Act was repealed. In 1980, when I began to pursue graduate studies in the United States, I selected the course "Money and Banking." The professor criticized the Glass-Steagall Act and left a deep impression on me. At that time, I had a superficial understanding of this issue. Subsequently, through continued research, teaching, and participation in international seminars and especially after joining the People's Bank of China, I conducted increasingly focused research and comparison of this issue from an international perspective.

Separate operation and mixed operation models both have their strengths and weaknesses. Generally speaking, the benefits of separate operations are that risks can be clearly identified and the regulatory responsibilities are well defined; the weaknesses of separate operations are that it may stifle financial innovation and cause lower efficiency. The mixed operation promotes financial innovation and new products but sometimes risks cannot be easily identified. Under the mixed operation and separate regulation model, it is difficult to define the regulatory responsibilities. European countries have adopted the mixed operation model, universal bank model, or financial supermarket model. The debate on the merits and drawbacks of the two alternative models goes on. Before the U.S. subprime crisis broke out, Chinese scholars had reached a consensus to gradually adopt the universal banking model. China can thus draw on the U.S. financial holding company model or the positive experiences of Europe and Japan.

History appears to award those who are thinking diligently. The U.S. subprime crisis repeatedly cast doubt over the universal banking model. By nature, separate operations segregates the risks of commercial banking (indirect financing) from the risks of investment banking (direct financing), whereas mixed operation (universal banking) causes the demarcation of commercial banking with investment banking and insurance to become increasingly fuzzy in respect to organization and product portfolio. "Would the subprime crisis have happened if the Glass-Steagall Act had not been repealed?" asked some scholars (including Stanley Fischer, former MIT professor and the former IMF Deputy Director). The impacts of the subprime crisis on the power of the universal banking model are profound and forceful.

In 1995, China decided to adopt the separate operation model; in 2003, it began to introduce the "one central bank, three regulatory commissions" system. Today, I do not want to draw any conclusion. China is lucky. Whenever we think about key issues, there are major events happening and telling us where risks are and helping us to chart the course of navigation. With such information and thinking available, China's financial industry can avoid taking experimental detours.

C. *The Basic Logic of Thirty Years of Bank Reform*

The replacing government funds for enterprises with bank loans to enterprises in 1979 was the starting point of transition from political incentives to economic incentives in financial sector reform. By replacing government funds for enterprises with bank loans to enterprises, enterprises began to feel the pressure of debt. As debt repayment entities, enterprises began to be bound by property rights. Meanwhile, banks also began to have every incentive to pursue profitability. In replacing government funds for enterprises with bank loans to enterprises on a larger scale and in a unified way, it then became imperative to change away from the bank system in which government and business functions are mixed. As a result, the People's Bank of China and the Industrial and Commercial Bank of China were separated. This also marked the beginning of the reform of separating government from business in the financial sector.

The need to set up policy banks after the mid-1990s showed that when government functions were mixed with business operations, commercial banks pursuing their own commercial interests ran on a collision course with their mandate of implementing state policies. Amid the increasing appeal for reform of economic incentives, the financial sector further kicked off the reform initiative of separating government from business functions. As the objectives of establishing a socialist market economy was realized, financial reform began on all fronts. Against this background, reforms gave commercial banks the most extensive authority and scope to date, set up a large number of non-bank financial institutions, and lent money through such institutions without quantitative restriction. Meanwhile, they also obtained licenses for entry into the equity, real estate, futures, and trust markets to conduct any operation permitted in the financial industry.

Reform at the time was not complemented with supporting measures. Externally, the concepts and system of financial regulation were not fully established; internally, financial institution reform had yet to start and the lack of external or internal disciplinary mechanisms naturally triggered financial chaos. After the Asian financial crisis broke out, financial risks were severely exacerbated. This situation showed that pure economic incentive reform, offering market entities greater economic incentives under the power-delegating and profit-sharing scheme, could not succeed by in a system where property rights were not clearly defined and financial institutions lacked sound corporate governance and internal disciplinary mechanisms. To the contrary, such reform became a game of interests between the state and enterprises and generated numerous moral hazards. It was be unable to reach the objective of truly boosting the internal check and balance of micro-entities. It was therefore critical for the Chinese financial industry in the late 1990s to undergo improvement and rectification and adopt the separate operation model.

The new round of financial reform, beginning at the end of 2003, has the distinctive features of property rights reform. Regardless of setting up share-holding corporations, introducing foreign investors or floating IPOs, the financial institutions have complied with corporate governance requirements for well-defined property rights under the modern enterprise system framework. This round of reform has enabled financial institution reform to shift from the external economic incentives such as power-delegating and profit-sharing into the property rights incentives of setting up modern enterprise systems and standardizing corporate governance. External market oversight and social supervision are strengthened by going public. As the property rights reform of financial institutions (especially state-owned commercial banks) deepens, the micro-basis of the entire financial sector is undergoing a fundamental change. Market forces will in turn spur the government to speed up function transformation and promote the change from governing the country by command and control to governing the country by law.

The intrinsic reasoning of the thirty-year process of bank reform has thus far been described based on the five characteristics of a market economy. Last but not least, we make an item-by-item review of the five characteristics to see whether the banking industry has been changed as expected after thirty years of reform. First of all, we assess whether property rights are more clearly defined than in the past. The answer is affirmative. In the past, the banking industry was dominated by the People's Bank of China; nowadays, there are hundreds of banks and thousands of relatively independent rural credit cooperatives. The capital adequacy ratios of financial institutions have significantly improved. In the past, banks served as the cashier of government and public finance and acted on the order of government; nowadays, they are market entities pursuing independent operation and allocating resources under market forces, suggesting that government and business have been separated to a great extent. In the past, administrative decrees took the place of laws; nowadays, the legislative construction has been well in place. The *Law on the People's Bank of China*, *the Law on Regulation of and Supervision over the Banking Industry* (银行业监督管理法), the *Commercial Bank Law* and the *Property Law* (物权法) have become the basis by which regulatory authorities and commercial banks regulate and operate by law. In the past, bank executives were rewarded with political promotion for good performance; nowadays, the banking industry offers enormous economic incentives. In the past, banks were not subject to social supervision; nowadays, they are required to disclose and publish their annual report each year. Publicly listed banks also need to consider share price performance and their operating and decision-making transparency has improved significantly. All these are the manifestations of social oversight and supervision.

In spite of remarkable accomplishments achieved thus far, banking industry reform still has a long way to go. Chairmen and presidents of state-owned holding banks are appointed and these banks are regulated under the command and control mode. This is also in line with China's unique situation and the piecemeal reform approach. In addition, state-owned banks are evaluated as per the operating metrics such as returns on assets (ROA), returns on capital (ROC), profit margin, and non-performing asset ratio. They also face increasingly fierce competition from domestic and foreign banks. Publicly listed banks need to keep a close eye on their share price and market capitalization. All these factors constitute external check and balance on the traditional system of state-owned banks. At present, the banking industry has exhibited significant mixed economic characteristics. The complicated environment in the transition process has resulted in higher transaction costs and given rise to rent-seeking (corruption) opportunities. Nowadays, the current system is still a viable option and no better alternative has emerged. As the global financial integration deepens, the pressure of international competitive will increase. Hong Kong, Macau, and Taiwan will be increasingly integrated into the economic life of mainland China and the ambitious blueprint for the unification of China has become increasingly clear. The Chinese banking industry will continue to advance towards its market-oriented destination. It may suffer temporary twists and turns but the reform and opening trend has become irreversible. In the foreseeable future, the Chinese banking industry will face the challenges of fluctuation of macroeconomic cycle, gradually moving to Renminbi convertibility and interest rate liberalization. I am confident that the Chinese banking industry will be able to overcome these three challenges.

Bibliography

Central Government of the PRC. "Tanhua nongcun xinyongshe gaige shidian fangan 深化农村信用社改革试点方案[Methods for Deepening Reform of Pilot Rural Credit Cooperatives]" Document No. 15 (2003). Available on the website of the Central Government of the People's Republic of China.

Central Committee of the CPC. "Zhonggong zhongyang guanyu wanshan shehuizhuyi shichangjingji tizhi ruogan wenti de jueding 中共中央关于完善社会主义市场经济体制若干问题的决定Decisions of the CPC Central Committee on Several Issues of Improving the Socialist Market Economy System]." In *Zhonggong zhongyang guanyu wanshan shehuizhuyi shichangjingji ruogan wenti dejueding, fudaoduben* 中共中央关于完善社会主义市场经济体制若干问题的决定-辅导读本 [*A Study Aid on the Decisions of the CPC Central Committee on Several Issues of Improving the Socialist Market Economy System*], compiled by the authors of this book, 1–26. The People's Press, 2003.

Central Party Literature Research Center. "Zhonggong zhongyang guanyu jianli shehuizhuyi shichangjingji tizhi ruganwenti de jueding 中共中央文献研究室编.中共中央关于建立社会主义市场经济体制若干问题的决定 [Decisions of the Party Central Committee Concerning Several Problems with the Establishment of a Socialist Market Economy]." In *Shisida yilai zhongyao wenxian xuanbian (xiace)* 十四大以来重要文献选编 (下册) [*Selected Documents from the Fourteenth Party Congress, (Volume 2)*], 519–548. The People's Press, 1999.

——. "Guowuyuan guanyu jinrong tizhi gaige de jueding 国务院关于金融体制改革的决定 [Decisions of the State Council Concerning Reform of the Financial System]." In *Shisida yilai zhongyao wenxian xuanbian (xiace)* 十四大以来重要文献选编 (下册) [*Selected Documents from the Fourteenth Party Congress, (Volume 2)*], 593–604. The People's Press, 1999.

Deng Xiaoping 邓小平. "Guanyu jingji gongzuo de jidian yijian 关于经济工作的几点意见 [Opinions on Economic Work]." In *Deng Xiaoping wenxuan* 邓小平文选 [*The Selected Works of Deng Xiaoping*], Vol. 3. The People's Press, 1994: 194–202.

Janos, Kornai. *Economics of Shortage* (Chinese Translation). Beijing: Economic Science Press, 1986.

People's Bank of China. "Difang zhengfu xiang gongyang zhuanye jiekuan guanli guiding 地方政府向中央专项借款管理规定 [Regulation on Local Governments' Progress Towards Centralizing Lending Management]." Bank Document No. 148 (2000).

People's Bank of China, Central Party Literature Research Center. "Zhonggong zhongyang, guowuyuan guanyu shenhua jinrong gaige, zhengdun jinrong zhixu, fangfan jinfrong fengxian de tongzhi 中共中央、国务院关于深化金融改革、整顿金融秩序, 防范金融风险的通知 [Notice by the Party Central Committee and State Council Concerning Deepening Financial Reforms, Consolidating Financial Order, and Avoiding Financial Risk]." In *Jinrong gongzuo wenxian xuanbian (1978–2005)* 金融工作文献选编 (1978–2005) [*Excerpts from Financial Documents (1978–2005)*], 281–293. China Financial Press, 2007.

State Council of the PRC. "Guowuyuan bangongting guanyu jinyibu shenhua nongcun xinyongshe gaige de shidian yijian 国务院办公厅关于进一步深化农村信用社改革的试点意见 [Opinions of the State Council on Deepening Reform of Pilot Rural Credit Cooperatives]." Document no. 66 (2004). Available on the website of the Central Government of the People's Republic of China.

Tang Shuangning 唐双宁. "Guanyu guoyou shangye yinhang gaige de jige wenti 关于国有商业银行改革的几个问题 [Several Issues with Reforming State-owned Commercial Banks]" Lecture given at the Annual Academic Conference of the China Finance Society, March 25, 2005. Available on the Banking Regulatory Commission website.

Yi Gang 易纲. "Shichang xiaolü yu chanquan jieding 市场效率与产权界定[Demarcating Market Efficiency and Production Power]." *China: Development and Reform* vol. 12 (1988).

Zhou Xiaochuan 周小川. "Zhongguo yinhangye gaige de changqixing, jianjuxing he fuzaxing 中国银行业改革的长期性、艰巨性和复杂性 [The Difficulty, Complexity, and Long-term nature of Reforming China's Banking Industry]." *Tansuo yu sikao—renminyinhang xueshu jiangzuo yu lingdao ganbu diaoyan baogao xuan* 探索与思考—人民银行学术讲座与领导干部调研报告选 [*Exploration and Reflection—People's Bank Selections from Academic Lectures and Government Research*]. People's Bank of China, 2006: 14–26.

CHAPTER FIVE

GOVERNMENT TRANSFORMATION AND PUBLIC FINANCE

Hu Angang[1]

I. *Introduction*

The thirty years of reform and opening has been a historical era, one that has witnessed China's drive toward modernization. During these thirty years, China's economy and society have undergone a "once in a thousand years" period of change, achieving unprecedented success from its development. In the period from 1978 to 2007, China's per-capita GDP increased from 217 US dollars per person to 2,360 US dollars per person, increasing annually by an average of 8.6 percent, thus resulting in China's historical leap from a low-income country to a moderate-income country.[2] China's human development index (HDI) has increased from 0.56 to 0.78, approaching the "high level" of development (an HDI higher than 0.8); already, over 30 percent of the total population in China has reached this "high level" of development.[3] The speed and scale of China's development are not only far higher than those of other countries during the same period, but even in historical terms, are an example of something few and far

[1] Director of Center for China Study, Tsinghua University, Chinese Academy of Sciences, and professor and doctoral tutor of School of Public Policy and Management, Tsinghua University.

[2] At the beginning of the reform and opening, China's per-capita GDP ranked as one of the lowest in the world. In the database of the World Bank, the author has analyzed statistics that show that in 1980 China's per-capita GDP ranked 134th out of 140 countries and regions, and that in 2005, China ranked 93rd out of 169 countries and regions.

[3] The per-capita GDP is calculated based on the US dollar prices in 2000; figures from 2008 are estimated by the author. Data from 1978 is quoted from the World Bank, "World Development Indicator 2008," 2008; the human development index in 2008 was estimated by the author and the data in 1978 is quoted from UNDP, "Human Development Report 2008," 2008.

between.[4] The "China Miracle" has turned from a dream into a reality, and the "Chinese Model" has gone from being merely a topic of interest to winning widespread recognition.

In analyzing China's reform and transformation, we find that it is, in truth, a combination of transformations of the largest scale in the history. We also find that these transformations are interrelated, intertwined, and interactive, including not only the transformation of the economic and political system, but also social transformation, the transformation of the style of governance, and opening to the world. But what has counted most in this multiplex of transformations has been the transformation of government functions, which is what provided the political and social basis for China to successfully realize its "market transformation," "political transformation," "social transformation," and "opening to the world."[5] The force behind China's economic wonder that has emerged over past thirty years has been the Chinese government; on one hand, it has acted as the guide, designer, and propeller of reform, while also taking the initiative in undertaking self-reform, self-adjustment, and self-adaptation; on the other hand, however, the government, as an integral part of the traditional system itself, has inevitably been the main subject of reform, and has created barriers to the deepening of reform and sided with vested interests against reform. Although this governmental transition and multifaceted transformation has had only thirty years for these competing forces to interact and adapt to each other, there have nonetheless been revolutionary and radical changes, changes that have been realized through gradual reform; it has been a process that has seen rational cooperation and power sharing between the government and the market and between the government and society, thus forming a model of social transformation and development with Chinese characteristics.

---

[4] According to the World Development Indicator database, published by the World Bank, the author found that during the period from 1980 to 2005, of China's 31 provinces (municipalities and autonomous regions), Zhejiang Province saw the fastest growth of its per-capita GDP, with the growth rate reaching 12.1 percent; Qinghai Province saw the slowest growth of its per-capita GDP, with the growth rate reaching 6.98 percent, exceeding the growth rates of all other countries other than China (South Korea's per-capita GDP grew by 5.81 percent during this period).

[5] Zou Zhizhuang is of the opinion that the economic transformation in China is, to a large extent, aimed at realizing China's economic modernization. He views this as an action taken by the government, though profit-seeking behavior by private individuals and enterprises also plays a role. (Zou Zhizhuang 邹至庄, *Zhongguo jingji zhuanxing* 中国经济转型 [*China's Economic Transformation*], 2005.)

This chapter studies the transformation of the Chinese government and analyzes the shift of the government's goals for development, the transformation of government functions, the transformation of decision-making mechanisms, as well as the change of the state finance system and the public payments model. The main questions to be addressed in this chapter include: Has the Chinese government truly transformed its functions over the past thirty years? If so, how have these changes occurred? What aspects have been transformed? What are the historical starting points for these transformations? What is the historical trajectory of their evolution? What have been the lessons from this experience? And finally, what challenges will there be in the future and what changes be made to meet them?

To answer these questions, this chapter is divided into four parts: the first part introduces the historical background and the main issues for discussion; the second part gives a comprehensive analysis of the transformation of the Chinese government's development goals, decision-making mechanisms, and government functions; the third part deals with the results of the transformation of the Chinese government, the transformation of the state revenue and expenditure systems, and discusses the transformation of the finance system from state finance to public finance—in terms of its absorption model, expenditure model, and transfer payments; finally, the fourth part contains concluding remarks which summarize the main features of the government's transformation and the transition to public finance as well as give an account of the possibilities of for future developments.

II. *Three-Dimensional Analysis of the Chinese Government's Transformation*

A. *The Analytical Framework of Government Transformation*

The economic reform in China is different from the economic transformation of most countries. It is a reform led by the government. The state has been the main guide and propeller of economic development, political change, social transformation, and changing international relations.[6] China's social transformation has been the result

---

[6] Wang Shaoguang 王绍光, Hu Angang 胡鞍钢, *Zhongguo guojia nenli baogao* 中国国家能力报告 [*Report on China's National Capabilities*], 1993: 1.

of a combination of various forces. It was the market economy that lit the fire of social change and helped these reforms gain great momentum. But in order to control this momentum, it has been the job of the state to act as a cohesive force, balancing and restraining some of this momentum in order to ensure long-lasting peace and order and to ensure the possibility for China to realize its goal of "improving people's livelihood and building up the country's national strength." But, only by working for government transformation could the state hope to successfully guide and lead the transformation of the whole society. Otherwise, social and economic transformation could not proceed smoothly, and could even have stopped altogether.

So, what has been the core of the government's transformation? In this author's view, in the transformation of any nation's government, there are three important questions. Firstly, what does the government say? Reform and development in a country must be carried out by the entity with a dominant voice and this voice is usually that of the government. With the passage of time, this voice becomes the political consensus of the ruling party and eventually the consensus of the whole society. This consensus reflects a country's development philosophy, development strategy, and development objectives; this is the "objective dimension" of transformation. Secondly, what will the government do? There is a huge difference between "saying" and "doing." Strategies laid down by some countries are well-reasoned and tightly argued, but are changed beyond recognition when put into practice. As a result, what the government will do and what roles it will play during the course of transformation is the second important aspect in the transformation of government functions, which is the "functional dimension." Thirdly, how will the government do it? Even with the same guiding principles, if the process for government decision-making is different and there is variation in the level of participation by different interest groups, there can be much difference in the formulation of policies. Therefore, the third aspect is the "mechanism dimension" of government transformation.

Based on these three dimensions of government transformation, this author has established and analyzed a comprehensive framework for transformation of the Chinese government. In this framework, public finance is an integral part as well as the direct manifestation of the government's transformation (See Figure 5.1).

On the whole, thirty years of reform have brought about significant changes to the functions of the Chinese government. The main path for this change has been the redefinition and readjustment of the

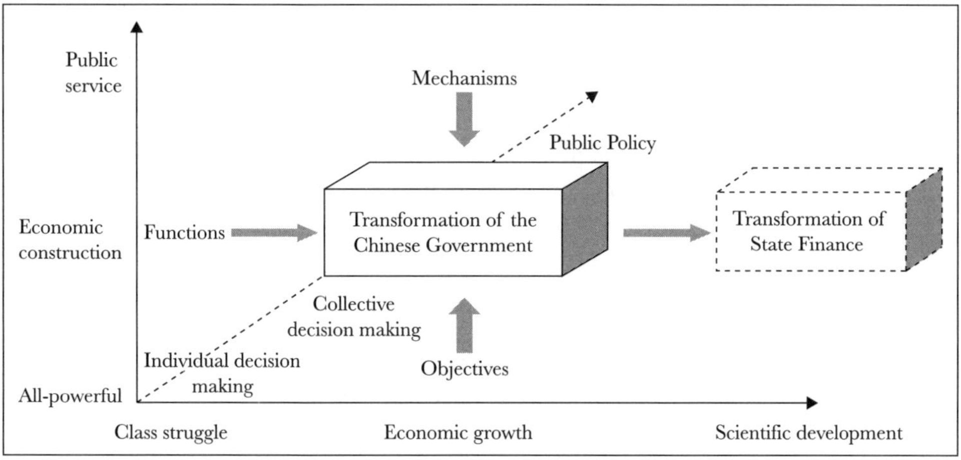

Figure 5.1. An Analytical Framework for the Transformation of the Chinese Government.

role played by the government in society and the market. In thirty years of reform and opening, the Chinese government has gradually turned from an all-powerful government in charge of everything to a government responsible for a limited amount of affairs, from a government that intervened excessively to a government that uses moderate intervention, from a government relying on personal decision-making to a government practicing scientific and democratic decision-making, and from a government focusing on economic construction to a government providing public services. Policy making by the government has shifted from emphasizing planning and administrative measures to relying mainly on economic and legal measures, and in the economy, indirect control has begun to take precedence over direct control. Also, the policy environment has been gradually changed from a "rule of man" environment to one characterized by "rule by law;" the government's actions are supervised and restricted by law, thus increasing the transparency and effectiveness of the government and providing a good environment for the development of the market economy.

B. *Change of the Government's Development Strategy: From Economic Construction to Scientific Development*

China's development model is in essence a catch-up model, that is, the Chinese government has set the basic objective of development as catching up with advanced industrialized countries. But in different periods, the Chinese government has chosen and implemented different development strategies and taken different outlooks on development. In the history of China's modernization drive since its founding in 1949, the outlook on development and the development strategy of the Chinese government have changed considerably every 25–30 years, which can be roughly divided into three periods: The period of Mao Zedong (1949–1976) and Hua Guofeng (1976–1978) was the first generation of development strategy; the period of Deng Xiaoping (1979–1991) and Jiang Zemin (1992–2001) was the second generation development strategy; and the period of Hu Jintao (2002–2012) and after is the third generation development strategy (See Table 5.1).

In this section, through analysis of the objectives set out in the five-year plans, we will analyze the evolution of the government's development objectives over the thirty years of reform and opening. During this period, the second generation's focus on "material first" was changed to the third generation's "people first", reflecting the changes in thinking within the Chinese government.

Table 5.1. China's Three Generations of Development Strategies

	First generation development strategy	Second generation development strategy	Third generation development strategy
Ruling philosophy	Philosophy of economic construction as the central task and class struggle as the guiding ideology	Philosophy of economic construction	Philosophy of social harmony
Development objective	"To gradually realize socialist industrialization and the socialist transformation of agriculture, handicraft industry, and capitalist industry and commerce;" "to catch up with Britain and surpass the United States;" to achieve the "Four Modernizations"[7]	To secure people's livelihood and triple industrial and agricultural output as well as the GNP	Construct of a well-off society in an all-around way

[7] During 1960s, Mao Zedong and Zhou Enlai summarized the objectives for China's socialist modernization as the "Four Modernizations": agriculture, industry, national defense, and science and technology.

Table 5.1 (*cont.*)

	First generation development strategy	Second generation development strategy	Third generation development strategy
Outlook on development	Placing politics in command; emphasis on revolution and advancing production; pursuing fairness and impartiality	Development is of overriding importance and is the primary task of the CCP to govern and rejuvenate the country.	People first; pursuit of humanistic development; prevention of polarization of the rich and poor
Means for development	Even development between coastal and inland areas	Uneven development strategy emphasizing development of coastal areas; strategy for the development of the western regions	Even development; rejuvenation of old industrial bases in Northeast China; lifting up Central China
Development and resources	Excessive development; destruction of resources; low-efficiency utilization	Excessive development; enhanced efficiency in utilization of resources	Establishment of a resource-conserving society; high-efficiency development
Reference model	Soviet model	East-Asia model (a model of mixed economies)	China's own road
Government function	All-powerful government; government of political movements	Development-centered government	Public-service government
Economic system	Command-style planned economy	Establishment of the socialist market economy	Improvement of the socialist market economy
Road to industrialization	National industrialization; exclusion of capital participation; elimination of private sector	National industrialization; allowing the participation of private capital; encouraging the development of the private sector	Advancing industrialization under state guidance and focusing on the private sector
Economy and society	Emphasis on social development	Emphasis on economic development	Coordinated economic and social development
Fairness and efficiency	Emphasis on social fairness and egalitarianism	Emphasis on efficiency with due consideration being given to fairness	Emphasis on social fairness, public service, and fairness in social distribution; boosting efficiency of the market mechanism

Table 5.1 (*cont.*)

	First generation development strategy	Second generation development strategy	Third generation development strategy
Development and environment	Black development; destruction of the environment; disregard of environmental protection	Development supreme at the cost of environment; destruction of the environment; unsustainable development	Establishment of an environmentally-friendly society; green development
Government and society	Government control over society; leader/follower society; charismatic leadership	Government control over the society; allowed public participation in a limited way.	Partnership between the government and the society; extensive participation; sharing of the fruits of joint governance
Political consensus	Preventing the restoration of capitalism; fighting and guarding against revisionism	Theory on becoming rich first; poverty is not socialism	Social fairness, social equality, and social harmony

Sources: Hu Angang 胡鞍钢 and Wang Yahua 王亚华, *Guoqing yu fazhan—zhongguo wuda ziyuan bendongtai bianhua yu changyuan fazhan zhan*国情与发展—中国五大资本动态变化与长远发展战略 [*National Conditions and Development—Dynamic Changes of China's Five Major Categories of Capital and the Strategy for their Long-term Development Strategy*], 2004: 163–165; as well as amendments by the author.

1. *Development Strategy Emphasizing Economic Construction (1978–1992)*

The Sixth Five-year Plan was the first five-year plan created after China put an end to the planned economy; the basic concept of the plan was to continually carry out adjustment, reform, and refinement to strive for fundamental improvement of China's finance system and economy and to make necessary preparations for developments planned for the Seventh Five-year Plan period.[8] The Sixth Five-year Plan was the first to bring social development into a five-year plan, with the plan being renamed "Plan for National Economy and Social Development;" unlike previous plans that set forth economic targets that emphasized high speed, high quantities, and high accumulation,

[8] In the Sixth Five-year Plan, it was stipulated that industrial and agricultural production was the priority and that, on the premise of improving economic performance, the average annual growth rate should reach 4 percent, and efforts should be made to increase it to 5 percent during the plan's implementation.

the economic strategy indicated in the Sixth Five-year Plan made steps in shifting the central task to improvement of economic performance.[9] The quantitative targets set in the Sixth Five-year Plan were quite different from the simple targets set for economic construction in the Second Five-year Plan. However, the central task was still economic construction, with the economic development targets taking up 60.7 percent of the plan and the social development targets making up the remaining 39.3 percent (See Table 5.2). This suggests that the central government had come to realize that not only did the state have economic functions, but also social functions.

The general train of thought in the Seventh Five-year Plan was focused on enlivening the Chinese economy and opening up to the outside world. Three major tasks were put forward in the plan. The first task was to carry out systematic reform in order to establish a new socialist economic system with Chinese characteristics, the second task was to maintain continuous and steady economic growth, and the third task was to improve the living standards of the people. The economic targets set in the Seventh Five-year Plan constituted 57 percent of the plan, while livelihood targets, concerning household income, medical care, and employment, increased to 32.1 percent.

The general train of thought indicated in the Eighth Five-year Plan was—based on ensuring continued economic and social stability—to deepen reform so as to better facilitate governance and adaptation. The economic targets set in the Eighth Five-year Plan constituted 57.7 percent of the plan, which for the first time included resource utilization targets, including quantitative targets such as energy consumption per 10,000 yuan of GNP.

Overall, during the time from the Sixth Five-year Plan to the Eighth Five-year Plan, China's outlook on development was "material centered," with the pursuit of the economic growth as the core; but the proportion of targets regarding people's living standards and public services also went up and population and resource targets began to be introduced. The government began to gradually withdraw from the microeconomic sphere; the number of physical output targets was reduced and the number of macro targets increased. The number of

[9] The first guiding ideology of the Sixth Five-year Plan was that "All economic activities must be centered on the improvement of economic performance and efforts should be made to seek the proportional, long-term, and steady growth of the national economy."

targets set by command plan was reduced and the number of guided planning targets increased. However, the government still intervened excessively in the economy until the introduction of the market mechanism, which had not yet become the basis for resource distribution.

2. *A Change to Public Service (1992–2003)*

The Ninth Five-year Plan was the first five-year plan created after China set the goal of establishing a socialist market economy; its general guiding slogan was "seize opportunity, deepen reform, promote opening up and development, and maintain stability." The Ninth Five-year Plan proposed two comprehensive changes of great importance. The proposed changes were the transition of the economic system from a traditional planned economy to a socialist market economy and the transition from an extensive economic growth strategy to an intensive one. The Central Committee of the Chinese Communist Party (CCP) put forward that the planning system, plan content, and planning methods should be reformed and that state plans should henceforth emphasize macro-level, strategic, and policy goals. The Central Committee mandated that planning targets be predictive and instructive.[10] They also mandated that the proportion of economic targets be reduced, and in the plan, less than 50 percent (47 percent) of the targets were economic in nature. Correspondingly, the proportion of targets pertaining to living standards, resources, the environment, and education went up drastically (to 53 percent), beginning to hold a dominant position.

The Tenth Five-year Plan was the first five-year plan to be created after the beginning of the third step in China's modernization drive; it was also the first five-year plan to begin establishing the socialist market economy. In the Tenth Five-year Plan, the plan targets were all the more concentrated in the fields of social development. In the Outline of the Tenth Five-year Plan, there was a reduction in the number of physical targets and an increase in the number of predictive targets, reflecting China's structural change and the plan's new emphasis on the role of the market and the use of economic policies and legal

[10] CCP Central Committee, *Zhonggong zhongyang guanyu zhiding guomin jingji he shehui fazhan "jiuwu" jihua he 2010 yuanjing mubiao de jianyi*中共中央关于制定国民经济和社会发展"九五"计划和2010年远景目标的建议 [*Suggestions of the CCP Central Committee on Formulating the Ninth Five-year Plan for the National Economy and Social Development and the Long-range Objectives for the Year 2010*], 1995.

Table 5.2. Different Types of Quantitative Targets and Proportion during Every Five-Year Plan Period (1981–2010)

Target	Sixth Five-year Plan period 1981–1985	Seventh Five-year Plan period 1986–1990	Eighth Five-year Plan period 1991–1995	Ninth Five-year Plan period 1996–2000	Tenth Five-year Plan period 2001–2005	Eleventh Five-year Plan period 2006–2010
Number (unit: planned items)						
Economic growth	5	6	7	4	3	3
Economic structure	15	10	8	4	7	6
Education, science, and technology	5	2	1	2	7	4
Population, resources, environment	1	1	2	2	6	13
People's living standards and public service	7	9	8	5	7	16
Total	33	28	26	17	30	42
Proportion (unit: %)						
Economic growth	15.2	21.4	26.9	23.5	10.0	7.1
Economic structure	45.5	35.7	30.8	23.5	23.3	14.3
Sub-total	60.7	57.1	57.7	47.0	33.3	21.4
Education, science, and technology	15.2	7.1	3.8	11.8	23.3	9.5
Population, resources, environment	3.0	3.6	7.7	11.8	20.0	31.0
People's living standards and public service	21.2	32.1	30.8	29.4	23.3	38.1
Sub-total	39.3	42.9	42.3	53.0	67.7	78.6
Total	100	100	100	100	100	100

Note: This data was compiled by the author according to various five-year plans.

measures to exert macro-control.[11] The Tenth Five-year Plan was a relatively complete and balanced plan, with the number of targets relating to population, resources, environment, living standards, education, science, and technology going up to 66.6 percent, while the proportion of economic targets dropped to 33.4 percent, which were all predictive targets. The plan was reflective of the gradual change toward a public-service oriented government.

3. *Construction of a Public-Service Oriented Government (2003–2020)*

The Eleventh Five-year Plan was the first five-year plan carried out under the guidance of the scientific outlook on development. In the Eleventh Five-year Plan, it was put forward that "development must be scientific development." This phrase was meant to emphasize the "scientific" in front of "development," meaning that China should adhere to the principle of "people first," change its outlook on development, pursue an innovative development model, improve the quality of development, and carry out the "Five Overall Plans" (五个统筹), so as to coordinate economic and social development and put them on the track of comprehensive and sustainable development. The objectives for economic and social development in the Eleventh Five-year Plan period were divided into four categories: economic growth, economic structure, public service and people's lives, and population, resources, and the environment, totalling 22 quantifiable targets. In terms of these targets, the plan emphasized those related to public service and resources and the environment, which made up 38 percent and 31 percent respectively, accounting for 79.1 percent of the total. Meanwhile, the number of economic targets was reduced to 21.4 percent of the total.

The most important change in the Eleventh Five-year Plan was that the plan defined the role of the government in terms of providing public services and social improvement and also in terms of public funds and spending, thus laying the foundation for the transformation of government functions in a real sense. In the 2006 Work Report of the Government, Wen Jiabao stressed that "We should be firm in our resolution to delegate tasks not handled by the government to the market,

[11] Zhu Rongji 朱镕基, "Guanyu guomin jingji he shehui fazhan dishi ge wunian jihua gangyao bao gao 关于国民经济和社会发展第十个五年计划纲要的报告 [Report on the Outline of the Tenth Five-year Plan for National Economy and Social Development]," 2001: 1685.

enterprises, social organizations, and intermediary agencies. We should consciously change the government's economic management methods and strengthen social management and public-service functions."[12] The Eleventh Five-year Plan marked a decisive step in the Chinese government's move towards becoming a public-service oriented government.[13] Although this transformation is far from finished, we should have confidence that by 2020, the Chinese government will have basically become a public-service oriented government in a real sense.

C. *Transformation of the Government's Decision-Making Mechanism: From State Decisions to Public Decisions*

The process usually determines the result. The kind of decision-making mechanism that a country adopts determines what goals can be placed on the government's agenda as well as what policies should be formulated to achieve these goals and ensure their implementation. As a result, transformation of the Chinese government's decision-making mechanism has been an important step in its overall transformation. In this section, we will examine the changes of government functions through the 60 years since the founding of the People's Republic of China by analyzing China's public policy decision-making methods and looking at these changes up to the period of the Eleventh Five-year Plan.

By probing into the history since new China's founding, we can see that the evolution of Chinese government's decision-making mechanism can be divided roughly into three periods:[14] arbitrary and

---

[12] Wen Jiabao 温家宝, *Zai dishijie quanguorenda sici huiyishang de zhengfu gongzuo baogao* 在第十届全国人大四次会议上的政府工作报告 [*Work Report of the Government at the Fourth Session of the 10th National People's Congress*], March 5, 2006.

[13] The author has directly participated in the designing and research of the targets as a member of the committee of experts on China's Eleventh Five-year Plan.

[14] It is important to point out that this is a rough division. There have also been changes to the decision-making mechanism within each period, especially with changes in leadership or guiding philosophies. For example, the period of the planned economy can be further divided into three periods: from the founding of the People's Republic of China to 1956; from 1957 to 1965; and from 1966 to 1976. During the first period, there was still centralized democratic decision making within the Party, leading to democratic consultation and collective decision making; later, the personal role of Mao Zedong in decision making became more and more important, and the number of arbitrary factors gradually increased; during the Cultural Revolution, the formulation of important policies was completely dependent on the personal wishes of Mao Zedong and the democratic decision-making mechanism was seriously

personality-based decision making during the period of the planned economy; collective rational decision-making from the reform and opening until 2001; and scientific and democratic decision making since the Sixteenth National Congress of the CCP held in 2002 (See Table 5.3).

Table 5.3. Evolution of the Three Generations of China's Decision-Making Mechanisms

	First generation decision-making mechanism	Second generation decision-making mechanism	Third generation decision-making mechanism
Type of decision-making	Personal decision making	Collective decision making	Public decision making
Objective of decision-making	Class struggle and prevention of the restoration of capitalism	Acceleration of development	All-round, coordinated, and sustainable development
Method of decision-making	Arbitrary decision making	Systematic and standardized decision making	Scientific and democratic decision making
Features of the decision-making	Dependence on personal experience	Collective and rational	Scientific and rational
Information source	Within the government and from restricted materials	Gradual opening of information within the government	From government, enterprises, and society; from China and other countries; open information
Information amount	Deficient	Limited	Plentiful
Information structure	Simplistic	Relatively simplistic	Diversified
Relationship between Party and government	Unified Party and government	Some division of labor between Party and government	Division of labor and co-operation between Party and government

undermined, even overturned; the period exemplified "the management of state affairs by word" (the Supreme Instructions) and "the personality-based arbitrary decision making." However, due to limited space, this section is mainly focused on the analysis of the dominant decision-making mechanisms during various periods, without elaboration of the detailed changes.

Table 5.3 (*cont.*)

	First generation decision-making mechanism	Second generation decision-making mechanism	Third generation decision-making mechanism
Relationship between the central government and local governments	Centralization of state power by the central government	Moderate power decentralization by the central government	Systematized decentralization of power
Relationship between the state and society	Government supremacy	Government dominance with limited participation by society	Government dominance with extensive participation by society

Source: Created by the author.

1. *Arbitrary Decision-Making*

From the founding of new China in 1949 to the Eighth National Congress of the CCP in 1956, there was a systematic decision-making model used by the government. Leaders like Mao Zedong took the lead in making investigations at the grassroots level and information was shared among Party leaders; the decision-making mechanism was based on multi-party consultation, co-operation, sharing, and participation, including discussion and debate by both Party and non-Party personages in the course of formulating important policies. The formulation of the First Five-year Plan took place through this systematized decision-making process, with participation by a wide range of contributors; it was then implemented according to the structured relations between the central government, the State Council, and the National People's Congress and in accordance with the rules stipulated in the Constitution; opinions from various sides were collected and taken into account, and a variety of different perspectives went into drafting the plan, thus ensuring scientific, democratic, and systematic decision making to a large extent. The period of the First Five-year Plan was the first golden age of development for China after 1949, with an average annual GDP growth rate of 9.2 percent and the proportion of China's GDP as a percentage of world total rising from 4.5 percent in 1950 to 5.5 percent in 1958.

But the systematic arrangement determined at the Party's Eighth National Congress was soon seriously undermined. The Nanning

Conference of 1958 and the Lushan Conference of 1959 signaled the end to democracy and normalcy within the Party, with commands by the top leader replacing democratic and centralized decision making. The Second Five-year Plan was a classic example of this change as well as an example of overall failure. In the first phase, the formulation of the Plan was carried out basically in accordance with the same procedures as adopted for the formulation of the First Five-year Plan. Initially, the State Planning Commission drew up the draft Second Five-year Plan as according to the unified plan of the central government; afterwards, at the Party's Eighth National Congress, the *Suggestions Regarding the Second Five-year Plan for the Development of the National Economy (1958–1962)* (关于发展国民经济的第二个五年计划的建议(1958年–1962年)) were put forward and submitted to the State Council for deliberation. At the forty-second meeting of the State Council on February 2, 1957, the *Suggestions* were approved and adopted, and the State Council instructed the State Planning Commission to draw up a draft of the plan to be prepared for review by the National People's Congress. But because Mao Zedong did not agree with the balanced and the steady development advocated in the *Suggestions*, at the Third Plenary Session of the Eighth Central Committee, he criticized the idea of "opposing premature advancement;" in May 1958, the Second Session of the Party's Eighth National Congress convened and new suggestions on the Second Five–year Plan were put forward; these new suggestions rejected those put forward at the Party's Eighth National Congress. Afterwards, the State Planning Commission submitted the new *Opinions on the Second Five-year Plan* (关于第二个五年计划的意见) to the central government, in which higher targets were put forward. On August 28 of the same year, the Political Bureau of the CCP Central Committee approved the *Opinions on the Second Five-year Plan*, which became implemented with the Plan. It was the replacement of collective decision making with the personal decision-making that resulted in the impractical Second Five-year Plan; it proved to be a total failure.

The formulation of the Third Five-year Plan and the Fourth Five-year Plan were carried out in an even less organized fashion, and the systematic arrangements in the government were further damaged. The Fifth Five-year Plan was also born of the arbitrary-decision-making model.

2. *Collective and Rational Decision-Making*

The bitter experiences of the Great Leap Forward and the Cultural Revolution caused Deng Xiaoping to realize not only the mistakes made by Mao Zedong, but also to engage in deep contemplation regarding serious problems in the Party's decision-making mechanism. As a result, when Deng Xiaoping returned to his leading post, he opened a new chapter in Chinese history, the reform and opening. Exhibiting strong resolve, he did away with the arbitrary decision-making model of Mao, brought back the collective decision-making model prescribed in the Constitution, and once again established a framework for systematic decision-making.[15]

The formulation of the Sixth Five-year Plan began in a systematized and scientific way, with the process being roughly divided into three steps. The first step was the drafting of the plan. The Sixth Five-year Plan was initially drawn up as a part of the draft of the *Outline of the Ten-year Plan for the Development of the National Economy During 1976–1985* (1976–1985 年发展国民经济十年规划纲要). In February, 1980, the State Council held a symposium on the plan and decided to draw up the Sixth Five-year Plan. Upon this decision, the State Planning Commission and other concerned departments conducted a series of investigations as well as a great deal of research and calculations; the commission also called in experts and specialists to provide scientific analysis. The second step was the submission of the plan for approval. At the national planning conference of 1982, the attendees engaged in a thorough discussion of the draft of the Sixth Five-year Plan. The third step was the official approval of the plan. In December of 1982, the Sixth Five-year Plan was officially approved by the Fifth Session of the Fifth National People's Congress. Thus, the systematic decision-making was reborn and the approval of the plan by the National People's Congress was strengthened.

The process of drafting the Seventh Five-year Plan and the Tenth Five-year Plan[16] had two important features. Firstly, the process of

[15] The *Resolution on Historical Issues of the Chinese Communist Party Since the Founding of the People's Republic of China* (关于建国以来党的若干历史问题的决议) declared that "according to the lessons of the Cultural Revolution and based on the Party's present conditions, we must build our Party into a party with sound democratic centralism."

[16] The drafting of the Fifth Five-year Plan occurred in the later days of the Cultural Revolution; it was a complex and tortuous process. However, the use of some systematic arrangements did resume. In January 1974, the State Planning Commission issued a notice on drawing up a ten-year plan. In 1975, the State Planning

drafting the plan was systematized according to a set of relatively fixed procedural steps. These five steps were: (1) the State Council and State Planning Commission drew up recommendations for the drafting of the plan; (2) the Party National Congress and Plenary Sessions of the CCP Central Committee released their suggestions for the Five-year Plan; (3) the State Council organized relevant departments for the formal drafting of the plan; (4) the State Council and the Politburo discussed and passed the draft plan and plan reports, and submitted the plan to the National People's Congress for review; (5) the National People's Congress officially reviewed and adopted the outline for the Five-year Plan.

Secondly, the formulation of the plan was carried out in relatively scientific and democratic way, and the elements of "collective decision-making" and "decision-making through consultancy" became more and more apparent. In formulating the plan, not only were leaders and state organs required to conduct decision-making in a collective way, but opinions from various sides at various levels were included. During this process, however, decision making mainly took place within government departments; participation by experts or specialists took place primarily through forums that were sporadic and narrow in scope. At this point, the system of planned, organized, and large-scale public policy research and input-seeking had not yet formed.

3. *The Public Policy Stage*

A diversity of participants and an open decision-making process are the basis tenants for public, scientific, and democratic decision making. In 2002, a report by the Sixteenth Party National Congress explicitly called for scientific and democratic decision making.[17] In 2004, the

---

Commission presided over the drawing up of the *Outline of the Ten-year Plan for the Development of the National Economy During 1976–1985 (Draft)* (1976–1985年发展国民经济十年规划纲要(草案)) and decided to conduct a trial implementation of the plan for one year after the outline was reviewed by the Politburo of the CPC Central Committee. The revised draft outline of the ten-year plan was adopted at the First Session of the Fifth National People's Congress in March, 1978. Some targets were adjusted after the Third Plenary Session of the Eleventh CPC Central Committee convened in 1978.

[17] The *Report on the Party's Sixteenth National Congress* called for: decision-making bodies at all levels to improve their rules and procedures regarding important decisions; the creation of a system to reflect social conditions and public opinions; the establishment of a system for public hearings for major events of importance or interest to the people; the improvement of the expert counseling system and should carry out the decision-making exposition; and responsibility system to guard against arbitrary decision-making. (Jiang Zemin 江泽民, "Quanmian jianshe xiaokangshehui, kaichuang zhongguo tese 全面建设小康社会，开创中国特色 [Build a Prosperous

revised *Working Rules of the State Council* (国务院工作规则) were revised to emphasize the requirement for law-observing, scientific, and democratic decision making; the rules also required further improvement of the decision-making mechanism by calling for mass participation and advice from experts. The process of creating the Eleventh Five-year Plan reflected the goal to make decision making systematic, scientific, and democratic; it's passage marked an important point in the government's transformation, the improvement of the decision-making mechanism, and the entry Chinese government into the period of open decision-making.

Formulation of the Eleventh Five-year Plan had three important features. (1) There was improved systematization and standardization in the drawing up of the plan. The National Development and Reform Commission (NDRC) and other departments released the *Regulations on Drawing Up the Eleventh Five-year Plan* (规划编制条例), specifying the procedures and various processes of drafting the plan. Also to this end, in October 2005, the State Council promulgated the *Views on Improving the Work on Drafting the Plan for the National Economy and Social Development* (关于加强国民经济和社会发展规划编制工作的若干意见). (2) Guarantees were introduced for the scientific development of the plan through standardized and large scale opinion-seeking and research. Starting in 2003, the NDRC adopted practices such as internal entrustment, open tendering, and cooperative research to investigate over 160 important topics, producing a research report of over five million characters long. (3) Finally, the formulation of the Eleventh Five-year Plan featured a heightened degree of democratization, achieved through extensive participation by people representing an array of social levels and different groups. During the course of formulating the plan, the NDRC established a governmental website to encourage people across the country to provide ideas and suggestions for the formulation of the Eleventh Five-year Plan; the NDRC also set up a committee consisting of 37 well-known experts to provide four rounds of exposition on the plan outline. The report of their work was submitted, with the outline, to the National People's Congress for reference. The formulation of the Eleventh Five-year Plan has come to

Society in an All-round Way and Open Up New Prospects for the Socialist Cause with Chinese Characteristics]," 2004.)

be regarded as a classic example of public policy-making and diversified, open decision-making.

D. *Transformation of Government Functions: From State Construction to Public Service*

Through reform, the functions of the Chinese government have gradually evolved from those of an all-powerful patriarch to those of a night watchman guarding over harmonious economic and social development. Under the government's current guise, its basic objectives are to carry out the national development strategy, ensure the all-round development of the economy and society, and enable the whole people to share the benefits of reform and opening. From the history of national development since the founding of New China, it can be seen that important transformations have tended to take place every 25–30 years. This is no less true for government functions. The transformation of government functions can be divided into three stages:

The first stage was that of the all-powerful nationalistic government (from 1950 to 1978). Upon its establishment, China imitated the model of the former Soviet Union and set up a unified and highly centralized management model, with the government in charge of everything. Under the economic and social circumstances at the time, productive forces were relatively low and the social order had yet not been completely established. Therefore, an all-round government was able to effectively centralize resources from various social spheres and concentrate manpower to accomplish goals.

The second stage was that of the development-oriented government focused on economic construction (from 1978 to 2002). In the beginning of the reform period, since developing the productive forces, promoting economic development, and improving people's living standards were the principal goals, the transformation of government functions began with its economic functions and then gradually expanded to the sphere of social development. The *Decisions of the CCP Central Committee on the Reform of the Economy* (中共中央关于经济体制改革的决定), adopted in 1984 by the Third Plenary Session of the Twelfth CCP Central Committee, called for the scope of command-planning to be reduced and for the scope of guided planning to be widened; it called for the price of products created by sideline businesses, small every-day-use items, wages in the service and repair industries, and some agricultural products to be freely determined by the market.[18] At the Thirteenth National Congress of the CCP, the relationship between the government and the market was clarified, depicting the relationship as "the state adjusting the market and the market guiding the enterprises;" the Party Congress also called for improved use of macroeconomic adjustments as a tool for indirect management. The Third Plenary Session of the Fourteenth CCP Central Committee specified guidelines for the establishment of the socialist market economy, with more prominence being given to the role of the government in supporting economic development; the plenary session also put forth the objective of "giving priority to efficiency while showing concern for fairness." Thus, the functions of the government in economic management gradually began to be confined to the spheres of macro-control, market supervision, social security, environmental protection, and management of state-owned assets.[19]

The third stage is the stage of public-service-oriented government focused on systematic construction (since 2002). The convening of the Sixteenth National Congress of the CCP marked the beginning of a new round of transformations for government functions. With the economic management functions of the government being continually improved, there has been a new emphasis put on strengthening the social functions of the government; as part of this, promoting all-round development and coordinating between economic growth, population, resources, and the environment have become the goals of this period.[20] The Seventeenth National Congress of the CCP put forward the objective of building a harmonious society, emphasizing a development model based on "people first." The range of government functions were increased and the importance was placed on the idea of making investments for the people, serving the people, developing for

[18] CCP Central Committee. "Zhonggong zhongyang guanyu jingji tizhi gaige de jueding 中共中央关于经济体制改革的决定 [Decision of the CCP Central Committee on the Reform of the Economic System]," 1986: 569, 573.

[19] CCP Central Committee. "Zhonggong zhongyang guanyu jianli shehuizhuyi shichang jingji tizhi tuogan wenti de jueding 中共中央关于建立社会主义市场经济体制若干问题的决定 [Decision of the CCP Central Committee on Issues Concerning the Establishment of the Socialist Market Economy System]," 1996: 530.

[20] CCP Central Committtee, "Zhongong zhongyang guanyu wanshan shehuizhuyi shichang jingji tizhi ruogan wenti de jueding 中共中央关于完善社会主义市场经济体制若干问题的决定 [Decision of the CCP Central Committee on Issues Concerning the Improvement of the Socialist Market Economy System]," 2004: 471.

the people, promoting human development, enhancing people's opportunities to develop, and increasing the benefits of development.[21]

The government functions during the above-mentioned three stages have had both similarities and differences; such systems have neither been completely different from each other nor completely separated. Throughout these stages, the government's varying functions have all come from a similar source; it has been the innovation of government functions that has been different. At every stage, the government functions are a direct reflection of the development strategy at the time but are also interrelated, linked to what came before and what went after. All are the result of constant innovation on the part of Chinese leaders at different times responding to the challenges of modernization and globalization.

III. *Transformation of the Finance System: From State Finance to Public Finance*

A capable and responsible government is essential for the orderly development of a country's economy and society. In China, it has been the reform of the finance system that has most embodied the government's transformation into a capable and responsible force. Over the past sixty years, changes to China's economic system have coupled with changes to its finance system. China's finance system has experienced repeated changes, centralizing and decentralizing its finance system, and gradually changing from a state finance system to a public finance system. Through this transition, the country has changed from a traditional "owner-state" to a "tax-state." Currently, China is changing into a modern "budget-state."[22]

---

[21] Hu Angang 胡鞍钢, Wang Yahua 王亚华, *Guoqing yu fazhan—zhongguo wuda ziyuan bendongtai bianhua yu changyuan fazhan zhan* 国情与发展—中国五大资本动态变化与长远发展战略 [*National Conditions and Development—Dynamic Changes of China's Five Major Categories of Capital and the Strategy for their Long-term Development Strategy*], 2005: 107.

[22] Domain-state" and "tax-state" are concepts put forward by Schumpeter. The main feature of the "domain state" describes a feudal system where a portion of the taxes collected by the king comes from his own domain, while the rest comes from tributes paid by dukes; the "tax-state" describes a system where the central government as well as lower governments absorb financial resources across the country through taxation. The concept of "budget state" was put forward by Wang Shaoguang; it refers to a country under the modern budgetary system. Such a system has two basic features: financial unity and budgetary supervision. (Wang Shaoguang 王绍光, "Cong

In order to accurately and comprehensively describe the transformation of China's finance system, we have further divided the system into three components (See Table 5.4). the first component is the method for absorbing fiscal revenue, which is the way that the primary collection of financial resources is arranged between the central and local governments; the second component is the fiscal expenditure system, which is the way that financial resources are divided between the central and local governments; the third is the finance redistribution system, which is the way that financial resources are transferred within the government. The different ways that a government goes about collecting revenue and making expenditures reflects the public service system of a government. The finance system is the way that resources and tools are provided to the government in order that it may carry out its powers and functions. China's finance model has been a reflection of, and adapted to, changes in government functions. We can thus see more clearly how the Chinese government has changed from an all-powerful government, to a government focused on economic construction, and then to a public-service-oriented government and how its finance system has changed from one of traditional state finance to modern public finance.

Table 5.4. Change of Government Functions and the Transformation to Public Finance (1952–2008)

	All-powerful government (1952–1977)	Government focused on economic construction (1978–2001)	Public-service-oriented government (2002–2008)
Fiscal absorption model	Centralized national income dominated by the central government	Scattered finance sources, co-existence of budgetary and extra-budgetary incomes; from local dominance to central dominance	A unified finance source, dominated by budgetary income, with the central government playing a leading role
Fiscal expenditure model	Highly centralized, with special emphasis on the increasing political power	Highly decentralized; serving economic construction	Limited decentralization, with special emphasis on supporting human development and public services

shuishou guojia dao yusuan guojia 从税收国家到预算国家 From a Tax-State to a Budget-State," 2007.)

Table 5.4 (*cont.*)

	All-powerful government (1952–1977)	All-powerful government (1952–1977)	Public-service-oriented government (2002–2008)
Fiscal redistribution model	Planned distribution	Centered on direct income quotas, with transfer payments playing a smaller role	Importance placed on both income distribution and transfer payments
Public-service supply model	Extensive coverage; unified state supply; relatively even supply between regions	Less coverage; scattered supply by local governments; widening disparity between regions	Extensive coverage, supplied jointly by central and local governments; a more equalized supply between regions

Source: compiled by the author.

A. *Transformation of the Absorption Model: From an Owner-State to a Tax-State*

From the beginning, the development of China's finance system has been focused on income; following the logic of keeping expenditures below income and tax-and-spend reasoning has always been the main logic behind finance system reform. Before economic reform began in 1978, China was an "owner-state," with state fiscal revenue mainly coming from the income generated by property owned by the state and the state generating its own revenue through state-owned enterprises; the economic reforms of 1978 not only radically changed China's economic system, but also began China's transition from an owner-state to a tax-state.[23]

In analyzing the changes in China's fiscal absorption mechanism since the beginning of reform, we can find three obvious features:

1. *From an Owner-state to a Tax-state*

First, the revenue absorption model has consistently become more standardized. Tax revenues have become the principal source of

[23] Ma Jun 马骏, *Zhongguo gonggong yusuan gaige: lixinghua yu minzhuhua* 中国公共预算改革: 理性化与民主化 [*Reform of China's Public Budget: Rationalization and Democratization*]: 2005: 33–43.

state income, signaling China's transition from an "owner-state" to a "tax-state."

In the time since the founding of new China, the changes in China's finance management model can be roughly divided into three periods: the "unified revenue and expenditure" period (1950–1979), the "separated revenue and expenditure" period (1980–1993) and the period of the "separated tax system" (1994–present) (See Table 5.5). Through continual reform and adjustment, China's finance system has gradually developed from a highly centralized system of unified revenue and expenditure to a modern public finance system of separated taxation.

Table 5.5. Change of China's Finance Management System (1950–2007)

Time of implementation		Changes to the finance system	Approving departments and relevant documents
Period of "unified revenue and expenditure"	1950	Highly centralized, unified revenue and expenditure.	*Decisions on Unifying National Fiscal and Economic Work*[24] issued by the Government Administration Council of the Central People's Government.
	1951–1957	Apportioning of revenues and expenditures between the central and local authorities, while holding the latter responsible for their own profits and losses; management at different levels.	*Decisions on Dividing the System of Fiscal Revenue and Expenditure in 1951*[25] issued by the Government Administration Council of the Central People's Government.
	1958	The tax-and-spend policy to be unchanged for five years.	*Regulations on Improving the Fiscal Management System*[26] issued by the State Council.
	1959–1970	Power of fiscal revenue and expenditure delegated to lower authorities; planned quotas, regional adjustments, proportional distributions to be changed every year.	*Regulations on Further Improving the Fiscal Management System and Reforming the Bank Credit Management System*[27] issued by the State Council.

24 关于统一国家财政经济工作的决定
25 关于1951年度财政收支系统划分的决定
26 关于改进财政管理体制的规定
27 关于进一步改进财政管理体制和改革银行信贷管理体制的几项规定

Table 5.5 (*cont.*)

Time of implementation		Changes to the finance system	Approving departments and relevant documents
	1971–1973	Specified revenue and expenditure, revenue and expenditure quotas, supply to higher authorities (or deficiency payments), use of retained balance to be specified every year.	*Notice of the Ministry of Finance on Implementing Fiscal Revenue and Expenditure Quotas.*[28]
	1974–1975	Income retained according to fixed ratios; proportion of retained excess income to be otherwise specified; expenditure to be spent according to quotas.	*Opinions of the Ministry of Finance on Improving the Fiscal Management System (for appraisal).*[29]
	1976–1979	Specified revenue and expenditure; revenue linked to expenditure; proportional distribution of the total amount, to be changed every year. Some provinces (municipalities) experimented with "linking revenue to expenditure and distributing the added income proportionally"	*Notice of the Ministry of Finance on Carrying out the Trial Implementation of the Finance System of "Distributing the Added Income Proportionally and Linking Revenue to Expenditure.*[30]
Period of "separated revenue and expenditure"	1980–1985	Apportioning of revenues and expenditures between the central and local authorities, while holding the latter responsible for their own profits and losses.	*Regulations of the State Council on the Trial Implementation of the Fiscal Management Measures of "Dividing Revenue and Expenditure and Practicing Graded Quotas,*[31]

[28] 关于实行财政收支包干的通知
[29] 关于改进财政管理体制的意见 (征求意见稿)
[30] 关于试行"增收分成、收支挂钩" 财政体制的通知
[31] 关于试行"划分收支、分级包干"财政管理办法的若干规定

Table 5.5 (*cont.*)

Time of implementation		Changes to the finance system	Approving departments and relevant documents
	1985–1988	Classification of items of taxation; verification of revenues and expenditures; graded quotas.	*Notice on Implementing the Regulations on Carrying Out the Fiscal Management System of "Classifying the Items of Taxation, Verifying Revenues and Expenditures and Practicing Graded Quotas*[32] issued by the State Council in the spirit of the Third Plenary Session of the Twelth CCP Central Committee
	1988–1993	Completion of assigned finance tasks	*Decisions of the State Council on Implementing the Measures for Completing Assigned Fiscal Tasks in Localities*[33]
Period of separated taxation	1994	The fiscal management system of separated taxation	*Decisions on Practicing the Fiscal Management System of Separated Taxation*[34] promulgated by the State Council in the spirit of the Third Plenary Session of the Fourteenth CCP Central Committee
	1998	Establishment of a framework for public finance	National conference on fiscal work
	2003	Improvement of the public finance system	Third Plenary Session of the Sixteenth CCP Central Committee
	2007	Improvement of the public finance system	Seventeenth National Congress of the CCP

Source: Compiled by the author.

From 1950 to 1978, although the national finance system and the enterprise finance system were adjusted many times, "state finance," the system of unified revenue and expenditure and the major mechanism for collecting revenue, was not radically changed. During the

32 关于实行"划分税种、核定收支、分级包干"财政管理体制的规定的通知
33 关于地方实行财政包干办法的决定
34 关于实行分税制财政管理体制的决定

recovery of the national economy and the socialist transformation, taxation held a dominant position in state finance. In 1950, taxation accounted for 78.8 percent of state revenue while the incomes of enterprises accounted for only 14.0 percent. However, through the process of socialist transformation, the overwhelming majority of profits made by the state-owned enterprises came to be owned by the state. Meanwhile the taxation reforms carried out in 1958 and 1973 focused on amalgamating the items of taxation and simplifying the tax system. As a result, the major source of state revenue gradually shifted to coming from the incomes of state-owned enterprises. This shift made China's finance system typical for that of an "owner-state," in which the national revenue comes mainly from profits made by state-owned property and tax revenues hold a secondary position. Statistics show that, after 1958, the proportion of the state revenue made up by taxation had reduced to less than 50 percent. In 1960, that proportion reached an all-time low of 35.6 percent, while the proportion from enterprises reached 63.9 percent. (See Table 5.6).

Table 5.6. China's Budgetary Fiscal Revenues (1950–2007)

Unit: %

Period	Revenue total	Various items of taxation	Incomes of the enterprises	Subsidies for the losses of the enterprises	Energy and communication construction funds	Budgetary adjustment funds	Additional educational expenses	Others
Recovery of the national economy (1950–1952)	100	63.1	26.7					10.2
First Five-year Plan (1953–1957)	100	52.3	43.9					3.8
Second Five-year Plan (1958–1962)	100	43.5	55.6					1.0
1963–1965	100	45.3	53.5					1.2
Third Five-year Plan (1966–1970)	100	44.6	54.7					0.7

Table 5.6 (*cont.*)

Period	Revenue total	Various items of taxation	Incomes of the enterprises	Subsidies for the losses of the enterprises	Energy and communication construction funds	Budgetary adjustment funds	Additional educational expenses	Others
Fourth Five-year Plan period (1971–1975)	100	44.4	54.6					1.0
Fifth Five-year Plan (1976–1980)	100	49.2	44.1					6.7
Sixth Five-year Plan (1981–1985)	100	68.8	16.4	−6.8	4.9			16.8
Seventh Five-year Plan (1986–1990)	100	99.1	2.3	−18.9	7.4	1.8		8.3
Eighth Five-year Plan (1991–1995)	100	96.7	0.8	−9.2	2.4	2.0	1.1	6.1
Ninth Five-year Plan (1996–2000)	100	93.9		−3.2			1.2	8.1
Tenth Five-year Plan (2001–2005)	100	92.0		−1.0			1.1	7.9
2007	100	88.9	–	–	–	–	–	11.1

Source: Editorial department of the *China Financial Yearbook*, *Zhongguo caizheng nianjian* 中国财政年鉴 2007 [*China Financial Yearbook 2007*], 2007; National Bureau of Statistics. *Zhongguo tongji nianjian* 中国统计年鉴 [*China Statistical Yearbook*], 2008.

At the end of 1978, China began to implement trial systems for the setting aside of funds from state-owned enterprises; also implemented were a variety of systems for the retention of profits as well as responsibility system for enterprises, making them responsible for their own profits and losses. Through the 1983 and 1984 reform of the enterprise tax system, substituting a tax based on profits as opposed to directly transferring profits to the state, China made the first steps in forming a multi-tiered and multi-faceted tax system. These steps began to standardize the fiscal revenue system. In 1985, tax revenue as a portion of total revenue reached 101.8 percent, while the revenue from enterprises reduced to 2.2 percent. From 1985 to 1993, the tax revenue as a portion of total revenues reached as high as 98.0 percent. As time passed, the standardization of the fiscal revenue system was pushed forward. After 1993, the incomes of enterprises were no longer included in the revenue budget. In 1996, construction funds for key energy and transportation projects as well as budgetary and regulatory funds left the scene, no longer included as a part of state finance. Although the proportion of the tax revenue as a portion of the total reduced after the implementation of the tax distribution system, (with tax revenue making up 91.7 percent of the total from 1994 to 2007), this merely demonstrated that an increasing amount of previously non-budgetary revenues sources were brought under budgetary management, such as specialized revenues obtained mainly by local governments, administrative charges, confiscated funds, etc. At this point, China had realized its transition from an "owner-state" to a "tax-state".

2. *Transition from a High Administrative Decentralization to Limited Economic Decentralization*

The second main feature of China's finance reform has been the change of the fiscal absorption model from a system of high administrative decentralization to a system of limited economic decentralization, resulting in continued improvement of absorption capacity.

In 1980, the State Council promulgated the *Provisional Regulations on Implementing the Fiscal Management System of "Apportioning Revenues and Expenditures Between Central and Local Authorities while Holding the Latter Responsible for Their Own Profits and Losses"* (关于实行"划分收支、分级包干"财政管理体制的暂行规定), clarifying the scope of revenues and expenditures between central and local treasuries and determining the bases for apportioning revenues and expenditures. The regulations also featured preferential treatment for the autonomous regions of ethnic minorities and economically underdeveloped regions. It also transitioned the country from the past system of unified revenues and expenditures to a system of apportioned revenues and expenditures.

However, with the development of the complete fiscal responsibility system, putting local governments in charge of their own profits or losses, the opportunities for their profit and loss gradually expanded, eventually resulting in a scenario where the maximization of profits and interests became the chief motivator for local government policy choices. Driven by this interest mechanism, local governments competed with one another in adopting measures to make their areas more favorable to the distribution of capital. Such tactics included reducing tax collection, turning budgetary incomes into extra-budgetary incomes, decreasing taxes and increasing tax exemption for enterprises important to the local economy, thereby allowing them to make great profits. The finance system that resulted from this system was a model that featured "each province enforcing its own system." Although this system gave full consideration to the differences between various regions, the overall unity of state finance was seriously affected. This decentralized system led directly led to the drastic fall in state's revenue absorption capabilities. Beginning in the late 1980s, the ratio of the government's fiscal revenue as a portion of GDP continued to fall, as did the central government's revenue as a percentage of total fiscal revenue. The result was to seriously limit the ability of the central government to engage in macroeconomic management. By 1993, the proportion of state revenue as a percentage of GDP had declined to 12.3 percent, and the proportion of central government revenue to that of the whole had reduced to 22.0 percent; if the budgetary revenue is included, the proportion of central government revenue to that of the whole can be considered an all-time low, at 20.8 percent (See Figure 5.2).

In order to jump start the economy and deal with the excessively decentralized finance system at the time, after the reform of the tax system, the Chinese government began to change from administrative decentralization to economic centralization. This was done by reducing the government's debt and centralizing fiscal revenue, thereby increasing the control of the central government. On December 15, 1993 the State Council promulgated the *Decisions on Implementing the Finance Management System of Separated Taxation* (关于实行分税制财政管理体制的决定), which officially implemented the division of tax revenues between the central government and local governments, implemented the division of duties and responsibilities as well as right of expenditure between the central government and local governments, and determined of the amount of tax revenue to be returned to local governments. With the implementation of this separated tax system as the demarcation point, China's finance system changed from one of administrative decentralization to one of economic decentralization. In the administratively decentralized system, the practice of "governments at various

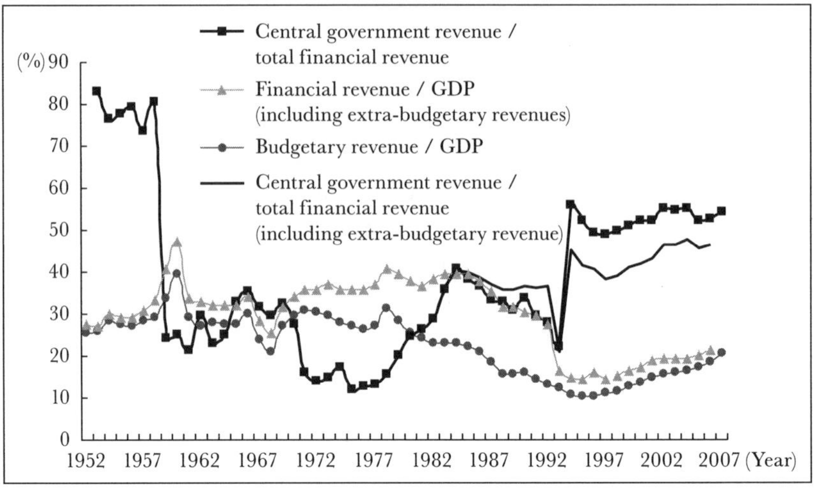

Sources: National Bureau of Statistics Department of Comprehensive Statistics, *Xinzhongguo wushiwunian tongji ziliao huibian* 新中国五十五年统计资料汇编 [*A Collection of Statistical Data from Over Fifty-five Years Since the Founding of New China*], 2005; National Bureau of Statistics, *China Statistical Yearbook*, 2006–2008.

Figure 5.2. Proportion of Fiscal Revenue as a Portion of GDP and the Proportion of the Revenues of the Central Government in Total Fiscal Revenues (1952–2007).

levels taking control of enterprises based on administrative subordination" remained unchanged and the powers of local governments were expanded. In the economically decentralized system, governments at various levels no longer took control of enterprises based on administrative subordination and their revenues were divided between governmental levels according to different categories of tax revenue.[35] In the end, implementation of the separated tax system was effective in tackling the problem of "the two low proportions" (total revenue and central government revenue), increasing the government's revenues, especially that of the central government. In 2007, fiscal revenue as a portion of GDP increased to 20.6 percent and central government revenue as a portion of total fiscal revenue reached 54.1 percent. Also resulting from this change, the size of the state's deficit as a portion

[35] Jia Kang 贾康, Zhao Quanhou 赵全厚 eds., *Zhongguo caishui tizhi gaige 30nian huigu yu zhanwang* 中国财税体制改革30年回顾与展望 [*Review and Outlook on the 30 Year's Reform of China's Financial and Tax System*], 2008: 44.

of GDP has reduced year by year, from 2.5 percent in 2000 to –0.7 percent in 2007. Whether calculated in terms of budgetary revenue and expenditure, extra-budgetary revenue and expenditure, or the percentage of social insurance funds collected and paid, all measures have shown similar changes. Since 2000, the gap in China's finances has obviously narrowed (See Figure 5.3).

3. *Unifying the Revenue System*

The third step in reforming China's finance system was unifying the revenue system. This was a change from a system that simultaneously had separate calculations for budgetary revenue, extra-budgetary revenue, and extra-system revenue to a unified and uniform system build around budgetary revenue. In the beginning of the reform and opening, the coexistence of three types of fiscal revenue caused disconnects in the information obtained by the central government and that obtained by local governments. Especially under the model of "streamlined administration and decentralized power" (简政分权), there was some degree of distorted behavior by local governments. As a portion of budgetary revenue, the extra-budgetary revenue increased from 48.1 percent in 1980 to 110.7 percent in 1992; over two-thirds of this extra-budgetary revenue was controlled by local treasuries, and thus became a secondary budget, free from supervision and control.

To bring these extra-budget and extra-system sources of fiscal revenue under budgetary control and further the transformation towards a public finance system, gradual reform was carried out to unify the fiscal revenue system. In 1993, the State Council promulgated new *General Rules on Enterprise Finance* (企业财务通则) and *Accounting Criteria for Enterprises* (企业会计准则), stipulating that the earmarked depreciation funds and the retained after-tax funds of state-owned enterprises should be allocated at their discretion and that such funds would no longer be managed as extra-budgetary funds. The scope of extra-budgetary funds was drastically reduced, leaving only the extra-budgetary funds of government treasuries and charges by administrative work units. In 1996, the State Council promulgated the *Decisions on Strengthening the Management of Extra-budgetary Funds* (关于加强预算外资金管理的决定), stipulating that budgetary appropriations and extra-budgetary revenues should be brought under unified accounting and management. The amount of extra-budgetary revenue as a portion of budgetary revenue went down from 52.6 percent in 1996 to

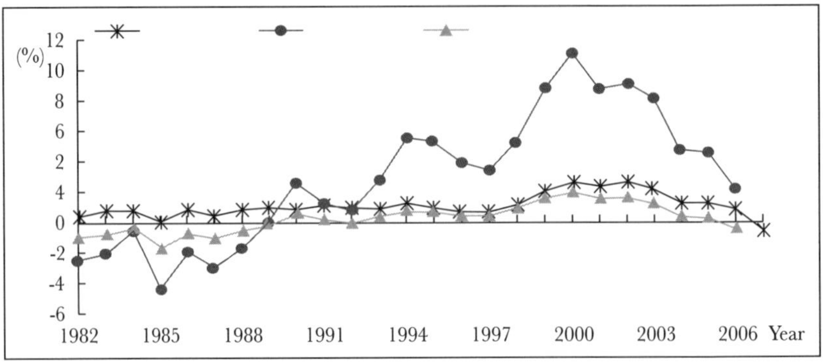

Note: Criterion I = [(Budgetary Expenditure—Budgetary Revenue) /GDP]; Criterion II = {(Budgetary Expenditure + Extra-budgetary Expenditure)—(Budgetary Revenue + Extra-budgetary Revenue)]/GDP}; Criterion III = {[(Budgetary Expenditure + Extra-budgetary Expenditure + Social Insurance Expenditure)—(Budgetary Revenue + Extra-budgetary Revenue + Social Insurance Revenues)]/GDP}.
Sources: National Bureau of Statistics Department of Comprehensive Statistics, *A Collection of Statistical Data from Over Fifty-five Years Since the Founding of New China*, 2005; National Bureau of Statistics, *China Statistical Yearbook*, 2008.

Figure 5.3. China's Deficit as a Portion of GDP (1982–2007).

32.7 percent in 1997. Since 1998, the Chinese government has implemented the system "fee to tax"[36] (费改税) to clean up and consolidate the system of extra-budgetary revenue. In 2001, the Ministry of Finance undertook management reform of budgetary units, called the "two lines of revenue and expenditure" reform (收支两条线), which cut the links between revenue and expenditure and implemented a system whereby revenue would be delivered to state treasuries or special finance accounts and expenditures would be determined for various units according to their respective duties; through this system, the reforms worked to gradually eliminate extra-budgetary funds. In 2002, the Ministry of Finance stipulated that the extra-budgetary revenues of various departments should be all brought under the budgetary supervision or be put into special finance accounts. By 2005, the amount of extra-budgetary revenue as a portion of budgetary revenue had been reduced to 17.5 percent.

[36] Editor's Note: Transforming administrative fees into taxes.

B. *Transformation of the Fiscal Expenditure Model: From Construction-Oriented to Livelihood-Oriented*

Since 1990, the fiscal expenditures published by Chinese authorities have been mainly composed of three parts: budgetary expenditures, extra-budgetary expenditures, and social insurance expenditures. In looking at statistics since 1993, it can be seen that China's fiscal expenditures as a portion of GDP, especially in terms of budgetary expenditures, have shown a clear upward trend. In 2007, budgetary fiscal expenditure accounted for 20.0 of GDP; however, this is still far lower than other countries in world, especially OECD countries (43.9 percent). However, studies made by Wong and Ma suggest that if extra-budgetary expenditures, which are not counted in statistics, were added into the official expenditures, the total expenditures of the Chinese government reached about 32 percent of GDP around the year 2000.[37] This amount of expenditure is not drastically lower than what would be expected by China's development level.

One could understand pre-1998 finance reform as being mainly focused on revenue and how to collect money, rather than how to manage and make good use of the money.[38] But after 1998, the Chinese government proposed the establishment of a public finance framework and began reforms of the departmental budgetary system, the state purchasing system, the system of centralized collection and payment, and the "two lines of revenue and expenditure" budgetary system. These efforts were indicative of the government beginning to place importance on fiscal expenditure as part of finance reform as well as its aim to set up a modern budgetary system standardizing the management of all government revenue and expenditure.

[37] Wong, Christine, "Fiscal Decentralization in China: the Problematic Outcomes of Unplanned Changes in Transition towards a Market Economy," 2001; Ma Jun 马骏, "Off-budgetary Activities of China Governments Since Economic Reform," 2000.

[38] At the National Conference on Finance Work held in December 1998, the then-State Council vice-premier, Li Lanqing, demanded that vigorous action be taken to establish a public finance framework. The then-vice-minister of finance, Xiang Huaicheng, expressly pointed out that efforts should be made to—within his time in office—set up a standardized budgetary management system to complement the socialist market economy. He called for a system that included within it budgets for public expenditure, the operation of state-owned assets, and social security. Since this point, establishment of a public finance became the direction for state finance reform.

Table 5.7. China's Total Fiscal Expenditures (1982–2007)

Year	Total fiscal expenditure (100 million yuan)	Budgetary expenditure (100 million yuan)	Proportion of GDP (%)			
			Comprehensive fiscal expenditure	Budgetary expenditure	Extra-budgetary expenditure	Social insurance expenditure
1982	1964.5	1230.0	37.10	23.23	13.87	–
1985	3379.3	2004.3	37.70	22.36	15.34	–
1990	5942.5	3083.6	32.04	16.63	14.59	0.82
1993	6438.8	4642.3	18.22	13.14	3.72	1.36
1994	8183.0	5792.6	16.98	12.02	3.55	1.41
1995	10032.1	6823.7	16.50	11.22	3.83	1.44
1996	12858.2	7937.6	18.07	11.15	5.39	1.52
1997	13258.3	9233.6	16.79	11.69	3.40	1.70
2000	21801.1	15886.5	21.97	16.01	3.56	2.40
2003	32822.7	24650.0	24.17	18.15	3.06	2.96
2004	37466.0	28486.9	23.43	17.82	2.72	2.89
2005	44573.6	33930.3	24.33	18.52	2.86	2.95
2006	52767.1	40422.7	24.90	19.07	2.77	3.06
2007	–	49781.4	–	19.95	–	3.16

Note: Extra-budgetary revenue and expenditure from 1993 to 1996 were adjusted respectively; they are incomparable to previous years. Beginning in 1997, extra-budgetary revenues and expenditures do not include the government funds (charges) that were brought under budgetary management. Beginning in 2004, extra-budgetary revenues and expenditures are considered to be revenues and expenditures of extra-budgetary special accounts.
Sources: National Bureau of Statistics Department of Comprehensive Statistics, *A Collection of Statistical Data from Over Fifty-five Years Since the Founding of New China*, 2005; National Bureau of Statistics, *China Statistical Yearbook*, 2008.

In 1998, China for the first time declared that the leading goal of finance reform was to gradually set up a sophisticated public finance system. In 2003, at the Third Plenary Session of the Sixteenth CCP Central Committee, the government officially called for the "establishment of a public finance system;" in 2007, at the Seventeenth National Congress of the CCP it was put forward that "the public finance system must be improved." Thus, the structure of government expenditure gradually came to be oriented around public finance and state funds were gradually withdrawn from normal, competition-based sectors of the economy; instead, government expenditure began to emphasize fulfilling the state's role in regulating the economy, supervising the market, providing social management, and providing public services. The goal of state expenditure shifted to providing public goods to meet the needs of citizens and to gradually equalize access to such goods. At the same time, the state strived to make the finance system more fair, open and transparent. In summary, since 1998, China's finance reform truly has worked for unification of the finance system and budget supervision. With the transition from a construction-oriented to a livelihood-oriented finance system, China began to transform from a "tax-state" to a "budget-state." The core philosophy of this public finance system is "to obtain it from the public and use it for people's livelihood."

Government expenditure has changed from being focused on economic construction to being focused on providing public services and from being aimed at boosting economic growth to promoting human development. Since the reform and opening, investment by the state has been the main driving force behind economic development. A huge amount of state funds were invested in capital construction, while investment for social development was obviously insufficient. In 1978, the state's capital expenditure amounted to 45.19 billion yuan, making up 40.3 percent of total state expenditure, while expenditure on culture, education, science, and public health amounted to 11.27 billion yuan and that on social security amounted to 1.89 billion yuan, accounting for merely 10.0 and 1.7 percent of total fiscal expenditure respectively.

Changes since 2000 indicate that recently social-oriented expenditure has been aimed mainly at rural issues, such as those pertaining to agriculture and farmers, social security, education, medical care, and public health. The amount of expenditure in these areas as a portion of total expenditure has become higher and higher, which fully reflects the change in government functions from an economic-and-construction-oriented to public-service-oriented government. In 2006, expenditures on science, education, culture, and public health had increased to 742.6 billion yuan, accounting for 18.4 percent of the total state expenditure, up 8.4 percent increase from 1978; expenditure on social security for the same year amounted to 436.18 billion yuan, making up 10.8 percent of total fiscal expenditure, a 9.1 percent increase from 1978. Meanwhile, the amount of capital expenditure as a portion of total expenditure decreased to 10.9 percent, down 29.4 percentage points since 1978 (See Table 5.8).

However, it should be pointed out that within China's finance system, quite a number of government expenditures are not included in the official budgets, which reduces the transparency of the system

Table 5.8. China's Fiscal Expenditures and Composition (1978–2006)

Item	Expenditure (100 million yuan)				Proportion of total expenditure (%)			
Year	*1978*	*1990*	*2000*	*2006*	*1978*	*1990*	*2000*	*2006*
Total expenditure	1122.1	3083.6	15886.5	40422.7	100	100	100	100
Capital expenditure	451.9	547.4	2094.9	4390.4	40.3	17.8	13.2	10.9
Allocation of circulating funds for enterprises		10.9	71.1	16.6	0.0	0.4	0.4	0.0
Funds for increased utilization and upgrading and expenses on science and technology	63.2	153.9	865.2	1744.6	5.6	5.0	5.4	4.3
Geological prospecting expenses	20.2	36.2	88.1	141.8	1.8	1.2	0.6	0.4
Costs for undertakings related to industry, communications, and information	17.8	46.9	150.1	581.3	1.6	1.5	0.9	1.4
Expenditure for supporting agriculture	77.0	221.8	766.9	2161.4	6.9	7.2	4.8	5.3
Expenditure on culture, education, science, and public health	112.7	617.3	2736.9	7426.0	10.0	20.0	17.2	18.4
Expenditure on social security	18.9	55.0	1517.6	4361.8	1.7	1.8	9.6	10.8
Expenditure on national defense	167.8	290.3	1207.5	2979.4	15.0	9.4	7.6	7.4
Administration fees	49.1	303.1	1787.6	5639.1	4.4	9.8	11.3	14.0
Policy expenditures as subsidies	11.1	380.8	1042.3	1387.5	1.0	12.3	6.6	3.4

Sources: National Bureau of Statistics, *China Statistical Yearbook*, 2007.

to a large extent. Extra-budgetary expenditures mainly include costs for administrative services and capital construction. Over the past ten year, the costs for administrative services have risen quickly. In 1996, the amount of administrative fees as a portion of extra-budgetary expenditure was 32.7 percent; by 2006, it had increased to 71.0 percent. Thus, it can be seen that reducing and eventually eliminating extra-budgetary accounts is not only a crucial step in implementing the government's improved public expenditure policy, but that it can also drastically reduce the number of illegal extra-budgetary activities and increase the transparency and legitimacy of the government.

C. *Transformation of the Fiscal Redistribution Model: From Return of Interests to Equalization of Interests*

In the beginning of the reform period, fiscal adjustment of the differences in revenues and expenditures between regions was quite simplified; the standardized and sophisticated inter-governmental transfer payment system had not yet been formed. In truth, transforming the transfer payment system has been a process of starting from scratch, developing the system piece by piece until eventually forming the whole.

To begin with, the transfer payments system became an important method for adjusting the fiscal relationship between governments. The transformation of the fiscal redistribution model was mainly been reflected in the changing nature of transfer payments made by the central government to local governments. Since 1994, the size of these transfer payments has grown rapidly. After the reform of the tax distribution system, transfer payments from the central government accounted for about 70 percent of local government revenues. From 2000 to 2007, the total value of transfer payments increased from 474.8 billion yuan to 1.811 trillion yuan, increasing by 281 percent, with an average annual rate of increase of 21.1 percent. During the same period, the value of the payments as a portion of GDP rose from 5.3 percent to 7.8 percent (See Table 5.9).

Secondly, the distribution of transfer payments became oriented towards providing equal access to public services. This was exhibited by more transfer payments, especially fiscal transfer payments and special transfer payments, being injected into underdeveloped areas in central and western China. In 2005, fiscal transfer payments totaled 329.9 billion yuan, 45.8 percent of which were directed towards central China and 45.5 percent toward western China, while the amount of transfer payments directed toward eastern China's accounted only for 8.7 percent. In the same year, special transfer payments totaled 374.5 billion yuan, of which payments to regions in central China made up 42.7 percent, payments to western regions made up 40.6 percent, and the payments to eastern regions made up 16.7 percent.

Table 5.9. Total Amount of Transfer Payments and Their Total as a Portion of Central Government Revenue and GDP (1986–2007)

Year	Total (100 million yuan)	Transfer Payments (%)			Proportion of transfer payments (%)	
		Tax revenue return	Finance capacity	Special project	Proportion of central government revenue	Proportion of GDP
1986	464	–	–	–	59.6	4.5
1990	585	–	–	–	58.9	3.2
1995	2533	73.7	5.3	14.8	77.8	4.3
2000	4748	46.5	11.6	34.7	67.9	5.3
2005	11474	34.1	33.2	32.6	69.4	6.2
2006	13491	32.0	35.1	32.7	66.0	6.4
2007	18112	–	–	–	65.3	7.8

Source: Li Ping 李萍, *Zhengfujian caizheng guanxi tujie* 政府间财政关系图解 [*Graphics Illustrating the Financial Relations Between Governments*], 2006; Editorial department of the *China Financial Yearbook*, *China Financial Yearbook 2007*, multiple years.

Next, there was consistent improvement of the transfer payment system to make it capable of equalizing the finance capacity of various regions. During the implementation of the fiscal responsibility system, the difference coefficient for both per-capita revenue and per-capita expenditure showed a downward trend year by year, basically following the changes in per-capita GDP of corresponding years;[39] After the separated tax system was implemented, the difference coefficient for per-capita revenue was relatively stable, whereas the coefficient for per-capita expenditure first went up before going down. Particularly after 2003, the decline was quite obvious. In order to measure the role played by the finance system in promoting the equalization of regional expenditure, this author has defined an equilibrium coefficient. Results from the calculation suggest that after the implementation of the fiscal responsibility system in 1980, the equilibrium coefficient exhib-

[39] It needs to be pointed out that, to a certain extent, the low differences between per-capita expenditure figures is somewhat misleading. The figures of per-capita revenue and per-capita expenditures are quite similar. This is in part because of the fact that there is a limit to the influence of fiscal regulatory measures such as transfer payment, but also because of the phenomenon of wealth being in the hands of citizens (and not the state) in urban areas. Both of these factors contribute to the abnormally small differences in per-capita expenditure.

ited a fast downward trend, hitting an all-time low in 1994. After the implementation of the separated tax system, the equilibrium coefficient began to rise year by year (See Table 5.10).

In addition, similar to the standardization and unification of the revenue system, the transfer payments system also went from being unstandardized to standardized, and from being focused on vested interests to being focused on equal access to public services. The categories of transfer payments are becoming more diverse and more and more transfer payments are calculated using standardized formulas.

D. *A Mixed Model: China's Current Finance System*

The finance system is an integral part of China's government and is adaptable to other aspects of the political system, such China's government hierarchy and structure. Compared to other countries, the Chinese government has two particularly different features. First, China is the only country with four levels of local government,[40] while the governments of most other major market-economy countries have two or three levels. Second, the population and the geographical area under the jurisdiction of governments at various levels or enjoying governmental services exceed that of other countries. Take the United States as an example. Although in terms of area, China and the United States are similar, the total population in China is 4.93 times higher than that of the United States, the average population of China's provinces is 7.26 times higher than the average state population in the United States; the average population of China's counties is 5.25 times higher than that of the United States; and the average population of every township in China 2.29 times higher than that of townships in the United States.

As the country with the largest population in the world, vast territory, and complex national conditions, it is impossible for the central government to take control of everything. But at the same time, China consists of regions with different geographical conditions and uneven political, economic, and cultural development. So it is equally impossible for local governments to take care of everything on their own.

[40] In fact, in total China's government has five-and-a-half levels: the central government, provincial governments, municipal governments at the prefectural level, county governments, township governments and fifteen sub-provincial municipalities between the provincial level and the municipal level.

Table 5.10. Differences in Fiscal Revenues and Expenditures between Various Provinces and Regions (1978–2007)

Year	Per-capita revenue			Per-capita expenditure			Per-capita GDP			Equilibrium coefficient
	Average	Minimum/ maximum	Difference coefficient	Average	Minimum/ Maximum	Difference coefficient	Average	Minimum/ maximum	Difference coefficient	
1978	159	171.2	1.87	96	8.0	0.69	461	14.3	0.98	1.18
1980	146	69.3	2.04	86	7.4	0.65	553	12.5	0.91	1.39
1985	164	50.5	1.74	152	8.2	0.73	974	9.2	0.73	1.01
1990	221	165.6	1.11	254	5.8	0.56	1842	7.3	0.61	0.55
1995	305	17.2	0.97	537	8.1	0.71	5258	10.2	0.68	0.26
2000	601	14.2	1.05	1069	7.9	0.72	8589	13.0	0.76	0.33
2005	1378	18.4	1.18	2538	7.9	0.73	16203	10.2	0.68	0.45
2006	1654	16.8	1.10	2995	6.5	0.67	18662	10.0	0.66	0.43
2007	2114	15.7	1.11	3750	5.9	0.66	21973	9.6	0.64	0.45

Note: Equilibrium coefficient = (Differentiation coefficient for per-capita fiscal revenues—differentiation coefficient for per-capita fiscal expenditures)

Source: National Bureau of Statistics Department of Comprehensive Statistics, *A Collection of Statistical Data from Over Fifty-five Years Since the Founding of New China*, 2005; National Bureau of Statistics, *China Statistical Yearbook*, multiple years.

Thus, China cannot holistically adopt a fully decentralized or centralized finance system, and instead must continue to abide by the principle of combining unity with diversity.[41] Thus China's model mixes the characteristics and advantages of both centralized and decentralized systems. In terms of the current system, China has adopted a mixed system of "centralized revenues with decentralized expenditures." The mixed nature of this system is primarily exhibited in three main areas:

Firstly, since the implementation of the separated tax system, the revenue of local governments as a portion of total government revenue has been declining continually. Meanwhile, the expenditure of local governments as a portion of total expenditure has been on the rise. As described before, implementing the separated tax system resulted in a substantial improvement in the absorption capacity of the central government as well as an increase in central government revenue as a portion of total revenue and the related decrease in the revenue proportion of local governments. At the same time, since 1978, the proportion of expenditures by local governments in total expenditures has been climbing, from 53.4 percent in 1978 to 76.9 percent in 2007, a change which has made local governments responsible for the majority of public expenditures. In describing this system, the Organization for Economic Co-operation and Development (OECD) reported that China's fiscal expenditures are highly decentralized, but that the independence of the local treasuries is restricted by the centralized control of the central government. The report also pointed out the great gap between revenue and expenditure of local governments.[42]

Secondly, the "livelihood-oriented" expenditures in China are characterized by a high degree of decentralization, with local governments

[41] This so-called unity is reflected in the role and functions of the central government, including its role in regulating the economy, providing social security, performing income redistribution, establishing a unified and fair domestic market system, unifying the nationwide tax system and tax rates, formulating criteria for public services and monetary policy, etc. Diversity is reflected by the roles and functions of local governments. According to the Constitution, localities have the right to formulate local laws and administrative regulations that do not conflict with national laws; within their jurisdictions, local governments have the right to boycott ordinances and regulations not in line with the written constitution. Wang Shaoguang 王绍光, Hu Angang 胡鞍钢, "Guanyu zhongguo guojia nengli de yanjiu baogao 关于中国国家能力的研究报告 [*Report on Research Regarding China's National Capabilities*]," 1996: 31–32.

[42] OECD. *Challenges Facing China's Public Expenditures: A Passageway to More Efficiency and Impartiality* (Chinese Version), 2006.

playing the primary role in making livelihood-oriented public expenditures. Quite a large portion of such local expenditures comes from tax returns and subsidies provided by the central government; the proportion of funds derived from tax returns and transfer payment in local government expenditures has increased from 38.4 percent in 1986 to 44.3 percent in 2006. Thus, decentralization doesn't mean to completely disperse the right of expenditure to various localities, but rather a formation of a model of mixed centralization-decentralization focused on localities. Using statistical criteria for fiscal expenditure from after the change in 2007, the breakdown of the mixed model can be seen more clearly. Expenditures on diplomacy and national defense are borne by the central government, as are expenditures on science and technology; based on the type of public expenditure, expenditures on communication and transportation, industrial, commercial and financial affairs, ordinary public services, public security, culture, sports, mass media, and others are to be mainly borne by local governments; expenditure on elementary public services such as those on agriculture, forestry, and water conservancy, social security and employment, education, environmental protection, medical care, public health, and affairs concerning communities in urban and rural areas are to be totally borne by local governments (See Table 5.11).

Table 5.11. Breakdown of Expenditures by the Central and Local Governments (2007)

Unit: %

Item	Central government	Local governments	Remark
Diplomacy	99.3	0.7	Centralized
National defense	98.0	2.0	
Science and technology	51.9	48.1	Dominated by the central government
Communication and transportation	40.8	59.2	Dominated by local governments
Industrial, commercial, and financial affairs	33.9	66.1	
Ordinary public services	25.4	74.6	
Other expenditures	19.5	80.5	

Table 5.11 (*cont.*)

Item	Central government	Local governments	Remark
Public security	17.4	82.6	
Culture, sports, and mass media	14.2	85.8	
Affairs concerning agriculture, forestry, and water conservancy	9.2	90.8	Decentralized amongst local governments
Social security and employment	6.3	93.7	
Education	5.6	94.5	
Environmental protection	3.5	96.5	
Medical care and public health	1.7	98.3	
Affairs concerning communities in urban and rural areas	0.2	99.8	
Total	23.0	77.0	Dominated by local governments

Source: National Bureau of Statistics, *China Statistical Yearbook*, 2008.

Thirdly, the central government has consistently improved its fiscal planning and coordination of expenditures on livelihood-related issues such as those regarding rural areas, agriculture, and farmers, as well as education, public health and social security. China's decentralized model of public expenditure has faced some severe challenges. The proportion of expenditure for the development of human resources, science and technology, and social welfares has been quite low, while too much is devoted to capital expenditures and administration costs. Also, financial expenditure has been far more decentralized than financial revenue, causing subordinate governments to be highly dependent on transfer payments from higher-level governments, which resulted in many local governments having a huge gap between their demand for financial resources and their revenue, especially governments in less-developed regions.[43] To resolve this, governments in China,

[43] OECD. *Challenges Facing China's Public Expenditures: A Passageway to More Efficiency and Impartiality* (Chinese Version), 2006.

especially the central government, has had to further improve the fiscal expenditure structure, provide subsidies and preferential conditions for public investment in poor and less-developed regions in accordance with their needs, emphasize the fair distribution of public investment, set reasonable ratios for local supporting funds, and do more to use public investment and public finance to provide equal access to public services. Some figures from recent years show that the central treasury has begun to play a more important role in providing such public services. In regard to issues pertaining to rural areas, agricultural, and farmers, between 2003 and 2007, the central treasury invested 1.5 trillion yuan in efforts aiming to improve support to rural areas. In regard to education, in 2006, the central treasury invested 15 billion yuan for the reform of the rural education system, including reform aiming to guarantee the financial support of rural schools through government finance. In terms of public health, between 2003 and 2006, the central treasury arranged a special fund for public health totaling 14.3 billion yuan to provide backing for the establishment of local public health systems. In terms of social security, from 2003 to 2006, central treasury subsidies for the pension insurance program totaled 232.1 billion yuan, increasing annually by an average of 17.4 percent. Finally, between 2003 and 2006, central treasury expenditure devoted to expanding employment and re-employment totaled 42.8 billion yuan, increasing by 51 percent annually.[44] These figures tell us two things. First, central government expenditure in "livelihood-oriented" spheres has incrementally increased. Second, this expenditure is first and foremost aimed at bringing benefit to disadvantaged groups. This is symbolic of the finance system's transformation from a state finance system into a public finance system and the Chinese government's transition from an economic-construction government to a public-service-oriented government, process that have both played an important role in improving the excessively centralized expenditures system.

[44] Source: Ministry of Finance of the People's Republic of China, *Gonggong caizheng yu baixing shenghuo* 公共财政与百姓生活 *Public Finance and People's Lives*, Beijing, China Financial & Economic Publishing House, 2007; *China Public Health Statistical Yearbook 2008; China Statistical Yearbook 2008.*

IV. *Concluding Remarks*

The Chinese government's transformation has been a process of gradual advancement through self-transformation, self-adjustment, and self-adaptation. It has included not only reforms conducted on the government's own initiative, but also reforms carried own in reaction to outside forces, reforms due to external pressure. During the planned economy period, China was a student of the Soviet Union, implementing their highly centralized political and economic models. However, facts and history have shown that such models are not suitable for China and that China's road of reform must be guided by its own unique characteristics. Obviously, such an exploration cannot be accomplished all at once; it must progress gradually. During the course of the transformation—by drawing upon the historical lessons from the serious mistakes made by Mao Zedong—the Chinese government, especially in terms of its main state leaders, has upheld a philosophy guided by pragmatism, abided by a governance model based on effective policy response to crises,[45] and made concerted effort to fully understand China's particular national conditions. The government has also strived to look objectively at China's development, put forward appropriate development objectives, and formulate workable development strategies. Since the founding of the People's Republic of China, China has given birth to three generations of different development strategies. The leading philosophy of the government has changed from class struggle, to nation building, and most recently to building a harmonious society. Likewise, the government has changed from an all-powerful government, to a government focused on economic construction, and finally to a public-service-oriented government.

After giving a brief account of the transformation of China's development strategy, decision-making mechanisms, and government functions, this chapter focused on the reform and transformation of China's finance system. All in all, the reform to a public finance system has been—in the course of the government fulfilling its duties—a constant process of self-study, self-improvement, and adaptation. The revenue absorption system has experienced a change from one of

---

[45] The challenges mentioned herein include the endogenous political, economic, and social challenges as well as extraneous international challenges. Particularly against the backdrop of ever-increasing economic and cultural opening, many policies have been adjusted in response to international pressure.

revenue coming from scattered sources, to a model of relatively unified absorption and relatively simplified division of revenues between central and local governments, and finally to a system of standardized division of revenue. The fiscal expenditure system has experienced a similar transformation from a highly decentralized model to one with limited decentralization and from centering on economic construction to centering on human development. The financial re-distribution system has advanced from a simple division of revenue to the establishment of a sophisticated network of financial relationships within the government; transfer payments have changed from small amounts of single-policy-oriented transfer payments to large amounts of transfer payments made to meet a variety of policy goals. Public service has gone from narrow coverage to extensive coverage, from a scattered supply in a few localities to a joint supply by both the central and local governments, gradually narrowing the gap in services between regions.

China is at a crucial period in achieving socialist modernization. To accomplish this, China must modernize the economy as well as the government. It is clear that through the process of economic transformation, China is also redefining the relationship between the state and the economy and between the state and society, reshaping the government's functions and its scope of intervention to something more suitable to the market economy, and adjusting government's duties, powers, style and priorities, transforming areas of its "absence" into "presence" and areas of "excess" into "restraint."

At present, China continues to push forward government transformation, constantly improving the public finance system and facilitating the comprehensive, coordinated, and sustainable development of the economy and society through the establishment of the "Four Public Systems" (public decision-making, public finance, public investment, and public services). As this transformation continues, China will be focused on establishing a supervised, public-service-oriented, limited, honest, responsible government supervised by the public and doing good for the people. The main functions of the government will be to deal with market malfunction by supplying public products and equal access to public services, so as to improve the overall living standards of the public and boost economic and social development.

In the future, China should continue to thoroughly reform the finance system by: improving the mechanisms for democratic decision-making; establish a national budgetary system for public finance, government funds, social security, and accounts for the operation of state-owned capital; pushing forward the implementation of this comprehensive budget system; pursuing reform and supervision of departmental budgets, the centralized payments system, and "two lines of revenue and expenditure" system;" and further the transformation from a "tax-state" to a "budget-state." At the same time, China should adjust and optimize the structure of its fiscal expenditures and ensure investment target towards rural areas, education, public health, employment, social security, and guaranteeing people's livelihoods. By the government effectively exercising its power and making reasonable expenditures, China can not only increase the scope and quality of public services, but can also, more importantly, provide citizens with equal opportunity, enabling people—especially disadvantaged groups—with different household registration and different incomes, to enjoy equal access to public services.

Bibliography

CCP Central Committee. "Zhonggong zhongyang guanyu jianli shehuizhuyi shichang jingji tizhi ruogan wenti de jueding 中共中央关于建立社会主义市场经济体制若干问题的决定 [Decision of the CCP Central Committee on Issues Concerning the Establishment of the Socialist Market Economy System]." Adopted at the Third Plenary Session of the Fourteenth CCP Central Committee on November 14, 1993. Published in *Shisida yilai zhongyao wenxian xuanbian* 十四大以来重要文献选编 [*A Selection of Important Documents Since the Fourteenth National Congress of the Chinese Communist Party*] (Volume One), compiled by the Party Literature Research Center, 530. Beijing: The People's Press, 1996.

——. "Zhonggong zhongyang guanyu jingji tizhi gaige de jueding 中共中央关于经济体制改革的决定 [Decision of the CCP Central Committee on the Reform of the Economic System]." Adopted at the Third Plenary Session of the Twelfth CCP Central Committee on October 20, 1984. Published in *Shierda yilai zhongyao wenxian xuanbian* 十二大以来重要文献选编 *A Selection of Important Documents Since the Twelfth National Congress of the Chinese Communist Party* (Volume Two), compiled by the Party Literature Research Center, 569, 573. Beijing: The People's Press, 1986.

——. "Zhongong zhongyang guanyu wanshan shehuizhuyi shichang jingji tizhi ruogan wenti de jueding 中共中央关于完善社会主义市场经济体制若干问题的决定 [Decision of the CCP Central Committee on Issues Concerning the Improvement of the Socialist Market Economy System]." Published in *Shiliuda yilai zhongyao wenxian xuanbian* 十六大以来重要文献选编 [*A Selection of Important Documents Since the 16th National Congress of the Chinese Communist Party*] (Volume One), complied by the Party Literature Research Center, 471. Beijing: The People's Press, 2004.

——. *Zhonggong zhongyang guanyu zhiding guomin jingji he shehui fazhan "jiuwu" jihua he 2010 yuanjing mubiao de jianyi* 中共中央关于制定国民经济和社会发展"九五"计划和2010年远景目标的建议 [*Suggestions of the CCP Central Committee on Formulating the Ninth Five-year Plan for the National Economy and Social Development and the Long-range*

Objectives for the Year 2010]. Adopted at the Fifth Plenary Session of the Fourteenth Central Committee of the Chinese Communist Party, September 28, 1995.

Editorial department of the *China Financial Yearbook. Zhongguo caizheng nianjian* 中国财政年鉴2007 [*China Financial Yearbook 2007*]. Beijing: China Financial & Economic Publishing House, 2007.

Hu Angang 胡鞍钢 and Wang Yahua 王亚华. *Guoqing yu fazhan—zhongguo wuda ziyuan bendongtai bianhua yu changyuan fazhan zhan* 国情与发展—中国五大资本动态变化与长远发展战略 [*National Conditions and Development—Dynamic Changes of China's Five Major Categories of Capital and the Strategy for their Long-term Development Strategy*]. Beijing: Tsinghua University Press, 2004.

Jia Kang 贾康, Zhao Quanhou 赵全厚 eds. *Zhongguo caishui tizhi gaige 30nian huigu yu zhanwang* 中国财税体制改革30年回顾与展望 [*Review and Outlook on the 30 Year's Reform of China's Financial and Tax System*], Beijing: The People's Press, 2008: 44.

Jiang Zemin 江泽民. "Quanmian jianshe xiaokangshehui, kaichuang zhongguo tese 全面建设小康社会, 开创中国特色 [Build a Prosperous Society in an All-round Way and Open Up New Prospects for the Socialist Cause with Chinese Characteristics]." In *Shiliuda yilai zhongyao wenxian xuanpian* 十六大以来重要文献选编 [*A Selection of Important Documents Since the Sixteenth National Congress of the Chinese Communist Party*] (Volume One), by the Party Literature Research Center. Beijing: The People's Press, 2004.

Li Ping 李萍. *Zhengfujian caizheng guanxi tujie* 政府间财政关系图解 [*Graphics Illustrating the Financial Relations Between Governments*]. Beijing: China Financial & Economic Publishing House, 2006.

Ma Jun 马骏. *Zhongguo gonggong yusuan gaige: lixinghua yu minzhuhua* 中国公共预算改革: 理性化与民主化 [*Reform of China's Public Budget: Rationalization and Democratization*]. Beijing: Central Compilation & Translation Press, 2005: 33-43.

——. "Off-budgetary Activities of China Governments Since Economic Reform." Paper presented at the Twelfth Annual Conference of the Association for Budgeting and Financial Management, Kansas City, USA, 2000.

Ministry of Finance of the People's Republic of China. *Gonggong caizheng yu baixing shenghuo* 公共财政与百姓生活 [*Public Finance and People's Lives*]. Beijing: China Financial & Economic Publishing House, 2007.

National Bureau of Statistics Department of Comprehensive Statistics. *Xinzhongguo wushiwunian tongji ziliao huibian* 新中国五十五年统计资料汇编 [*A Collection of Statistical Data from Over Fifty-five Years Since the Founding of New China*]. Beijing: China Statistics Press, 2005.

National Bureau of Statistics. *Zhongguo tongji nianjian* 中国统计年鉴 [*China Statistical Yearbook*]. Beijing: China Statistics Press, Various Years.

——. *Zhongguo weisheng tongji nianjian*中国卫生统计年鉴2008 [*China Health Statistics Yearbook 2008*]. Beijing: China Statistics Press, 2008.

OECD. *Challenges Facing China's Public Expenditures: A Passageway to More Efficiency and Impartiality* (Chinese Version). Beijing: Tsinghua University Press, 2006.

UNDP. "Human Development Report 2008." 2008.

Wang Shaoguang 王绍光. "Cong shuishou guojia dao yusuan guojia 从税收国家到预算国家 [From a Tax-State to a Budget-State]." *Dushu* 读书 [*Reading*] No. 10 (2007): 3–13.

Wang Shaoguang 王绍光 and Hu Anggang 胡鞍钢. *Zhongguo guojia nengli baogao* 中国国家能力报告 [*Report on the Abilities of the Chinese State*]. Liaoning People's Press, 1993.

Wang Shaoguang 王绍光, Hu Angang 胡鞍钢. "Guanyu zhongguo guojia nengli de yanjiu baogao 关于中国国家能力的研究报告 [*Report on Research Regarding China's National Capabilities*]." In *Jiquan yu fenquan—zhongyang yu difang guanxi de goujian* 集权与分权—中央与地方关系的构建 [*Centralization and Decentralization—Structure of the*

Relations Between the Central Government and the Local Governments], by Dong Fureng 董辅礽 et al., 31–32. Beijing: Economic Science Press, 1996.

Wang Shaoguang 王绍光, Hu Angang 胡鞍钢. *Zhongguo guojia nenli baogao* 中国国家能力报告 [*Report on China's National Capabilities*]. Liaoning People's Press, 1993.

Wang Shaoguang 王绍光, Ma Jun 马骏. "Zouxiang 'yusuan guojia'—caizheng zhuanxing yu guojia jianshe 走向 "预算国家"—财政转型与国家建设 [Towards a 'Budget State'—State Building and the Transformation of Public Finance]. *Gonggong xingzheng pinglun* 公共行政评论 [*Public Administrative Review*] No. 1 (2008): 6.

Wen Jiabao 温家宝. *Zai dishijie quanguorenda sici huiyishang de zhengfu gongzuo baogao* 在第十届全国人大四次会议上的政府工作报告 [*Work Report of the Government at the Fourth Session of the 10th National People's Congress*]. Speech given on March 5, 2006.

Wong, Christine. "Fiscal Decentralization in China: the Problematic Outcomes of Unplanned Changes in Transition towards a Market Economy." Paper presented at the Asian Development Forum, Bangkok, 2001.

World Bank. "World Development Indicator 2008." Washington D.C., 2008.

Zhu Rongji 朱镕基. "Guanyu guomin jingji he shehui fazhan dishi ge wunian jihua gangyao bao gao 关于国民经济和社会发展第十个五年计划纲要的报告 [Report on the Outline of the Tenth Five-year Plan for National Economy and Social Development]." In *Shiwuda yilai zhongyao wenxian xuanpian* 十五大以来重要文献选编 [*A Selection of Important Documents Issued Since the 15th National Congress of the Chinese Communist Party*] (Volume II), by the Party Literature Research Center, 1685. Beijing: The People's Press, 2001.

Zou Zhizhuang 邹至庄. *Zhongguo jingji zhuanxing* 中国经济转型 [*China's Economic Transformation*]. Beijing: Renmin University Press, 2005.

CHAPTER SIX

CHINA'S INTEGRATION WITH THE WORLD: DEVELOPMENT AS A PROCESS OF LEARNING AND INDUSTRIAL UPGRADING

Justin Yifu Lin and Yan Wang

> The way to make the transition from a traditional planned economy to a market economy is just like crossing the river by groping the stones beneath the surface.
>
> —Deng Xiaoping

I. *Introduction*

In the past thirty years, China has achieved unprecedented economic growth and the most rapid poverty reduction in human history. Real gross domestic product (GDP) has expanded at an average annual rate of more than 10 percent.[1] China has grown to be the fourth-largest economy and second-largest trading nation in the world. A 2008 study by Chen and Ravallion found that using the World Bank's $1.25 US per day consumption measure, the proportion of the population living in poverty fell from 84 percent in 1981 to 15.6 percent in 2005, lifting nearly 600 million people out of poverty.[2]

China is unique in many ways. It is the largest developing country in terms of population, and it was a closed economy thirty years ago. After the country embarked on its transition from a centrally planned economy to a market economy, it had to combine the three daunting tasks of structural transformation, economic liberalization,

[1] The "World Bank, Global Economic Prospects 2009," December 2008.

[2] Chen and Ravallion, "China is Poorer than we Thought, But No Less Successful in the Fight against Poverty," 2008. This paper uses the new PPP data (2008) and finds that though China is poorer than previously thought, it is no less successful in poverty reduction. The different of PPP conversion factor does not change the conclusion that China has had the largest and fastest poverty reduction in history (World Bank, "Global Economic Prospects 2009," 2008).

and institutional transition into one—i.e., "three into one." And China did it remarkably well.

China's incremental and experimental strategies for economic reform and pragmatic and gradual liberalization have been unique and unorthodox. This approach has been piecemeal, partial, incremental, and often experimental. It has not been guided by well-founded theory or followed a pre-determined blueprint. In the late 1980s, many observers predicted that the reforms in China would lead nowhere. The success of China's approach to transition so far has posed many challenges to the conventional wisdom of economic theory. This approach violates almost all the basic propositions for successful transition that were identified by many economists advising the former socialist countries in the early phase of their transition. The success has also puzzled many economists.[3] Some economists suggest that China's success poses a challenge to the wisdom of the Washington Consensus, which considers stabilization, market liberalization, and privatization as necessary components to successful transition. The Chinese experience demonstrates the superiority of evolutionary, experimental, and bottom-up reforms over the comprehensive and top-down, big-bang approach. Key questions/debates include:

- Why have unorthodox reform approaches and openness helped China to achieve the most rapid economic growth and poverty reduction in human history? Have these strategies, including home-grown and "second-best institutions" like Special Economic Zones (SEZs), affected the patterns of trade?
- Has China followed a comparative advantage defying (CAD) or comparative advantage following (CAF) strategy (as defined in Lin[4]) in the transition process?
- Which positive and negative experiences and lessons from China are relevant for other developing countries?

This study aims to review and synthesize China's reform and trade integration with the world economy, with a focus on China's unique approach to reform (改革) and opening (开放) since 1978. We argue

[3] Nolan, "Political Economy and the Reform of Stalinism: The Chinese Puzzle," 1995.
[4] Lin, "Development and Transition: Idea, Strategy, and Viability," 2007.

that China's reforms follow the logic of a comparative advantage-following strategy[5] and the logic of "development as a process of learning and innovation."[6]

The framework of the paper is based on the following premises:

- An economy's factor endowments, which are given at any point in time and can be changed over time, are an important starting point for an enquiry about economic development in a country. The factor endowments in an economy determine its total budget and relative factor prices—the two most important economic parameters at any given time. The structure of its factor endowments determines endogenously its optimal industrial structure.
- Development is a process that is full of uncertainties, and economic transition even more so. Because of this uncertainty and different country specificity, development must be a process of *learning, selective adaptation, and innovation*. When China started the reform, it faced tremendous uncertainty, so it is only natural that the Chinese leaders adopted a pragmatic reform strategy that allowed for nation-wide incubation, trial and error, selection of what worked, and removal of what did not.
- In the transformation from a comparative advantage-defying (CAD) strategy to a comparative advantage-following (CAF) strategy, the optimal industrial structure will upgrade according to the changes in its endowment structure. The upgrading of industrial structure requires learning in areas where it is needed the most (with greater returns). Different from *knowledge*, which is a stock concept, *learning* is a series of actions to acquire knowledge, build capacity, and adapt to new technologies, industries, and institutions. Just as growth is a *flow* concept, learning is also a *flow* concept: it involves the accumulation of knowledge in a dynamic process that empowers actors, learners, businesses, local governments, and other entities to take action. Learning itself is a process of upgrading a country's human capital—key to successful industrial upgrading. Learning effort is a function of the expected

[5] Lin, 2003; "Development and Transition: Idea, Strategy, and Viability," 2007.

[6] Wang "Development as a process of Learning and Innovation: Lessons from China," 2005.

rate of return in a subsector, market conditions, and the macro environment.

This paper is written for Chinese readers who are seeking a summary of the thirty years of economic reforms as well as for an international audience interested in understanding the "why" and "how" of China's economic success. The paper is organized as follows: Section II provides a historical review of China's development strategy before the economic reforms. Section III reviews China's dual track approach to reform and opening, which followed the logic of learning to shift away from a CAD strategy to a CAF strategy. Section IV evaluates the causes behind the rapid trade integration and economic growth. Section V analyzes some positive and negative lessons for developing countries, in particular those in Africa. And the last section concludes with some policy implications.

II. *Why Was China Closed? The High Cost of Industrialization Using CAD Strategy*

In 1978 when reform started, China was a low-income country with agriculture as its largest sector in terms of employment. This structure is similar to that in many countries in Africa. The Chinese economy at that time was closed, oriented toward heavy industry, had few labor-intensive manufacturing exports, and had to export raw materials such as crude coal, crude oil, minerals, and agricultural products to earn foreign exchange.

China at that time was like other low-income countries in that its endowment structure was one of relative abundance in natural resources and/or unskilled labor, with a scarcity of human and physical capital. In these countries, only the labor-intensive and resource-intensive industries had comparative advantage in open, competitive markets.[7] Before the reform in 1979, the Chinese government adopted a comparative advantage-defying (CAD) and heavy industry-oriented development strategy. This strategy meant that the economic system in China was distorted and closed.

[7] Ohlin, Bert, "Interregional and International Trade," 1967; Heckscher, Eli, "The Effect of Foreign Trade on the Distribution of Income," 1991.

At the founding of the People's Republic in 1949, the Chinese government inherited a war-torn, agrarian economy in which 89.4 percent of the population resided in rural areas and the industrial sector accounted for only 12.6 percent of the national income. At that time, the heavy-industry sector was the symbol of the nation's power and economic achievement. It was lack of industrialization that had forced China, India, and other developing countries to yield to the colonial powers. Therefore, the government set the development of heavy industries as high priority.

Heavy industry is capital-intensive. In the 1950s, China was a capital-scarce, low-income, agrarian economy. Therefore, capital-intensive heavy industry was not China's comparative advantage at that time. The construction of a heavy-industry project in a developing country requires a long gestation period, bulky investments, and imported equipment. When the Chinese government initiated this strategy in the early 1950s, the economy had limited capital, a high interest rate, and scarce foreign exchange. Its exportable goods were limited and primarily consisted of low-price agricultural products. Because the three characteristics of the Chinese economy were mismatched with the three characteristics of a heavy industry project, spontaneous development of capital-intensive industry was impossible.

Due to this mismatch, a set of distorted macro policies was required for the development of heavy industry. At the beginning of the first Five-Year Plan, the government instituted a policy of low interest rates and over-valued exchange rates to reduce the costs of both interest payments and imported equipment. Meanwhile, in order to secure enough funds for industrial expansion, a policy of low input prices—including nominal wage rates for workers and prices for raw materials, energy, and transportation—evolved alongside the adoption of the development strategy. Private enterprises were soon nationalized and new key enterprises were owned by the State so that it could secure control over profits for reinvesting in heavy-industry projects. *Trade protection was also endogenous.* In order to protect domestic industry, high import tariffs and nontariff barriers were put in place to shield the otherwise nonviable industries from international competition. Exporting was considered the only way to earn the foreign exchange needed to import advanced technology. In addition to providing cheap food for industrialization, agriculture was the main foreign-exchange earner. In the 1950s, agricultural products alone made up more than 40 percent of all exports. If processed agricultural products are also counted, agriculture contributed more than 60 percent of China's foreign exchange earnings up to the 1970s. Because foreign exchange was as important as capital for the CAD strategy, the country's capacity to import capital goods for industrialization in the early stages of development clearly depended on its agricultural performance.

Low interest rates, high tariffs, and over-valued exchange rates; low nominal wage rates; and low prices for raw materials and living necessities constituted the basic macro policy environment of the CAD strategy.

The above macro policies induced a total imbalance in the supply and demand for credit, foreign exchange, raw materials, and other necessities. The government set plans and administrative controls to allocate scarce credit, foreign reserves, raw materials, and basic commodities, ensuring that the limited resources would be used for the targeted projects. Moreover, the state monopolized banks, foreign trade, and material distribution systems, and was able to mobilize and invest massive resources in heavy industries. More than three-quarters of the population earned a living in agriculture and labor-intensive light industries, which were consistent with the country's comparative advantage. However, agriculture and light industries each received less than 10 percent of State investment in the period 1953–1985, while 45 percent went to heavy industry. As a result, the share of heavy industry in the combined total value of agriculture and industry grew from 15 percent in 1952 to about 40 percent in the 1970s.

Judging from China's sector composition, the *trinity* of the traditional socialist economic structure—a distorted macro-policy environment, a planned allocation system, and micro-managed institutions—did accomplish its goal of accelerating the development of heavy industry. However, China paid a high price for such an achievement. The economy was very inefficient due to low allocative and technical efficiency. The most important indicator that reflected this inefficiency was the extremely low growth rate of total factor productivity. A World Bank study shows that, even calculated using the most favorable assumptions, the growth rate was merely 0.5 percent between 1952 and 1981, only a quarter of the average growth rate of the 19 developing countries included in the study.[8] Moreover, the total factor productivity of

[8] World Bank, "China: Long-term Issues and Options." 1985.

China's state-owned enterprises (SOEs) was in a state of stagnation or decline between 1957 and 1982.[9]

In summary, although the adoption of a CAD strategy can in some cases establish some advanced industries in some developing countries, it inevitably leads to inefficient resource allocation, suppresses worker incentives, provides fertile grounds for rampant rent-seeking and corruption, leads to mushrooming nonviable enterprises, and causes deterioration in income distribution and poor economic performance. In the end, there is "more haste, less speed." The adoption of a CAD strategy will not narrow the gap between developing and developed nations; instead, it will widen the gap.

III. *Reform That Follows the Logic of Learning and Innovation*

China's rapid growth and poverty reduction are attributable to its market-oriented reforms, openness to trade and investment, and transformation from a CAD to a CAF strategy—approaches that followed the logic of learning and innovation to explore its comparative advantage. China started with the "easier" reforms, relying on homegrown institutions in rural areas—the household responsibility system (HRS)—followed by an expansion of township and village enterprises (TVEs), a gradual liberalization of trade regimes via special economic zones (SEZs), liberalization of prices at the margin, and opening up to the global economy.

The more complex reforms started relatively late in the process: fiscal reforms (1994) and financial reforms (after 2000). (The process is illustrated in Figure 6.1.) "Crossing the river by groping the stones beneath the surface" became the hallmark of China's economic reform—implementing partial reforms in an experimental manner, often in a few regions, and expanding them based on proven success. This approach also explains the relatively stable and continuous contribution of total factor productivity to growth over the reform period.

First, when China's leaders set out to reform the economic system, they "had no blueprint." Instead of being designed *a priori*, the choice of specific reform measures and the sequence of transition reflected

[9] World Bank, "China: Economic Structure in International Perspective," 1985.

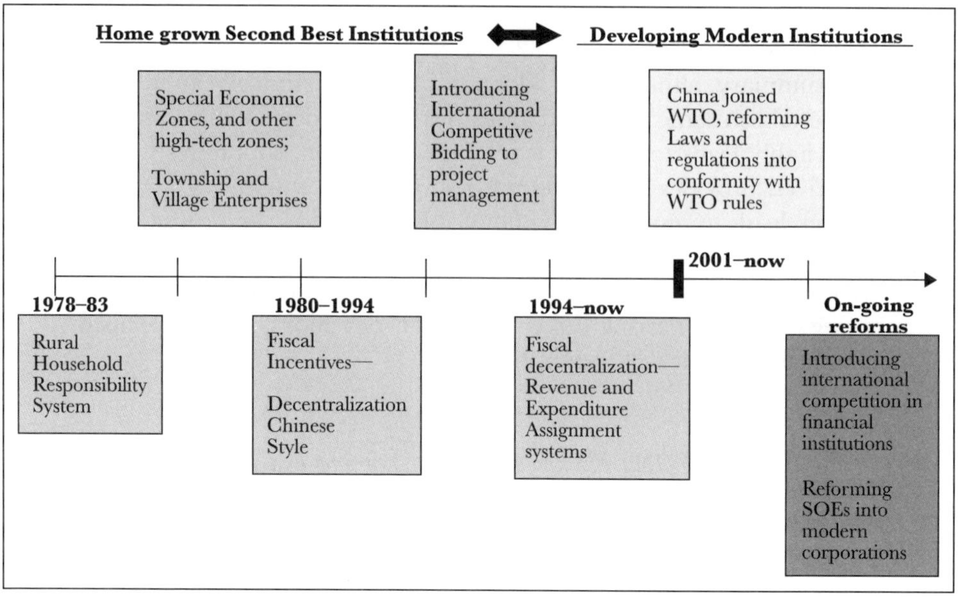

Source: Wang, Yan, "Development as a process of Learning and Innovation: Lessons from China," 2005.

Figure 6.1. Institutional Development: From Home-Grown to Modern Institutions.

the government's pragmatism toward the problems or crises that emerged in the economic system and the opportunities that could be utilized to mitigate or solve the problems. Second, retrospectively, the transition process in China followed a logical process that is predictable from the internal logic of a Soviet-type economy.[10] The Chinese approach in essence is a "micro" first approach,[11] which is different from the "macro" first approach to transition. In China, the transition started with improvement of incentives through decollectivization of agriculture, improvement of the governance of state-owned enterprises by expanding enterprise autonomy, improvement of resource allocation by the promotion of non-state enterprises that faced hard budget

[10] Lin, Justin Yifu 林毅夫, Cai Fang 蔡昉, and Li Zhou 李周, *China's Miracle: Development Strategy and Economic Reform*, 2003: Chap. 5.

[11] McKinnon, Ronald I., "Taxation, Money and Credit in the Transition from Central Planning," 1995.

constraints, and introduction of a dual-track system for prices and the exchange rate before their liberalization.

Third, the reform process in China followed the logic of learning and experimentation, in which all economic agents—including local governments and the private sector—are encouraged to try and solve the pressing issues during the transition. It was a process of "letting a thousand flowers bloom" to try and solve the problems of the sectors that needed it the most.

Kaufman and Wang[12] developed a simple model for human capital production in which the gain in learning is a function of demand for and supply of sector-specific knowledge, as well as indicators reflecting market conditions and the macro-environment. Intuitively, an economic agent, be it an individual or a firm, is motivated to learn in a specific sector if the expected rate of return from engaging in that sector is higher than the financial and opportunity costs of learning. When prices are liberalized, learning gain is the largest (rate of return highest) in sectors where the price differentials are the highest, provided there are clearly defined property rights, freedom of entry, labor market flexibility, and a stable macro environment. That is,

$$L_i = f(R_i, M_i; Macro)$$

where learning in sector *i* is a function of the expected net rate of return in sector *i*, the market conditions in sector *i*,[13] and a vector of variables reflecting the macro-environment in the country, including property rights, openness, law and order, inflation, national security, etc. The rate of return, *R*, in sector *i* would in turn depend on the level of price differentials between domestic and imported goods, cost structure, and ultimately, whether the country has comparative advantage in this sector. Where there is a large price difference, the incentive for learning would be high.

We submit the hypothesis that in China, private sector learning happened most rapidly in sectors where prices were liberalized early on, and entry and exit were allowed. And this was in the labor

---

[12] Kaufmann, Daniel, and Yan Wang, "The Impact of Macroeconomic Policies on Project Performance in the Social Sectors: A Framework of Analysis and Evidence," 1995.

[13] M could be a vector of variables reflecting the degree of freedom for entry and exit, investment climate, market size, or proximity to a large market, infrastructure, concentration, and labor market condition in that sector i.

intensive sectors. From the following discussion, one can see that this is the main reason why China is able to catch up in these sectors and to become more successful in labor-intensive exports.

A. *In Terms of Institutional Transition, What Happened and When?*

The institutional-reform and opening-up processes are intertwined. This section examines the two processes separately and step by step. In terms of the sequence of China's transition, the country conducted the easier micro-management reforms first, and then moved to the more complex macro-policy environment issues at a later stage.

1. *The Micro-Management System Reforms*

The most important change in the micro-management system was the replacement of collective farming with a household-based system, now known as the household responsibility system (HRS). In the beginning, the government had not intended to change the farming institutions. Starting in a village in Anhui in late 1978, HRS was scaled up to 45 percent of agriculture in 1980 and to 98 percent in 1983. The land lease was limited to only 1–3 years at the beginning, later extended to fifteen years, and later still to thirty years after the expiration of the first contract. Empirical estimates show that almost half of the 42.2 percent growth of output in the crop sector from 1978 to 1984 was driven by productivity change brought about by the reforms. Furthermore, almost all of the above productivity growth could be attributed to the changes resulting from the introduction of the household responsibility system.[14]

Unlike the spontaneous nature of farming institution reform, the reform in the management system of the SOEs was initiated by the government. These reforms have undergone three stages: the initial expansion of enterprise autonomy in 1984–86; a formal contractual responsibility system (1987–1992); and the "corporatization" process from 1993 to the present, in which small SOEs were sold to the

[14] Fan, S. "Effects of technological change and institutional reform on production growth in chinese agriculture," 1991; Lin, Justin Yifu 林毅夫, "Rural Reforms and Agricultural Growth in China," 1992; McMillan, J., J. Whalley, and L. Zhu, "The Impact of China's Economic Reforms on Agricultural Productivity Growth," 1989; Wen, Guanzhong James, "Total Factor Productivity Change in China's Farming Sector: 1952–1989," 1993.

private sector (according to the Zhucheng model), and large SOEs were restructured and listed in the equity market through IPOs (抓大放小). Production function estimates in several studies find that, for industry, the increase in enterprise autonomy increased productivity in SOEs.[15] Therefore, the reforms in the micro-management system in both agriculture and industry have created a flow of new resources, an important feature of China's reforms.

An unexpected effect of the relaxation of the resource allocation mechanism was the rapid growth of non-State enterprises, especially TVEs. Rural industry already existed under the traditional system as a result of the government's decision to mechanize agriculture and develop rural processing industries to finance the mechanization in 1971. In 1978 the entry and exit of TVEs were allowed in a large number of sectors, and the output of TVEs consisted of 7.2 percent of the total value of industrial output in China. In 1981–91, the number of TVEs, employment, and total output value grew at average annual rates of 26.6 percent, 11.2 percent, and 29.6 percent, respectively. The annual growth rate of TVEs in total output value was three times that of the state firms in the same period. In 1993, the output of TVEs accounted for 38.1 percent of total industrial output in China. The share of industrial output from non-state enterprises increased from 22 percent in 1978 to more than 75 percent in 2003.

The rapid entry of TVEs and other types of non-state enterprises exerted pressure on the SOEs and triggered the state's policy of delegating more autonomy to SOEs. And the development of TVEs and non-state enterprises significantly rectified the misallocation of resources. In most cases, non-state enterprises had to pay market prices for their inputs, and their products were sold at market prices. The price signals induced non-state enterprises to adopt more labor-intensive technologies and concentrate on more labor-intensive small industries, much more so than SOEs. Therefore, the production structure of non-state

[15] Groves, T. et al., "The change in productivity of Chinese state enterprises," 1994; Wang and Yao, "Sources of China's Economic Growth," 2003; Chen, Kuan et al., "Productivity change in Chinese industry: 1953–1985," 1988; Gordon, Roger H. and Wei Li, "The change in productivity of Chinese state enterprises, 1983–1987," 1995; Dollar, David, "Economic Reform and Allocative Efficiency in China's State-Owned Industry," 1990; Li, Wei, "The Impact of Economic Reform on the Performance of Chinese State Enterprises: 1980–1989," 1997; Jefferson, G.H., T.G. Rawski, and Y. Zheng, "Growth, Efficiency and Convergence in China's State and Collective Industry," 1992.

enterprises was more consistent with the comparative advantages of China's endowments.

2. *Reforms of the Macro-Policy Environment*

In the trinity of the traditional economic system, the distorted macro-policy environment was linked most closely to the development strategy, and its effects on allocative and technical efficiency were indirect. The reforms of the macro-policies were thus the most sluggish. We will argue later that most of the economic problems that appeared during the reforms—for example, the cyclical pattern of growth and rampant rent-seeking—can be attributed to the inconsistency between the distorted policy environment and the liberalized allocation and semi-private enterprise system.

Changes in the macro-policy environment started with the commodity price system. Material supplies were progressively de-linked from the plan, and the number of controlled items was incrementally reduced. Centralized credit rationing was also delegated to local banks at the end of 1984. In the same year, the government introduced the dual-track price system, which allowed SOEs to sell their output in excess of quotas at market prices and to plan their output accordingly. The aim of the dual-track price system was to reduce the marginal price distortion in SOEs' production decisions while leaving the state a measure of control over material allocation. As the share of a commodity that was allocated under the planned price was gradually reduced due to the growth of non-state sectors and the outside-the-plan production activity of the SOEs, the government would then give up the planned price, allowing the price to converge to market prices. By 1988 only 30 percent of retail sales were made at planned prices, and the SOEs obtained 60 percent of their inputs and sold 60 percent of their outputs at market prices.[16] By 1996, with the exception of a few raw materials and coal, fuel, and transportation, the prices of most commodities and services had been liberalized.

The second major change in the macro environment occurred in foreign exchange rate policy. In 1979–80, the official exchange rate was roughly 1.5 yuan per US dollar. The rate could not cover the costs of exports, as the average cost of earning one US dollar was around

[16] Zou, G., "Modelling the Enterprise Behavior under the Two-tier Plan/Market System in the PRC," 1993.

2.5 yuan. A dual rate system was adopted at the beginning of 1981. Commodity trade was settled at the internal rate of 2.8 yuan per dollar; the official rate of 1.53 yuan per dollar continued to apply to non-commodity transactions. After 1985, the proportion of retained foreign exchange, which was introduced in 1979, was gradually raised, and enterprises were allowed to swap their foreign exchange entitlements with other enterprises through the Bank of China at rates higher than the official exchange rate. Restrictions on trading foreign exchange were further relaxed with the establishment of a "foreign exchange adjustment center" in Shenzhen in 1985, in which enterprises could trade foreign exchange at negotiated rates. By the late 1980s, such centers were established in most provinces in China and more than 80 percent of the foreign-exchange earnings were swapped in these centers.[17] The climax of foreign exchange rate policy reform was the establishment of a managed floating system and unification of the dual rate system on January 1, 1994. By that time, 80 percent of foreign exchange had already been allocated through the swap markets. Therefore the significant devaluation at the time of unification did not produce a big shock to the economy. After the Asian financial crisis in 1997, the exchange rate was pegged to the dollar and kept stable. After July 2005, due to the large current account surplus, RMB was allowed to appreciate gradually, from 8.7 yuan to the dollar in 1994, to 6.8 yuan to the dollar in 2008. Since August 2008, due to global financial crisis and economic slowdown, the RMB appreciation has slowed and essentially stopped.

Interest-rate policy is the least affected area of the traditional macro-policy environment. Under the heavy industry-oriented development strategy, the interest rate was kept artificially low to facilitate the expansion of capital-intensive industries. After the reforms started in 1979, the government was forced to raise both loan rates and savings rates several times. However, throughout the reform process, the rates were maintained at levels far below market-clearing rates. Three development banks were established in 1994 to finance long-term projects, imports and exports, and agricultural infrastructure at subsidized rates. The promulgation of the *Law on the People's Bank of China* (中国人民银行法) (the central bank) and the *Commercial Bank Law* (商业银行法) in 1995 and 1996 strengthened the authority of People's Bank of

[17] Lardy, Nicholas R., *Integrating China into the Global Economy*, 2002.

China (PBoC) and provided commercial banks with a legal framework for operation. Until recently, however, interest rates had been tightly controlled by the PBoC. The mentality of the heavy industry-oriented development strategy is deeply rooted in the mind of China's political leaders. To accelerate the development of capital-intensive industry in a capital-scarce economy, a distorted macro-policy environment—at the very least in the form of a low interest-rate policy—is essential. First, inter-bank lending rate was liberalized; then, after several years in the WTO and the introduction of competition from foreign banks, the lending rate was gradually made flexible.[18] Until 2003, the state sector received a disproportionate share of credit but only produced 23 percent of GDP, whereas the private sector produced 52 percent of GDP but accounted for 27 percent of outstanding loans.[19] Currently, lending rates to small and medium enterprises are more flexible, but the prime lending rate and deposit rate have not yet been liberalized. This low interest rate policy has played an important role in the expansion of China's capital-intensive industries.[20]

B. *Terms of Trade Reforms and Export Upgrading: What Happened and When?*

In contrast to the institutional reforms, the opening up process in China's trade and investment can be divided into four stages:

(1) 1979–1987: Reforms aimed to break the state monopoly in trade, to experiment with Special Economic Zones (SEZs), and to provide incentives for exporters. Foreign borrowing and direct investment were encouraged, but foreign direct investment (FDI) was small, mainly from Hong Kong and Taiwan (85 percent), and located in SEZs.

---

[18] For post-WTO financial sectors reforms, See: Allen, Qian, Qian, and Zhao "Review of China's Financial System and Initiatives for the Future," 2008; Lardy, *Foreign trade and economic reform in China, 1978–1990*, 1992; and Zhao, Longyue and Yan Wang, "Trade Remedies and Non-market Economies: Economic Implications of the US First Countervailing Duty Case on China," 2008.

[19] McKinsey Global Institute, "Putting China's Capital to Work: the value of financial system reform," May 2006.

[20] On distortion in financial structure and industrial structure, see Lin, Justin Yifu 林毅夫, "Rebalancing equity and efficiency for equitable and sustainable growth," 2008.

(2) 1988–1993: Reforms fostered market development, introduced the responsibility system and the shared foreign exchange revenue system to promote export at all levels—the center, local, and enterprises—and the dual exchange rate system was implemented at this stage, and import tariffs were beginning to be reduced.
(3) 1994–2001: Reforms established the market oriented international trade system, unified the foreign exchange rate in 1994, reduced tariffs unilaterally from an average of 40 percent to 16 percent, and actively prepared for WTO accession.
(4) 2001–present: There has been rapid growth in trade and foreign investment as a result of China joining the WTO, locking-in liberalization of trade in goods and in services, making China's laws and institutions conform with international standards, and providing a more certain policy and legal environment for investors. Total trade has been expanding at an annual average rate of more than 35 percent, and export structure has been upgrading rapidly since China's accession.[21] Total trade value exploded from 510 billion USD in 2001 to 2,174 billion USD in 2007. That same year, China became the third largest trading nation in the world.

In the late 1970s and early 1980s, China's exports were concentrated in resource-intensive raw materials and primary products, such as coal, crude oil, minerals, grains, and food and vegetables. This was consistent with China's natural endowment at that time,[22] despite of the government's efforts at building heavy industries. But differing from other low-income countries, China did have some manufacturing exports, and machinery accounted for 5 percent of total exports. This was a result of many years of Soviet-type CAD strategy. However, China did not have sufficient home-grown knowledge and skills that were consistent with its comparative advantage, such as how to make labor-intensive textiles, clothing, shoes, and toys that were exportable. Thus, foreign investors, including overseas Chinese, brought this

[21] National Bureau of Statistics (NBS), *Zhongguo tongji nianjian* 中国统计年鉴 [*China Statistical Yearbooks*]. China Statistics Press, Various Years; and Ministry of Commerce of PRC.
[22] World Bank, "China: Long-term Issues and Options," 1985.

practical know-how about the international market and taught Chinese workers and engineers hands-on skills.

It is noteworthy that China's two parallel processes of reform and opening have been intertwined, sequential, and mutually reinforcing. The first line of action established four "Special Economic Zones" in the late 1970s, where regulations streamlined for trade promotion and preferential treatment were enacted to attract foreign direct investment. The second parallel line of action is domestic fiscal decentralization, which began with a fiscal contract system in which local governments entered long-term fiscal contracts with higher-level governments and retained some of the incremental revenues at the margin ("fiscal reform, Chinese style").[23] This system, albeit imperfect and eventually replaced by a tax assignment system in 1994, provided large incentives for local governments to develop local economies by opening to trade and foreign investment and learning from them, so that local revenue would grow. The autonomy assigned to local governments included foreign exchange revenue sharing, fiscal revenue retention, approval of investment projects under a certain amount, and expenditure decisions, which gave local governments more opportunities to engage in initiatives promoting the local accumulation of capital via trade, FDI, and development of TVEs (semi-private).

From 1979 to 1991, foreign borrowing dominated FDI. After the establishment of four SEZs, setting up joint ventures and joint cooperation companies were the main mode of cooperation. During that period, 85 percent of foreign capital came from Hong Kong, Macau and Taiwan, and other Asia countries. Foreign investors played a vital role in providing the market connections on what types of products were needed by the international market, how to get orders for exports, and how to get access to the technology that was suitable for the development stage of the country. Thus, labor-intensive industries were able to expand rapidly.

---

[23] This argument has been supported by many empirical studies. For example, see: Qian, Yingyi and Barry R. Weingast, "Federalism as a Commitment to Market Incentives," 1997; Cao, Yuanzheng, Yingyi Qian, and Barry R. Weingast, "From Federalism, Chinese Style, to Privatization, Chinese Style," 1999; Qian, Yingyi, "The process of China's market transition, 1978–1998: the evolutionary, historical and comparative perspectives," 2000.

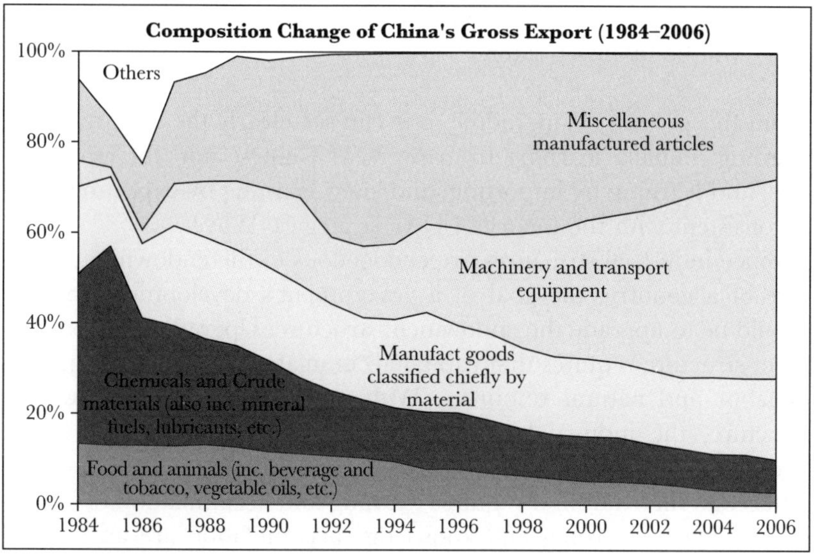

Source: Based on data from the UN COMTRADE website.

Figure 6.2. China Has Been Following Its Comparative Advantage: From Raw Materials in the 1980s, to Labor Intensive Manufacturing Products in the Mid-1990s.

(1) The first industrial upgrade happened in 1986, when exports of textiles and clothing exceeded crude oil. This point in history signified China's transition from exporting resource-intensive products to labor-intensive textile and clothing products, which was consistent with China's comparative advantage.

(2) The second upgrade happened in 1995, when China's export of machinery and electronics exceeded textiles and clothing. This indicated that China started the transition from exporting traditional labor-intensive exports to non-traditional labor-intensive products.

(3) The third upgrade happened after China's accession to the WTO, when high-tech exports grew rapidly, and the level of product sophistication increased. The central and local governments conducted regulatory reforms to improve the investment climate, and provided incentives for FDI, export expansion, and private sector development. Many exporters have become an integral part of the global supply chains of multinationals in automobiles, computers, and airplanes (Figure 6.2). There is,

however, a myth on the level of export sophistication, which will be discussed later.

From this process of upgrading, one can see clearly the importance of learning: initially learning from overseas Chinese and foreign investors, and learning by importing, and later, learning by exporting. This is consistent with the theory of CAF strategies. Why?

Since industrial structures are endogenous to the endowment structure of a country, the goal of a government's development strategy should be to upgrade the endowment structure. Upgrading the endowment structure requires that capital accumulate faster than the growth of labor and natural resources. With upgrading of the endowment structure, the industrial/technology structure of the economy also needs to be upgraded. As the upgrading of industrial/technology is, by nature, an innovation, it requires learning and accumulation of knowledge. That is, learning and knowledge accumulation are an integral process in the upgrading of an economy's endowments, technology, and industry.

IV. *Why Was China Able to Achieve Rapid Growth?*

Both China and Vietnam have been able to maintain rapid growth during the transition process. The above discussion provides us some explanations for the success. First, micro-institutional reforms have provided incentives for SOEs and farms to produce more efficiently, and the macro-management environment has been gradually opened/liberalized, allowing the market price to play a role *at the margin*. Second, market reforms have allowed prices to better reflect scarcities in the economy (except in a few cases regarding interest rates, land and other resources, and the exchange rate), which in turn allows firms to specialize according to comparative advantage and to compete in the international market. The power of specialization is endless, and China is a living example of it.

The question is, how best to explain the dramatic trade expansion and upgrading of the industrial sector? Has China really followed its comparative advantage? This section will discuss some misunderstandings about China's trade pattern and export sophistication.

A. *Measurement Issues of Trade Integration*

A commonly used measure for trade integration is the exports-to-GDP ratio. According to this ratio, China is extremely successful: its exports-to-GDP rose from only 9 percent in 1980 to over 36 percent in 2006. However, this ratio may be a misleading indicator of an economy's actual dependence on trade in the presence of processing trade. This is due to the geographical segmentation of world production: intermediate goods may cross country borders many times before they become exports of final products. This is also why world trade growth has been much faster than global GDP growth in past three decades. The fundamental reason is that exports and GDP are measured by different accounting standards. The size of an economy is measured by GDP, which is a net or value-added concept, while exports are still measured in gross terms containing both domestic and imported content.

A recent paper by Koopman, Wang, and Wei[24] shows two interesting points. First, the exports-to-GDP ratio for China and Mexico, at 36.7 and 29.8 percent, respectively, in 2006, are extraordinarily high for large economies. This compares with 7.9 percent for the United States, 12.1 percent for the EU, 14.9 percent for Japan, 12.9 for Brazil, and 13.2 percent for India in the same year. Second, the exports-to-GDP ratio of Mexico and China increased dramatically when major trade liberalization packages were implemented: NAFTA in 1994 for Mexico, and China's WTO accession at the end of 2001.

Related to the fragmentation of global production, there is a rapid expansion of processing trade in developing economies, especially China. Based on China's customs statistics, processing exports accounted for more than 55 percent of manufacturing exports during past decades. This type of exports is characterized as "importing for export"—firms import parts and other intermediate materials from abroad, duty free, and then re-export the processed or assembled final products to the international market. Ignoring such a difference in production structure will overestimate the domestic value-added share

[24] Koopman, Robert, Zhi Wang, and Shang-jin Wei, "How Much of Chinese Export Is Really Made in China: Assessing Domestic Value-Added when Processing Trade Pervasive," 2008.

in gross exports for economies that are heavily involved in the global supply chain and processing trade, such as China and Mexico.[25]

B. *Upgrading Factor Endowments*

The third reason for China's success is that it has continuously upgraded its factor endowments through learning and capital accumulation. Capital has accumulated at a faster pace than growth of labor and natural resources, which allows the factor endowments to be upgraded. One of the reasons is improved incentives for reforms in micro management and resource allocation. Productivity and investment have increased dramatically. A second key factor is the inflow of FDI. Along with improvement of the investment climate from 1992 to 2001, FDI exceeded indirect financing, and the number of solely foreign-owned enterprises increased rapidly. There was a remarkable growth among foreign investors from Europe and North America in the manufacturing sector.

Table 6.1 shows clearly how China has been augmenting its endowments intensively in terms of both physical and human capital. The accumulation of physical capital has been more rapid than the economic growth rates in both reform periods I and II. Total factor productivity grew more rapidly in reform period I, reflecting rapid institutional change and reallocation of resources to more productive sectors. More recently, physical capital stock has grown dramatically in reform period II (2000–2005), although human capital accumulation has slowed in the post-reform period. Unskilled labor is still more abundant, as reflected in the low relative wages for unskilled workers. However, growth accounting analysis also shows that in the recent years, China has been overly reliant on physical capital accumulation, while productivity gains (TFP growth) have declined.[26]

---

[25] Koopman, Robert, Zhi Wang, and Shang-jin Wei, "How Much of Chinese Export Is Really Made in China: Assessing Domestic Value-Added when Processing Trade Pervasive," 2008.

[26] Wang, Yan and Yao Yudong, "Sources of China's Economic Growth 1952–1999: Incorporating Human Capital Accumulation", 2003.

Table 6.1. Sources of China's Growth: Augmenting Physical and Human Capital in Addition to Productivity Growth, 1953–2005

Item	Pre-reform (1953–77)	*Reform period I* (1978–1999)	*Reform period II* (2000–2005)
Average annual growth rate			
Output	6.12	9.56	9.17
Physical capital stock	6.14	8.97	12.47
Labor	2.24	2.13	1.00
Human capital stock	5.46	2.14	1.28
Total factor productivity	–0.80	2.94	1.79
Contribution to GDP growth (percent)			
Physical capital stock	50.2	56.9	68.0
Labor	18.3	11.1	5.5
Human capital stock	44.6	11.2	7.0
Total factor productivity	−13.1	30.7	19.5

Source: Wang, Yan and Yao Yudong, "Sources of China's Economic Growth 1952–1999: Incorporating Human Capital Accumulation", 2003; and updated by Wang, Yan.

1. *Labor Reallocation and Human Capital Augmentation: Learning Must Be in Sectors Where Prices Have Been Liberalized and Comparative Advantage Exists*

China has invested greatly in the health and education of its population since the founding of the Republic. At the end of the 1970s, the human development indicators of the Chinese population were higher than those of developing countries at the same income level. However, investment in human capital has not exceeded the pace of physical capital accumulation.

The most remarkable feature has been the private-sector-led learning and catch-up. Since prices in labor intensive sectors were liberalized early in the reform process, learning first happened in those sectors where the cost advantage (or rate of return of learning) was high. In those sectors in the early 1980s, TVEs and small private firms started to learn from SOEs to meet domestic demand much before they were able to export. This could be considered the stage of "learning for import substitution." Examples include the better designed clothing produced in Shenzhen, goods for sale in the domestic market, and the upgrading of bicycle companies into motorcycle companies. When domestic prices of these manufactured goods are higher than international prices, there is a huge incentive for private sector firms to learn to produce to meet domestic demand.

Several remarkable features are particularly noteworthy.

First, private sector development has been most rapid in the labor-intensive sectors where prices were liberalized early on, and entry and exit were allowed. New private firms mushroomed in the early stage of reforms, and they were able to learn initially from SOEs and to attract their technological know-how. The SOEs could not compete with the private firms in those sectors, and became nonviable.[27] Between 1981 and 1991, TVEs' annual growth rate in total output value was three times that of the state firms in the same period. By 1993–95, thanks to the famous "Zhucheng model," local governments were able to sell or privatize most of the small-to-medium size loss-making SOEs without causing large displacement of workers.

Second, there was a massive reallocation of labor, along with human capital, from public to private and export sectors, from capital-intensive to labor-intensive sectors where the rate of return to learning was higher. Cadres and fresh graduates "plunged into the sea" to seek higher salaries in those sectors where prices and wages were liberalized—which were labor intensive sectors. In particular, there was a massive reallocation of labor from the primary sector to the secondary and tertiary sectors, which are more labor intensive (see Figure 6.3). Today, there is still a huge potential for China to develop its service sector, which is labor-intensive and underdeveloped; by 2007, the tertiary sector accounted for 40 percent of GDP.

Third, in the manufacturing sector, there has been labor reallocation from capital-intensive to labor-intensive subsectors. Figure 6.4 shows that, in recent years (1998–2006), even when the entire manufacturing industry has shed labor, the labor-intensive subsectors—such as apparel, footwear, leather, sporting goods, and furniture—still expand rapidly, gaining larger shares in total manufacturing employment. The share of employment in the labor-intensive sector rose from 52 to 57 percent in total manufacturing. During this period, employment in the

[27] Liberalizing entry and exit is crucial to learning based on comparative advantages, similar to Schumpeter's idea of creative destruction (1942) which stresses new products and new services: new entrants with better products/services drive the old firms out, which is good for productivity; and the endogenous growth model where monopolistic rents provide the payoff for research, and better products/services render previous ones obsolete. (Aghion, Philippe and Peter Howitt. "A Model of growth through Creative Destruction," 1992; Melitz, Marc J. "The Impact of Trade on Intra-industry Reallocations and Aggregate Industry Productivity," 2003.)

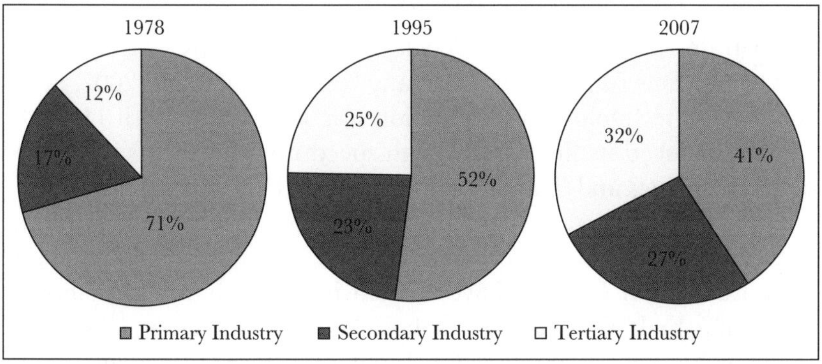

Source: based on data from NBS, *China Statistical Yearbook*, 2008.

Figure 6.3. The Composition of Employment in China, 1978, 1995, 2007.

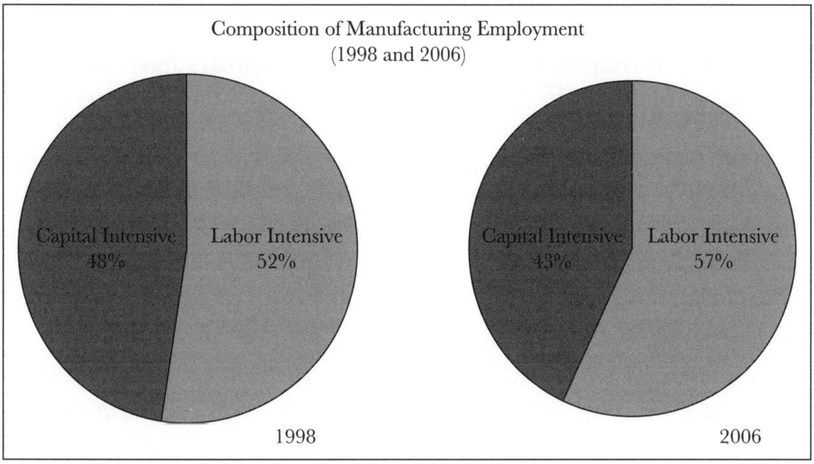

Source: NBS, *China Labor Statistical Yearbook*, various years from 1998 to 2007.

Figure 6.4. Composition of Manufacturing Employment: Labor or Capital-Intensive Sectors.

manufacturing sector decreased by 1.55 percent, whereas, for apparel, footwear, leather, sporting goods, and furniture, it grew more than 6.5 percent annually. Employment in communications and computer assembly grew remarkably, at 11.6 percent annually.

In addition to labor reallocation, China has been investing in formal education as well as on-the-job learning. Each year, China sends many official delegations for study-tours, although data is sketchy.

For example, in order to learn the technology related to the high-speed trains from Siemens, 97 delegations or groups with a total of 580 technicians were sent to Germany between 2006 and 2007, and a contract on technological cooperation was signed. On April 11, 2008, China produced its first CHR3 high-speed rail motor-cars, now used between Beijing and Tianjin with a top speed of 350km per hour.[28]

Since 1979, when Deng Xiaoping visited U.S. President Jimmy Carter and agreed to expand the student exchange programs, more than 1.2 million students have studied in more than 100 countries. According to UNESCO, China has the largest number of students studying abroad, accounting for 1 out of 7 foreign students in the world. In 2007 alone, 144,000 went abroad, of which 129,000 are studying at their own expense.[29] There are also many who joined the "work-study" training programs in Japan. According to the Ministry of Commerce, more than 450,000 work-study students have gone to Japan, received apprenticeship/vocational training, and came back to China. These trained workers and returned scholars have played an important role in China's rapid growth and export development.

2. *Rapid Physical Capital Augmentation: Market-Driven or Government-Driven?*
One special example is the significant investment in infrastructure. The Chinese government's proactive fiscal policy and public investment have played an important role in infrastructure improvement. During the past twenty years, investment in public infrastructure increased rapidly. For example, in transportation, investment in fixed assets increased from RMB 33.37 billion in 1990 to RMB 1,122.45 billion in 2006. Since 1998, total expenditure on transport infrastructure has exceeded 5 percent of GDP annually.[30]

After thirty years of intensive capital augmentation, China now has the second highest length of expressways in the world, and six out of ten of the largest ports in the world.

Better infrastructure has significantly reduced the transportation cost for manufacturing exports, creating a new comparative advantage that other developing nations do not have. This rapid development of infrastructure is partially market-driven and partially government

[28] *People's Daily*, November 24, 2008: 8.
[29] *People's Daily*, November 28, 2008: 6.
[30] World Bank, "China: Poverty Assessment," 2007.

driven, since there is market pressure to lower transportation costs for various localities to be able to export to the international market. Thus, the local governments have an incentive to meet this market demand and build infrastructure for reducing the cost of trade. China's fiscal decentralization has provided great incentives for provincial and local governments to augment physical infrastructure.

3. *Augmentation by Foreign Direct Investment and Technology*

Figure 6.5 shows that foreign direct investment has been concentrated in the area of manufacturing, while the primary and tertiary sectors have been largely ignored. This pattern of FDI inflow is consistent with China's comparative advantage, since foreign investment attempts to utilize China's low-cost labor in order to compete in the international market. China does not have comparative advantage in land-intensive agriculture or most other resource-intensive sectors; thus, the primary sector is not attractive for FDI. And, until recently, the service sector was protected.

Openness and competition are crucial for learning and knowledge transfer, as there are at least three channels of knowledge transfer: (a) technology can be embodied in imported equipment; (b) entry of more efficient (foreign) firms can lead to the exit of less efficient firms; and (c) foreign investors bringing not only capital, but also better products/services and practical sector-specific skills. They have the incentives to train workers and managers through apprenticeships and on-the-job training. Following the same logic of learning as described above, when prices are liberalized and entry and exit are allowed, learning gains from foreign investors for the export market are high, and there is a strong incentive for the private sector to learn from foreign investors via joint ventures and learning-for-exporting.

As mentioned earlier, from 1992 to 2001, FDI inflows to China exceeded indirect flows, and the number of wholly-foreign-owned enterprises firms rose rapidly. Multinational manufacturing firms from OECD countries moved into China on a large scale, bringing advanced technology. After China joined the WTO in 2001, this trend continued. Governments at all levels have attached more importance to attracting high-tech firms, managerial know-how, and talent. China has become an integral part of the global supply chain, and the manufacturing center of the world.

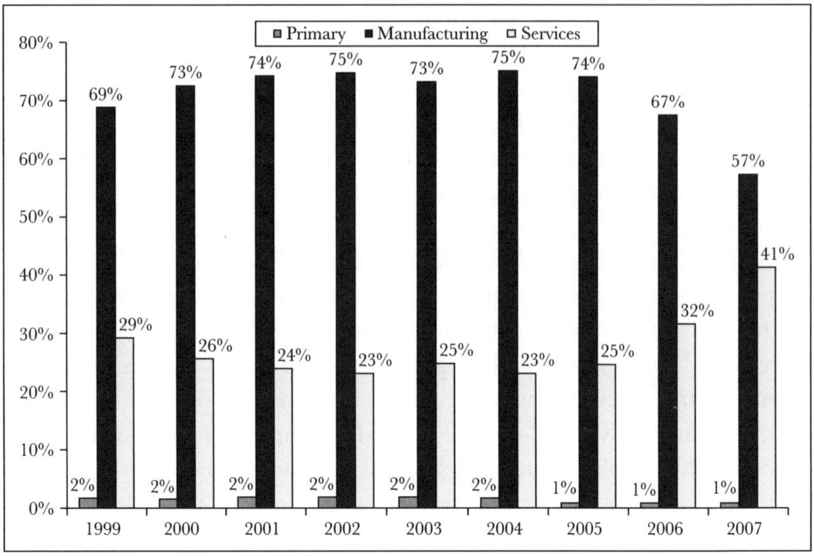

Source: based on data from NBS, *China Statistical Yearbook*, 2001–2008.

Figure 6.5. Sector Composition of FDI Stock in China: Concentration in the Manufacturing Sector.

C. *Caveats: Overinvesting in Physical Capital and Under-Investing in Human and Natural Capital?*

However, China's investment is generally considered to be at a higher level than is desirable or sustainable, and many domestic and international observers argue that in order for growth to be sustainable, it needs to be rebalanced away from an excessive reliance on investment and exports, and toward consumption.[31]

Currently, a key concern is that the low cost of capital (the real rate of interest is less than half the level of the real GDP growth rate), together with the low cost of other inputs, such as energy and land prices, and externalities such as pollution, have contributed to excessive levels of investment. High levels of investment raise the risk of excess capacity in some sectors, contributing to price declines that in turn could lead to increases in nonperforming loans and associated economic and financial disruptions. Moreover, the low cost of capital has shifted production toward capital intensive methods that entail

[31] Aziz, Jahangir and Steven Dunaway, "China's Rebalancing Act," 2007.

relatively little job creation, as is evident in the negative job growth in the manufacturing sector.

He and Kujis[32] show that China is one of the most industry-led economies in the world, second only to Malaysia in terms of share of industry in value added, and its capital intensity is rising, as measured by investment over GDP. The service sector accounts for about 40 percent of GDP, and is stagnating. This pattern of development creates few jobs, and is inequitable and unsustainable, as shown below.

D. *China's Economic Growth is Too Capital Intensive and Imbalanced*

The gross investment share of the economy increased from about 35 percent at the beginning of the decade to a record high of 45 percent of GDP in 2006. Compared with Japan and Korea, China has an unusually high share of investment. In contrast to the investment share, the private consumption share of GDP declined to less than 40 after accession to the WTO. A World Bank study found that China's growth pattern is increasingly capital intensive, with increasingly high levels of saving and investment.[33] China's gross fixed capital formation—in factories, buildings, and infrastructure—has always been relatively high. It increased further from 35 percent of GDP in 2000 to an estimated 45 percent of GDP in 2006. This was combined with a rise in (gross domestic) saving from 37 percent of GDP in 2000 to an estimated 51 percent in 2006. In contrast to conventional understanding, the bulk of China's investment is financed domestically, much of it by enterprises. Conventional wisdom has long held that enterprise investment was largely financed by household savings, and many studies of China's high saving still focus mainly on household savings. However, much of China's high savings is done by enterprises, while the government also saves considerably. With household income around 60 percent of GDP, and with households now saving 25–30 percent of their income, down from more than 30 percent a decade ago, household saving has not been the driving force behind the impressive increase in China's domestic saving rate over the last decade.

---

[32] He, Jianwu and Louis Kuijs, "Rebalancing China's Economy—Modeling a Policy Package," 2007.

[33] He and Kuijs, "Rebalancing China's Economy—Modeling a Policy Package," 2007.

A recent IMF Working Paper found that the decline of household income is the main reason for the decline in the consumption share.[34] Despite the remarkably high national economic growth, the share of Chinese household income has declined across all major sub-categories of wages, investment incomes, and government transfers.[35] In China, wage income consists of more than 86 percent of the total household disposable income. The share of wage income is estimated to have dropped from about 67 percent of GNP in the early 1980s to the current level of 56 percent. The share of investment income is very small and falling due to several reasons. First, ownership of Chinese firms is not widely held by households. Second, even listed firms have not distributed dividends, but instead reinvested most profits. Third, until recently, SOEs did not pay dividends to the government. Lastly, bank deposits are the main savings vehicle of Chinese households but the interest rate on household deposits has been kept very low by the government.

Job creation in China has been relatively slow in contrast to soaring GDP growth in recent years. In addition to the problem of under-employment in the countryside, unemployment of the urban population is rapidly growing. China's urban unemployment stems from two sources: one is the continuously enlarging urban labor supply due to the combination of the current increase in population and rural-to-urban migration; another is massive layoffs from the restructuring and downsizing of SOEs that are mostly located in urban areas. China's official numbers on unemployment soared to 8.4 million in 2005. However, independent estimates, by Chinese economists using measures similar to those used in market economy countries, suggest that China's urban unemployment rate has been 11 to 12 percent in recent years, almost three times more than the official rate.[36] Low employment leads to low disposable household income.

Income inequality has been rising. While economic growth has brought unprecedented prosperity to China, income inequality has experienced a significant increase. China's Gini coefficient, a standard

---

[34] Aziz, Jahangir, and Li Cui, "Explaining China's Low Consumption: The Neglected Role of Household Income," 2007.

[35] Government transfer is part of government expenditure directed to support the poor and vulnerable households such as conditional cash transfers, unemployment benefit, medicare and social security.

[36] Bergsten, C. Fred, Bates Gill, Nicholas R. Lardy, and Derek Mitchell, *China: The Balance Sheet—What the World Needs to Know Now about the Emerging Superpower*, 2006.

measure of a country's overall income inequality, increased from 0.30 in 1981 to 0.43 in 2002, and rose to 0.45 in 2005.[37] This figure represents an inequality level that is higher than that of the United States and Russia. A World Bank report showed that China's income inequality has grown wider in comparison other countries as well. The rapid increase in inequality is in part related to the distortions caused by the partially liberalized price system and the lack of competition in many sectors.[38] As discussed above, China has been following a low-interest-rate policy for a long time, and over 80 percent of low-interest loans have been obtained by the state sector, which is more capital intensive. These low interest loans represent a capital subsidy to make capital cheaper for the state sector, providing incentives for developing capital-intensive products. Fewer jobs are being created in such a capital-intensive industrial structure, and income inequality is higher in part because subsidies are given to owners of capital, not to labor, and in part because of the dual structure farmers are not able to share equally in the benefits of pro-industry and pro-urban growth.

E. *A Myth about China's Export Structure: CAD or CAF?*

Six years after WTO accession, some economists argue that that China's export bundle resembles that of a country with an income per-capita level three times higher than China's.[39] Using another approach, Schott[40] finds that the overlap between China's exports to the US and those of OECD countries to the US increased from 15 percent in 1994 to 21 percent in 2005. These studies, however, neglect two important caveats.

One caveat is that foreign invested enterprises (FIE) have played a very important role in China's trade expansion and industrial upgrading. From 1985 to 2007, the share of FIE's exports and imports increased from less than 10 percent to about 60 percent today. In the trade of certain advanced technology products (ATPs), the share of FIE is even higher. Recently, the United States International

[37] Ravallion, Martin and Shaohua Chen, "China's (uneven) Progress against Poverty," 2007; World Bank, "China: Poverty Assessment," 2007.

[38] Lin, Justin Yifu 林毅夫, "Rebalancing equity and efficiency for equitable and sustainable growth," 2008.

[39] Rodrik, Dani, "What's so Special About China's Exports?" 2006.

[40] Schott, Peter K., "The Relative Sophistication of China's Exports," 2008.

Trade Commission (USITC) conducted a study on China's trade in ATPs. The results showed that while China ran a $41–$49 billion surplus with the U.S. in 2006 based on the U.S. Census ATP definition, a huge gap still exists between Chinese ATP exports to the U.S. and U.S. ATP exports to China. In addition, more than 95 percent of China's ATP exports were processing exports from 1995 to 2006, more than 90 percent of China's ATP exports to the U.S. were produced by FIEs in China, and in 2006 about 65 percent of China's ATP exports to the U.S. were from various policy zones.[41]

Another caveat is the practice known as processing trade. A large and increasing share of China's exports involve assembling duty-free imported inputs for export, a practice known as processing trade. The share of processing trade in China's exports has risen from 47 percent in 1992 to 55 percent in 2007. The share of processing trade varies across industries. In the high export growth machinery sector, most of this growth is indeed due to growth in processing trade.[42] Ferrantino et al.[43] find that 90 percent of China's expanding ATP exports to the U.S. are in processing trade.

The role of processing trade in the upgrading of skills is debatable. Amiti and Freund[44] calculated the skill content of only those exports that exclude processing trade. Interestingly, they found that, for China's non-processing exports, between 1992 and 2005 there was no change in the skill content. Thus *all* the skill upgrading observed in total exports was due to the high skill content in processing trade. One implication of this finding is that China has a great distance to go before the skill content in its non-processing exports comes even close to that of processing trade.

A recent study has methodically calculated the total domestic value added in China's exports.[45] It shows that the shares of domestic and foreign value added in total exports are about 50:50, but that

[41] Ferrantino, Michael et al. "Classification of Trade in Advanced Technology Products and its Statistics Reconciliation: The Case of China and the United States," 2007.

[42] Amiti, Mary and Caroline Freund, "An Anatomy of China's Export Growth," 2008.

[43] Ferrantino et al., "Classification of Trade in Advanced Technology Products and its Statistics Reconciliation," 2007.

[44] Amiti and Freund, "An Anatomy of China's Export Growth," 2008.

[45] Koopman, Robert, Zhi Wang, and Shang-jin Wei, "How Much of Chinese Export Is Really Made in China: Assessing Domestic Value-Added when Processing Trade Pervasive," 2008.

domestic value added is much lower than foreign value added in processing trade.

- First, the authors estimate that the level of foreign content in Chinese exports is close to 50 percent, almost twice as high as what another group of authors found.
- Second, they find interesting heterogeneity across sectors: those sectors that are likely to be labeled as sophisticated or high-skilled, such as computers, electronic devices, and telecommunication equipment, tend to have an especially low share of domestic content.
- Conversely, many sectors that are relatively intensive in low-skilled labor, such as apparel, are likely to exhibit a high share of domestic content.[46]
- Again, this study reveals that China has gone a long way in upgrading, but it has been only partially successful. China has yet to become competitive with industrial countries in high-tech sectors. In other words, China still has a long way to go in climbing the technological ladder. This confirms that China's export structure is still consistent with its comparative advantage, if one looks carefully beneath the surface, and differentiates between domestic and foreign value added.

V. *Lessons Learned from China's Experience*

China has experienced dramatic expansion in its trade and changes in its export composition. In manufacturing, it has moved from labor intensive goods, such as apparel, textiles, footwear, and toys, to more sophisticated manufactured machinery and equipment. What lessons can be learned from China's experience? Are these lessons relevant for Africa?

(1) Liberalizing imports alone is not sufficient to jump-start exports. China's average tariffs were not significantly lowered until the mid-1990s, although effective tariffs were reduced for processing trade and SEZs. The Chinese strategy consists of two equally important

[46] Koopman, Wang, and Wei, "How Much of Chinese Export Is Really Made in China," 2008.

parts: economic system reform and the gradual opening of its markets to the outside world. Neither one is dispensable for achieving stability and dynamic growth. This is relevant in Africa, as imports are liberalized in many countries but exports have yet to expand. There are also many issues related to the development stage the country is in and the country's comparative advantage, requiring country-specific analysis. In general, a country cannot go beyond its development stage or export in sectors where there is no comparative advantage. In addition, regulatory reforms to reduce entry barriers and institutional reforms to provide incentives for the private sector to invest, learn, and produce for the domestic market must be implemented before it is possible to export to neighboring countries.

(2) Import substitution vs. export promotion? It depends on a country's development stage and its comparative advantages. China has experimented with Special Economic Zones and opening to FDI, which allowed the transformation from a heavy-industry and primary goods exporter to labor-intensive manufacturing exporter, consistent with its comparative advantages. Price liberalization and entry and exit played an important role in this process. Many export processing zones (EPZs) have been established in Africa, which is the right step. However, the incentive structure must be in place for the private sector to produce where there is a cost advantage or comparative advantage.

In many African countries, there are large price differentials between imported goods at home and those on the international markets. One example is motorcycles, which offer relatively low-cost transportation and greatly expand the market size for farmers and other producers. While in some African countries, motorcycle use has been minimal due to prohibitively high costs, demand for motorcycles in Nigeria has grown in recent years. A roadside assembly operation can generate income of $9 US per motorcycle, sold for $400 US to $700 US depending on the model. This is where the learning gain could be large for the country's growth and development. A similar example where there is also a large price difference is water pumps. A country may have to go through a period of "import substitution" in order to meet domestic demand and promote private sector growth, before it can be successful in meeting international demand.

Another example is the computer assembly cluster in Nigeria, with firms in Lagos importing components, assembling them, and selling them on the domestic market. Having begun with desktops, the firms now assemble laptops too. Again, it is labor-intensive work with the potential for incremental technological upgrading over time. Now, this computer cluster is able to export to neighboring countries as well.[47]

(3) What African countries should avoid is long-term price distortions. One of the lessons from China's partial and piecemeal reform is that some distortions were kept for too long, including low interest rates and controlled prices for energy, water, electricity, and land. As discussed earlier, a low interest rate has distorted the financial and industrial structure toward more capital-intensive industries. This could also lead to higher income inequality, as discussed above. Low and subsidized prices for energy have encouraged high energy consumption, low-energy efficiency, high emissions, and pollution.

China has paid a high social and environmental cost for its rapid growth, which arguably could have been avoided. This can be seen most clearly in excessive energy consumption and serious environmental degradation and pollution. A recent World Bank study found that the health cost of air and water pollution in China amounts to about 4.3 percent of its GDP. Adding the non-health impacts of pollution, estimated at about 1.5 percent of GDP, brings the total cost of air and water pollution to about 5.8 percent of GDP.[48] Fully aware of this issue, the Chinese government set up targets for saving energy and reducing pollutant emissions in its eleventh Five-Year Plan. This is of vital importance in efforts to change the pattern of economic growth and to increase energy conservation and environmental protection. However, China fell short of the targets set at the beginning last year for cutting energy consumption per unit of GDP by about 4 percent and total discharge of major pollutants by 2 percent. Energy efficiency declined from the 1980s to the 2000s but rebounded after 2003. To make growth more sustainable, China needs to reduce subsidies to energy, water, and land, and rebalance away from heavy and energy-intensive industries toward the service sectors. Fiscal policy can be used to spend more on providing public goods and social services, and encourage the development of green technology.[49]

---

[47] See also Zeng, Douglas Zhihua, ed., "Cluster-based growth in Africa," 2008, on cluster-based growth in Africa.

[48] World Bank, "China: Poverty Assessment," 2007.

[49] See Lopez, Ramon, Vinod Thomas, and Yan Wang, "The Quality of Growth: Fiscal Policies for Better Results," 2008, for details.

VI. *Conclusion*

> Comparative advantage still explains much, perhaps most of world trade. However, both traditional location theory and recent work in economic geography generally assume away inherent differences between locations, and instead explain regional specialization in terms of some kind of external economies.
>
> Paul Krugman, 1995

One does not need to look far in order to understand China's rapid trade integration with the world. As acknowledged by Paul Krugman, due to different stages of development, trade between countries with different endowment structures can be better explained by the Heckscher-Ohlin model. Krugman's own model assumes that the endowment structures are the same across countries (and regions). In a sense, he assumes away the inherent difference in factor endowments. Therefore, in his model trade is determined by (regional) specialization. In fact, most trade occurs between countries at a similar stage of development, which have a similar endowment structure. That is why Krugman's contribution to trade theory won a Nobel Prize. However, his theory is not intended to explain trade between countries with different endowment structures and at different stages of development.

In addition to CAF, what more can China's experience tell us? The power of market-based learning.[50] China has been a proactive and selective learner. The entire thirty years of reform can be rightly described as a process of learning, selective adaptation/acquisition, augmentation, and industrial upgrading. Experimentation, trial and error, incubation, and innovation have played important roles in its success.

Three more takeaways:

First, the learning process that we stress here should be used to help a country specialize in certain industries that are consistent with its comparative advantages so that it can trade not only with countries having different endowment structures, but also with countries having a similar endowment structure. The argument should not be used to support a country that attempts to go against its comparative advantages, determined by its endowment structure, to develop

[50] As described in the simple model in Section II, market-based learning happens when and where there is a cost advantage or comparative advantage. Market is a benchmark for selection.

certain capital-intensive or technology-intensive industries to compete with high-income countries. This is because the specialization in a capital-intensive good that a capital-scarce low-income country can reach, a capital-abundant high-income country can also reach easily. With a similar specialization, the capital-intensive good produced by a high-income country will be cheaper than that produced by a low-income country.

Second, to achieve export competitiveness, it is crucial to liberalize prices, and reduce barriers to entry and exit in most sectors, so that private sector firms can select the right subsector and products where they have true comparative advantage. Providing subsides to certain export industries would make them nonviable and vulnerable to shocks in the external environment. Learning would happen when and where the expected rate of return is high and uncertainty in the macro environment is low. Consistent with the theory of creative destruction,[51] firms armed with new products and services will drive out firms with obsolete products, and hence gain from learning and innovation. This is the true driver of industrial upgrading.

Third, the pace of reforms, adaptation, and innovation should be commensurate with a country's development stage and regulatory capacity. China certainly did not do everything right during the trials and experimentations of the past thirty years of reforms. It paid dearly in high "tuition." But, as a good student, China has been learning, selectively, from the experiences of other developed and developing countries—learning well and fast. Through learning-by-doing, China is catching up at a pace that is consistent with its institutional capacity and national objectives. It is noteworthy that the pace of reforms has seldom been allowed to go beyond institutional and regulatory capacity. In other words, China has been engaging in experiments that are controllable—one example is China's cautious attitude toward capital account liberalization and financial innovations including securitization (e.g. the initiate-and-distribute model in mortgage backed securities). The government has been reluctant to go along with a policy reform that is too complex to be able to be fully understood and controlled by regulators. With the benefit of hindsight, it is apparent that this cautious attitude toward certain complex reforms/financial

[51] Schumpeter, Joseph A., *Capitalism, Socialism, and Democracy*, 1976.

instruments (such as Credit Default Swaps, CDS and Collateralized Debt Obligations, CDOs) is wise and prudent.

Looking forward, China is now better positioned than it was before to meet complex development challenges by drawing on its own experience as well as the experience of others, and by continuing to combine openness with institutional reform and capacity building. Recently, there are signs of an accelerating pace of reform: in announcing the $586 billion US stimulus package for growth, policymakers have shown a strong determination to reform fiscal policies to correct the remaining price distortions, including subsidies for water, fuel, and other natural resources. It is thus transforming fiscal policies from aiming for industrialization to focusing on public services in order to build a people-centered and harmonious society. Many new reform measures to make the growth pattern more equitable and more sustainable have been announced. It is for this reason that researchers are confident that over time, the strong commitment to continuous openness and institutional reforms will allow China to make greater progress towards its own national objectives as well as to influence others positively, most notably through South-South learning and exchange of experiences.

Bibliography

Allen, Qian, Qian, and Zhao. "Review of China's Financial System and Initiatives for the Future," Wharton Financial Institutions Center Working Paper No. 08–28 (2008). Available at SSRN: http://ssrn.com/abstract=1185877.

Aghion, Philippe and Peter Howitt. "A Model of growth through Creative Destruction." *Econometrica* Vol. 20, No. 2 (1992): 323–351.

Amiti, Mary and Caroline Freund. "An Anatomy of China's Export Growth." In *China's Growing Role in World Trade*, edited by Robert Feenstra and Shang-Jin Wei. Cambridge, Massachusetts: National Bureau of Economic Research, 2008.

Aziz, Jahangir, and Li Cui. "Explaining China's Low Consumption: The Neglected Role of Household Income." IMF Working Paper No. 07/181 (2007).

Aziz, Jahangir and Steven Dunaway. "China's Rebalancing Act," *IMF F&D* Vol. 44, No. 3 (2007).

Bergsten, C. Fred, Bates Gill, Nicholas R. Lardy, and Derek Mitchell. *China: The Balance Sheet—What the World Needs to Know Now about the Emerging Superpower.* Washington DC: The Center for Strategic and International Studies and the Institute for International Economics, 2006.

Bhattasali, Deepak, Shantong Li and Will Martin. *China and the WTO: Accession, Policy Reform, and Poverty Reduction Strategies.* Washington DC: World Bank and Oxford University Press, 2004.

Cao, Yuanzheng, Yingyi Qian, and Barry R. Weingast. "From Federalism, Chinese Style, to Privatization, Chinese Style." *Economics of Transition* Vol. 7, No. 1 (1999): 103–31.

Chen, Shaohua and Martin Ravallion. "China is Poorer than we Thought, But No Less Successful in the Fight against Poverty." World Bank Policy Research Working Paper No. 4621 (2008).

Chen, Kuan et al. "Productivity change in Chinese industry: 1953–1985." *Journal of Comparative Economics* Vol. 12, No. 4 (1988): 570–591.

Cui, Li. "China's Growing External Dependence." *IMF F&D* No. 44, Vol. 3 (2007).

Dollar, David. "Economic Reform and Allocative Efficiency in China's State-Owned Industry." UCLA Department of Economics Working Paper No. 489 (1990).

——. "Lessons from China for Africa." World Bank Policy Research Working Paper No. 4531 (2008).

Fan, S. "Effects of technological change and institutional reform on production growth in Chinese agriculture." *American Journal of Agricultural Economics* No. 73 (1991): 266–275.

Ferrantino, Michael et al. "Classification of Trade in Advanced Technology Products and its Statistics Reconciliation: The Case of China and the United States." Brookings-Tsinghua Center for Public Policy Working Paper Series No. 20070907EN (2007).

Gordon, Roger H. and Wei Li. "The change in productivity of Chinese state enterprises, 1983–1987." *Journal of Productivity Analysis* Vol. 6, No. 1 (1995).

Groves, T. et al. "Autonomy and incentives in Chinese state enterprises." *The Quarterly Journal of Economics* Vol. 109, (Feb. 1994).

He, Jianwu and Louis Kuijs. "Rebalancing China's Economy—Modeling a Policy Package." The World Bank China Research Paper No. 7 (2007).

Heckscher, Eli. "The Effect of Foreign Trade on the Distribution of Income." In *Heckscher-Ohlin Trade Theory*, by Eli Heckscher. Cambridge, MA: The MIT Press, 1991.

Jefferson, G.H., T.G. Rawski, and Y. Zheng. "Growth, Efficiency, and Convergence in China's State and Collective Industry." *Economic Development and Cultural Change* (January, 1992).

Kaufmann, Daniel, and Yan Wang. "The Impact of Macroeconomic Policies on Project Performance in the Social Sectors: A Framework of Analysis and Evidence." *World Development* Vol. 23, No. 4 (May 1995): 751–65. Originally published by the World Bank, WPS #939 (July, 1992).

Koopman, Robert, Zhi Wang, and Shang-jin Wei. "How Much of Chinese Export Is Really Made in China: Assessing Domestic Value-Added when Processing Trade Pervasive." NBER Working Paper No. 14109 (2008).

Lardy, Nicholas R. *Integrating China into the Global Economy*, Brookings Institute Press, Washington DC, 2002.

——. *Foreign trade and economic reform in China, 1978 1990*, Cambridge: Cambridge University Press, 1992.

Li, Wei. "The Impact of Economic Reform on the Performance of Chinese State Enterprises: 1980–1989." *Journal of Political Economy* Vol. 105, No. 5 (1997): 1080–1106.

Lin, Justin Yifu 林毅夫. "The Household Responsibility System in China's Agricultural Reform: A Theoretical and Empirical Study." *Economic Development and Cultural Change* Vol. 36, No. 3 (Supplement, April 1988): S199–S224.

——. "Rebalancing equity and efficiency for equitable and sustainable growth." In *China: Growth, the Environment and Climate Change*, edited by Song, L., W.T. Woo, and R. Garnaut. Asia Pacific Press, the Brookings Institution Press, and Social Sciences Academic Press, 2008.

——. "Rural Reforms and Agricultural Growth in China." *American Economic Review* Vol. 82, No. 1 (March 1992): 34–51.

Lin, Justin Yifu 林毅夫, Cai Fang 蔡昉, and Li Zhou 李周. "The Lessons of China's Transition to a Market Economy." *Cato Journal* Vol 16, No. 2 (fall 1996): 201–31.

Lin, Justin Yifu 林毅夫 Cai Fang 蔡昉 and Li Zhou 李周. "Competition, Policy Burdens, and the State-owned Enterprise Reform." *American Economic Review: Papers and Proceedings* Vol. 88, No. 2 (May 1999): 422–7.

Lin, Justin Yifu 林毅夫 and Guofu Tan. "Policy Burdens, Accountability, and the Soft Budget Constraint." *American Economic Review: Papers and Proceedings* Vol. 89, No. 2 (May 1999): pp. 426–31.

Lin, Justin Yifu 林毅夫, Cai Fang 蔡昉, and Li Zhou 李周. *State-owned Enterprise Reform in China*. Hong Kong: The Chinese University Press, 2001.

Lin, Justin Yifu 林毅夫, Cai Fang 蔡昉, and Li Zhou 李周. *China's Miracle: Development Strategy and Economic Reform*, (revised edition). Hong Kong: Chinese University Press, 2003. First published in English in Hong Kong: The Chinese University of Hong Kong Press, 1996. Originally published in Chinese in Shanghai: Shanghai Sanlian Press, 1994.

Lin, Justin Yifu 林毅夫. "Development and Transition: Idea, Strategy, and Viability." Marshall Lectures, Cambridge University, London, 2007.

Lopez, Ramon, Vinod Thomas, and Yan Wang. "The Quality of Growth: Fiscal Policies for Better Results". IEG working paper, September (2008).

Maddison, Angus. "Dynamics of Development in the New China" and "Problems and Prospects: The Outlook for China and the World Economy, 2003–2030." In *Chinese Economic Performance in the Long Run*, Chapters 3 and 4. OECD Development Center Studies, 2007.

McKinnon, Ronald I. "Taxation, Money and Credit in the Transition from Central Planning." In *From Centrally Planned to Market Economies: The Asian Approach* (Vol. 1), edited by Pradumna B. Rana, 35–72. Hong Kong: Oxford University Press, 1995.

McKinsey Global Institute. "Putting China's Capital to Work: the value of financial system reform." McKinsey & Company, 2006.

McMillan, J., J. Whalley, and L. Zhu. "The Impact of China's Economic Reforms on Agricultural Productivity Growth." *Journal of Political Economy* Vol. 97, No. 4 (August 1989): 781–807.

Melitz, Marc J. "The Impact of Trade on Intra-industry Reallocations and Aggregate Industry Productivity." *Econometrica* Vol. 71, No. 6 (2003): 1695–1725.

Ministry of Commerce of the PRC website: http://english.mofcom.gov.cn/

Murphy, Kevin, Andrei Schleifer, and Robert Vishny. "The Transition to a Market Economy: Pitfall of Partial Reform." *Quarterly Journal of Economics* Vol. 107, No. 3 (August 1992): 889–906.

National Bureau of Statistics. *China Labor Statistical Yearbook*. China Statistics Press, Various Years.

——. *Zhongguo tongji nianjian* 中国统计年鉴 [*China Statistical Yearbooks*]. China Statistics Press, Various Years.

Nolan, Peter. "Political Economy and the Reform of Stalinism: The Chinese Puzzle." In *The Transformation of the Communist Economies*, edited by Ha-Joon Chang and Peter Nolan. London: Macmillan, 1995.

Ohlin, Bert. "Interregional and International Trade." *Harvard Economic Studies* No. 39 (1967).

People's Daily (Overseas edition), November 24, 2008: 8.

——, November 28, 2008: 6.

Prasad, E. and S.J. Wei. "The Chinese Approach to Capital Inflows: Patterns and Possible Explanations." IMF Working Paper WP/05/79, Washington DC: International Monetary Fund, 2005.

Qian, Yingyi. "The process of China's market transition, 1978–1998: the evolutionary, historical and comparative perspectives." *Journal of Institutional & Theoretical Economics* Vol. 156, No. 1 (2000): 151–171.

Qian, Yingyi and Barry R. Weingast. "Federalism as a Commitment to Market Incentives." *Journal of Economic Perspectives* Vol. 11, No. 4 (Fall 1997): 83–92.

Qian, Yingyi and Chenggan Xu. "Why China's Economic Reforms Differ: The M-Form Hierarchy and Entry/Expansion of the Non-state Sector." *The Economics of Transition* Vol. 1, No. 2 (June 1993): 135–70.

Ravallion, Martin. *Are There Lessons for Africa from China's Success against Poverty?* World Bank Policy Research Working Paper No. 4463 (2008).
Ravallion, Martin and Shaohua Chen. "China's (uneven) Progress against Poverty." *Journal of Development Economics* 82 (2007): 1–42.
Ravallion, Martin. *Geographic Inequity in a Decentralized Anti-Poverty Program: a Case Study of China*. World Bank Policy Research Working Paper No. WPS 4303 (2007).
Rodrik, Dani. "What's so Special About China's Exports?" NBER Working Paper No. 11947, Cambridge, Massachusetts: National Bureau of Economic Research, 2006.
Sachs, Jeffrey D. and Wing Thye Woo. "China's Economic Growth after WTO Membership." *Journal of Chinese Economics and Business Studies*, Vol. 1, No. 1(2003): 1–31.
Schott, Peter K. "The Relative Sophistication of China's Exports." *Economic Policy*, January (2008): 5–49.
Schumpeter, Joseph A. *Capitalism, Socialism, and Democracy*. New York: Harper and Brothers, 1976. Originally published in 1942.
Wang, Yan. "Development as a process of Learning and Innovation: Lessons from China." In *Reducing Poverty on a Global Scale: Findings from the Shanghai Global Learning Initiative*, edited by Moreno-Dodson, Chapter 3. Washington DC: World Bank Publication, 2005.
Wang, Yan and Yudong Yao. "Sources of China's Economic Growth 1952–1999: Incorporating Human Capital Accumulation." *China Economic Review* Vol. 14, No. 1 (2003): 32–52.
Wen, Guanzhong James. "Total Factor Productivity Change in China's Farming Sector: 1952–1989." *Economic Development and Cultural Change* Vol. 42, No. 1 (October 1993): pp. 1–41.
World Bank. "Global Economic Prospects 2009." World Bank, December 2008.
——. "China: Poverty Assessment." 2007.
——. "China: Long-term Issues and Options." Paper published for the World Bank. Oxford: Oxford University Press, 1985.
——. "China: Economic Structure in International Perspective," Published as an annex to "China: Long Term Issues and Options." Washington, D.C.: the World Bank, 1985.
Zeng, Douglas Zhihua, ed. "Cluster-based growth in Africa." World Bank, 2008.
Zhao, Longyue and Yan Wang. "Trade Remedies and Non-market Economies: Economic Implications of the US First Countervailing Duty Case on China." World Bank Policy Research Working Paper No. 4560 (2008).
Zou, G. "Modelling the Enterprise Behavior under the Two-tier Plan/Market System in the PRC." World Bank, 1993.

CHAPTER SEVEN

BEYOND THE EAST ASIAN MIRACLE: LOOKING BACK AND FUTURE PROSPECTS FOR CHINA'S ECONOMIC GROWTH MODEL

Wu Jinglian and Fan Shitao

After analyzing empirical statistics from major industrial countries in Western Europe and North America during the middle of the 20th century, Simon Kuznets, a Nobel Prize laureate in economics, pointed out that rapid economic growth is truly a modern phenomenon. He divided economic growth into two stages, namely "early-stage economic growth" and "modern economic growth." Between the first Industrial Revolution in the late 18th century and the second Industrial Revolution in the late 19th century, leading industrial countries all devoted large amounts of resources to capital-intensive machine building, as well as other heavy industries, which served as the foundations to industrialization. As manual labor was gradually replaced by machine processing and natural resources were no longer crucial to economic growth, the economies of this period grew rapidly. This type of growth is considered to be of the "early-stage economic growth model." However, since the second Industrial Revolution in the late 19th century, the science-related development of modern technology and increased production efficiency, rather than capital accumulation, has been the major impetus for economic growth. This type of economic growth is of the "modern economic growth model." Kuznets asserted that economic growth relies on the advancement of technology and corresponding adjustments to the economic system and ideologies.[1] The growth models developed by Kuznets were commonly accepted as truth by contemporary economic scholars and since have been widely cited.[2] Another Nobel Prize winner, Robert Solow,

[1] Kuznets, Simon, *The Economic Growth of Nations*, 1971.

[2] From its earliest editions all the way to the eighteenth, Paul A. Samuelson has devoted a chapter of his pioneering textbook *Economics* to "growth theory," writing that the economic growth of modern industrialized nations can be divided into three

developed the "neo-classical exogenous growth model." Based on quantitative analysis, he pointed out that economic growth in the United States mainly relies on technical improvement and higher efficiency, instead of factor investment. This chapter uses the ideas of extensive and intensive growth, used widely in socialist countries, to analyze Kuznets' models of early and modern economic growth.

Within this framework, we shall examine China's sustained and rapid development over the past thirty years. From 1978 to 2007, the average growth rate of GDP was as high as 10 percent, growing by a total of over seventeen fold; in 2007, the average annual disposable income of urban residents and the average annual net income of rural residents had increased from 343 yuan and 134 yuan in 1978 to 13,786 yuan and 4,140 yuan respectively. Meanwhile, China's economic growth model has undergone changes since the reform and opening, but these changes have been temporary and the nature of China's economic growth, boosted by factor infusion into the economy, especially capital, has remained unchanged. Since the mid-1990s, China's export-oriented economic policy has been an important reason behind its extensive economic growth, but these authors believe that this model is not sustainable. In order to maintain the rapid growth of the Chinese economy, we must accelerate the transformation from extensive growth to intensive growth and from the early growth model to the modern growth model. To achieve this transformation, China must accelerate the improvement of the market economy, create economic policy that steps beyond the growth pattern that formally supported the "East Asian miracle," change its export-oriented strategies and policies, reduce governmental intervention through industrial policy and "administrative guidance," maintain economic stability, and stimulate economic entities to actively participate in the process of transition.

---

stages: the "pre-development stage;" "early-stage economic growth;" and "modern economic growth" (refer to Hayami Yujiro, *Development Economics—From Poverty to the Wealth of Nations*, 1998). In *National Competitiveness*, Michel E. Porter, a leading authority on competitive strategy, divides national competitiveness into four stages: (1) the factor-driven stage, in which the competitive advantage arises from basic factors of production, such as cheap labor and natural resources; (2) the investment-driven stage, in which improvements in competitiveness rely mainly on large-scale investment in technologies and advanced machines; (3) the innovation-driven stage, in which companies

I. *China's Economic Growth Model before Reform and Opening*

China's pre-reform economic growth model was based on that of the Soviet Union. From the first Five Year Plan (1928–1932) until the 1950s, the Soviet Union regarded the investment-driven growth model as the theoretical foundation of economic planning. When summarizing the Soviet Union's economic development, Stalin asserted categorically that the idea of "[capital] accumulation being the only way to expand reproduction" was one of the six "fundamentals" in Karl Marx's "theory of reproduction."[3] When it came to choosing an investment model, Stalin was partial to heavy industry, seeing the preferential growth of heavy industry as an essential part of "socialist industrialization." Besides bringing into play large investments from the state, planning authorities also deliberately set lower prices for production factors and arranged for compulsory savings targeted towards expanding heavy industry. As a result, the Soviet economy experienced a period of astonishingly rapid growth, bringing Khrushchev to boast that his country would out-do the United States and bury capitalism through "peaceful economic competition." To achieve this goal, in 1959 the Soviet Communist Party Congress approved an ambitious plan, pledging to surpass the United States within 15 years.

In its first Five Year Plan (1953–1957), China accepted the validity of the Soviet Union's "socialist industrialization" policy of "giving priority to heavy industry." Along this line, Mao Zedong himself drafted a programmatic document, the *Outline for Study and Promotion of the General Line for the Transition Period* (过渡时期总路线学习和宣传提纲), saying that the task of the Party and the Chinese people, after the

improve their competitiveness through continuous innovation in products, processing technology, marketing, etc.; (4) the wealth-driven stage, in which economic growth is driven mainly by the pursuit of comprehensive development and pursuit of a higher quality of life. The first three stages in Porter's theory are quite similar to those in Samuelson's. (Porter, Michael E., *National Competitiveness*, 1990.)

[3] In "Economic Problems of Socialism in the USSR," Stalin condensed Karl Marx's "theory of reproduction" into six fundamentals: "the division of social production into the production of means of production and the production of means of consumption; the relatively greater increase of production of means of production in reproduction on an extended scale; the correlation between Departments I and II; surplus product as the sole source of accumulation; the formation and designation of social funds; accumulation as the sole source of reproduction on an extended scale." Refer to: Stalin, Joseph, "Economic Problems of Socialism in the USSR" (Chinese Version), 1979.

success of the revolution, was to "achieve socialist industrialization, so that China can rely on its own advanced heavy industry to produce industrial equipment and so that modern industry can lead the entire economy, gaining overwhelming predominance over agriculture, making socialist industry the only industry in China." He also specially emphasized that "heavy industry is the linchpin of the nation's socialist industrialization."[4] Around the same time, in his "Ten Major Relationships" (论十大关系), Mao Zedong showed some signs of rethinking this strategy, recognizing that over-development of heavy industry impaired agriculture and light industry, and that striking a balance between these three sectors was necessary. Shortly after, however, the Great Leap Forward retained the emphasis on heavy industry, putting forth the slogan "steel is the basis" (以钢为纲) and leading to a 30 percent increase in the accumulation rate, with most investment at the time emphasizing heavy industry. In the end, the Great Leap Forward led to economic disaster and the loss of tens of millions of lives. In 1961 and 1962, industrial production declined by 38.2 percent and 16.6 percent respectively; more specifically, light industry declined by 21.6 percent and 8.4 percent, while heavy industry dropped by 46.6 and 22.6 percent respectively. After the adjustments during 1961–1963, the accumulation rate fell below 20 percent; by 1965, although the gross output value of industry and agriculture in 1965 exceeded the corresponding figure in 1957, people's standard of living was still lower than it was in 1957.[5] More importantly, the flawed guidelines for economic development as well as the strategy for industrialization remained unchanged. Thus the economic growth model relying heavily on resources, factor accumulation, and government investment (especially in heavy industry) determined economic policy from the period from the first Five Year Plan (1953–1957) to the end of the Cultural Revolution (as shown in Table 7.1). Even after the Gang

---

[4] Publicity Department of the CCP Central Committee, "Wei dongyuan yiqie lilian ba woguo jianshe chengwei yige weida de shehui zhuyi guojia er douzheng—guanyu dang zai guodu shiqi zongluxian de xuexi he xuanchuan tigang 为动员一切力量把我国建设成为一个伟大的社会主义国家而斗争—关于党在过渡时期总路线的学习和宣传提纲 [Mobilize All Possible Forces and Strive to Transform China into a Great Socialist Country—Outline for Study and Promotion of the General Line for the Transition Period]," 1957.

[5] Xue Muqiao 薛暮桥, "Tiaozheng guomin jingji, gaohao zonghe pingheng 调整国民经济, 搞好综合平衡 [Adjust the Economy, Achieve a Comprehensive Balance]," 1981.

of Four was arrested in October, 1976, and the Cultural Revolution put to an end, government leaders in charge of managing the economy still refused to criticize the Great Leap Forward, instead insisting on continued support for the "three red flags,"[6] which included the Great Leap Forward. Leaders at the time believed that "another opportunity for a leap was nigh" and attempted to "leap forward with the help of imported equipment."[7] Thus, as inferred by Zou Zhizhuang, the Total Factor Productivity (TFP) did not see any growth from 1952 to 1978.[8]

Table 7.1. Distribution of China's Investment in Infrastructure

	1953–57	1958–62	1963–65	1966–70	1971–75	1976–80
Agriculture	7.1	11.3	17.7	10.7	9.8	10.5
Industry	42.5	60.4	49.8	55.5	55.4	52.6
Heavy Industry	36.1	54.0	45.9	51.1	49.6	45.9
Light Industry	6.4	6.4	3.9	4.4	5.8	6.7
Geological Exploration	2.4	1.2	0.4	0.5	0.7	1.3
Construction Industry	3.7	1.3	2.1	1.8	1.6	1.8
Transportation, Postal Services, Telecommunications	15.3	13.5	12.7	15.4	18.0	12.9
Commerce	3.6	2.0	2.5	2.1	2.9	3.7
Science, Education, Public Health	7.6	3.8	5.7	2.8	3.1	5.4
Urban Public Facilities	2.5	2.3	2.9	1.8	1.9	4.1
Others	15.3	4.2	6.2	9.4	6.6	7.7

Source: Maruyama, Nobuo. *Industrialization and Technological Development in China*, 1992: 59, table 2–7.

In their book, Justin Yifu Lin, Cai Fang, and Li Zhou call the strategy of GDP growth driven by a large government investment the "overtaking strategy." In their work, they root out and analyze the problems created by this strategy, including, for instance, the distortion of industrial structure, low economic performance, and shrinking public

[6] "Red Flags" refers to a series of policies put into effect in 1958, which included calls to continue pursuing the goals of the "Great Leap Forward, the People's Communes, and making every effort to build socialism with more results, higher speed, better quality, and lower costs."

[7] Xue Muqiao, "Adjust the Economy, Achieve a Comprehensive Balance," 1981.

[8] Chow, Gregory C., "Capital Formation and Economic Growth in China," 1993; Zou Zhizhuang 邹至庄. *Zhongguo jingji zhuanxing* 中国经济转型 [*China's Economic Transformation*], 2005.

welfare.[9] But, they also point out that from 1953 to 1978—while maintaining a high savings and investment rate (the average accumulation rate was 29.5 percent)—China still managed to achieve 8.2 percent annual growth in the total output of industry and agriculture (average annual growth rate of GDP was 6 percent) (As shown in Table 7.2).

Table 7.2. Economic Growth Index from 1952 to 1978 Unit: (%)

	Social Total Output Value	gross output value of industry and agriculture	GDP	National Income	Accumulation Rate
First Five Year Plan Period	11.3	10.9	9.1	8.9	24.2
Second Five Year Plan Period	–0.4	0.6	–2.2	–3.1	30.8
1963–1965	15.5	15.7	14.9	14.7	22.7
Third Five Year Plan Period	9.3	9.6	6.9	8.3	26.3
Fourth Five Year Plan Period	7.3	7.8	5.5	5.5	33.0
1976–1978	8.1	8.0	5.8	5.6	33.5
1953–1978	7.9	8.2	6.0	6.0	29.5

Note: the growth rates are calculated based on price comparison; the accumulation rates are calculated based on current prices.
Source: National Bureau of Statistics, *Zhongguo Tongji Nianjian* 中国统计年鉴 [*China Statistical Yearbook*], Various Years; Lin, Cai, and Li, *The China miracle: development strategy and economic reform*, 2003: 69.

However, decades of growth in the output values of industry and agriculture neither modernized the Chinese economy nor lifted the country above the poverty line. Quite the contrary, the four "Asian Dragons," who's economies started developing almost at the same time as China, left China far behind. Lin, Cai, and Li attribute China's relative backwardness to the fact that the remarkable growth rate of the total output value does not reflect real economic growth, and more importantly, to China's abnormal industrial structure and low economic efficiency brought by its chosen path for industrialization.

[9] Lin, Justin Yifu 林毅夫, Cai Fang 蔡昉, and Li Zhou 李周, *Zhongguo de qiji: Fazhan zhanlüe yu jingji gaige* 中国的奇迹: 发展战略与经济改革 [*The China miracle: development strategy and economic reform*], 2003: 69.

In fact, Karl Marx once carried out a thorough analysis of economic growth models based on the experiences of leading industrial countries. He asserted that as the capital-labor ratio (called the "organic composition of capital" in Marxian theory) rose due to investment-driven economic growth, the proportion of variable capital (capital that is used to pay salaries) in gross capital would begin to decline, thus inevitably bringing about two phenomena: the drop in average profit margin and the increase of excess population (i.e. the unemployed). Marx termed these two phenomena as "laws" and further stated that the drop in margins would cause capital concentration and monopolization whilst the rise in excess population would bring down the proportion of labors' income as a portion of national income and impoverish the proletariat.[10] Based on this analysis, in the chapter entitled "Historical Tendency of Capitalist Accumulation" of *Capital*, Volume I, Marx asserted that "the demise of capitalism is nigh."[11] Unfortunately, in the late 19th century, Western countries successfully transformed their investment-driven growth models to the technology and productivity-driven model. Meanwhile, Stalin established the "socialist path of industrialization," which was equivalent to the early development model already abandoned by Western capitalist countries. If one is to acknowledge that, beginning in the late 1960s, the Soviet growth model struggled with declining marginal returns and a declining growth rate, then one must also see that during the 1970s, China's economy, even its whole society—which after adopting the Soviet industrialization model and dealing with the failure of the Great Leap Forward went on to begin the Cultural Revolution— was taken to the brink of utter disaster.

II. *Changes to the Growth Model after the Reform and Opening*

With the arrest of the Gang of Four in October, 1976, the Cultural Revolution came to the end. However, this did not mean the outmoded economic growth model had been changed. On the contrary, the "disharmony between heavy industry, light industry, and agriculture" and the "imbalance between accumulation and consumption" deteriorated

---

[10] Marx, Karl. *Capital, Vol. I.* (Chinese Version), 1975.
[11] Marx, Karl. *Capital, Vol. I.*, 1975.

further in 1977–1978 during the Great Leap Forward with Overseas Help (洋跃进). On August 14, 1979, Chen Yun and Li Xiannian wrote to the Chinese Communist Party (CCP) Central Committee, suggesting that the Party take stringent measures to redress imbalances in the economy within two or three years. During the meeting of the Politburo of the CCP Central Committee (March 21–23, 1979) and the Working Conference of the CCP Central Committee (April 5–28 of the same year), it was decided to redress China's economy within three years; the meetings also marked the official release of the "Eight-character policy" (八字方针): adjustment, reform, rectification, and improvement (调整、改革、整顿、提高). The policy focused on cutting down investment on infrastructure, reviving agriculture, revitalizing light industry, and developing commerce. In other words, the policy aimed to heal the "economic wounds" caused by the extensive growth model and the mass input of resources. Furthermore, as required by the "Eight-character policy," the Party and government revised the 1979 National Economic Plan, slashing infrastructure investment by 26 percent and reducing the number of large-scale projects from 1,187 to 912.

However, owing to the widespread and deep-rooted influence of the traditional growth model—and the lack of market discipline caused by the hasty withdrawal of administrative restrictions on state-owned enterprises during the "reform of enterprise autonomy" in the late 1970s—before long, a dramatic upsurge in investment aiming to accelerate economic growth occurred. Thus, contrary to the government's expectations, the investment in infrastructure increased in 1980, and the demand for steel, cement, and timber far exceeded supply, leading to even worse imbalances in the national economy (refer to Figure 7.1).

At the Working Conference of the CCP Central Committee, which took place from December 16 to December 25 in 1980, it was decided to "further rectify the national economy," strengthen the concentration of political power, and ensure the "sufficient reduction" of investment. To achieve these objectives, the Party and government were even willing to temporarily sacrifice the growth rate of industry, especially heavy industry. In 1981, the GDP growth rate fell to 5.2 percent while the primary, secondary, and tertiary industries saw growth rates of 7.0, 1.9, and 10.4 percent respectively. In 1982, the GDP growth rate rebounded to 9.1 percent. That same year, primary, secondary, and tertiary industries grew by 11.5, 5.6, and 13.0 percent respectively. By 1983, after the "adjustment" and "readjustment" of the national

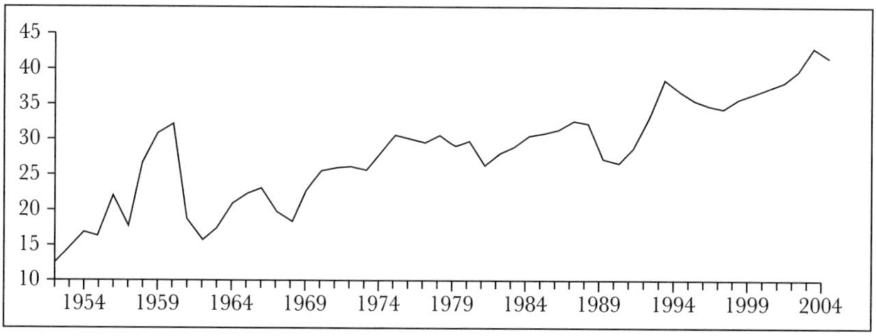

Source: China Economic Information Network, "Zhongjing wang tongji shujuku 中经网统计数据库 [China Economic Information Network Statistics Database]."

Figure 7.1. China's Investment Rates from 1952 to 1986 (%).

economy, the abnormal structure of the Chinese economy had been corrected to some degree.

However, both the "adjustment" of national economy in 1979 and the "readjustment" in 1981 used administrative means to deal with the negative effects of the extensive growth model, without touching on the fundamental reasons behind these effects, i.e. the command economic system and the growth model driven by resource input (the so-called Socialist industrialization path).

It is noteworthy that the Party still did not have clear criteria for determining the right path, especially in terms of creating policy. Shortly after the beginning of the "readjustment of national economy" in early 1981, a theorist who worked with the development of ideology began to insist that Xue Muqiao's statement that "the first Five Year Plan made a mistake in giving priority to heavy industry" was "an erroneous deviation" in ideology and theory. He went on to deliver a speech entitled "The Fundamentals of Marx's Reproduction Theory Must be Upheld" (马克思主义再生产理论的基本原理必须坚持), arguing that Stalin's "Socialist Path to Industrialization" and the policy of emphasizing the development of heavy industry were "fundamentals to Marx's theory of reproduction" and must be adhered to. This speech was transcribed and printed serially over three issues of Red Flag, a magazine featuring writings on Communist theory released by the CCP Central Committee. Thus, the speech became very influential at the time.[12]

[12] Deng Liqun 邓力群. *Shier ge chunqiu* 十二个春秋 [*Twelve Years*], 2006.

As a result, driven by the traditional growth model, the investment rate began to rise once again after 1984 and the negative effects of the model once again began to emerge. Between 1985 and 1992, there were a number of economic fluctuations caused by economic overheating and poor macro-control. Liu Zunyi (Lawrence J. Lau) and others have carried out detailed analysis of the sources of growth during this period. Boosted by the input of resources and production factors, the growth model remained unchanged even after the beginning of the reform and opening.

Based on a quantitative study of the TFP in East Asian economies by Lawrence J. Lau and Alwyn Young, one can draw the conclusion that the rapid economic growth in East Asian nations and territories, with the exception of Japan, can almost completely be attributed to increased investment rather than increased productivity. Paul Krugman summarized the results of Lau and Young's research in his article "The Myth of Asia's Miracle," which was published in *Foreign Affairs* in 1994; he concluded that, due to the diminishing marginal returns of investment resulting from insufficient improvement in productivity, the economic growth in East Asia would, sooner or later, grind to a halt. Furthermore, by comparing the growth of East Asia and the Soviet Union, Krugman pointed out that, just like the Soviet Union's prosperity in the 1950s and 1960s, the East Asian miracle was the result of "sweat" instead of "inspiration." He argued that the East Asian "Miracle" is, in fact, a misnomer. He further predicted that because the growth of productivity lagged far behind economic growth, East Asian economies would see diminishing returns and a rise in the incremental capital output ratio (ICOR),[13] similar to the Soviet Union. East Asian countries refuted Krugman's prediction, but soon after, the East Asian financial crisis broke out. Since then, the crisis-stricken countries have adjusted their economic structure in order to resume rapid growth through innovation and increased productivity.

Although in the beginning China was not counted as one of the "miracles" in East Asia,[14] Lawrence Lau still applied his research

[13] ICOR refers to the ratio of investment to growth which equals to RMB 1. The higher the ICOR, the lower the productivity of capital.

[14] The World Bank's report The East Asian Miracle in 1993 only analyzed the economic growth in Hong Kong, Indonesia, Japan, South Korea, Malaysia, Singapore, Taiwan (China), and Thailand, because "China's economic performance is far behind that of the other eight Asian economies." Refer to World Bank, "An East Asian Renaissance: Ideas for Economic Growth," 2007.

methods to China. He found the contribution of three key factors to China's economic growth—capital, labor, and technical progress—were 92.2 percent, 9.2 percent, and −1.4 percent respectively; in contrast, the corresponding figures for Singapore were 60 percent, 20.9 percent, and 19.1 percent; Japan's were 62.9 percent, 4.7 percent, and 32.4 percent; and those of the United States were 32.95 percent, 26.2 percent, and 40.9 percent. It is apparent that China's economic growth is driven mainly by investment, especially investment in physical assets such as buildings, equipment, and infrastructure. Thus, China's growth has relied on "sweat" rather than "brains," i.e. investment rather than technical progress and increased TFP. If the impact of the TFP on economic growth is ignored, the growth in physical assets still accounts for 80 percent of the observable economic growth.[15]

Why does this reliance on the input of resources and production factors remain a basic characteristic of the Chinese growth model? Now that market-oriented reforms have brought about a dramatic increase in productivity, why is the impact of this productivity on China's economic growth imperceptible?

One reason is that the analysis of a country's growth model is conducted at the level of the aggregate economy, through research on overall factors causing efficiency and inefficiency. When the improvements in efficiency are not enough to counteract the impact of inefficient factors, the effect of these improvements will not be reflected in the efficiency analysis. Although the reform of ownership rights, the migration of surplus labor, and price reform have brought exciting changes to China, we must nonetheless keep an eye on the inefficient factors ubiquitous in the Chinese economy. These factors counteract the effects of improved efficiency, leading to the overall lack of measurable improvement in efficiency and technical progress in the economy. If there is reliable evidence of improvements in efficiency, then it can be confirmed that the continued influence of inefficient factors is the reason why the growth model has not fundamentally changed.[16]

---

[15] Liu Zunyi 刘鐏义, "Dongya jingji zengzhang de yuanquan yu zhanwang 东亚经济增长的源泉与展望 [The Source of and Future of East Asian Economic Growth]," 1997.

[16] Wu Jinglian 吴敬琏 and Huang Shaoqing 黄少卿, "Chuangxin haishi xunzu—Zhongguo zhuanxingqi zhidu huanjing yu qiyejia xingwei 创新还是寻租—中国转型期制度环境与企业家行为 Innovation or Rent-seeking: Institutional Environment and Entrepreneurs' Behaviors in China during the Transition Period," 2007.

The continued and pervasive presence of these inefficient factors is closely associated with the distinctive manner of China's reform.

Prior to the economic reforms, the entire country was organized as a "national syndicate,"[17] where all economic resources were in the government's hands and the talented could not use their abilities to receive maximum benefits unless they entered the government hierarchy and held relatively high ranks. In order to change this situation, reform before 1994 consisted of adopting a series of policies aiming to bring market functions into full play while still under the control of the government. The intentions of this reform became evident in the decentralization of administrative power and the "double-track pricing system." The "decentralization" was initiated in 1980, when the central government began to reform its system of "total control over revenue and expenditure." The reforms consisted of allocating budgetary revenue—in accordance with a predefined scheme—between the central and primary-level local governments (except for those of Beijing, Tianjin, and Shanghai). This allocation of revenue enabled local governments to handle some of their own financial affairs. The "double-track pricing system" emerged in the late 1970s; at the time, reforms allowing the "expansion of enterprise autonomy" and the "decentralization of power and transfer of profits" gave state-owned enterprises a degree of autonomy in determining their production zand sales. When these enterprises' excess production over the planned amount was sold through the "negotiated price" system, the "second track" of distribution and price determination—through the market—was born. In 1985, the "double-track" system was formally recognized by the government.

Apart from stimulating the rise of private enterprise, the aforementioned policies also stimulated nonproductive rent-seeking. Take, for example, the double-track price system. Due to the huge disparity between planned prices and market prices (for example: there was a wide gap between the official exchange rate for the RMB and market exchange rate; the market price for steel in 1985 was twice the allocation price; and loan interest rates were divided into the market rate and the official rate), the total amount of economic rent within the economy was astonishingly high. In 1987–1988, economic rent in China accounted for 20–40 percent of the national income; in the

[17] Lenin, Vladimir. *The State and Revolution* (Chinese Version), 1972.

mid-1990s, it was 32 percent.[18] As for the "expansion of enterprise autonomy" reform, managers of state-owned enterprises and collectively-owned enterprises abused their unrestrained power to embezzle public property and "kept the profits for themselves and left debts to the country;" or, to aid in the tunneling of profits, authorized management representatives of state-owned enterprises would have accomplices set up subsidiary companies and then transfer management power to their accomplices; following their example, the accomplices would do the same, transferring power down to subsidiary companies, forming a "multi-level legal person" and accelerating the loss of public assets. Various other methods of rent-seeking emerged with changes in policy. This economic rent-seeking pushed the economy further down the road of relying on the massive input of resources and production factors to stimulate growth.

In 1994, China's reform entered a stage of general progress. This stage witnessed not only the emergence of efficiency-oriented reforms like strategic restructuring of the state-owned economy, but also the consolidation of administrative power over resource allocation. This consolidation was primarily reflected by intervention into production factors market and increased control over the so-called "strategic industries."

First, increased administrative power over resource allocation was chiefly manifested in the control of land, which, like fresh water, is a "non-tradable commodity"—difficult or impossible to acquire via international trade. In China, land per capita is much lower than the world average and population distribution is uneven, with 94 percent of the population living on just 46 percent of the land. Therefore, it is essential to protect land resources. Although the *Decisions by the CCP Central Committee on Issues Regarding Perfecting the Socialist Market Economic System* (中共中央关于完善社会主义市场经济体制若干问题的决定) states that "property rights are the core and main content of the ownership system," and proclaims the goal to "build a modern property rights system with clear rights to ownership, precise system of rights and responsibilities, strict protection, and smooth circulation," Article 2

[18] Hu Heli 胡合立, "1988nian woguo zujin de gusuan 1988 年我国租金的估算 [Estimation of Rents in China-1988]," 1993; Wan Anpei 万安培, "Zhongguo jingji zhuanxing shiqi de zujin goucheng ji zhuyao tedian fenxi 中国经济转型时期的租金构成及主要特点分析 [Analysis of the Composition and Characteristics of Rents during the Transition Period]," 1996.

of the *Land Management Law* (土地管理法) clearly states that land is owned by the whole people, i.e. the State Council shall exercise the right of ownership on behalf of the nation. However, the central government did not take on its responsibility as the land owner. So, since the role of the owner is unclear, municipal governments at different levels have become the actual owners of land in their administrative areas. Thus, for municipal governments, property tax and land transfer fees levied on real estate development companies have become the primary source of revenue. In many places, income from the development of farmland constitutes over a half of the local government revenue; more specifically, land tax revenue accounts for 40 percent of budgetary revenues nationwide, and land transfer fees account for 60 percent of non-budgetary revenue nationwide.[19] Stimulated by these profits, local governments are keen to get land from farmers at low prices and convert the farmland into "image" and "political achievement" projects, characterized by gigantic buildings or residences, huge squares, and vast "economic development" zones, which encourage development in their cities by boosting the real estate market. According to a report released by the Ministry of Land and Resources in 2004, in recent years 6,866 such economic development zones have been established by governments, covering a total area of 38,600 square kilometers.[20] The government's enthusiasm for real estate can also reflected in the amount of farmland occupied by construction sites. Since 1994, the proportion of farmland converted into construction sites had been frighteningly high. But even so, the figure climbed to new heights in 2001.[21] As land leasing is normally decided via negotiation and "approved" by the authorities, the cost of leasing is so low that the precious farmland is actually sold at 50 percent discount or presented to developers under the semblance of "fair transaction." These factors have resulted in a tremendous amount of rent-seeking as well as a serious waste of land resources, such as the one-storey "garden factories," which cover over a thousand *mu*, that can be seen all across China.

[19] (*Caijing*, 2006).

[20] (Ministry of Land and Resources, 2004).

[21] Qu Futian 曲福田, Chen Jianglong 陈江龙, Chen Huiguang 陈会广, *Jingji fazhan yu zhongguo tudi feinongye* 经济发展与中国土地非农化 [*Economic Growth and Farmland Conversion in China*], 2007.

Second, looking at the financial market, administrative departments have, to a large extent, intervened in the allocation of financial resources. The four biggest state-owned specialized banks have nominally been converted to commercial banks, but their management is still interfered with by governments at different levels, therefore most of their loans are given to state-owned enterprises. It is estimated that in the mid-1990s, 70 percent to 80 percent of the loans issues by the four biggest state-owned commercial banks were made to state-owned enterprises that created just 30 percent of GDP. Local governments have even encouraged state-owned enterprises to evade debts by declaring bankruptcy. When the stock market opened in the early 1990s, companies could not go public to raise funds on the stock market unless their applications were approved by both their local and the central government. The quotas for listing were usually transfers of tens or even hundreds of millions of yuan; meanwhile, high efficiency small and medium-sized private companies could not receive support from the financial system.

Third, the examination and approval system protects the monopoly of state-owned enterprises in so-called "strategic industries," which refers to industries in fields that are crucial to the development of national economy. Strategic industries include sectors which are associated with national security, those with natural monopolies, those that provide essential public products and services, and those that form the backbone of the high-tech industry or the entire economy. Although the constitution was amended in 1998 to reflect the recognition of the non-publicly-owned economy as an "organic component of the socialist market economy," and although during the negotiations prior to China's entry into the World Trade Organization (WTO), the CCP Central Committee pledged to open most industries and markets to private enterprise, releasing the *Several Opinions of the State Council on Encouraging, Supporting, and Guiding the Development of Individual and Private Economy and Other Non-Public Sectors* (国务院关于鼓励支持和引导个体私营等非公有制经济发展的若干意见) in 2005, in reality, governments at all levels have established high barriers for accessing these strategic industries. Private enterprises' applications for access to these monopolized markets are strictly controlled by government departments at different levels so that the leading position of state-owned enterprises remains stable. Under the protection of the government, state-owned enterprises have realized a constant growth in margins for ten consecutive years. In 1998, there were 238,000 state-owned enterprises in China; in 2006, the figure was 119,000; the total profits of state-owned companies in 1997 was merely 80 billion yuan, by 2006, the figure jumped to 1.2 trillion, up 1400 percent from 1997. The enterprises achieved profits of 768 billion yuan and paid 682 billion yuan in taxes. High profits, on one hand, show the improvement in state-owned enterprises' profitability; on the other hand, they are representative of monopoly profit and loss of efficiency.

Not every factor that causes the inefficient allocation of resources has been mentioned above. There are certainly others. For example, the price of energy and other resources are undervalued by administrative restriction, which leads to the excessive use and abuse of these resources. This and the examples described above illustrate that inappropriate, delayed reform measures can cause an inefficient allocation of resources. The growth model cannot be fundamentally changed because the market is still not the foundation for the allocation of resources; instead, the government still has great power over allocation.

In regard to the potential of the Chinese economy to continue growing through this investment-reliant strategy, Professor Lau is optimistic. Only three or four years ago, however, Wu Jinglian used the word "decisive" to describe the urgency of changing China's growth model. The basis for his judgment lies mainly in the fact that there are clear signals indicating that reduced returns on investments have already begun to impact the economy.[22]

The first sign is that investment-driven growth has led to a gradual but continuous increase in the investment rate. The amount of investment as a proportion GDP rose has risen from 25 percent at the beginning of the reform and opening period to over 44 percent in 2004. This is the highest investment rate ever recorded in world history,[23] let alone Chinese economic history (refer to Figure 7.2).

Second, China's industrial structure has become more and more unbalanced. Because of the fact that investment has tended to flow towards more capital-intensive secondary industry, the proportion

---

[22] (Wu Jinglian, 2005).

[23] This figure is much bigger than the highest rate (34%) achieved by Japan during its rapid growth period, which was also characterized by excessive investment. According to the statistics provided by Shan Weijian, the investment rate of the US did not exceed 20% even in during rapid industrialization in the late nineteenth and early twentieth centuries, as well as in the recovery period after World War II. In Japan, the investment rate reached its historical height (32%) during 1960s–1970s. (Refer to Shan, Weijian, "China's Yuan is Overvalued," 2005.)

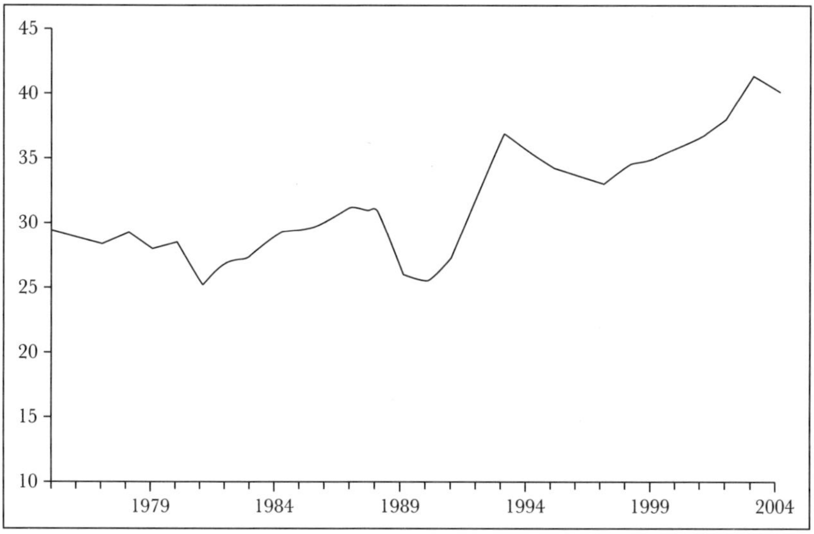

Source: China Economic Information Network, "China Economic Information Network Statistics Database."

Figure 7.2. Investment Rates in China from 1975 to 2004 (%).

directed towards the service industry declined between 2002 and 2004 as well as between 2005 and 2007. (Refer to Table 7.3.)

Third, the investment and consumption structure has become distorted. Due to the fact that China's investment rate has tended to be high and its consumption rate quite low, the Tenth Five Year Plan resolved to raise the consumption rate to around 50 percent and reduce the capital assets investment rate to about 35 percent. However, opposite from what had been planned for, during the first four years the investment rate unexpectedly increased while consumption decreased (See Table 7.4).

Finally, the ICOR has continued to rise, reflecting the decline in investment efficiency. In 2004, Ma Kai, the then-Director of National Development and Reform Commission (NDRC), pointed out that the investment rates of the United States, Germany, France, and India accounted for 10–20 percent of their GDP, while China's was 40–45 percent of GDP. For the countries listed above to increase of their GDP by 100 million dollars/yuan, they must invest 100–200 million; China, however, must invest 500 million for the same gain.[24]

[24] Ma Kai 马凯, "Shuli he luoshi kexue fazhanguan, tuijin jingji zengzhang fangshi de genbenxin zhuanbian 树立和落实科学发展观, 推进经济增长方式的根本性转变

Table 7.3. The Change in Output Value of Tertiary Industry since 1980*

Unit: %

	1980	1984	1990	2000	2001	2002	2003	2004	2005	2006	2007
Output Ratio	21.4	24.7	31.3	33.4	34.1	34.3	33.4	31.9	39.9	39.4	39.1

* At the end of 2005, the National Bureau of Statistics published the results of the first economic census, which showed a substantial increase in the GDP and tertiary industry figures. According to the census, the total value of the GDP in 2004 was 2.3 trillion yuan higher than that listed in the accounting report from that year, an increase of 16.8 percent; the census also showed that the value of tertiary industry was higher than as listed in the report, changing from 15.2, 52.95, and 31.9 percent for primary, secondary, and tertiary industry to 13.1, 46.2, and 40.7 percent respectively; this represented an 8.8 percent increase in the overall value of tertiary industry over the data found in the report of that year. Due to the fact that data from after 2004 uses the adjusted standard based on the census, the proportion of tertiary industry in 2005 shows a substantial increase.

Source: National Bureau of Statistics. *China Statistical Yearbook*, Various Years; National Bureau of Statistics, *2007nian guomin jingji he shehui fazhan tongji gongbao* 2007 年国民经济和社会发展统计公报 [Report on Development Statistics of the National Economy and Society].

Table 7.4. Investment and Consumption Rates in China (%)

	Capital Formation Rate (Investment Rate)	Fixed Capital Formation Rate (Investment Rate for Fixed Capital)	Final Consumption Rate (Consumption Rate)	Resident Consumption Rate
2000	36.4	36.5	61.1	48.0
2001	38.0	37.3	59.8	46.6
2002	39.2	38.9	58.2	45.3
2003	42.4	42.2	55.4	43.9
2004	44.2	43.8	53.0	41.4

Source: China Economic Information Network, "Zhongjing wang tongji shujuku 中经网统计数据库 [China Economic Information Network Statistics Database]."

There are signals of declining turns elsewhere as well. In the first twenty years of reform and opening, China doubled its energy consumption and quadrupled GDP, maintaining an energy elasticity of about 0.5. After the start of the twenty-first century, however, the energy elasticity increased rapidly to 1.0. Also, while energy and pollution-intensive sectors have grown, increasing their share in the economy, the relatively efficient service sector contributes less to GDP than it did

[Build up and Put into Effect the Scientific Outlook on Development, Advance the Fundamental Change in Economic Growth Model]," 2004.

before. Another symbolic indicator, the rate of household consumption, decreased from 63.8 percent in 2000 to 38.5 percent in 2005.[25] According to the NDRC, in 2006 China accounted for 5.5 percent of the global GDP and 15 percent of the global energy consumption (as well as 30 percent of the global steal and iron consumption and 54 percent of the global cement consumption). In terms of efficiency, China's energy consumption is much higher that of the developed countries, using 15 percent more energy to produce one ton of steel, 20 percent more coal to generate electricity in thermal power plants, 23.6 percent more energy to produce cement, and an average of 20–25 percent more oil to drive a vehicle one hundred kilometers. Meanwhile, China's rate of mineral resource recycling is about 30 percent, 20 percentage points lower than developed countries. If the price of ecological damage is taken into account, the wealth produced by China's economy is nowhere near that indicated by the GDP.[26]

III. *The Export-Oriented Strategy and the Ongoing Extensive Growth Mode*

Why is it that, despite the fact that the negative characteristics of China's economic growth model were clearly revealed in the mid-1990s, China's economy has been able to continue its high speed growth for over a decade since? One of the key reasons is that China has been following a strategy of export-oriented growth, a path pioneered by Japan, Hong Kong, Singapore, Taiwan, and Korea, as well as used by other countries and regions. Using this strategy, growth of China's exports is able to make up for insufficient domestic demand caused by the investment-driven economic growth model. In this way, China has managed to maintain a kind of rapid economic growth by means of using excess capacity—the result of excessive investment—to manufacture huge amounts of cheap products for export.

One of the most important tools used by countries that adopt the export-oriented strategy is to undervalue the country's currency, which is

[25] Different statistical methods make the consumption rates here a bit different from those in Table 7.4, but the tendency reflected by them is the same.

[26] Chen Qingtai 陈清泰, "Xinxihua zhutui fazhan fangshi zhuanbian 信息化助推发展方式转变 [Informatization Accelerates the Transformation of Growth Model]," 2007.

further supported by measures such as subsidizing exports, tax exemption for exports, export tax rebates, and low interest rates.

Since establishing a stable diplomatic relationship with the United States in 1972, China has abandoned its closed-door policy and began to trade with the West. However, China did not adapt the export-oriented policy used by other East Asian countries at the time, but instead a policy of import substitution, the objective of which was to promote the domestic production of goods that would otherwise need to be imported. To match with this strategy, China adopted a policy of maintaining a high RMB exchange rate, which meant that the official exchange rate was always much higher than market rate.

In the late 1970s, China's government announced its intentions to adopt an open policy in a bid to maximize China's comparative advantage of low-cost labor[27] and to earn foreign exchange through exports following the "three plus one" trading scheme (processing supplied materials, assembling supplied materials, manufacturing based on samples, and compensation trade). In fact, before undertaking reform of its foreign exchange regime on January 1, 1994, China kept its policy of maintaining a high RMB exchange rate needed for the import substitution strategy; this was due in part to historical inertia, but even more so, it was due to the influence of companies who prospered from the import quotas and accompanying foreign currency, by which they could benefit from the exchange difference. From 1985 to 1993, China had an exchange rate system featuring the co-existence of an exchange rate set by the government and a rate determined by the market. In other words, China had two sets of exchange rates at the same time: the official one featuring an overvalued RMB and the market one featuring an undervalued RMB. Before the above-mentioned reform in 1994, one USD equaled 5.76 RMB according to the official exchange rate, but 8.6 RMB on the market. Using this system of an overvalued RMB, the amount of exports as a portion of GDP rose from 4.6 percent in 1978 to 16.1 percent in 1990. However, exports at the time did not contribute significantly to economic growth.[28]

The critical moment in China's move towards an export-oriented economic growth strategy occurred on January 1, 1994. In 1993, the

---

[27] Certainly, this is a low-level and static comparative advantage, which China cannot continue to depend on. More detailed discussion of this topic appears later.

[28] Wu Jinglian 吴敬琏. *Dangdai zhongguo jingji gaige* 当代中国经济改革 *Economic Reform in Contemporary China*, 2004.

Third Plenary Session of the Fourteenth Central Committee of the CCP passed the *Decisions on Issues Regarding Improvement of the Socialist Market Economy System* (关于建立社会主义市场经济体制若干问题的决定). One of these decisions was to do away with the dual exchange-rate system in two steps, first for domestic companies and then for foreign, and to adopt a single exchange rate and free floating (but managed) RMB for calculating current account. The system, which had no official exchange rate and instead featured a market-determined exchange rate based on supply and demand—but still under the control of the government—began being implemented on January 1, 1994. In accordance with this change, individuals began buying and selling foreign exchange and banks began to make exchanges in inter-bank foreign exchange markets, which gave rise to a market-determined exchange rate. At the same time, the central bank set a scope for exchange rate fluctuation and, through market management, began to maintain a stable RMB exchange rate. On January 1, 1994, the USD-RMB market exchange rate was 1 USD = 8.72 RMB, which was a 51 percent drop from the former official value of the RMB (1 USD = 5.76 RMB). In the time from then until when the East Asian financial crisis broke out in October 1997, the USD-RMB exchange rate rose to 1:8.28. In the aftermath of the crisis, other countries requested that the exchange rate of the RMB be fixed in order to stabilize the Asian economy. China granted this request, and thereafter played an important role in putting an end to the financial crisis. Afterwards, China kept the RMB exchange rate pegged to the USD. The RMB-USD exchange rate basically stayed at 1:8.27, fluctuating a little from time to time but within a limited range, until July 21, 2005, when the next reform of the exchange rate system began.

With the devaluation of the RMB and the full-scale adoption of the export-directed growth strategy, China's exports soared (see Figure 7.3). This was especially true after China became a member of the WTO in November 2001, which was the result of a fifteen year negotiation process, during which China took many measures to improve its trade policy, including drastically reducing tariffs and customs barriers, eliminating import quotas, and scaling back trade protection by the government. Additionally, as stipulated in the WTO agreement, beginning on January 1, 2002, China lowered the tariff for more than 5,300 imported items, the average tariff being cut from 15.3 percent to 11.3 percent. China's economy began to become fully integrated with the international market. During the period of the Tenth Five-year Plan,

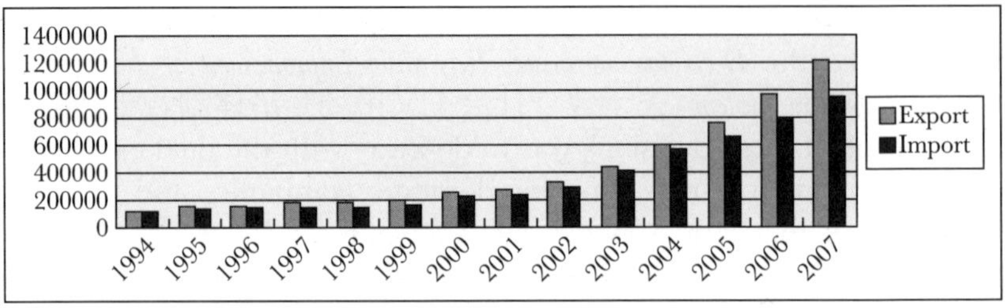

From: China Customs.

Figure 7.3. China's Import/Export since 1994 (unit: millions of USD).

from 2001 to 2005, China's economy witnessed the fastest growth in trade in its history and the balance of trade rose sharply. (See Figure 7.4)

In the late 20th century, when hundreds of millions of rural laborers were searching for work in China's urban industrial and commercial sectors, these export-oriented policies played a very important role in China's economic development. The strong demand for exports fueled China's economy, and brought it into a new stage.

However, ten years after adopting the strategy, some of the problems it has caused are obvious. China is experiencing exactly what other East Asian countries and regions that adopted this system—the so-called "neo-mercantilism"—experienced in 1990s.

In regard to the microeconomic situation, just as pointed out by Joseph Stiglitz, the export-oriented growth strategy allows demand to be free from the limits of domestic revenue, but it can also lead to overspecialization in labor-intensive manufacturing and impair long-term growth potential while leaving non-export sectors at a low level of development.[29] This is exactly what China is experiencing now. Since the adoption of the aforementioned "three plus one" trading scheme in the 1980s, processing trade has grown much faster than other types of trade; ever since 1996, when the volume of processing trade surpassed that of normal trade, processing trade has been China's single largest form of trade. This type of trade features deep involvement in the worldwide division of labor and engagement in low value-added processing and manufacturing for the industrial supply chain. Intermediate-level inputs are imported from Japan, Korea, Chinese Taiwan

[29] Stiglitz, Joseph E. *Economics* (Chinese version), 2000.

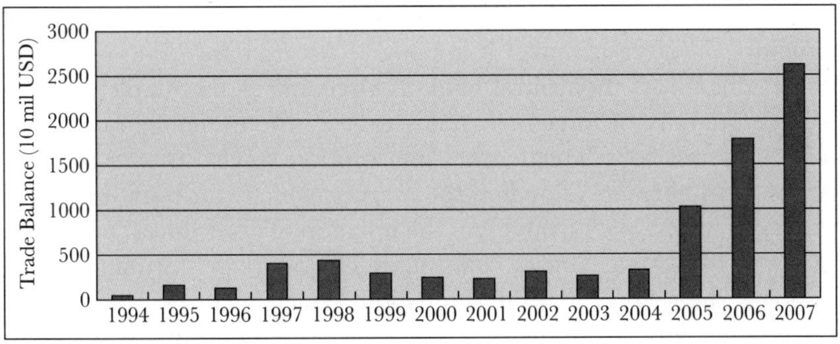

From: China Customs.

Figure 7.4. China's Balance of Trade since 1994 (unit: 10 million USD).

and so forth, and then assembled by companies with foreign equipment and cheap Chinese labor; finally, these products are exported to the United States, Japan, and Europe. Although China seems to have become the world's factory, this is only in terms of export volume. The value-added created by processing and manufacturing is very low and only a small amount of "hard-earned money" can be earned from such export. Moreover, this kind of export structure severs the link between exported products and domestic demand; as a result, companies oriented toward the domestic market are generally much less specialized than those directed towards export. Finally, the negative characteristics of the high investment, low output extensive growth model are not changed as a result of adopting export-oriented policy; on the contrary, they become more entrenched.

In regard to the macroeconomic situation, although the combination of the export-oriented policy and the investment-driven growth model played a significant role in supporting the fast economic growth of the late 20th century, its negative impacts has become obvious since the beginning of the 21st century. It has lead to an unbalanced external economy. This unbalance is primarily reflected by the fact that China has accumulated an enormous trade surplus, while meanwhile there has increasing friction between China and its trading partners, which has put huge pressure on China to allow its currency to appreciate.

Currently, if there were to be reform of China's exchange rate regime to base the rate on the market (i.e. liberalization), currencies from countries with trade surpluses would naturally appreciate, thus restoring the international balance of payments. However, such a reform would also put huge pressure on export companies to update their technologies and products. Usually, the inertia of the original structure of interests makes it impossible for exchange rate reform to occur; this forces the central bank to intervene in the market, buying a large quantity of foreign currency to keep the exchange rate of the local currency low. This market intervention results in over-issuance of the local currency, flooding the market, which can result in one of three situations: one possibility is the inflation of asset prices, where the prices of real estate, stocks, collectibles, etc., increase, forming market bubbles; the second is normal inflation, which involves a rise in the price of general goods; the third possibility is a mix of these two kinds of inflation. In the end, no matter which situation emerges, as soon as there is some internal or external shock, the country will be faced with serious and systematic risk, which could cause long-term economic recession.

In most of the East Asian countries and territories that adopted the export-oriented growth strategy, due to the fact that they could not implement currency reforms in time or failed to reform their government-led financial systems, currency became over issued and massive market bubbles developed. In the end, some external force caused these bubbles to burst and the economies of these countries fell into long-term economic recession. Take Taiwan as an example. Its 1958 foreign exchange reform transitioned it away from the import substitution strategy to export promotion, allowing it to achieve rapid economic development. If in the 1960s it had made the best of export promotion and improved its trade balance by gradually eliminating export subsidies, relaxing its restrictions on imports, and adjusting its exchange rate to fix the overly-low New Taiwan Dollar (TWD), it would have been able to raise its resource utilization rate, thus achieving a higher economic growth rate and relieving the economic recession that followed the 1974 oil crisis. However, even in the 1980s, when Taiwan had accumulated huge amounts of foreign exchange and had the second largest reserves of USD in the world (only after Japan), Taiwan's authorities were still not willing to allow the TWD to appreciate. Instead, the government delayed de-regulating its foreign exchange regime and adjusting the TWD exchange rate, while at the same time controlling the currency's appreciation by purchasing large amounts of USD. It was the dramatic increase in the money supply resulting from this purchase that caused the inflation of asset prices and the bubble in the late 1980s. In the end, external economic shock burst the bubble in Taiwan's market. Nearly every financial group with construction companies as subsidiaries incurred heavy financial debts. Countless companies sank into financial trouble as their assets shrank. Banks were so heavily burdened by the soaring number of non-performing assets that they had to seek help from the government, which paid bad debts with taxpayers' money. In retrospect, the Taiwanese economist Sun Zhen pointed out, "If the Taiwanese authorities had made serious efforts to implement the liberalization policy promptly after announcing it, and allowed the currency to naturally rise as required by the situation, the expected appreciation would never have occurred, nor would there have been the huge flood of international capital, increase of monetary supply, or inflation of asset prices. The production sector could have easily adjusted to changes in the exchange rate and people could have enjoyed the increase in economic well-being and the fruits of economic growth. Moreover, the government would not have needed to be so busy regulating."[30] From Japan to Korea to Malaysia, East Asia is full of many stories of economic woe similar to Taiwan's.

In the autumn of 2003, there began to be extensive debate among economic scholars regarding RMB revaluation and the foreign exchange regime. Professor Yu Yongding pointed out the risks associated with a dramatic increase in foreign exchange reserves, insisting that measures be taken to "eliminate the phobia of RMB revaluation and shift to balanced economic development," and to "restore the floating exchange rate as soon as possible."[31] Some economists worry that the long-term pursuit of export-directed growth and the accompanying low factor prices and exchange rate will lead to companies resting on their laurels, lacking the pressure to update their industry or adopt new technologies. Due to such concerns, many such economists support Professor Yu Yongding's views.

Unfortunately, like Taiwan's authorities in the past, the decision makers in China are also worried that RMB revaluation will reduce exports and economic growth. For this reason, it was not until July 21, 2005 that China's government announced its plans to launch a new

[30] Sun Zhen 孙震, "Taiwan jingji ziyouhua de jingyan yu jianlun 台湾经济自由化的经验与检讨 [Economic Liberalization: Taiwan's Experieces]," 2006.

[31] Yu Yongding 余永定, "Xiaochu renminbi shengzhi kongjuzheng, shixian xiang jingji pingheng fazhan de guodu 消除人民币升值恐惧症, 实现向经济平衡发展的过渡 [*Eliminating the Fear of RMB Revaluation and Realizing the Shift Balanced Economic Development*]," 2003.

RMB exchange rate regime that features a controlled floating exchange rate system wherein the RMB's value would not be matched to the USD, but instead use a basket of currencies as reference. Since then, the RMB exchange rate against the USD has continued to rise. As of July 21, 2008, the central parity rate of interbank foreign exchange reached 1 RMB = 6.827 USD.

The gradual revaluation of the RMB has not harmed the economy or export companies to any great degree. However, it has led to a wave of "hot money" flowing in from overseas to gain benefits from the RMB's revaluation; this put a great deal of pressure on the RMB's price to appreciate faster. In order to keep RMB appreciating at reasonable speed, the central bank has had to frequently intervene in the market, buying foreign exchange such as USD. Accordingly, these purchases have accelerated the growth of China's foreign exchange reserve. Over the course of 2003, the central bank purchased an average of 0.1–0.2 billion USD every day; this number went up to USD 0.7–0.8 billion in 2006. Since then, the amount of USD purchased has continued to rise faster and faster (as shown by Figure 7.5). In 2005, China already had currency worth USD 853.6 billion , ranking first in the world; by the end of 2006, this number broke through the one trillion dollar mark, hitting USD 1.0663 trillion; at the end of 2007, the number reached USD 1.53 trillion. By the end of the first half of 2008, the foreign exchange reserve was worth USD 1.8088 trillion, more than the combined reserves of seven Western developed countries.

This large quantity of foreign exchange has been purchased using high-powered currency issued by the central bank (the so-called "foreign exchange funds"), and then converted to real purchasing power through issuing currency by commercial banks. For instance, to acquire USD 1.8 trillion in foreign exchange reserves, the People's Bank of China released 15–16 trillion of this high-powered currency, which when magnified by the money multiplier (about five fold), amounted to a 60 trillion dollar increase in the money supply.

The consequences of over issuing currency and excess liquidity were first seen in asset markets, such as those of real estate, stocks, and collectibles. The soaring price of real estate and decline of rent at the beginning of the 2000s indicated the formation of a bubble in the real estate market. As for the stock market, share prices have been going up since the spring of 2006. At the end of 2005, the composite index of the Shanghai Stock Exchange (SSE) was 1,161; the closing value at the end of 2006 was 2,675; and on October 16, 2007, the index

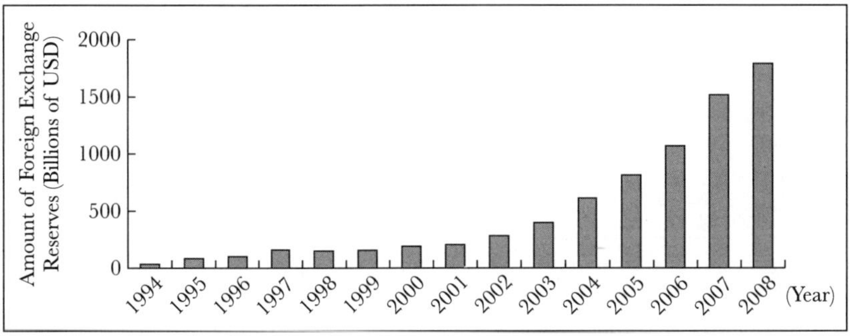

Figure 7.5. China's Balance of Foreign Exchange Reserves from 1994 to the First Half of 2008 (unit: USD 1 bn).

reached its all-time high of 6,124. (See Figure 7.6) In less than two years time, the Shanghai and Shenzhen stock markets grew by nearly fivefold, reaching a total value of 33.62 trillion yuan with a static price-to-earnings (P/E) ratio of 72. Upon examination of earnings at the time, including non-repeatable earnings such as interest on stock investments, the dynamic P/E ratio was even higher. All told, the stock market in China is a bubble ready to burst, and "there is no bubble that will not burst." Since 2006, the stock market has been teetering on the brink of collapse.

Due to the lag effect of inflation, the consumer price index (CPI) increased slower than real estate and stock prices. Even so, the effect of inflation did become visible in 2007. In March 2007, the CPI rose by more than 3 percent; by July of the same year, it had already exceeded the "mild inflation marker," reaching 5.6 percent. Since then, it has continued to rise, reaching 7.9 percent in the first half of 2008. China's real interest rate of residents' deposits has already gone into negative numbers. This has forced the government into a difficult situation. On one hand, it needs to deal with inflation to stabilize the price of everyday goods; on the other hand, it must be careful to avoid causing the bubbles in real estate and securities assets to explode, which would be risky on a systematic scale. Meanwhile, increasing the interest rate could lead to financial difficulties or even bankruptcy for small and medium-sized companies, but even the effects of such an increase would be impaired by the need to preserve the undervalued RMB exchange rate. What's worse, the central government has taken a series of administrative measures to control the prices of food, petroleum products, and electricity in a bid to control the increase of

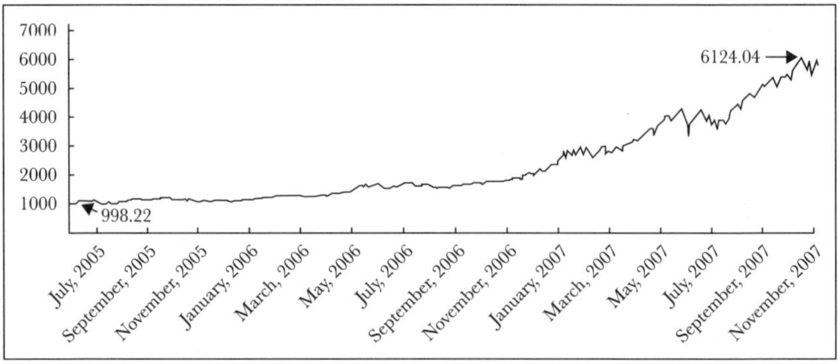

Figure 7.6. Shanghai Stock Exchange Composite Index.

nominal CPI and PPI. These measures make it difficult for the balancing mechanisms of the market to have full effect.

IV. *Pushing forward Market-Oriented Reform and Speeding the Transformation of the Economic Growth Model*

The need to transform China's economic growth model became a hotly debated topic among economic scholars in 2004 and 2005. More and more economists began to recognize that the existing model of economic growth could not continue for much longer. They recommended that China learn from the experiences of developed countries, which made similar transitions at the end of the 19th century, to help China transition to a modern economic growth model. Economists called for progress in four different areas. (1) The first was a call to speed up scientific development and technological innovation. Scholars called for efforts to promote the wide application of science-intensive technology throughout the economy, encourage technological innovation and product updating, and increase society-wide investment in basic research and development of generic technologies. (2) The second part was a call for advancement of the service sector, especially producer services. Different from the manufacturing systems of the 19th century, modern manufacturing is integrated with the service sector. Accordingly, the development of a modern manufacturing sector must have effective support from producer services. (3) The third component of the recommended strategy was to let Information Technology (IT) lead the development of industry. Economists called for the wide use of information & communications technology (ICT) to improve the productivity of the industrial and service sectors. (4) Finally, economists called for promoting the transition of the surplus rural labor force into the non-agricultural urban workforce and for measures to be taken to increase employment opportunities for such workers in urban industrial and commercial sectors.[32] In response to these recommendations and the widespread debate among economists, the *Recommendations of the CCP Central Committee on the Eleventh Five-year Plan for National Economic and Social Development* (中共中央关于制定国民经济和社会发展第十一个五年规划的建议) was passed in October 2005. In the document, "accelerating economic restructuring and transformation of the growth pattern" (called 'economic development model' in official documents since 2007) is considered to be the most serious challenge and most pressing task included in the Eleventh Five-year Plan. In the Plan, passed and adopted by the National People's Congress the following year, it was confirmed that "the unreasonable structure and extensive growth model of the economy are the essential reasons behind many of the problems currently challenging China's economic growth." It called for China to transition from a "high investment, high consumption, high emissions, and low efficiency" extensive model of economic growth to a "low investment, low consumption, low emissions, and high efficiency" resource-saving and environmentally-friendly growth model.

Although the government announced that the objective of the Eleventh Five-year Plan was to change China's economic growth model, actually making this change has been a difficult, slow, and small-scale process. For example, the imbalanced ratio of investment and consumption has continued to expand. In 2007, China had the smallest share of consumption as a portion of GDP in history, but investment accounted for nearly 50 percent of GDP. Moreover, the size of secondary industry as a portion of GDP has kept increasing, while that of the service industry has declined. Also, the share of foreign demand as a portion of the GDP has continued to go up. In addition, the efforts to accomplish another goal put forth in the plan—to increase the value added of exports by improving technology, updating products, and upgrading industry—have not been nearly enough. Finally,

[32] Wu Jinglian, *Zhongguo jingji zengzhang moshi jueze* 中国经济增长模式抉择 [*Choosing China's Economic Growth Model*], 2006.

the amount of energy consumed and volume of emissions needed to produce one unit of GDP (energy intensity) have been higher than as stipulated in the plan.

The underlying reasons for this slow change are the persistent systematic barriers. In other words, it is because the old growth model is based on the traditional command economy. Unless this traditional command system, wherein the government possesses immense authority in resource allocation, is completely changed, China will never be able to truly change its economic growth model. Since the implementation of the reform and opening policy, China's economic system has changed a lot, but even so, many negative characteristics, more suited to the command economy, remain. Thus, the market is unable to play a fundamental role in resource allocation. Specifically, characteristics "inherited" from the old system include:

(1) Governments at various levels still have the authority to allocate important economic resources. Take land for example, which is critical for urban and industrial development. Due to the fact that rural residents have no clear title to their land, governments are aggressive in using farmland for construction to stimulate the housing market, thereby profiting from the land transfer fees and property tax. This has been a big driver of the consumption of land.
(2) The rate of GDP growth has become one of the main indicators for assessing the performance of Party members and government officials. Many officials abuse of their authority by using large amounts of resources to construct projects devoted to helping their "image" or documenting their "political achievements."
(3) Deficiencies in the finance and tax systems have caused the finances of local governments to be closely tied to the GDP growth rate. In term of revenue, tax revenue comes primarily from value-added taxes, with about half coming from production value-added tax. This has led to governments using their resource allocation authority to promote increased production (regardless of market supply and demand). In terms of the structure of the fiscal expenditure system, too much fiscal responsibility for critical public services, such as social security and education, is placed on governments at or below the county level. These low-level governments are not given the financial support that would enable them fulfill their responsibilities, so

they become directly responsible for finding their own sources of revenue and investment. Thus, they are forced to rely on control over enterprises to ensure their revenue.

(4) The distortion of factor prices encourages companies to support increased production value through high volume investments and resource consumption. Currently, commodity prices in China are based primarily on the market, but factor prices are set by administrative decision. In setting these prices, the government has continued to undervalue the price of energy and resources, suppressing the costs of labor and capital (by put a ceiling on salaries and interest rates). The price of petroleum products are a good example. In China, the price of such products is much less than in the international market, even after being adjusted upwards in June, 2008. This pricing policy obviously does not create the conditions necessary for developing a resource-conserving circular economy, not to mention making progress in terms of environmental protection and transition of the economic growth model. Another example is the underdevelopment of the labor market. In recent years, the wages of migrant workers have started to rise, but the average wages for employees of town/county-level enterprises have been growing slowly. If inflation is taken into account, the real interest rate is already negative.

(5) Departments of science, research, and education are bureaucratic and organized according by official rank. Competition is the main mechanism that ensures the effective and efficient operation of scientific institutions; the system of official ranking and bureaucratization of scientific institutions negatively influences the originality and creativity of research.

Looking at China's economy from another perspective, the underlying reason for the slow transition to a new economic growth model is that market-oriented reform has been weak and distorted. This has made it impossible for the market mechanism to become a fully active force in resource allocation.

Therefore, to transform the economic growth model in China, there must be reforms cementing the market system, causing resource allocation to be fundamentally based on price and competition. In regard to this, in the last chapter of his book, *Choosing China's Economic Growth Model*, Wu Jinglian gives a detailed summary of the changes that need to be made. This chapter will not offer a complete account; instead, it will address some of the institutional problems that must be promptly addressed, as well as issues that need to be stressed or revisited.[33]

China should solve the following problems as soon as possible.

First of all, large-scale control should be maintained to keep the macro-economy stable. As pointed out above, the underlying reasons for the external and internal imbalance of China's macro-economy are the investment-led economic growth model and export-oriented strategy. In terms of the micro-economy, inflation of asset prices have disturbed price signals, which are no longer reliable indicators of resource shortage, which is not beneficial for changing the economic growth model. Some worry that if China were to take decisive policy action to stabilize the economy, it would burst the bubble in asset prices, leading to the same sort of crisis that happened in Japan and Southeast Asia. It is apparent that the Chinese government faces a macroeconomic dilemma; there is a little space for it to take macroeconomic measures to resolve the current economic problems. Under such circumstances, the government can do nothing except use policy measures and tools to stabilize the economy in a short term and shield it from external shocks caused by drastic fluctuations in the financial system.

Secondly, the exchange rate regime needs to be further based on the market. This is a lesson economists have learned from those East Asian countries that faced serious problems resulting from their own export-led economic growth model.[34] Although since July 2005, China has resumed "a managed floating exchange rate," there still is too much "management" by the government and not enough floating. Increasing the floating of the exchange rate could be an effective means of avoiding an extremely complex set of problems that could be caused by the combination of huge foreign exchange reserves and macroeconomic risk.[35]

Thirdly, China needs to relieve restrictions on factor prices to allow the market to play a more effective role. The unclear rights to land ownership, nonstandard market order, policy of low interest in the

---

[33] Wu Jinglian, *Choosing China's Economic Growth Model*, 2006.

[34] Sun Zhen 孙震, "Taiwan jingji ziyouhua de jingyan yu jianlun 台湾经济自由化的经验与检讨 [Economic Liberalization: Taiwan's Experieces]," 2006.

[35] AOKI Masahiko considered "How does China Learn from the Asian Crisis," by YOSHITOMI Masaru to be "the most important lecture listened to in his lifetime." (Yoshitomi, Masaru. "How China Learns from the Asian Crisis" (Chinese version), 2004.)

capital market, and under-developed labor market have caused abuse of scarce resources. After inflation began to be a problem in the second half of 2007, the authorities frequently used administrative measures to deal with rising prices, putting ceilings on prices rise of grain, petroleum products, energy, and other products whose prices tended to increase rapidly. This kind of administrative regulation is worse than the disease China's economy originally had. On one hand, these administrative actions result in increased demand and more inflation pressure. On the other hand, these actions further promote investment-led economic growth, which works against the transformation of the economic growth model. Only when prices accurately reflect the relative scarcity of resources can the market direct resources to be used for technology, improved efficiency, and transformation of the economic growth model.

Fourthly, policies allowing entry into all industries not forbidden by policy as well as policy opposing monopoly should be implemented to encourage new competitors to enter the market. After a thirteen-year legislation process, the *Anti-monopoly Law* (反垄断法) was officially put into effect on August 1, 2008. However, this law only forbids monopoly activities that have "harmful effects," not all monopoly activities. So, before the *Anti-monopoly Law* is amended, the regulation calling for equal treatment of the public economy and the non-public economy, adopted by the Seventeenth National Congress of the CCP, should be implemented, ensuring easy industry access and encouraging new competitors, thus improving economic efficiency.

The above-mentioned problems are those that must be urgently solved in view of the current situation. It is worth emphasizing that the success or failure of the transition to a new model of economic growth is dependent on whether or not a limited and effective government can be established.

As for the issue of limited government, through examining the process of economic restructuring during the late 1990s, one can see clearly that the underlying reason for excessive investment and a worsening industrial structure is that the government, instead of the market, was the main body adjusting economic structure. In accordance with the goal of establishing a socialist market economy and to promote economic efficiency and change of the economic growth model, China must limit the authority of the government to allocate resources and intervene in the microeconomic decision-making of companies and individuals. In addition, China must realize the "separation of the government from the Party and separation of the government from enterprise," a point repeatedly emphasized by Deng Xiaoping. The government should not do anything beyond its duties; the responsibility for managing things that the government should not manage should be delegated to the market, businesses, chambers of commerce, or other social organizations. The key to correcting the distorted prices of real estate, capital, and other production factors is to let the market determine their prices. Only when factor prices are determined by their relative scarcity, instead of by administrative officials, can the market play a fundamental role in resource allocation, which is an essential prerequisite to changing the economic growth model. The government should not intervene in microeconomic matters; it should not directly intervene in resource allocation between regions, sectors, or companies. Even in the case of market failure, when the government must play a macroeconomic role, it should do so in an indirect way, coordinating with the mechanisms of the market. For example, there are two possible ways to achieve increased energy efficiency: one way is for the government and economic planning department to determine which companies they consider to have energy-efficient production, and then to supply these companies with energy; the other way is for the government to lift restrictions on energy prices and use taxes to force energy-intensive companies with low-value-added production to either close or move elsewhere. The second solution is a better one.

As for the issue of effective governance, the idea that the government should delegate tasks that don't fall under its responsibilities to companies, social organizations, and the market does not mean that the government can reduce its responsibilities or idle about. The modern market system can only run successfully when the government fulfills its own duties in an efficient way. Those duties consist of: (1) providing a rule-of-law economic environment and impartial law enforcement; (2) stabilizing the economy by means of macroeconomic control; (3) providing basic social security to low-income groups and protecting social fairness; and (4) providing free compulsory education and building a national education system.

To build a limited and effective government, political reform must keep up with economic reform. As put it by Deng Xiaoping, "Political and economic reform should depend on and cooperate with each other. Economic reform cannot succeed without support from reform of the political system."

In conclusion, the Chinese economy is now at a critical period where it would be difficult to continue with the outdated economic growth model, but a new one has yet to be established. In the short term, China faces the risk of a hard economic landing. In the medium/long term, China has the huge task of transforming its model of economic growth. Thus, at this critical point, it is particularly important for reform in China to unswervingly push forward.

Bibliography

Chen Qingtai 陈清泰. "Xinxihua zhutui fazhan fangshi zhuanbian 信息化助推发展方式转变 [Informatization Accelerates the Transformation of Growth Model]." *Zhongguo xinxijie* 中国信息界 *China Information Times* No. 18 (2007).

China Economic Information Network. "Zhongjing wang tongji shujuku 中经网统计数据库 [China Economic Information Network Statistics Database]." http://ibedemo.cei.gov.cn/index/showdoc.asp?blockcode=DBjjnj_gdp&filename=200510252771

Chow, Gregory C. "Capital Formation and Economic Growth in China." *The Quarterly Journal of Economics* Vol. 108, No. 3 (August 1993): 809–42.

Deng Liqun 邓力群. "Makesi zaishengchan lilun de jiben yuanli bixu jianchi 马克思再生产理论的基本原理必须坚持 The Fundamentals of Marx's Reproduction Theory must be Adhered to." *Hongqi* 红旗 [*Red Flag*] No. 5–7 (1982).

——. *Shier ge chunqiu* 十二个春秋 [*Twelve Years*]. Hong Kong: Strong Wind Publishing House, 2006.

Gu Chongqing 谷重庆. "Zhongguo jingji de fangbodi: you kongzhi de tigao huilü linghuoxing 中国经济的防波堤: 有控制地提高汇率灵活性 [*The Breakwater for China's Economy: the Flexibility of Exchange Rate Control*]." *21shiji jingji baodao* 21 世纪经济报道 [*21st Century Economic Herald*], February, 14, 2008.

Hayami, Yujiro. *Development Economics—From Poverty to the Wealth of Nations*. Trans. into Chinese by Li Zhou 李周. Social Sciences Academic Press, 2003.

Hu Heli 胡合立. "1988nian woguo zujin de gusuan 1988 年我国租金的估算 [Estimation of Rents in China—1988]." In *Fubai: quanli yu jinqian de jiaohuan* 腐败: 权力与金钱的交换 [*Corruption: Exchange of Power and Money (2nd Edition)*], edited by the board of editors of *Jingji shehui tizhi bijiao* 经济社会体制比较 [*Comparative Economic and Social Systems*]" magazine. China Economic Publishing House, 1993.

Krugman, Paul. "The Myth of Asia's Miracle." *Foreign Affairs* Vol. 73, No. 10–12 (1994): 62–78.

Kuznets, Simon. *The Economic Growth of Nations*. Trans. into Chinese by Chang Xun 常勋 et al. Beijing: Commercial Press, 1985.

Lau, Lawrence J. "Long-Term Economic Growth in the PRC and Its Sectoral Implications." Report No. 2 in *The Economy of the PRC: Analysis and Forecasts, Studies by the. Salomon Brothers Panel of PRC Experts*, edited by A. Freris, 35–43. New York: Salomon Brothers, 1996.

——. "Sources and Prospects for the East Asia's Economic Growth." *Journal of Quantitative & Technical Economics* No. 10 (1997).

Lenin, Vladimir. *The State and Revolution* (Chinese Version). The People's Press, 1972.

Lin, Justin Yifu 林毅夫, Cai Fang 蔡昉, and Li Zhou 李周. *Zhongguo de qiji: Fazhan zhanlüe yu jingji gaige* 中国的奇迹：发展战略与经济改革 [*The China miracle: development strategy and economic reform*] (Chinese version, enlarged edition). Shanghai: Shanghai Sanlian Press, Shanghai People's Publishing House, 2003.

Liu Zunyi 刘尊义. "Dongya jingji zengzhang de yuanquan yu zhanwang 东亚经济增长的源泉与展望 [The Source of and Future of East Asian Economic Growth]." *Shuliang jingji jishu jingji yanjiu* 数量经济技术经济研究 [*Journal of Quantitative and Technical Economics*] No. 10 (1997).

Ma Kai 马凯. "Shuli he luoshi kexue fazhanguan, tuijin jingji zengzhang fangshi de genbenxin zhuanbian 树立和落实科学发展观, 推进经济增长方式的根本性转变 [Build up and Put into Effect the Scientific Outlook on Development, Advance the Fundamental Change in Economic Growth Model]." Speech at the China High-ranking Annual Conference on March 21, 2004. Script available at People's Daily Online: http://www.people.com.cn/GB/jingji/8215/32688/32689/2403665.html

Maruyama, Nobuo. *Industrialization and Technological Development in China*. Trans. into Chinese by Gao Zhiqian 高志前, Liang Ce 梁策, and Wang Zhiqing 王志清. China Renmin University Press, 1992.

Marx, Karl. *Capital, Vol. I* (Chinese version). The People's Press, 1975.

National Bureau of Statistics. *Zhongguo Tongji Nianjian* 中国统计年鉴 [*China Statistical Yearbook*]. Various Years.

——. *2007nian guomin jingji he shehui fazhan tongji gongbao* 2007 年国民经济和社会发展统计公报 [Report on Development Statistics of the National Economy and Society]. 2007.

Porter, Michael E. *National Competitiveness*. Trans. into Chinese by Li Mingxuan 李明轩 and Qiu Rumei 邱如美. Huaxia Press, 2002.

Publicity Department of the CCP Central Committee. "Wei dongyuan yiqie lilian ba woguo jianshe chengwei yige weida de shehui zhuyi guojia er douzheng—guanyu dang zai guodu shiqi zongluxian de xuexi he xuanchuan tigang 为动员一切力量把我国建设成为一个伟大的社会主义国家而斗争—关于党在过渡时期总路线的学习和宣传提纲 [Mobilize All Possible Forces and Strive to Transform China into a Great Socialist Country—Outline for Study and Promotion of the General Line for the Transition Period]." In *Shehuizhuyi jiaoyu kecheng de yuedu wenjian huibian* 社会主义教育课程的阅读文件汇编 [*Socialist Education Curriculum: Reading Collection*] (First Edition, Vol. 1) by the Publicity Department of the CCP Central Committee. The People's Press, 1957.

Qu Futian 曲福田, Chen Jianglong 陈江龙, Chen Huiguang 陈会广. *Jingji fazhan yu zhongguo tudi feinongye* 经济发展与中国土地非农化 [*Economic Growth and Farmland Conversion in China*]. Commercial Publishing House, 2007.

Shan, Weijian. "China's Yuan is Overvalued." *The Asian Wall Street Journal*, June 23, 2005.

Stalin, Joseph. "Economic Problems of Socialism in the USSR." In Selections from Joseph Stalin Vol. 2, by Joseph Stalin (Chinese version). The People's Press, 1979.

Stiglitz, Joseph E. *Economics* (Chinese version). China Renmin University Press, 2000.

Sun Zhen 孙震. "Taiwan jingji ziyouhua de jingyan yu jianlun 台湾经济自由化的经验与检讨 [Economic Liberalization: Taiwan's Experiences]." *Bijiao* 比较 [*Comparisons*] No. 25 (2006).

Wan Anpei 万安培. "Zhongguo jingji zhuanxing shiqi de zujin goucheng ji zhuyao tedian fenxi 中国经济转型时期的租金构成及主要特点分析 [Analysis of the Composition and Characteristics of Rents during the Transition Period]." In *Jianshe shichang jingji de zongti gouxiang yu fangan sheji* 建设市场经济的总体构想与方案设计 [*Blueprint and Scheme Design for the Construction of the Market Economy*], by Wu Jinglian 吴敬琏 et al. Central Compilation and Translation Press, 1996.

World Bank. "An East Asian Renaissance: Ideas for Economic Growth." Trans. into Chinese by Huang Zhiqiang 黄志强 and Yu Jiang 余江. China Citic Press, 2007.

Wu Jinglian 吴敬琏. *Dangdai zhongguo jingji gaige* 当代中国经济改革 [*Economic Reform in Contemporary China*]. Shanghai Far East Publishers, 2004.

——. *Zhongguo jingji zengzhang moshi jueze* 中国经济增长模式抉择 [*Choosing China's Economic Growth Model*]. Shanghai Far East Publishers, 2006.

Wu Jinglian 吴敬琏 and Huang Shaoqing 黄少卿. "Chuangxin haishi xunzu—Zhongguo zhuanxingqi zhidu huanjing yu qiyejia xingwei 创新还是寻租—中国转型期制度环境与企业家行为 [Innovation or Rent-seeking: Institutional Environment and Entrepreneurs' Behaviors in China during the Transition Period]." In *Huhuan fazhi de shichang jingji* 呼唤法治的市场经济 [*Calling for a Rule-of-Law Market Economy*] by Wu Jinglian 吴敬琏. Sanlian Press, 2007.

Xu Keqiang 徐可强 and Luo Xiaojun 罗小军. "Zhuanjia cheng renminbi buyinggai shengzhi meihuilü baofuan bu heli 专家称人民币不应该升值美汇率报复案不合理 [Expert Says RMB should not Appreciate, America's Diplomatic Policy on Exchange Rate is Unreasonable]." *21 shiji jingji baodao* 21 世纪经济报道 [*21 Century Economic Report*], April 20, 2005.

Xue Muqiao 薛暮桥. "Tiaozheng guomin jingji, gaohao zonghe pingheng 调整国民经济, 搞好综合平衡 [Adjust the Economy, Achieve a Comprehensive Balance]. *Jingji yanjiu* 经济研究 [*Economic Research Journal*] No. 2 (1981).

Yoshitomi, Masaru. "How China Learns from the Asian Crisis" (Chinese version). *Bijiao* 比较 [*Comparisons*] No. 11 (2004).

Yu Yongding 余永定. "Xiaochu renminbi shengzhi kongjuzheng, shixian xiang jingji pingheng fazhan de guodu 消除人民币升值恐惧症, 实现向经济平衡发展的过渡 [*Eliminating the Fear of RMB Revaluation and Realizing the Shift Balanced Economic Development*]." *Guoji jingji pinglun* 国际经济评论 [*International Economic Review*] No. 5 (2003).

Zhang Zhuoyuan 张卓元. "30nian guoyou qiye gaige de huigü yu zhanwang 30 年国有企业改革的回顾与展望 [Looking Back and Future Prospects after Thirty Years of State Owned Enterprise Reform]." *Qiye wenming* 企业文明 [*Enterprise Civilization*] No. 2 (2008).

Zou Zhizhuang 邹至庄. *Zhongguo jingji zhuanxing* 中国经济转型 [*China's Economic Transformation*]. China Renmin University Press, 2005.

CHAPTER EIGHT

ECONOMIC GROWTH AND INCOME DISTRIBUTION: AN EMPIRICAL ANALYSIS OF CHINA'S EXPERIENCES

Li Shi[1]

I. *Introduction*

Economic growth and income equality are both essential objectives of governments across the world. In the past half century, the relationship between economic growth and income distribution has been one of the main focal points for the research of economists. In mid-1950s, Simon Kuznets's paper "Economic Growth and Income Inequality" was published,[2] which triggered an intense debate that lasted for a long time. Using data from Great Britain, the United States, and Germany Kuznets found that in these countries during the early 20th century (even earlier in Great Britain) income inequality among individuals reduced to some extent. Based on this phenomenon, he hypothesized that developing countries undergo periods where income inequality increases or shrinks. He summarized that changes in income distribution have a strong connection to different stages of the economic development. He also observed that this happened not only in developed countries but also in some relatively "younger" countries. These observations and his theory amount to what is now famously known as the "Kuznets Hypothesis," or the "Kuznets Curve."

One of the major reasons why this hypothesis has generated such long-lasting debate is that it has strong implications for economic policy. If the pattern of income inequality is related to the different phases of economic development and if, in the early stage of the economic development, increased income inequality is inevitable, then the government's use of policy to redistribute income would serve little purpose, or at least would be more of a loss than a gain. What would

[1] Many thanks go to Dr. Deng Quheng 邓曲恒, who has provided data and help for this paper.

[2] Simon Kuznets, "Economic Growth and Income Inequality," March 1955.

be needed instead would be policy that accelerated economic growth and development. Only when the economy reached a certain stage would income inequality reduce by itself automatically. If this is true, governments should devote themselves to promoting economic development rather than using policy to redistribute the income. In other words, if this hypothesis is true, increasing income inequality would be inevitable in the early stage of economic development but the duration of it could be reduced by accelerating economic development.

In the academic world, this debate still rages. Some scholars have attempted to use data from China to verify the veracity or falsity of the Kuznets Hypothesis, seeing whether it can uncover the relationship between economic growth and income inequality or explain the changing pattern of income inequality in China. To date, there has not been any research that shows that China's of income inequality is following the Kuznets curve.[3]

The main objective of this chapter is to, based on further examination of the Kuznets Curve, clarify the relationship between China's economic growth and its income distribution, and to elaborate on the characteristics of China's income inequality. This chapter provides explanations for increasing income inequalities from multiple angles, examining the impact of economic development, economic transition, and government policy.[4] It is organized as follows: the second section is devoted to summarizing the empirical analysis of the "Kunznets hypothesis." The third section describes the statistical data regarding China's economic growth and income distribution changes.

[3] Li Shi 李实, "Zhongguo jingji fazhanzhong de shouru fenpei 中国经济发展中的收入分 [The Income Distribution in China's Economic Development]," 1993; Knight and Song, 1993; Li Shi 李实, Zhao Renwei 赵人伟, and Zhang Ping 张平, "Zhongguo jingji gaige guochengzhong de shouru fenpei biandong 中国经济改革过程中的收入分配变动 [Shifting Income Distribution During China's Economic Reform]," 1998; Wang Xiaolu 王小鲁 and Fan Gang 樊钢, "Zhongguo shouru chaju de zoushi he yingxiang yinsu fenxi 中国收入差距的走势和影响因素分析 [Analysis of the Contributing Factors to the Trend of Income Inequality in China]," 2005; Cai Fang 蔡昉, "Quanqiuhua zenyang huiji putong laodongzhe—zhongguo jingji fazhan zhuanzhedianshang de zhengce xuanze 全球化怎样惠及普通劳动者—中国经济发展转折点上的政策选择 [How Can Globalization Benefit Average Workers: policy options at the turning point of the economic development in China]," 2006.

[4] Zhao Renwei 赵人伟 and Li Shi 李实, "Zhongguo jumin shouru chaju de kuo da jiqi yuanyin 中国居民收入差距的扩大及其原因 [Expanding Income Inequality of the Residents in China and Its Reason]," 1997; Li Shi 李实 and Zhao Renwei 赵人伟, "Zhongguo jumin shouru fenpei zaiyanjiu 中国居民收入分配再研究 [Re-examining Income Distribution in China]," 1999.

The fourth section analyses the relationship between China's economic growth and income inequality. The fifth section attempts to explain the changes in China's income inequality. Finally, the last section offers a summary of the points raised in this chapter.

II. *The Latest Empirical Analysis of the "Kunznets Hypothesis"*

Kuznets did not only point out the relationship between income inequality and economic development, but also made great efforts to prove a causal relationship between the two phenomena; he believed that each stage of economic development had its own driving forces for income inequality change. Kuznets explained the inverted U-shaped curve of income inequality as result of transitional process in two economic sectors: the traditional rural sector and newly emerged urban sector. According to Kuznets, society consisted of these two sectors. Compared with urban sector, the rural sector had a relatively low income level and low income inequality. In this model, during industrialization and urbanization, even if income disparity between individual members of the urban rural sectors remained unchanged, the increasing urban population would still result in income inequality for society as a whole.[5] In this case, the income inequality of the whole society would be largely dependent on income changes within the urban sector. And how does the income inequality within the urban sector get reduced? According to Kuznets, there are two contributing factors. First, the children of rural-urban migrants in urban areas would be increasingly competitive in the labor market as they gradually adapted to urban life. Second, the increasingly large number of migrants would acquire more social influence and become able to influence the creation of income redistribution policy by the government, thereby making themselves the beneficiaries of social policy.

Since the mid 1950s, many economists have carried out both theoretical and empirical research to verify Kuznets hypothesis. The hypothesis has been engaged from different theoretical angles and the authors of works regarding the hypothesis have come to different

---

[5] Kuznets, "Economic Growth and Income Inequality," March 1955.
For explanation on the Kuznets hypothesis, please refer to Robinson, Sherman, "A Note on the Hypothesis Relating Income Inequality and Economic Development," 1976.

conclusions. Some research has been shown to support the hypothesis other research hasn't.

Most of the research regarding the Kuznets hypothesis tends to be empirically based, which involves testing the hypothesis against first-hand experience. Generally speaking, most research done before the 1990s was supportive of the hypothesis.[6] However, after 1990s, less and less research supported the hypothesis. Nowadays, most economists agree that economic growth does not have any systematic impact on income inequality.[7] For the relevant literature, please refer to Deininger and Squire,[8] Chen and Ravallion,[9] Easterly,[10] and Dollar and Kraay.[11]

The data used in the empirical studies that supported the Kuznets hypothesis were basically cross-country cross-sectional data, while more recently, Deininger and Squire[12] used cross-country panel data. The advantage of panel data lies in the fact that the impact of country-specific characteristics can be recognized and accounted for in the model estimation. After taking into account the country-specific factors, their results showed not only that the estimated coefficients for income levels were not only statistically significant, but also that their sign was opposite to what the Kuznets hypothesis predicts.[13] Furthermore, by using different sample countries, they found that the results for most countries (about 80 percent) show that the estimated coefficients of the income variables were insignificant. Moreover, even when the income coefficients were significant, their sign was the opposite of Kuznets hypothesis. In the end, only 10 percent of the sampled

---

[6] Among the related literature, the most representative paper is by Montek S. Ahluwalia (Ahluwalia, "Inequality, Poverty, and Development," 1976). He utilized 60 sample countries (including 14 developed countries, 40 developing countries, and 6 socialist countries) to verify Kuznets hypothesis. The results of his analysis are in line with the Kuznets Hypothesis.

[7] Please refer to the following website for conclusions regarding the researches on economic development and income inequality: http://web.worldbank.org/WBSITE/EXTERNAL/TOPICS/EXTPOVERTY/EXTPGI/0,,contentMDK:20263391~menuPK:577810~pagePK:148956~piPK:216618~theSitePK:342771,00.html

[8] Deininger, Klaus and Lyn Squire, "New Ways of Looking at Old Issues: Inequality and Growth," 1998.

[9] Chen, Shaohua and Martin Ravallion,"How have the world's poorest fared since the early 1980s?" 1997.

[10] Easterly, William, "Life During Growth," 1999.

[11] Dollar, David and Aart Kraay, "Growth Is Good for the Poor," 2002.

[12] Deininger and Squire, "New Ways of Looking at Old Issues: Inequality and Growth," 1998.

[13] Ibid.: 278.

countries were in line with Kuznets hypothesis. Finally, their study also showed how cross-sectional data could induce results favorable for the Kuznets hypothesis; data that favored the hypothesis was that from Latin-American countries. This is because in Latin-American countries, the per capita income was roughly middle level but the income inequality ranked the highest in the world. When data from these Latin-American countries was eliminated, the results showed that the Kuznets hypothesis could not hold water.[14]

The analysis of Ravallion and Chen[15] was based on the data from 67 developing and transitional countries; for 42 of these countries, there was data documenting at least a two years span. Through analyzing the relationship between the range of income (consumption expenditure) inequality and the growth rate of consumption expenditure at different periods in the 42 countries since the 1980s, they found that there was a correlation between rising consumption expenditure and shrinking inequality. However, once data from Eastern European countries and Central Asian countries was excluded, there was no apparent relationship whatsoever.

Dollar and Kraay[16] utilized a much bigger cross-country sample to estimate the effect of economic growth on poverty reduction. They found that economic growth can promote income growth for impoverished populations. The relationship between these two variables was one-to-one, that is to say, the income growth for an impoverished population increased directly with economic growth. However, because their research did not find that income growth for impoverished groups exceeded that of non-impoverished groups during economic development, their study failed to show that economic growth reduced income inequality.

The cross-country data used by Easterly[17] used data measuring the change of 81 indicators from four different years (1960, 1970, 1980, and 1990) directly or indirectly related to quality of life—including per capita income and income inequality indicators—to find out the impact of economic development on quality of life. Easterly analyzed the data from these 81 indicators one by one and found out that

[14] Ibid.: 282.

[15] Chen and Ravallion, "How have the world's poorest fared since the early 1980s?" 1997.

[16] Dollar and Kraay, "Growth Is Good for the Poor," 2002.

[17] Easterly, William, "Life During Growth," 1999.

growth of per capita income positively impacted 61 of these indicators. However, in his study, a country's income level bore no relationship to its income distribution. To account for this problem, Easterly[18] used models and data from a study carried out by Deininger and Squire,[19] and still came to almost the same conclusion.

Over the past 20 years, studies on the relationship between economic development and income distribution have tended to approach the topic from a different angle, which is exploring the effect of income inequality on economic development. Studies on this topic have not only been based in theory but also on empirical analysis. At present, results from these studies have not produced any consensus. Some results show that income inequality negatively impacts economic development,[20] while others suggest that income inequality promotes economic development.[21] Other studies have not discovered any relationship between these two.[22] Due to the limits on space, however, this chapter cannot review these results and their relevance to China's experience in more detail.

But if economic development has an impact on income inequality, then through what kinds of mechanisms does it occur? Many scholars have made efforts to determine the key contributing factors. One that has been uncovered is education. In regard to the role of education, research has shown that the popularization of education is beneficial not only in terms of promoting economic development, but also in lowering income inequality. In his work, Ding Bogen[23] pointed out that changes in income inequality are, to a great extent, determined by technological progress and the expansion of education. Technological progress determines the demand for technically skilled people, while education determines the supply. Ding has also suggested that the relationship between economic growth and income inequality is determined by a race between technological progress and education.

---

[18] Ibid.

[19] Deininger and Squire, "New Ways of Looking at Old Issues: Inequality and Growth," 1998.

[20] (Alesina, A. and D. Rodrik, "Distributive Politics and Economic Growth," 1994; Perotti, R., "Growth, Income Distribution and Democracy," 1996.

[21] Li and Zhou, 1998; Forbes, K., "A Reassessment of the Relationship between Inequality and Growth," 2000.

[22] Lopez, H., "Pro-Poor-Pro-Growth: Is There a Trade-Off?" 2004.

[23] Ding Bogen (1995).

III. *Economic Growth and Income Distribution in China*

The relationship between economic growth and income distribution in China must be understood with the backdrop of China's economic transition. China's economic transition and institutional innovation have positively impacted economic growth. Under the traditional planned economy, the economy was stifled by inefficiency and economic growth was hindered by the economic system. Under this system, egalitarianism was the main principle of income distribution. Wage determination and distribution could not fulfill their role of incentivizing work. Due to centralized control by the government, income inequality was limited to a minimum. It is well known that at the time, the economy was one of low growth, low efficiency, and small income differentials. As the economy has transitioned from a planned economy to market economy, both economic growth and income inequality have simultaneously emerged. Currently, economic reform has the most direct influence on both economic growth and rising income inequality. The effect of economic growth or development on the changes in income inequality is deserving of further research.

A. *Economic Growth and Income Inequality*

Thirty years of reform has put China's economy on the fast track for development. From 1978 to 2007, the annual growth rate of GDP has been 9.8 percent; the annual growth rate of GDP per capita has been 8.6 percent. Accompanying this rapid economic growth has been the equally rapid growth of incomes for both urban and rural residents, as is shown in Figure 8.1. Between 1978 and 2007, the real income of urban and rural residents has increased substantially; in 2007, average income had increased to about six times higher than it was in 1978. One interesting characteristic of this growth is that, when calculated in 2006, the real income growth rate of urban citizens was equal to that of rural residents when compared to their respective levels in 1978. The real income growth rate of urban residents did not exceed that of rural residents until 2007. However, this does not necessarily mean that rural and urban residents enjoyed the same income growth rate every year between 1978 and 2006. Before 1989, the growth rate of the real income of rural residents exceeded that of urban residents. But for the years after 1989, rate of income increase for urban and rural residents has shown the opposite trend. This can all be clearly

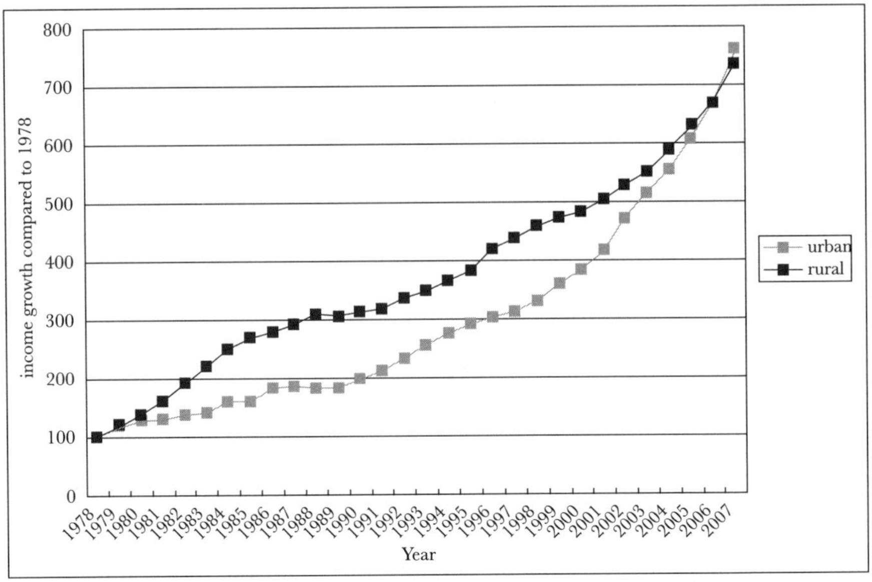

Source: National Bureau of Statistics, *Zhongguo tongji zhaiyao* 中国统计摘要 2008 [*China Statistics Abstract 2008*], 2008: 101.

Figure 8.1. Real Income Growth in China between 1978 and 2007.

seen in Figure 8.1. Figure 8.2 shows even more clearly the difference in income growth rate for urban and rural residents during these two periods. Before 1989, the income growth of rural residents had always been higher, with the exception of the year 1986. Since 1989, the income growth of urban residents has exceeded that of rural residents, with the exception of the years 1996 and 1997.

It is precisely this difference between the income growth rates of rural and urban residents during these two periods that resulted in the different degrees of income inequality during these two periods. As is shown in Figure 8.3, when using the 1978 value to evaluate income change, the directions of income change for rural and urban residents around 1988–1989 were totally different. At the beginning of China's reform, the income difference between rural and urban residents was relatively high, with the urban residents' income roughly 2.6 times that of rural residents. But from the start of reforms until 1989, the urban-rural income gap was basically shrinking, with urban residents' income lowered to roughly 1.5 times that of rural residents in 1988, which was lowest point in the past thirty years. However, pushed by further market-oriented reforms in urban areas, urban residents have

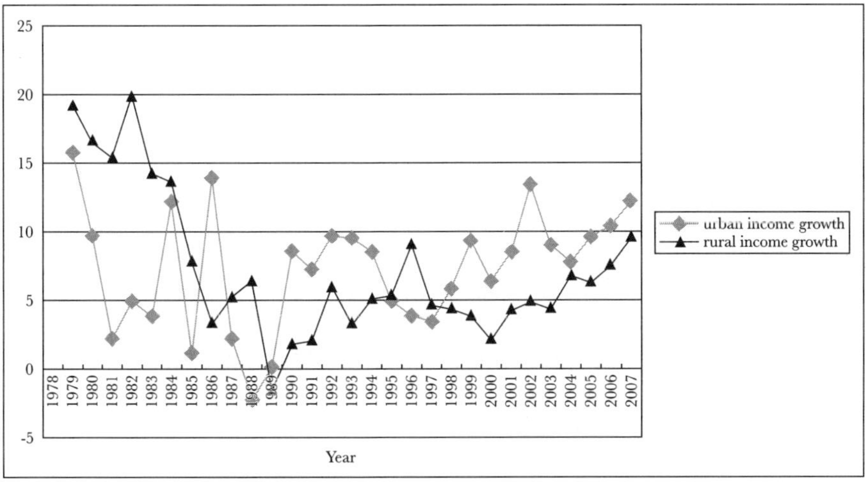

Source: National Bureau of Statistics, *China Statistics Abstract 2008*, 2008: 101.

Figure 8.2. Growth of Per Capita Income in China between 1979 and 2007.

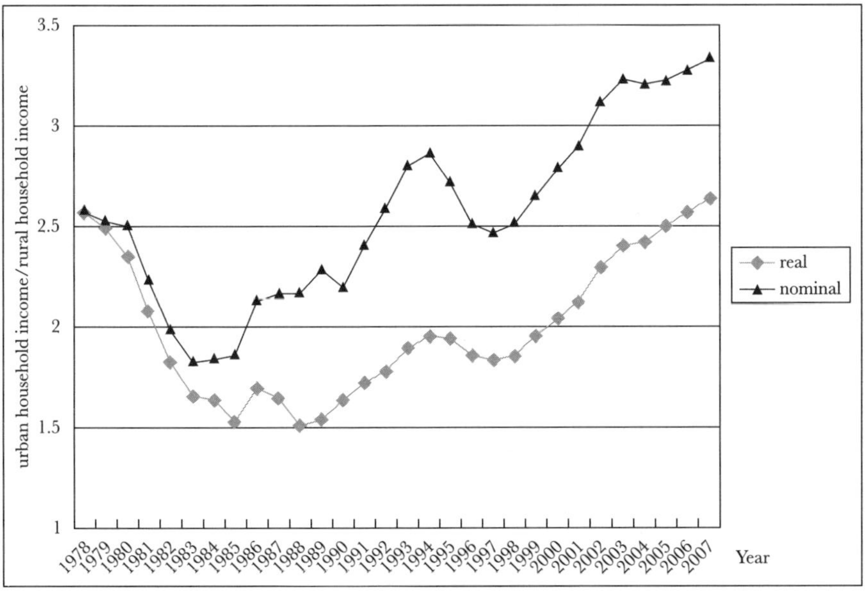

Note: The actual income gap is obtained from the computation of the real income of urban and rural residents in 1978 prices.
Source: National Bureau of Statistics, *China Statistics Abstract 2008*, 2008: 101.

Figure 8.3. China's Urban-Rural Income Gap from 1978 to 2007.

seen a rapid rise in income, and the urban-rural income gap has been expanding ever since. In 2006, the urban-rural income ratio reached the level of 1978, and expanded further in 2007, reaching the highest point in 30 years. In regard to this income pattern over the last few years, the urban-rural income gap keeps hitting new records because it is difficult to find any factors that can cause the income growth of rural residents' to overtake that of urban residents.

Urban and rural income growth has been accompanied by widening urban-rural income gap, which can be clearly seen in Figure 8.4. Due to the fact that comparable national Gini coefficients could only be assembled for the period between 1981 and 2002, Figure 8.4 shows the growth path of China's national GDP per capita and the Gini coefficient during this period. The two paths are similar, both exhibiting an upward growth pattern. During this period, the GDP per capita increased by about fivefold, with the Gini coefficient indicating national income distribution rising by 50 percent, from 0.3 in 1981 to 0.46 in 2002.

The same pattern of growth occurred in rural and urban areas. Figure 8.5 shows that the rural net per capita income and income distribution have also been on an upward path. Between 1978 and 2005, the net income of rural residents has risen over fivefold; during the same period, the Gini coefficient within rural areas has gone from 0.23 to 0.38, rising about 60 percent. Figure 8.6 shows the same story of synchronized growth for urban residents' income and income disparity between 1978 and 2005, with the disposable per capita income in urban areas increasing fivefold and its Gini coefficient doubling, rising from 0.16 to 0.35.

However, this phenomenon of simultaneous rise of income and expansion of the income gap often leads to the mistaken conclusion that income growth causes income difference; others conclude that income difference is one of the necessary factors to promote income growth. And some suggest that the widening income gap is not necessarily "bad" because it is beneficial to economic development and the income growth overall.

B. *Economic Growth and Income Inequality*

The description above is not sufficient enough to accurately depict the relationship between economic growth and income inequality. Further examination of the relationship between income growth and changes

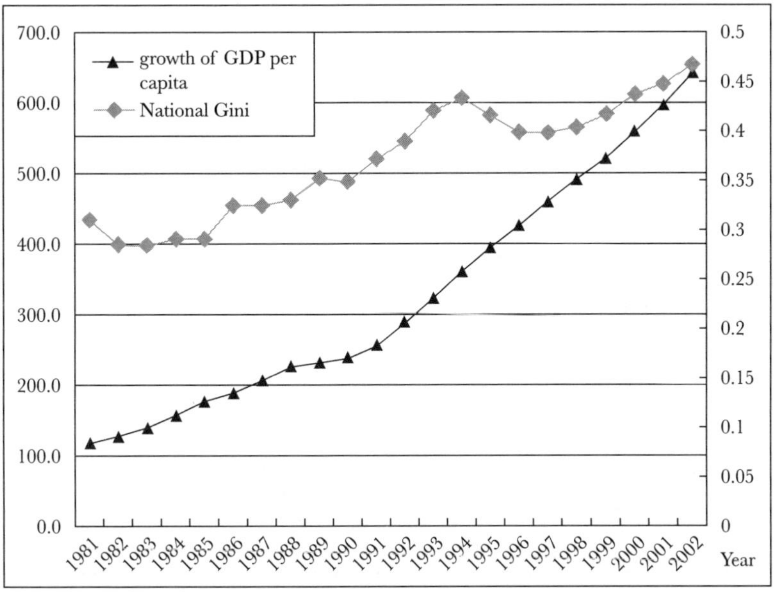

Source: The growth pattern of GDP per capita was calculated using data from National Bureau of Statistics, *China Statistics Abstract 2008*, 2008: 24; the data for national Gini coefficients are from Ravallion, Martin and Shaohua Chen, "China's (Uneven) Progress Against Poverty," 2004.

Figure 8.4. National Per Capita Income and Gini Coefficient in China.

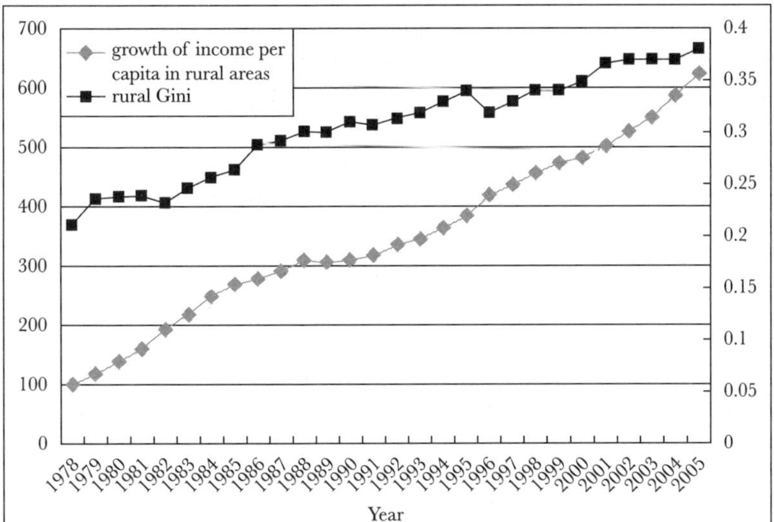

Source: The per capita income growth pattern of the rural residents was based on National Bureau of Statistics, *China Statistics Abstract 2008*, 2008: 101; The rural Gini coefficients were from the appendix Table 8.1 in this paper.

Figure 8.5. Per Capita Income and Gini Coefficient in Rural Areas.

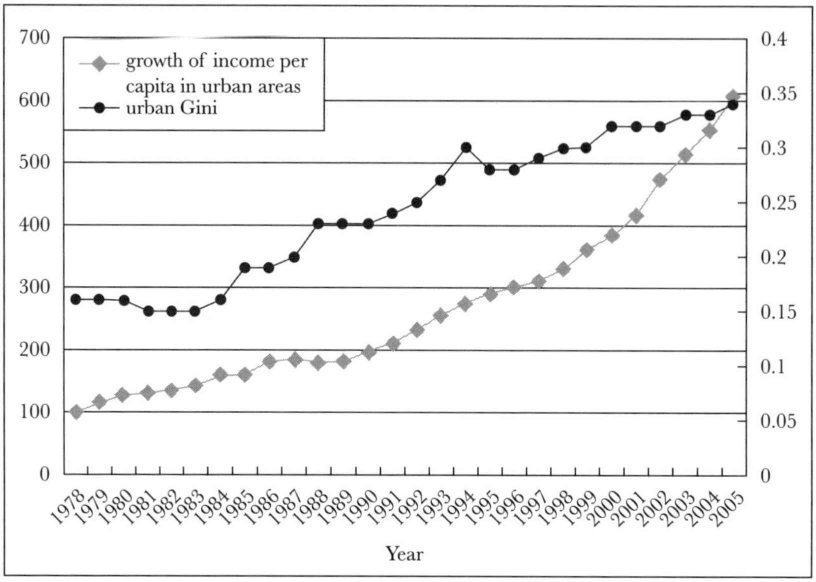

Source: The per capita income growth of urban residents was based on the data from National Bureau of Statistics, *China Statistics Abstract 2008*, 2008: 101; The rural Gini coefficients were from the Appendix Table A8.1 in this paper.

Figure 8.6. Per Capita Income and Gini Coefficient in Urban Areas.

in income inequality is needed. If a strong correlation exists between economic growth and income equality, then changes in income growth rate will result in corresponding changes in income inequality. Some simple analysis will help clarify this relationship.

Figure 8.7 illustrates the relationship between the growth rate of rural per capita income and changes in the rural Gini coefficient, in which the horizontal axis represents the annual growth rate from 1978 to 2005 and the vertical axis representing changes in the Gini coefficient at a specific annual growth rate. Figure 8.7 shows clearly that there is no apparent correlation between changes in the Gini co-efficient and income growth rate. If an income growth rate of 5 percent is set as a baseline, the Gini coefficient fluctuates at an average annual rate of 0.8 percentage points in those years when the annual growth rate is below 5 percent. During the years when the annual growth rate of income is over 5 percent, the Gini coefficient also fluctuates at an average annual rate of 0.5 percentage points. If we exclude the Gini coefficient from 1996, when it dropped drastically, the average annual fluctuation rate for Gini coefficient would be 0.7

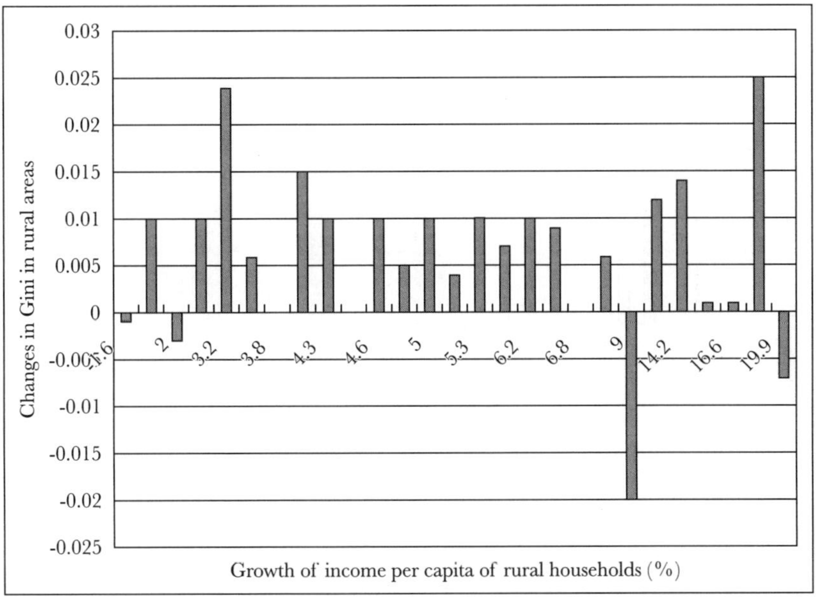

Figure 8.7. Relationship between the Growth Rate of Rural Per Capita Income and the Rural Gini Coefficient.

percentage points. This data shows no apparent difference between the rates of change for the Gini coefficients between these two different income growth rate ranges, which at the very least shows no connection between rising income inequality and faster income growth.

The relationship between the rural income growth rate and the rural Gini coefficient is not very clear either. As is illustrated in Figure 8.8, increasing income disparity corresponds not only with a lower income growth rate but also with a higher income growth rate. In other words, if the growth rate of income is higher, income inequality can increase greatly, increase by a low amount, or even diminish. Moreover, if the income growth rate is set at 7 percent as a boundary, the average variation of the Gini coefficient is about the same in years either over or under the boundary. This data shows that there is no evidence that fast income growth in urban areas results in relatively large expansion of the income gap.

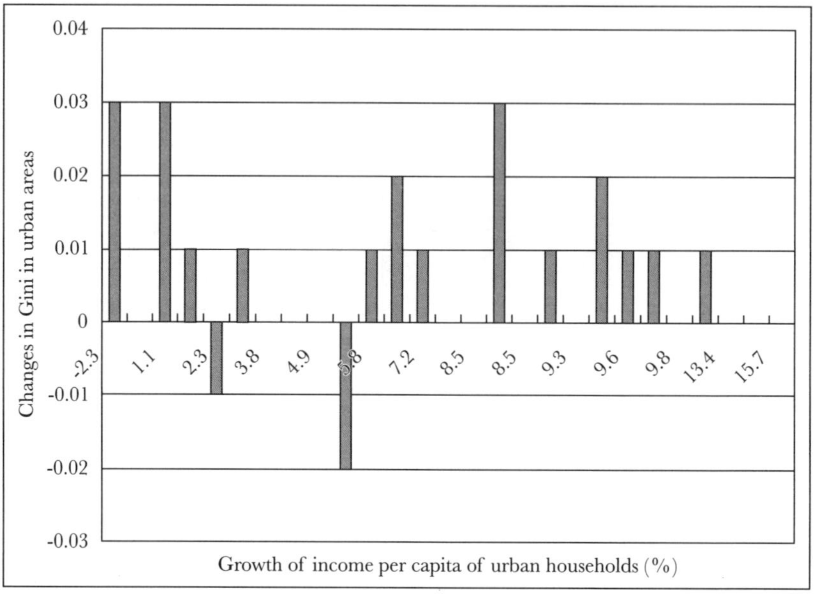

Figure 8.8. Relationship between the Growth Rate of Urban Per Capita Income and the Gini Coefficient.

IV. *Verifying the Causality between China's Economic Growth and Its Income Inequality*

The above description of the income growth and income inequality in rural and urban areas in China is only a rough outline. But it is nevertheless helpful in allowing us to form a general judgment about the relationship between income growth and income inequality. But the above analysis neither determined the nature of their relationship nor uncovered causality in their relationship. Even if it is a causal relationship, it would still difficult to determine which one is the cause and which is the result. Does income growth cause income inequality or vice versa? Further analysis and tests still needed in order to verify the nature of this relationship.

With the aim to verify their relationship empirically, the relationship between income growth and income inequality can be expressed in the following formula:

Formula 1

$I_t = b_0 + b_1 \log Y_t + b_2 (\log Y_t)^2 + e_t$

In this equation, I is a variable representing income inequality, which can be either the Gini coefficient or other measures of income inequality. Y_t represents income level, usually shown as a logarithm of per capita income and e_t is an error term. The introduction of $(\log Y_t)^2$ here is to verify whether or not the path of income inequality shows an inverted U-shaped curve. If the coefficient b_1 is a statistically significant positive integer and b_2 is negative, it will produce an inverted U-shaped path of income inequality.

If income growth has an impact on income inequality, the income growth rate should also influence the scale of income inequality. The above Formula 1 can be changed into the following formula:

Formula 2

$$\Delta I = b_0 + b_1 (\Delta y) + b_2 (\Delta y^2) + e$$

In this formula, ΔI and Δy represent the scale of income inequality and the income growth rate respectively.

Table 8.1 shows the relationship between income growth and income inequality, with one estimation set expressing the relationship between the income level and income inequality and the other showing the relationship between the income growth rate and the change in income inequality. Each group includes 3 models, using national, rural, and urban data. In these models, the dependent variables are the Gini coefficients or changes in the coefficient at the national, rural, and urban levels and the independent variables are the logarithm of national GDP per capita or its growth rate, the logarithm of rural net per capita income or its growth rate, and the logarithm of urban deposable per capita income or its growth rate.

From the first group of results comparing income level and income inequality, it is not hard to see that the estimations of the 3 models are completely different. In the national model, the estimated coefficient of income shows that the Gini coefficient first rose with the GDP per capita and then dropped down, but these estimated coefficients are not statistically significant. In this case, there is no apparent relationship between Gini coefficient and GDP per capita. In the rural model, the data is for the period from 1978 to 2005, in which the estimation shows a U-shaped curve of income inequality, which means that income inequality first dropped with the rise of per capita income, followed by a rise. This curve is against the Kuznets hypothesis. However, if the estimated range is limited to 1984–2005, the results would show an inverted U-shaped development path. Moreover, in producing a multiplier of over 10 percent, the first power term and the squared term of income change would be statistically significant; the computed Gini coefficient at the inflection point would be 0.41. These results are highly dependent on the choice of the specific range of 1984–2005 and the relationship between the income level and income inequality within those years. Different data from different periods would result in different estimations. Therefore, the estimation within this particular period only reflects the relationship between the income level and income inequality during this period; it does not mean that this kind of relationship would remain unchanged in the future.

In the urban model, the period under examination is also between 1978 and 2005. The results show that the path of income inequality is a clear inverted U-shaped curve. The coefficients on the income variable and its squared term are both significant. At the inflection point, the disposable per capita income is nearly 27 times that of 1978. According to the results, if the urban per capita income continues to grow at 10 percent per year, it would not be until the year 2018 that inequality would finally begin to decrease, with the Gini coefficient reaching 0.42. This means even if the relationship between urban income growth and income inequality remains unchanged in the long term, the widening income inequality would still last for another 10–15 years.

The second set of estimation results are disappointing but within expectation. The estimation results do not support the hypothesized inverted U-shaped curve of income inequality change either at the national level or for urban and rural areas. None of the estimation results in the three models have statistically significant coefficients on any of the independent variables. Even if the squared terms of income growth in the models are eliminated, the first power term of income growth rate is still not statistically significant. In other words, the growth rate of income and changes in income inequality do not have a linear relationship. Again, these results show that income growth rate does not have a clear impact on income inequality, even if there is a hypothesis on existence of this impact.

The cross-sectional data at a particular point in time can be utilized to estimate the above Formula 1 so as to test the relationship between income level and income inequality. Table 8.2 shows the results of these estimations from different cities based on data from the 2005 survey of 1 percent of the national population. The data from this 2005 sampling survey includes personal income information from which the mean income of the economically active population, the Gini coefficients of personal income, the mean income of highest and lowest

Table 8.1. Testing the Relationship between China's Income Growth Rate and Income Inequality: Time Series Data

	National	Rural	Urban
$I_t = b_{t0} + b_{t1}\log Y_t + b_{t2}(\log Y_t)^2 + e_t$			
b_0	−0.5181 (−0.58)	0.7962*** (2.80)	−1.8307*** (−2.98)
b_1	0.1505 (0.59)	−0.2736*** (2.81)	0.492** (2.69)
b_2	−0.0033 (−0.18)	0.0317*** (3.82)	−0.027* (−2.00)
Adj-R^2	0.8752	0.9471	0.9317
Income at the turning point	—	—	9055
Gini coefficient at the turning point	—	—	0.417
$\Delta I = b_0 + b_1(\Delta y) + b_2(\Delta y^2) + e$			
b_0	0.0205 (0.98)	0.0064 (1.36)	0.0122 (2.33)
b_1	−0.0038 (−0.73)	−0.0000 (−0.04)	−0.0015 (−0.99)
b_2	0.0002 (0.77)	2.08e−06 (0.03)	0.0001 (0.69)
Adj-R^2	−0.0753	−0.0832	−0.0240

Notes: (1) Estimations at the national level are based on data from 1981 to 2001; estimations for the urban and rural models are based on data from 1978 to 2005. (2) The income level is measured using 1978 values.

Sources: (1) The Gini coefficients of rural income distribution are from National Bureau of Statistics. *Zhongguo nongcun zhuhu diaocha nianjian* 中国农村住戶调查年鉴 [*China Rural Household Statistical Yearbook*]; the Gini coefficients of urban income distribution are from National Bureau of Statistics. *Zhongguo chengzhen zhuhu diaocha nianjian* 中国城镇住戶调查年鉴 [*China Urban Household Statistical Yearbook*]; the Gini coefficients of national income distribution are from Ravallion and Chen, "China's (Uneven) Progress Against Poverty," 2004. (2) National GDP per capita, urban disposable per capita income, and rural net per capita income are from the *China Statistics Yearbook* of relevant years.

10 percent, and other relevant indicators can be calculated for our estimation. In order to account for the variables that can influence income inequality, the urban unemployment rate (Unem), the ratio between migrant labor and total labor (MIGR) and its squared term ($MIGR^2$), and the ratio between the mean income of migrant labor and urban per capita income are used in this estimation. Formula 1 can be expanded into the following Formula 3:

Formula 3

$$I_i=b_0+b_1\log Y_i+b_2(\log Y_i)^2+b_3 Unem_i+b_4 MIGR_i+b_5 MIGR^2_i +b_{i6} MYR_i+e_i$$

Among the models using the Gini coefficient as a dependent variable, model 1 uses only the logarithm of per capita income and its quadratic term as dependent variables. The estimated coefficients of the two independent variables are statistically significant. But their signs show that the change of the Gini coefficient follows a U shape: first decreasing followed by an increase instead of the reverse U-shaped suggested

Table 8.2. Testing the Relationship Between Income Growth and Income Inequality in China: Urban Cross-sectional Data

Dependent variables: Gini coefficient	Model 1	Model 2	Model 3	Model 4	Model 5
b_0	2.20***(3.28)	0.95*(1.70)	2.04***(3.06)	0.75 (1.35)	4.205***(–3.57)
b_1	–0.54***(–2.72)	–0.25 (–1.53)	–0.48**(–2.38)	–0.17(–1.05)	–1.19***(–3.57)
b_2	0.04***(2.70)	0.02* (1.89)	0.03**(2.22)	0.02(1.25)	0.09***(3.67)
b_3		0.79***(12.86)		0.79***(13.15)	0.78***(13.0)
b_4			0.18***(3.30)	0.16***(3.56)	0.20***(4.43)
b_5			–0.19**(2.41)	–0.15**(2.32)	–0.20***(–3.07)
B_6					0.02**(2.55)
Adj-R^2	0.016	0.336	0.049	0.369	0.401
Urban sample quantity	344	344	344	344	342
Dependent variables: ratio of the income of the highest 10 percent to mean income	Model 6	Model 7	Model 8	Model 9	Model 10
b_0	47.73***(3.75)	33.96***(2.71)	45.35***(3.72)	30.79***(2.58)	31.58***(2.71)
b_1	–13.61***(-3.64)	–9.92***(2.71)	–12.56***(3.51)	–8.64**(–2.47)	–9.10***(–2.67)
b_2	1.03***(3.74)	0.78***(2.89)	0.92***(3.49)	0.65**(2.54)	0.69***(2.78)
b_3		3.51***(5.32)		3.53***(5.67)	3.84***(6.29)
b_4			2.10***(4.35)	1.96***(4.24)	2.16***(4.68)
b_5			–1.55**(2.23)	–1.31*(–1.96)	–1.44**(–2.19)
B_6					0.37***(4.38)
Adj-R^2	0.074	0.143	0.172	0.241	0.279
Urban sample quantity	343	343	343	343	342

Notes: In order to get a better picture of income inequality, besides the Gini coefficient as a dependent variable, the ratio of the mean income of the top 10 percent of income to urban mean income is also used to measure income inequality. Table 8.3 shows 5 models with the Gini coefficient and the income ratio as dependent variables. Each model has its own independent variables. However, all the models have two common independent variables, which are $\log Y_{i,}$ the mean per capita income of the urban economic active population, and its squared term $[(\log Y_i)^2]$.
Source: Data from the 2005 sampling survey of 1 percent of the national population.

in the Kuznets Hypothesis. According to this model's estimations, the lowest Gini coefficient is 0.36, followed by an increase along with the increase of income. When the monthly per capita income reached 500 yuan (calculated based on the 2005 value), the Gini coefficient rose to 0.5. In the other models, models 2 to 5, other controlled variables were introduced. When the variable representing the urban unemployment rate was introduced in model 2, the estimated coefficient on the income variable became insignificant while the estimated coefficient on the unemployment variable became highly significant. This shows a strong correlation between changes in income inequality and the urban unemployment rate. In the 344 urban samples, the average unemployment rate is 7.8 percent; the estimated coefficient shows that whenever the unemployment rate goes up by 1 percent, the Gini coefficient will increase by nearly 0.8 percent.

In model 3, the proportion of migrant labor in a city and its squared term are introduced as control variables in with an aim to measure the impact of labor structure on income inequality. The results suggest that the estimated coefficients of the two labor structure variables are both statistically significant. Their signs show that with increasing levels of migrant labor, income inequality first goes up and then drops. Also, the estimated coefficients of the income variables are not affected significantly upon introduction of the two variables. Based on models 3 to 5, we can see that income inequality expands with the increase of the proportion of migrant labor. When the proportion reaches its highest point of 45–50 percent, it begins to decline. According to the data from the 1 percent of the population survey, the average proportion of migrant labor in the sampled cities is around 20 percent. This implies that the continued movement of migrant labor into cities will continue to generate income inequality for quite a long time.

Besides the proportion of migrant labor, differences in the incomes of migrant and local labor are also a major factor contributing to urban income inequality. In model 5, the ratio of migrant labor income to local labor income is introduced, the estimated coefficients of which are statistically significant. Surprisingly, however, its sign turns out to be positive. This means that as the income gap between local and migrant laborers becomes smaller, overall urban income inequality increases instead of decreases. How do we explain this result? To a greater extent, this result has to do with income inequality among migrant laborers. Due to the large income gap between members of this group, especially between migrant workers from rural areas and migrant workers in cities who have already achieved some degree of success, the expansion of income inequality within this group is substantial and long term, which inevitably leads to increasing income inequality within urban areas as a whole.

V. *How Do We Explain Changing Income Inequality in China?*

Most of the results from the empirical studies above do not support the Kuznets Hypothesis. But, if economic growth is not responsible, or has very limited responsibility, for income inequality, how do we explain the trend of rising income inequality in China over the past thirty years? First, we must understand that China is not only a developing country but also a transitional country. During the economic transition, reform of economic system has made itself felt not only on the production side but also in income distribution (both primary distribution and redistribution). The impact of economic transition on the income distribution pattern should be fully considered. The income distribution trend that has emerged out of this process can, to a certain extent, be attributed more to economic reform than to economic development. Frankly speaking, it is hard to differentiate the impact of economic transition from that of economic development because China's experience over the past thirty years has featured a complementary and interconnected relationship between these two processes.

To understand the changing income inequality in China, we must take its regional characteristics into consideration. Due to the historically different policies for cities and the countryside, income inequality change in China as a whole can be understood from the change of income inequality within urban areas, or from the change in income inequality within rural areas, or from the income disparity between rural and urban areas. Income inequality is affected by different factors, therefore, when we analyze the trend and reasons for the income inequality, we must analyze from multiple perspectives instead using a single factor, such as economic growth. Comparatively, the change in income inequality within the rural areas is more likely to be affected by economic development, while the change in income inequality within urban areas is more affected by economic transition. Finally, the income disparity between urban and rural areas is more likely affected by economic policies.

A. *Explaining Income Inequality in Rural Areas*

Since early 1980s, income inequality within rural areas has increased over 60 percent, with its Gini coefficient rising from 0.23 in 1980 to 0.38 in 2005 (see Figure 8.5). The privatization of land-use in the early 1980s was a major institutional change that definitely impacted income distribution. However, this was a positive change, reducing income inequality instead of enlarging it. This is because this reform promoted the rapid growth of agricultural income for the farmers and narrowed the income disparity between agricultural and industrial workers. It is precisely this kind of income disparity (between agricultural and industrial workers) that serves as one of the major causes of income inequality in rural areas.[24] This reform narrowed the income gap between agricultural regions and relatively industrialized regions.

Since mid-1980s, economic development has gradually come to play a major role in income inequality, which can be seen in the development of the non-agricultural sector and increased employment in non-agricultural industries within the rural areas, due in part to restrictions on migration to urban areas. During the early stage of economic opening, the development of the non-agricultural sector was concentrated in the relatively wealthy coastal regions. There was still a scissors gap between the industrial and agricultural products. Therefore, the development of the non-agricultural sector promoted rapid economic development in coastal regions, enlarging the income gap between these regions and agriculture-dependent regions as well as income inequality within the coastal regions. This income inequality was mainly a result of the disparity between families in non-agricultural and agricultural sectors. In relatively less developed regions, even if there were limited opportunities for non-agricultural employment, the farmers who had access to these opportunities were mainly from relatively better off families.

The abolition of the food rationing system made possible the migration of rural laborers into cities. Also, the relaxation of employment regulations for urban state-owned and collective enterprises and private enterprises' demand for rural laborers made migration even more

[24] Khan, Azizur, Keith Griffin, Carl Riskin and Zhao Renwei, "Household Income and Its Distribution in China," 1992; Khan, Azizur, and Carl Riskin, "Income and Inequality in China: Composition, Distribution and Growth of Household Income, 1988 to 1995," 1998.

possible. But one thing that should not be overlooked is the high cost of migration in the 1990s, which could not be afforded by poorer rural families.[25] Therefore, the pattern of migration during the early stage of economic development was as follows: migrant laborers from relatively developed regions were mostly from middle income families and migrant laborers from less developed regions were mainly from high and middle income families. This pattern enlarged income inequality within rural areas instead of reducing it, especially in poorer regions.[26]

Due to the factors mentioned above, income inequality in rural areas has been on the increase since the mid-1980s. Since then, increasing non-agricultural employment opportunities in less developed regions, the increase in the number of migrant workers from middle and low income families, and the government's subsidies to grain farmers and relief to poverty-stricken families have all played a role in alleviating income inequality in the rural areas. However, the persistent influence of factors that enlarge income inequality have offset the positive impact of the above-mentioned factors to a great extent. The result is the continually expanding income inequality that we see in rural regions today.

Some factors that have increased income inequality in rural areas since late 1990s cannot be overlooked. First of all, income growth for high-income households and their further wealth accumulation has been a virtuous circle. Thus growing income inequality has been accompanied by unequal distribution of income as well, which has been an important phenomenon over the past ten years.[27] The households that got rich first have since begun to use their accumulated wealth to become entrepreneurs and investors. The ratio of their property income to their total income has been increasing. Meanwhile, the income of the middle and low income groups in rural areas is

[25] Zhao Yaohui, 赵耀辉, "Zhongguo nongcun laodongli liudong ji jiaoyu zai qizhong de zuoyong 中国农村劳动力流动及教育在其中的作用 The Migration of Rural Labor in China and the Role of Education in Migration," 1997; Cai Fang 蔡昉 and Wang Dewen 王德文, "Migration as Marketization: What Can We Learn from China's 2000 Census Data?" 2003.

[26] Li Shi, 1999.

[27] Zhao Renwei 赵人伟 and Ding Sai 丁赛, "The Distribution of Wealth in China," 2008; Li Shi 李实, Wei Zhong 魏众, and Ding Sai 丁赛, "Zhongguo jumin caichan fenbu bujundeng jiqi yuanyin de jingji fenxi 中国居民财产分布不均等及其原因的经验分析 [Economic Analysis of China's Unequal Wealth Distribution and the Reasons Behind It]," 2005.

constantly unstable, with their income level hovering around the poverty line.[28] Secondly, the impoverished population has not been given proper assistance. The academic world, both at home and abroad, has reached a consensus that the scale of rural poverty in China has been underestimated.[29] However, further relief measures to aid impoverished people have not been elevated to the level of national policy. Although the rural subsistence system has been initiated, the standard is still too low.[30] The new rural cooperative medical care system aims to cover all rural residents but a majority of the low income population still faces large medical expenses due to low rates of reimbursement. Finally, disease or sickness-induced poverty among farmers has yet to be completely eliminated.

B. *Explaining to Income Inequality in the Urban Areas*

The causes for income inequality within urban areas are different from those of rural areas. Before the implementation of the reform and opening policy, the urban economy was directed under the planned economic system. Under the public-ownership and uniform wage standard, the small degree of income inequality that existed was determined by the plan. Moreover, there was a great deal of ideological pressure to promote egalitarian income distribution. All these factors caused urban income inequality during the period of the planned economy to be reach its lowest level in China's history. According to estimates by the National Bureau of Statistics (NBS), the Gini coefficient of the income of urban residents in 1978 was 0.16 (see Table 8.6). However, the problems that this income distribution pattern brought about, such as low efficiency due to lack of incentive, were self-evident. It was these problems that provided the opportunity to carry out reform of the income distribution system.

---

[28] Whalley, John and Ximing Yue, "Rural Income Volatility and Inequality in China," 2007; Yue, Ximing, Terry Sicular, Li Shi and Bjorn Gustafsson, "Explaining Incomes and Inequality in China," 2008.

[29] The opinions regarding this issue can be found in *China Development 2007: Eliminating Poverty in Economic Development* by China Development Research Foundation.

[30] The average annual subsistence allowance was 840 yuan per person in the rural areas in 2008, the average monthly subsidy was 37 yuan per person(see the *China Development 2008: Constructing China's Social Security System (discussion version)* by the China Development Research Foundation.

In terms of changing the income distribution system, the reforms that contributed most to income inequality in urban areas were those in the following four areas: (1) first, one of the most important reform processes was that of allowing state-owned and collective enterprises a higher degree of economic freedom and promoting the development of the private sector, which introduced the market mechanism in wage determination. Though limited in number and size, private and individual enterprises began to emerge in 1980s, generating heated debate regarding their income distribution model, which was different from the egalitarian system. The development of these enterprises and their large profits resulted in the rapid rise of income inequality within the private sector. (2) Second, the reform of the wage system in state-owned enterprises was very significant. The wage distribution system that emerged from reform was based on the principle of efficiency-first, and aimed at increasing income disparity within firms so as to improve the incentive effect of wages. This reform took place not only within state-owned and collective enterprises, but also within government departments and public institutions. Although the ratio of managers' wages to that of employees in state-owned enterprises is controlled by their supervisory departments, this ratio has nonetheless consistently been on the rise. Every reform of the wage system within government and public institutions has set newer, higher standards for the wages of their managers. These reforms have by and large increased income inequality among urban workers. (3) Third, the restructuring of the state-owned enterprises increased unemployment, which has definitely been one of the most important factors contributing to income inequality in urban areas. The results from models of income inequality in different cities in 2005 have also provided evidence that supports this conclusion. The goal of state-owned enterprise restructuring was to "downsize for efficiency." In late 1990s, due to the absence of the social security system, laid-off employees lost not only their jobs but also their income security. Suddenly, many previous employees were thrown into the low income group, which resulted in increased urban poverty.[31] The employees who hadn't been laid-off benefited from increased "efficiency" through the rapid growth of their wages.[32] (4) Fourth, the rapid growth of incomes in industries

[31] (Li Shi, Sato Hiroshi, 2002).

[32] The number of urban self-employed people reached 4.5 million in 1985, the number of employees in the cooperative enterprises (a different form of private enter-

with monopolies resulted in the sudden expansion of the income disparity between different industries, which was an important contributor to growing income inequality within urban areas.[33] In early 1990s, income inequality between industries was nothing worth mentioning. There were hardly any differences between the wages of monopolized industries, such as finance, electricity, and telecommunications, and the manufacturing industry.[34] In 2006, however, the wages in these industries were 2–3 times those in the manufacturing industry.

The above explanations of urban income inequality have concentrated on the impact economic transition. However, this does not mean that economic development and policies have not played a role in income inequality. For example, the increasing returns on education have led to rising income disparities between people with different educational backgrounds and people in different professions. To some extent, income inequality is the result of changes in the structure of the urban labor market. A large amount of rural laborers with less education have entered the urban labor market, causing supply of labor to exceed demand, while the economic structure has been upgraded constantly due to efforts by the government. On one hand, this restructuring has led to decreased employment elasticity for urban industries;[35] on the other hand, it also led to demand for skilled labor to exceed supply, which has resulted in increased wages for educated workers and consequently increased returns on education.

C. *Explaining Income Disparity Between Urban and Rural Areas*

The income disparity between urban and rural areas is a result of the legacy of the planned economy as well as new factors coming from economic transition. During the period of the planned economy—on the basis of "catching up" with the West—the Chinese government

prise) were 380,000. The total number of both accounted for 3.8 percent of the total urban employees (See National Bureau of Statistics, *China Statistics Abstract 2008*: 45).

[33] Li Shi 李实, Sicular 史泰丽, and Gusstafsson 古斯塔夫森, *Zhongguo jumin shouru fenpei yanjiu III* 中国居民收入分配研究Ⅲ [*Researching China's Income Distribution Vol. 3*], 2008.

[34] Since 1999, the wage growth rate of the state-owned enterprises has exceeded 10 percent, much higher than the average growth rate of the wage of urban employees (See National Bureau of Statistics, *China Statistics Abstract 2008*: 45).

[35] Li Shi 李实, "Gaige kaifang sanshi nian zhongguo shouru fenpei de bianhua 改革开放三十年中国收入分配的变化 [Changes in Income Distribution over Thirty Years of Reform and Opening]," 2008.

adopted a growth strategy prioritizing heavy industry, and accumulated capital for the development of heavy industry by depriving farmers of their surplus. One result of this ill-envisioned strategy is the vast income disparity between urban and rural areas.[36] At the beginning of the reform and opening period in 1978, urban households earned nearly 2.6 times more than rural households and the ratio between the expenditure per capita of urban households and that of rural households was almost 2.7.[37]

In the early 1980s, when agricultural reform was carried out, the income disparity between urban and rural areas declined for certain amount of time, reaching its lowest point in the mid-1980s. When calculated using the 1978 value, the ratio between the per capita income of urban households and that of rural households dropped to 1.7 in 1985.[38] The decreasing income disparity between urban and rural areas can be attributed to the income growth of farmers, which had overtaken that of urban households.[39] Both reform and government policy played a role in the income growth of farmers. In this, reform refers to the privatization of land-use, which motivated and incentivized agricultural production. Policy refers to government policies raising the prices of agricultural products, which brought about income growth for farmers. In this case, reform and marketization did not necessarily lead to widening income disparity.

However, since the mid-1980s, the urban-rural income gap has been expanding (See Figure 8.9). In 2003, it reached its highest point in history. In recent years, it has been fluctuating around this level. Compared with other developing countries, the income disparity between the rural and urban areas in China ranks the highest.[40] Moreover, the impact of the urban-rural income disparity on income inequality

[36] Lin, Justin Yifu 林毅夫, Cai Fang 蔡昉, and Li Zhou 李周, *Zhongguo de qiji: Fazhan zhanlüe yu jingji gaige* 中国的奇迹, 发展战略与经济改革 [*The China miracle: development strategy and economic reform*], 1994.

[37] See National Bureau of Statistics, *China Statistics Abstract 2008*: 101–102.

[38] Li Shi, Sicular, and Gusstafsson, *Researching China's Income Distribution Vol. 3*, 2008.

[39] Between 1978–1983, the per capita income of the urban households increased by 40 percent, while the per capita income of the rural households increased by 120 percent, 3 times of that of the urban households. (See National Bureau of Statistics, *China Statistics Abstract 2008*: 101).

[40] Sicular, T., X. Yue, B. Gustafsson, and S. Li, "The Urban-Rural Income Gap and Inequality in China," 2007; Dollar, "Poverty, Inequality and Social Disparities during China's Economic Reform," 2007.

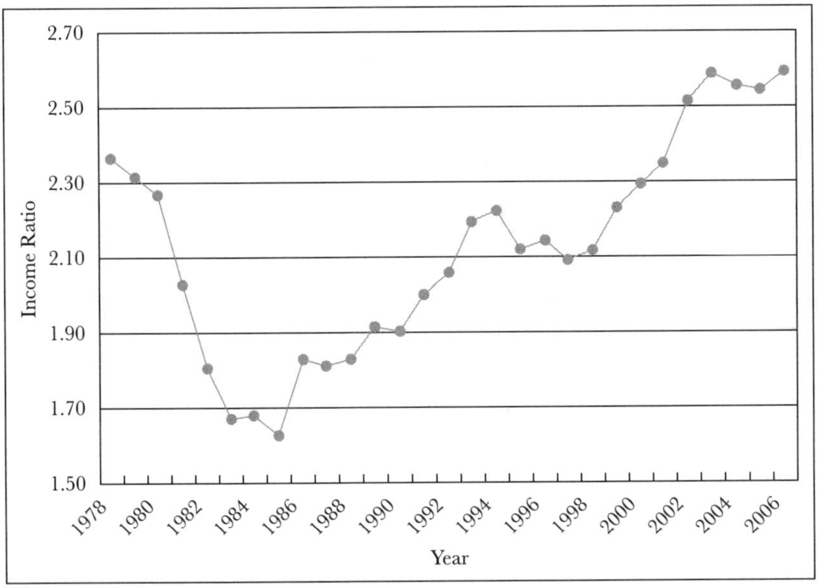

Y Axis: Income Ratio
X Axis: Year
Note: This figure is based on the data of the per capita income and price index of urban and rural residents from the *China Statistics Abstract* of different years. The per capita income of urban and rural residents in each year was measured according to 1978 prices. The rural consumer price index between 1978 and 1984 was replaced by the national consumer price index.

Figure 8.9. Ratio between Real Per Capita Income of Urban and Rural Workers in China.

nationwide has become stronger, with its share of national income inequality rising from 37 percent in 1988 to 41 percent in 1995 and to 46 percent in 2002.[41]

How do we explain the increasing income disparity between urban and rural areas since the mid 1980s? It is not difficult to fathom that the income growth of urban households exceeded that of the rural households. However, it still leaves one wondering if the income growth of urban households was abnormal or if the income growth of rural households was insufficient. Between these two, the latter problem is much more serious than the former one. The reason is that the growth rate for the income of urban households is synchronized

[41] Li Shi, Sicular, and Gusstafsson, *Researching China's Income Distribution Vol. 3*, 2008.

with the growth rate of GDP, while the income growth rate of rural households is much lower than the GDP growth rate.[42] Therefore, our analysis here will be concentrated on the reasons behind the slow growth of rural income.

First, the systemic and policy constraints on the free flow of labor during the planned economy period did no good for the income of farmers. Due to China's "different administrative policies for the cities and countryside" in labor management, the development of China's labor market has always lagged behind the development of its commodity market. Even after the turn of the new century, the migration of rural surplus labor to cities has been restrained by various systems, laws, regulations, and "local policies," instead of being encouraged and supported by the government. The free movement of rural laborers has yet to be fully realized. With the growing amount of the rural laborers in the countryside, delaying the migration of rural labor to cities has made its size bigger and bigger.[43] This has not only caused farmers to miss great opportunities to make money, but has also resulted in a longer-term oversupply of unskilled laborers in the urban labor market. Research suggests that the income growth of the farmers would have been faster if the restrictions on the free flow of the labor had been lifted.

Secondly, the government has always overlooked investing in social development and human capital in rural areas, which is a major factor contributing to the slow income growth of farmers. As known to all, the social development of rural areas in China has always lagged

---

[42] During the period between 1986 and 2006, the annual growth rate of GDP was 9.7 percent, the annual growth rate of the urban per capita income was 7.1 percent, and the annual growth rate of rural residents was 4.4 percent, less than half of the growth rate of GDP.

[43] Due to the complexity in estimating the size of the rural labor surplus, we could only approach this question based on other relevant data. The rural laborers rose from 306 million in 1978 to 490 million in 1997 (See National Bureau of Statistics, *China Statistics Abstract 2008*: 45). During this period, the local township enterprises absorbed 102 million laborers (Li Shi, "Rural Migrant Workers in China: Scenario, Challenges and Public Policy," 2007), the migrant laborers numbered 60–70 million, with a 30 million increase in the number of rural laborers. Besides this, agricultural mechanization and technology progress have created an even bigger labor surplus. As far as the number of employed persons in the three industries is concerned, the employed persons in the first industry with agriculture as its major have been increasing between 1978 and 1991, having increased by 110 million. The number have been declining gradually since 1991, reaching its lowest point in 1996, which was about 350 million followed by an increase, reaching 370 million in 2002 (See National Bureau of Statistics, *China Statistics Abstract 2008*: 44).

behind, manifested by the lack of public services and insufficient social securities, which are in stark contrast to those of urban residents.[44] The investment in human capital in particular, which is closely related to income growth, has been too little to even be worth mentioning. Before the implementation of the economic reform and opening policy, the poverty rate in the rural areas was very high. Hunger and malnutrition were commonplace.[45] One can imagine that the health of those born in 1960s and 1970s will be affected by their malnutrition as a child. This group of laborers will be more vulnerable to sickness and disease over the long term. But the current state of the rural medical care system is enough to make one cringe. Although some regions have implemented programs to cover basic medical costs, the vast majority of farmers must still cover their own medical expenses.[46] Factor in the fact that medical expenses keep growing and it is not too difficult to imagine how the difficulty in accessing and the high cost of medical care have lead to "sickness-induced poverty." Sickness can make it impossible for farmers to making profits from their work and delay their income growth. Also, the government's inadequate investment in education in rural areas has led to a long-term decline in income growth. Even though the average years of schooling among rural laborers have been increasing steadily and the illiteracy rate has been declining gradually, the human capital of rural areas is still lagging behind that of cities. According to data from the Fifth National Population Census (第五次全国人口普查), the illiteracy rate among the rural population over the age of 15 was 2.5 times higher than that

---

[44] China Development Research Foundation, UNDP. *China Human Development Report 2005: Toward Human Development with Equity*, 2005; Dollar, "Poverty, Inequality and Social Disparities during China's Economic Reform," 2007.

[45] Some relevant data shows that the calorie intake of the rural residents from 1996 to 1997 didn't even reach the level of 2100 calorie per day per person. According to the nutrition standard, 40–50 percent of the rural population was in poverty (See Zhou Binbin 周彬彬, "Renmin gongshe shiqi de pinkun wenti 人民公社时期的贫困问题 Poverty During the Period of the People's Communes," 1991). If calculated based on the poverty line of 1 US dollar per day per person, the estimated poverty occurrence rate would be 64 percent in 1981, dropping to 16.6 percent in 2001 (See Chen, and Ravallion, "How have the world's poorest fared since the early 1980s?" 2004).

[46] A survey carried out by the Ministry of Health shows that less than 10 percent of farmers have participated in the rural collective medical care system, and those who participated in the commercial insurance made up 8.5 percent. 79 percent of farmers don't have any kind of medical care at all and pay in full for their medical expenses (See *China Public Health Statistical Abstract 2008* online at: http://202.96.155.169/publicfiles/business/htmlfiles/zwgkzt/ptjty/200805/35671.htm)

of the urban population. For the population between 20 and 24 years old, the percentage of people with a junior high school education or below in 2000 was 45 percent in urban areas and 88 percent in the rural areas. These numbers just point out the differences in quantity, but the difference in educational quality is even more significant, which is clearly reflected in the distribution of educational investment. In 2001, the average educational budget expense per student in primary schools of the rural areas was 85 percent of the national level, and the average educational budget expense per student in junior high schools of rural areas was about 80 percent of the national level. The public expense per student in rural primary and junior high schools compared to the national level were even less, about 62 percent and 54 percent of national level respectively.[47] Only in the past two years has the situation begun to improve.

Finally, farmers in China have had both low incomes and high taxes for a long time. Before the agricultural tax was repealed, the Chinese taxation system was strongly regressive, which can be seen from the following two aspects. First, there was disunity and disconnect between the taxation systems of urban and rural areas. Low-income rural households shouldered much higher tax rates than high-income urban households. Second, most of the taxes were levied according to the size of one's land and the number of household members, so even within rural areas the low income households could face a higher tax rate than the high income households. The effect of the taxation system was to increase income inequality within rural areas as well as between urban and rural areas; it did nothing to alleviate the poverty, and even caused poverty.[48] This tax system completely lacked social fairness. At the beginning of this century, the central government began to realize the consequences of the taxation system and started to eliminate the various agricultural taxes in the rural areas step by step; agricultural taxes and fees were totally repealed in 2007.

[47] China Development Research Foundation, *China Development Research Report 2008: Constructing the Social Welfare System in China (Discussion Version)*, 2008.

[48] A simple simulation shows that, if the rural households were exempted from all the taxes and fees, the per capita income would increase by 5.4 percent, the income disparity between the rural residents and urban residents would decrease by 13 percent, and the Gini coefficient would drop by 1.4 percent. (Li Shi 李实 and Yue Xixin 岳希新, "Zhongguo chengxiang shouru chaju diaocha 中国城乡收入差距调查 [Investigation on the Urban-Rural Income Gap]," 2003).

VI. *Conclusions and Policy Implications*

This chapter has carried out an empirical study analyzing the relationship between income growth and income distribution, focusing especially on the impact of economic growth on income inequality based on data from China. Our results do not support the Kuznets hypothesis or its "inverted U-shaped curve," which means that income distribution in China has its own characteristics. Therefore, we analyzed separately income inequality and its changing pattern within rural areas and urban areas, as well as the income disparity between urban and rural areas. Our explanations emphasized not only the impact of economic development, but also the impact of economic transition and government policy, on income distribution. In the end, we found that these factors can both increase and reduce income inequality. But, since the un-equalizing effects have exceeded the equalizing effects, the result that we see now in China is expanding income inequality. But, even with the increase in income inequality, it can still be either fair or unfair. In creating economic policy to address these issues, mechanisms aimed at eliminating unfair income distribution should be taken into consideration.

The adverse effects of income inequality urgently require attention. Reform and policy measures should be taken to meet the challenge of unfair income distribution. Therefore, this paper proposes the following policy suggestions:

First, our analysis shows that unemployment is a major contributing factor to the growing income inequality. The Gini coefficient has a strong correlation with the unemployment rate, and unemployment is a major reason for change of the Gini coefficient. Therefore, one policy that would work to prevent growing income inequality is to improve employment opportunities by improving the allocative efficiency of rural labor and reducing surplus rural labor.

Second, the huge income disparity between urban and rural areas, the great regional disparities, and the growing income inequality between industries in China all suggest that there is severe segmentation in the labor market and a systematic obstacle to movement of workers. Therefore, accelerating the development of a more open labor market with more mobility will be an effective way to narrow the urban-rural, regional, and industrial disparities. Removing these systematic obstacles to labor migration not only includes abolishing the policies that directly prevent labor migration, such as the household registration system and the restrictions on migration to cities, but also includes eliminating the discriminatory provision of public services by including migrant workers and their children in the urban public education system, medical care system, and housing system. At the same time, steps must be taken to break up industrial monopolies, whose negative impacts on income inequality can be seen not only in high monopoly profits and income, but also, more seriously, in its appropriation of consumer surplus by manipulating prices, which encroaches on the public interest.

Third, income distribution policy aimed at protecting vulnerable groups must be enacted. Vulnerable groups not only include the impoverished populations of both the rural and urban areas, but also other groups who are in a disadvantaged position within the market economy, such as farmers who have lost their land, migrant workers in the cities, and laid-off workers. These groups of people are low income groups because they lack the potential to earn high incomes. Therefore, a key point of income redistribution policy should be to enhance their potential, including creating more employment opportunities, providing necessary educational subsidies, medical care, and other social security measures.

Fourth, the fiscal transfer from the central government to rural areas and less developed regions must be increased, so as to narrow the gap in public expenditure between urban and rural areas and different regions. Under the market economy, the major function of central finance should be shifted from supporting economic construction to providing public services, with emphasis on public security, public health, public education, professional training, a public relief system, infrastructure, etc., so as to resolve social conflicts, maintain social stability, and realize the national equalization of public services. Through transfer payments, investment in infrastructure in rural areas and relatively less developed areas can be increased and disparities in the public services between urban and rural areas and different regions—induced by the differences in fiscal income—can be closed. Transfer payments from the central government should emphasize public services and social protection, such as elementary education, medical care, and social relief.

Fifth, a more equalizing taxation system needs to be established. The progressive nature of the income tax should be increased, meaning that high-income earners pay a higher rate while low-income earners pay a lower rate and poverty-stricken people are subsidized with the transfer payments and pay no taxes. Such property taxes can be used to account for the vast the differences in wealth.

Sixth, the pace of the transition of the government's functions must be sped up, so as to eliminate unfair social distribution brought by power and corruption. Equalization of income distribution is closely related to the government's functions and style. A concentration of political power and lack of democratic supervision can lead to rent-seeking corruption. This unfair social distribution induced by corruption has a high degree of social sensitivity. The negative impact of corruption on income equality is the most serious problem. Therefore, in order to reduce the chances of the intermingling of political power and vested-interests, the transition of government functions needs to be accelerated.

Appendix Table A8.1. The Urban-Rural Income Disparity in 1978–2006 (Gini Coefficient)

Year	Rural	Urban	National	National with Adjustment
1978	0.212	0.16	n.a.	n.a.
1979	0.237	0.16	n.a.	n.a.
1980	0.238	0.16	n.a.	n.a.
1981	0.239	0.15	0.310	0.280
1982	0.232	0.15	0.285	0.259
1983	0.246	0.15	0.283	0.260
1984	0.258	0.16	0.291	0.269
1985	0.264	0.19	0.290	0.265
1986	0.288	0.19	0.324	0.292
1987	0.292	0.20	0.324	0.289
1988	0.301	0.23	0.330	0.295
1989	0.300	0.23	0.352	0.318
1990	0.31	0.23	0.349	0.316
1991	0.307	0.24	0.371	0.331
1992	0.313	0.25	0.390	0.342
1993	0.329	0.27	0.420	0.367
1994	0.321	0.30	0.433	0.376
1995	0.342	0.28	0.415	0.365
1996	0.323	0.28	0.398	0.351
1997	0.329	0.29	0.398	0.350
1998	0.337	0.30	0.403	0.354
1999	0.336	0.30	0.416	0.364
2000	0.354	0.32	0.438	0.385
2001	0.36	0.32	0.447	0.395

Appendix Table A8.1 (*cont.*)

Year	Rural	Urban	National	National with Adjustment
2002	0.365	0.32	0.468	n.a.
2003	0.368	0.33	n.a.	n.a.
2004	0.369	0.33	n.a.	n.a.
2005	0.375	0.34	n.a.	n.a.
2006	0.374			

Source: (1) Tang Ping 唐平, "Woguo nongcun jumin shouru shuiping ji chayi de fenxi 我国农村居民收入水平及差异的分析 [The Analysis of the Income Level and Inequality of the Rural Residents in China]," 1995. (2) Ren Caifang 任才方 and Cheng Xuebin 程学斌, "Cong chengzhen jumin shouru kanfenpei chaju 从城镇居民收入看分配差距 [The Impact of Income of Urban and Rural Residents on Income Distribution Disparity]," 1996. (3) The Gini coefficient after 1996 is provided by the Department of Urban and Rural Survey Organization at the National Bureau of Statistics. (4) From the National Bureau of Statistics, *China Statistical Yearbook* of relevant years. (5) Ravallion, Martin and Shaohua Chen, "China's (Uneven) Progress Against Poverty," 2004. (6) Li Shi 李实, Sicular 史泰丽, and Gusstafsson 古斯塔夫森. *Zhongguo jumin shouru fenpei yanjiu III* 中国居民收入分配研究Ⅲ [*Researching China's Income Distribution Vol. 3*] (7) Li Shi, "Changes in Income Distribution over Thirty Years of Reform and Opening," 2008.

Bibliography

Ahluwalia, Montek S. "Inequality, Poverty, and Development." *Journal of Development Economics* No. 3 (December 1976): 307–312.

Alesina, A. and D. Rodrik. "Distributive Politics and Economic Growth." *Quarterly Journal of Economics* Vol. 109, No. 2 (1994). Available online at: http://povlibrary.worldbank.org/library/view/13191/

Cai Fang 蔡昉. "Quanqiuhua zenyang huiji putong laodongzhe—zhongguo jingji fazhan zhuanzhedianshang de zhengce xuanze 全球化怎样惠及普通劳动者—中国经济发展转折点上的政策选择 [How Can Globalization Benefit Average Workers: policy options at the turning point of the economic development in China]." *Zhongguo quanwei jingjilun wenku* 中国权威经济论文库 *Collected Works of Leading Economists* (2006).

Cai Fang 蔡昉 and Wang Dewen 王德文. "Migration as Marketization: What Can We Learn from China's 2000 Census Data?" *The China Review* Vol. 3, No. 2 (2003): 73–93.

Chen, Shaohua and Martin Ravallion. "How have the world's poorest fared since the early 1980s?" World Bank Discussion Paper No. WPS3341 (2004).

China Development Research Foundation, UNDP. *China Human Development Report 2005: Toward Human Development with Equity* (Chinese Translation). Beijing: China Translation and Publishing Corporation, 2005.

——. *China Development Research Report 2007: Eliminate Poverty in the Economic Development* (Chinese Translation). Beijing: China Development Press, 2007.

——. *China Development Research Report 2008: Constructing the Social Welfare System in China (Discussion Version)* (Chinese Translation). 2008.

Deininger, Klaus and Lyn Squire. "New Ways of Looking at Old Issues: Inequality and Growth." *Journal of Development Economics* Vol. 57 (1998): 259–287.

Dollar, David. "Poverty, Inequality and Social Disparities during China's Economic Reform." World Bank Policy Research Working Paper No. 4253 (June 2007).

Dollar, David and Aart Kraay. "Growth Is Good for the Poor." World Bank Policy Research Working Paper No. 2587 (April 2001).

Easterly, William. "Life During Growth." *Journal of Economic Growth* Vol. 4, No. 3 (September 1999): 239–275.

Forbes, K. "A Reassessment of the Relationship between Inequality and Growth." *American Economic Review* Vol. 90, No. 4 (2000).

Khan, Azizur, Keith Griffin, Carl Riskin and Zhao Renwei. "Household Income and Its Distribution in China." *China Quarterly* (December 1992).

Khan, Azizur, and Carl Riskin. "Income and Inequality in China: Composition, Distribution and Growth of Household Income, 1988 to 1995." *China Quarterly* (June 1998).

Knight, John. "Reform, Growth, and Inequality in China." *Asian Economic Policy Review* Vol. 3, No. 1 (June 2008): 140–158.

Kuznets, Simon. "Economic Growth and Income Inequality." *American Economic Review* No. 45 (March 1955):1–19.

Li, H. and H. Zou. "Income Inequality is not Harmful for Growth: Theory and Evidence." *Review of Development Economics* Vol. 2, No. 3: 1998.

Li Shi. "Rural Migrant Workers in China: Scenario, Challenges and Public Policy." ILO Discussion Paper (2007).

Li Shi 李实. "Zhongguo jingji fazhanzhong de shouru fenpei 中国经济发展中的收入分 [The Income Distribution in China's Economic Development]." In *Xiaolü, gongping yu shenhua gaige kaifang* 效率、公平与深化改革开放 [*Efficiency, Impartiality and the Deepening of the Economic Reform and Opening*], edited by the Society of Chinese Economists and the China Economic Forum. Beijing: Peking University Press, 1993.

—— 李实. "Gaige kaifang sanshi nian zhongguo shouru fenpei de bianhua 改革开放三十年中国收入分配的变化 [Changes in Income Distribution over Thirty Years of Reform and Opening]." Paper for the Reform and Opening Memorial Conference on Economic Research for the 100 Year Anniversary of Sun Zhifang, Hong Kong, October 21–22, 2008.

—— 李实, Sicular 史泰丽, and Gusstafsson 古斯塔夫森. *Zhongguo jumin shouru fenpei yanjiu III* 中国居民收入分配研究Ⅲ [*Researching China's Income Distribution Vol. 3*]. Beijing: Normal University Press, 2008.

—— 李实 and Yue Xixin 岳希新. "Zhongguo chengxiang shouru chaju diaocha 中国城乡收入差距调查 [Investigation on the Urban-Rural Income Gap]." *Caijing* 财经 [*Caijing*] No. 3 and 4 (combined edition) (2004).

—— 李实, Zhao Renwei 赵人伟, and Zhang Ping 张平. "Zhongguo jingji gaige guochengzhong de shouru fenpei biandong 中国经济改革过程中的收入分配变动 [Shifting Income Distribution During China's Economic Reform]." *Guanli Shijie* 管理世界 [*Management World*] No. 1 (1998): 43–57.

—— 李实 and Zhao Renwei 赵人伟. "Zhongguo jumin shouru fenpei zaiyanjiu 中国居民收入分配再研究 [Reexamining Income Distribution in China]." *Jingji yanjiu* 经济研究 [*Economic Research Journal*] No. 4 (1999).

—— 李实, Wei Zhong 魏众, and Ding Sai 丁赛. "Zhongguo jumin caichan fenbu bujundeng jiqi yuanyin de jingji fenxi 中国居民财产分布不均等及其原因的经验分析 [Economic Analysis of China's Unequal Wealth Distribution and the Reasons Behind It]." *Jingji yanjiu* 经济研究 [*Economic Research Journal*] No. 6 (2005).

Lin, Justin Yifu 林毅夫, Cai Fang 蔡昉, and Li Zhou 李周. *Zhongguo de qiji: Fazhan zhanlüe yu jingji gaige* 中国的奇迹: 发展战略与经济改革 [*The China miracle: development strategy and economic reform*] (Chinese version). Shanghai: Shanghai Sanlian Press, Shanghai People's Publishing House, 1994.

Lopez, H. "Pro-Poor-Pro-Growth: Is There a Trade-Off?" World Bank Policy Research Working Paper No. 3378 (2004).

National Bureau of Statistics. *Zhongguo chengzhen zhuhu diaocha nianjian* 中国城镇住戶调查年鉴 [*China Urban Household Statistical Yearbook*], Various Years.

National Bureau of Statistics. *Zhongguo nongcun zhuhu diaocha nianjian* 中国农村住戶调查年鉴 [*China Rural Household Statistical Yearbook*], Various Years.

——. *Zhongguo Tongji Nianjian* 中国统计年鉴 [*China Statistical Yearbook*].Various Years.

Perotti, R. "Growth, Income Distribution and Democracy." *Journal of Economic Growth* No. 1 (1996).

Ravallion, Martin. "Growth, Inequality, and Poverty: Looking Beyond Averages." *World Development* Vol. 29, No. 11 (November 2001): 1803–1815.

Ravallion, Martin and Shaohua Chen. "China's (Uneven) Progress Against Poverty." World Bank Policy Research Working Paper Series No. 3408 (2004).

——. "What Can New Survey Data Tell Us about Recent Changes in Distribution and Poverty?" *World Bank Economic Review* Vol. 11, No. 2 (1997): 357–82.

Ren Caifang 任才方 and Cheng Xuebin 程学斌. "Cong chengzhen jumin shouru kanfenpei chaju 从城镇居民收入看分配差距 [The Impact of Income of Urban and Rural Residents on Income Distribution Disparity]." Jingji yanjiu cankao 经济研究参考 [*Review of Economic Research*] No. 157 (1996).

Robinson, Sherman. "A Note on the Hypothesis Relating Income Inequality and Economic Development." *American Economic Review* No. 66 (June 1976): 437–8.

Sicular, T., X. Yue, B. Gustafsson, and S. Li. "The Urban-Rural Income Gap and Inequality in China." *Review of Income and Wealth* Vol. 53, No. 1 (2007): 93–126.

Tang Ping 唐平. "Woguo nongcun jumin shouru shuiping ji chayi de fenxi 我国农村居民收入水平及差异的分析 [The Analysis of the Income Level and Inequality of the Rural Residents in China]." *Guanli shijie* 管理世界 [*Management World*] No. 2 (1995).

Tinbergen J. *Income Distribution: Analysis and Policies*. Amsterdam: North-Holland, 1975.

Whalley, John *and* Ximing *Yue*. "Rural Income Volatility and Inequality in China." NBER Working Paper No. 12779 (2006).

Wang Xiaolu 王小鲁 and Fan Gang 樊钢. "Zhongguo shouru chaju de zoushi he yingxiang yinsu fenxi 中国收入差距的走势和影响因素分析 [Analysis of the Contributing Factors to the Trend of Income Inequality in China]." *Jingji yanjiu* 经济研究 [*Economic Research Journal*] No. 10 (2005): 24–36.

Yue, Ximing, Terry Sicular, Li Shi and Bjorn Gustafsson. "Explaining Incomes and Inequality in China." In *Income Inequality and Public Policy in China*, edited by Bjorn Gustafsson, Li Shi and Terry Sicular. Cambridge University Press, 2008.

Zhao Renwei 赵人伟 and Ding Sai 丁赛. "The Distribution of Wealth in China" (Translated into English). In *Income Inequality and Public Policy in China*, edited by Bjorn Gustafsson, Li Shi and Terry Sicular. Cambridge University Press, 2008.

Zhao Renwei 赵人伟 and Li Shi 李实. "Zhongguo jumin shouru chaju de kuo da jiqi yuanyin 中国居民收入差距的扩大及其原因 [Expanding Income Inequality of the Residents in China and Its Reason]." *Jingji yanjiu* 经济研究 [*Economic Research Journal*] No. 9 (1997).

Zhao Renwei 赵人伟, Li Shi 李实, and Carl Riskin (eds.). *Zhongguo jumin shouru fenpei zaiyanjiu* 中国居民收入分配再研究 *Reexamining the Income Distribution of Chinese Residents*. China Financial and Economic Publishing House, 1999.

Zhao Yaohui, 赵耀辉. "Zhongguo nongcun laodongli liudong ji jiaoyu zai qizhong de zuoyong 中国农村劳动力流动及教育在其中的作用 The Migration of Rural

Labor in China and the Role of Education in Migration." *Jingji yanjiu* 经济研究 *Economic Research Journal* No. 2 (1997).

Zhou Binbin 周彬彬. "Renmin gongshe shiqi de pinkun wenti 人民公社时期的贫困问题 Poverty During the Period of the People's Communes." *Jingji fazhan luntan* 经济发展论坛 *Economic Development Forum* No. 3 (1991).

CHAPTER NINE

WOMEN'S CONTRIBUTION TO ECONOMIC DEVELOPMENT: THIRTY YEARS OF RURAL LABOR MARKET DEVELOPMENT AND WOMEN'S PARTICIPATION AND CONTRIBUTION

Linxiu Zhang and Team[1]

I. *Introduction*

Since reforms began in China in the late 1970s, the nation has experienced rapid economic growth, much of which has been fueled by increased employment in non-agricultural sectors. The expansion of the rural economy has driven a large part of the growth of the income in these sectors.[2] Rural labor markets have changed dramatically over the past thirty years and their emergence has contributed to the success of the rural economy.[3] Many observers agree that the success of rural labor in raising incomes and productivity can account for a significant part of the rise in rural welfare.[4]

The rise of rural labor markets, however, is more important than just its role in providing rural residents with a means to raise their incomes;[5] in fact, part of China's success in its modernization efforts during the past two decades has been due to the improvement of rural

[1] This chapter is mainly based on a newest labor dataset that collected by the Center for Chinese Agricultural Policy of the Chinese Academy of Sciences in 2008. However, the work is built on from previous works by the author and the collaborative team. The core team members include: Scott Rozelle, Alan de Brauw, Xiaofei Li, Chengfang Liu, Jikun Huang, and Qiang Li.

[2] Putterman, Louis, "Dualism and Reform in China," 1992; Perkins, Dwight, "Completing China's Move to the Market," 1994.

[3] Solinger, Dorothy, *Contesting Citizenship in Urban China: Peasant Migrants, the State, and the Logic of the Market*, 1999; West, Lorraine and Yaohui Zhao, *Rural Labor Flows in China*, 2000; World Bank, "The Alleviation of Poverty in China," 2001.

[4] Parish, William, Xiaoye Zhe, and Fang Li, "Nonfarm Work and Marketization of the Chinese Countryside," 1995; Rozelle, Scott, "Stagnation Without Equity: Changing Patterns of Income and Inequality in China's Post-Reform Rural Economy," 1996.

[5] Todaro, Michael, "Internal Migration in Developing Countries: A Review of Theory, Evidence, Methodology and Research Priorities," 1976; Stark, Oded, "Rural

labor markets. For a nation to modernize, it must rely on labor markets to facilitate the economy's transformation from a largely rural population to an urban one. Without well-functioning labor markets, it would be difficult to switch the primary mode of production in the economy from agriculture to industry. Hence, it would seem that the question of whether or not rural labor markets have emerged in a way that will allow them to facilitate the transformation of China's economy is at least as important as assessing their contribution to per capita rural income. In previous studies,[6] we have shown that China's rural labor force is increasingly migrating to cities and is creating a class of young workers that have fewer ties to the land. Mohatrapra[7] illustrates that rural labor markets are one of the main conduits for the structural change occurring in China.

Despite the shifts in employment patterns and the important contributions that labor market development has made to the economy as a whole, scholars do not agree on the role that labor markets have played in contributing to the welfare of rural women. Some researchers believe that significant barriers still exist for women in China's rural labor markets. For example, Chan and Senser[8] believe that although women began working more frequently during the 1990s, their positions were generally demeaning. Solinger[9] describes interviews with migrants who, despite having jobs, believe they are being disenfranchised and treated unfairly. Maurer-Fazio et al.[10] show that as labor markets liberalized in the 1990s, discrimination towards women, as measured by the male-female wage gap, reemerged. Their work, however, was confined to urban labor markets. Song and Jiggins[11] suggest that the adverse impacts of labor market trends spill over into agriculture; since women are being left to tend the fields and have

to Urban Migration and Some Economic Issues: A Review Utilizing Findings of Surveys and Empirical Studies Covering 1965–1975 Period," 1976.

[6] eg. de Brauw, Alan and Scott Rozelle, "Reconciling the Returns to Rural Education in Non-agricultural Employment in Rural China," 2002.

[7] Mohapatra, Sandeep, "The Evolution of Modes of Production and China's Rural Economic Development," 2001.

[8] Chan, Anita and Robert A. Senser, "China's Troubled Workers," 1997.

[9] Solinger, Dorothy, *Contesting Citizenship in Urban China: Peasant Migrants, the State, and the Logic of the Market*, 1999.

[10] Maurer-Fazio, Margaret, "Earnings and education in China's transition to a market economy—Survey evidence from 1989 and 1992," 1999.

[11] Song, Y., and Janice Jiggins, "Feminization of Agriculture and Related Issues: Two case studies in Marginal Rural Areas in China," 2000.

inferior access to resources, they earn less than men for their on-farm work.

In contrast, others believe that rural labor markets are not only spearheading China's drive towards modernization, they have created new opportunities for women. For example, Rozelle et al.[12] and Lohmar, Rozelle, and Zhao[13] have show that, between 1988 and 1995, women entered the non-agricultural sector at higher rates than men. Meng[14] shows that as rural labor markets have liberalized, women have been earning the same wages as men, all other things being equal. Wan[15] finds that despite the move by many women into jobs far from home under conditions that would be considered deplorable in developed countries, women are actually satisfied with their work and prefer working in the non-agricultural sector. Finally—although not many studies, to our knowledge, have quantified the effect of the rise of participation of women in farming—given the rapid increase in the agricultural sector's productivity during the 1990s,[16] it seems unlikely that the feminization of agriculture has had a very large adverse effect on agriculture output or incomes.

We believe that these fundamental disagreements continue to be unresolved largely as a result of previous analyses considering only part of the labor market or focusing on only part of the country. Few have attempted to quantify certain key issues, such as the feminization of agriculture, to empirically assess if the rising of women in farming is helping or hurting their performance in the agricultural sector. Perhaps due simply to the magnitude of the questions being asked, it is natural that the individual bits and pieces found in the literature seem inconsistent or contradictory.

Therefore, the overall goal of this chapter is to contribute to the ongoing assessment of China's rural labor markets, paying special attention to whether these markets are developing in a way that is helping or hurting the interests of women. Specifically, we have three objectives.

---

[12] Rozelle, Scott et al., "Leaving China's Farms: Survey Results of New Paths and Remaining Hurdles to Rural Migration," 1999.

[13] Lohmar, Bryan, Changbao Zhao, and Scott Rozelle, "Rural to Rural Migration: New Channels of Non-agricultural Employment in Rural China," 1998.

[14] Meng, Xin, "Regional Wage Gap, Information Flow, and Rural-Urban Migration," 1996.

[15] Wan, Donna. "Women in China and Off Farm Employment Decisions," 1993.

[16] Jin, S.Q., S.D. Rozelle, J.K. Huang, and R.F. Hu, "The Creation and Spread of Technology and Total Factor Productivity in China's Agriculture," 2002.

First, we provide an update of the trends in non-agricultural labor participation and will especially try to estimate the nation's aggregate non-agricultural participation rates, focusing on the participation of rural women during the reform era (between 1980 and 2007). Second, we analyze the implications of non-agricultural development on the participation of rural women to see if, with all other factors being held constant, women are making gains. Finally, we measure how the increasing role of women in the agricultural sector affects the efficiency of farming in order to understand whether or not their participation in agriculture undermines farm income.

To meet these objectives, the rest of the paper is organized as follows: In the next section, we describe the source of our data. Then, we describe how the overall rural labor market has evolved (by describing employment trends between 1981 and 2007) in the past thirty years using various data sets collected by the authors and their collaborators. Section IV discusses how such general trends of the labor market's development have impacted women's participation in it. The fifth section examines how women's participation in agriculture—either as heads of household or as field workers—affects the efficiency of crop production. Finally, the last section offers some conclusions.

II. *Data*

The two surveys referred to in this chapter were conducted in 2005 and 2008 respectively and focus on (1) a time period which spans from 1995 to the year before the implementation of the first wave of the survey (2004) and (2) a time period which spans from 2005 to the year before the implementation of the second wave of the survey (2007). The first round of the survey was conducted in April 2005 using a randomly selected, nationally representative sample of 101 rural villages in five provinces (Jiangsu, Sichuan, Shaanxi, Jilin and Hebei). For more details on the exact method of sample selection see Zhang et al.[17] The second survey was conducted in April 2008. The enumeration teams visited the same provinces, counties, townships, villages, and households that had been sampled and surveyed in 2005. During the

[17] Zhang, Linxiu, Renfu Luo, Chengfang Liu and Scott Rozelle, "Investing in Rural China: Tracking China's Commitment to Modernization," 2006.

second round, the surveyors implemented a household survey that was given to twenty households per village. In total the household survey covered 2,020 households and 8,471 individuals.

The survey teams gathered detailed information on household demographic characteristics, wealth, agricultural production, non-agricultural activities, and investment. Several parts of the survey are designed to learn about the household's migration decisions as well as its participation in other labor market activities over time. For all of the households in the first wave of the survey, a nine-year employment history form was completed for each household member and all the children of the head of the household, even when they were no longer considered household members. For each year between 1995 and 2004, the questionnaire tracks each individual's participation in non-agricultural employment, the main type of non-agricultural work performed, the place of residence while working within or outside the village, the location of non-agricultural employment, and whether or not each individual was self-employed or wage earning.[18]

Using the employment history data, we separate non-agricultural jobs into four types: migrant wage earners (henceforth, migrants); self-employed migrants; local wage earners; and local self-employed. Migrants were identified as people who had non-agricultural jobs but did not live in the household while working. Local wage earners were identified as people who had non-agricultural employment, were not self-employed, and lived at home while they worked. All people who reported being self-employed off the farm were categorized as such. The definitions held for both members of the household and children of the head of the household. We also asked about the extent of the participation of each member, in each year, in the household's agricultural activities. A household labor force measure was created by

[18] Enumerators attempted to ask the employment histories from each individual themselves. If a household member or one of the children of the household head was not present, the respondent (which was almost always the household head or spouse of the household head) answered. Extensive pre-testing found that the data are fairly accurate. In addition, we conducted a practical test to see whether or not a respondent bias problem exists in the employment history part of our data. We replicated the analysis after excluding observations on individuals whom we did not interview directly and found that the results did not change. This same method for collecting data has been used by authors of de Brauw et al., "The Evolution of China's Rural Labor Markets during the Reforms," 2002, in China; and Taylor et al. (2007) in Mexico. In fact, the authors in these papers ask households for 20-year employment history and believe they have high quality data.

aggregating all individuals in the households above the age 16 who indicated that they were either working in or searching for employment in agricultural and/or industry in each year. If a person over sixteen indicated he had retired, could not work for health-related reasons, or was enrolled in school full-time, he/she was not included in the labor force total. Descriptive statistics for selected variables are included in Table 9.1.

III. *Evolution of the Rural Labor Market*

Building on the previous work of de Brauw et. al[19] on the trend in rural labor market development, this section uses a newer rural household survey to update the trends of rural labor market development and its dis-aggregated trends according to different groups.

A. *Expansion of Rural Labor Markets in the Late 1990s and Early 2000s*

Consistent with previous findings of other national studies of rural non-agricultural employment,[20] data from our survey show the non-agricultural labor force expanded steadily between 1995 and 2007

Table 9.1. Descriptive Statistics for Selected Variables

Variable	Mean	Standard deviation
Gender(1=male)	0.51	0.50
Years of education	8.0	2.89
Skill training, 2004(1=yes)	0.161	0.367
Household's total land area, 2007(mu)	6.96	38.71
Value of durables, 2007(yuan)	4926	11685
Household's labor force	2.89	1.17
Household size	4.29	1.58

Source: Authors' survey.

[19] de Brauw et al., "The Evolution of China's Rural Labor Markets during the Reforms," 2002.

[20] E.g., de Brauw et al., "The Evolution of China's Rural Labor Markets during the Reforms," 2002.

(the period covered by our employment history data). From around 31 percent in 1995, our survey estimates that by 2004 more than 50 percent of the rural labor force found some non-agricultural employment (Figure 9.1, Panel A). In other words, 2004 can be thought of as a watershed year, since (according to our data) it is the first year that more than half of the rural labor forces was engaged in some kind of off-farm work (either wage earning, self employment, or both). By assuming that neighboring provinces similar to those surveyed have identical rates of non-agricultural labor participation, we estimate that non-agricultural rural employment in China rose from less than 150 million in 1995 to more than 250 million rural residents in 2004, a growth in non-agricultural employment of more than 100 million people.

Although based on a relatively small sample, these numbers also demonstrate the consistency of our data with much larger national studies by China's National Bureau of Statistics (NBS),[21] de Brauw et al.[22] and the 1995 national community survey described in Rozelle et al.[23] The estimate from our survey data of the 1995 employment rate is almost the same as both the NBS's estimate of the non-farm labor force (31 percent), the 2002 study by de Brauw et al. (32 percent) and a 1995 community questionnaire-based estimate of rural non-agricultural employment (34 percent) that was published in 1999.[24]

Despite the large investment into rural areas during the first term of the Wen-Hu regime (2003 to 2008[25]) and despite the rising unskilled wage rate after 2004,[26] our data shows that rural non-agricultural employment continued expanding between 2004 and 2007 (Figure 9.1, Panel A). By 2007, around 57 percent of rural individuals were participating in non-agricultural work, a rise of around 6 percentage points between 2004 and 2007. If this is representative of the entire country, this means that around 300 million rural residents worked off the farm in 2007, a rise of almost 50 million workers during the

---

[21] National Bureau of Statistics (NBS), *Zhongguo Tongji Nianjian* 中国统计年鉴 [*China Statistical Yearbook*], 1996.

[22] de Brauw et al., "The Evolution of China's Rural Labor Markets during the Reforms," 2002.

[23] Rozelle et al., "Leaving China's Farms: Survey Results of New Paths and Remaining Hurdles to Rural Migration,"1999.

[24] Rozelle et al., "Leaving China's Farms: Survey Results of New Paths and Remaining Hurdles to Rural Migration,"1999.

[25] Luo et al., 2007.

[26] Park, Albert, Fang Cai and Wang Du, "Can China Meet Her Employment Challenges?" 2008.

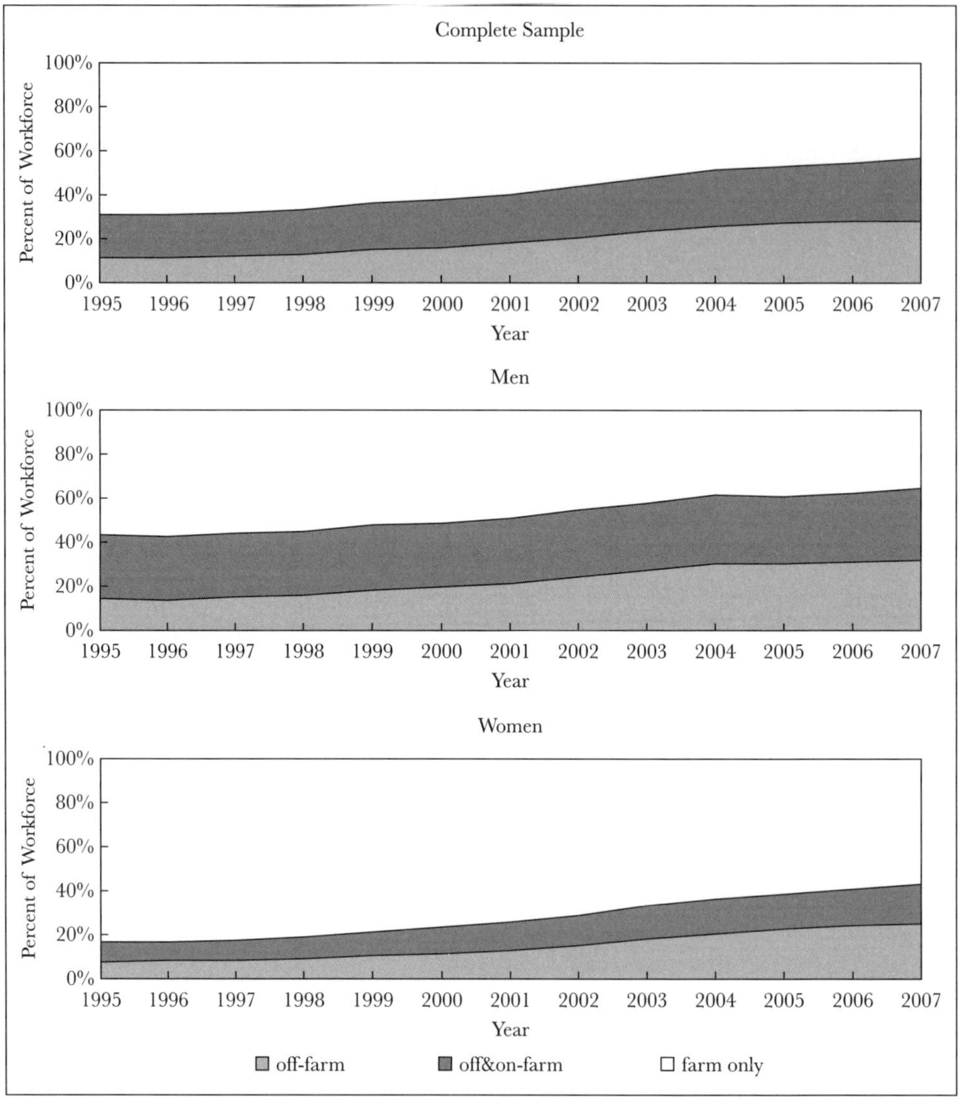

Notes: Each line shows cumulative percentages of all individuals, men, or women in the labor force. The gap between the top horizontal line of each panel (100%) and the upper most trend line is the percentage of people in full time farming. Off-&on-farm refers to individuals who work both off- and on-farm.

Source: Authors' survey.

Figure 9.1. Percentage of Rural Labor Force Engaged in Non-Agricultural and On-Farm Employment.

mid-2000s. Such a large increase in labor flow would be one indicator that China's labor market is well functioning.

B. *Rural Labor Market Development by Category and from Regional Perspective*

By deconstructing China's labor trends, our data demonstrates that labor markets are providing more than just non-agricultural income to rural residents. Trends by employment type show clearly that the target destination of workers over the past decade or so has shifted from rural to urban (Figure 9.2, Panel A).

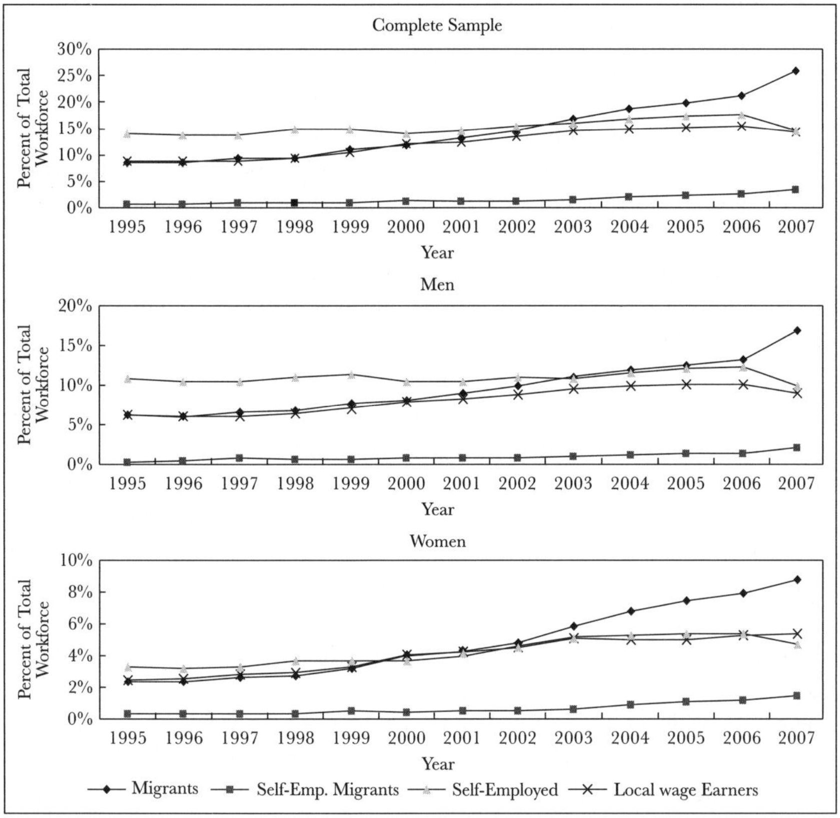

Notes: Each line shows total percentages of all individuals (men or women) engaged in that type of work.
Source: Authors' survey.

Figure 9.2. Percentage of Total Labor Force Engaged in Different Types of Non-Agricultural Work.

In 1995, most rural individuals (nearly 70 percent) spent all of their time in farming. Individuals who worked off the farm were more than twice as likely to live at home and work within or close to the village (14 percent were local self-employed plus 9 percent were local wage earners) than to work outside of the village and live away from home (around 1 percent were self-employed migrants plus around 8 percent were migrants). By 2007, however, the situation had changed radically. According to our data, almost exactly as many non-agricultural workers were living away from home (26 percent wage-earning migrants *plus* 3 percent self-employed migrants) as were living at home (14 percent local wage-earning workers *plus* 15 percent local self-employed). Migrants composed both the largest and fastest growing component of the rural labor force. At the same time, as described by Li and Rozelle,[27] local enterprises during this time were in the midst of their own major reform, shifting from local state-owned to private. During this reform local employment stagnated, both due to the shutting down of many locally-state owned township and village enterprises (TVEs) and due to layoffs that sometimes occurred when a TVE was sold to a private individual.

Over the past twenty years, migrants have also been venturing further from home, a trend that has continued in recent years (Table 9.2). In 1995 around 65 percent of migrants worked within their own province (row 2, column 1 and 2); while only around 35 percent went out of the province in search of work (row 2, column 3). By 2007, nearly half (46 percent) of migrants left their provinces for work (row 1, column 3). Even more striking than the changes for the average rural individuals were the changes for workers under 30 years old (henceforth, *young workers*). In 1995, 38 percent of young workers were leaving home, whereas more than half (54 percent) were leaving home in 2007 (rows 3 and 4, column 3). In contrast, the trend is much less pronounced, or nearly non-existent, among workers older than 30 (rows 5 and 6). These observations are consistent with the 1995 community-based questionnaire. Rozelle et al.[28] found that, while only 25 percent of workers moved out of the province in 1988, roughly 40 percent did by 1995.

The contours of labor movement created from the non-agricultural employment histories of different age cohorts add more detail to the

---

[27] 2004.

[28] Rozelle et al., "Leaving China's Farms: Survey Results of New Paths and Remaining Hurdles to Rural Migration," 1999.

Table 9.2. Comparison of Location of Migrant Employment in Percentage of Migrants Working in Specific Locations by Age in 1995 and 2007

	Off farm job located within:		
	Own county	Province, but outside of county	Another Province
All Non-agricultural Workers			
2007	30	24	46
1995*	36	29	35
Workers under 30 years old			
2007	21	25	54
1995	31	31	38
Workers over 30 years old			
2007	35	35	30
1995	40	32	28

* For example, the table compares workers who were 25 years old in 1995 with workers who were 25 years old in 2007.
Source: Authors' survey.

understanding of these trends and demonstrate one of the most striking characteristics of China's changing employment patterns: the youngest age cohort (i.e., those under 30) have almost completely shifted the focus of their employment to the non-agricultural sector (Table 9.3 and Figure 9.3).[29] Workers in all age cohort categories participated at nearly similar rates until as late as 1990 (Figure 9.3). In 1990, participation rates of all age cohorts fell into a narrow range from 20.5 to 33.6 percent (Figure 9.3 and Table 9.3, column 1). There was no clear progression when moving from the oldest to youngest cohorts.

However, by 2004 the rise in the non-agricultural participation rates of younger workers had greatly accelerated relative to older ones and a distinct ranking appeared as one's analysis moved from the oldest to the youngest cohort (Table 9.3, column 2). In 2004, young workers in the 16 to 20 year old cohort participated at rates more than three times (78.6 percent) those of 16 to 20 year olds in 1990 (23.7 percent). Those in the 21 to 25 year old cohort (82.8 in 2004) and those in the

[29] Table 9.3 and Figure 9.3 were created in order to allow us to compare the non-agricultural labor participation rates of individuals belonging to different age categories during different years. For example, when comparing the participation of 16 to 20 year olds in 2007 with those in 1995 in Table 9.3, we are actually looking at the participation in 1995 of those individuals who are currently 28 to 32 years old.

Table 9.3. Comparison of Labor Participation Rates in Percentage of Individuals That Participate in the Non-Agricultural Labor Force by Age Categories, 1990, 2004 and 2007

age cohorts	Percentage with non-agricultural work in: 1990 (from de Brauw et al. (2002)	2004 (our data)	2007 (our data)
16–20*	23.7	78.6	93.1
21–25	33.6	82.8	87.5
26–30	28.8	71.0	76.4
31–35	26.9	65.1	67.2
36–40	20.5	54.0	65.7
41–50	20.8	44.0	54.1

* For example, the table compares workers who were between ages16 and 20 in 1990 with workers who were ages 16 to 20 in 2007.

26 to 30 year old cohort (71.0 in 2004) more than doubled the non-agricultural participation rates of their 1990 cohorts (33.6 percent and 28.8 percent, respectively). In contrast, *older workers* (e.g., those over 40), while still increasing their participation rates (by 23 percentage points—from 20.8 to 44.0), worked off the farm at a rate that was nearly half the rate that of those in the 16 to 30 year old cohorts.

The rate of increase of workers in all age cohorts accelerated even faster between 2004 and 2007. According to our data, almost all of those in the youngest cohort (who are not in school and who are not sick) are employed and working off the farm. Indeed, less than 7 percent did not have a job! The rate is almost as high for the 21–25 year old cohort; 87.5 percent of these rural individuals have an off farm job. More than three out of four (76.4 percent) of those in the 26–30 year old cohort also have a job off the farm.

The work behavior of younger rural residents also illustrates the increasing specialization in the non-agricultural sector (Figure 9.3). For example, in 1990, of those in the younger cohorts who had off farm jobs (just 20 percent), more than half spent time working on the farm either part-time or during the busy season.[30]

[30] de Brauw, Alan et al., "The Evolution of China's Rural Labor Markets during the Reforms," 2002.

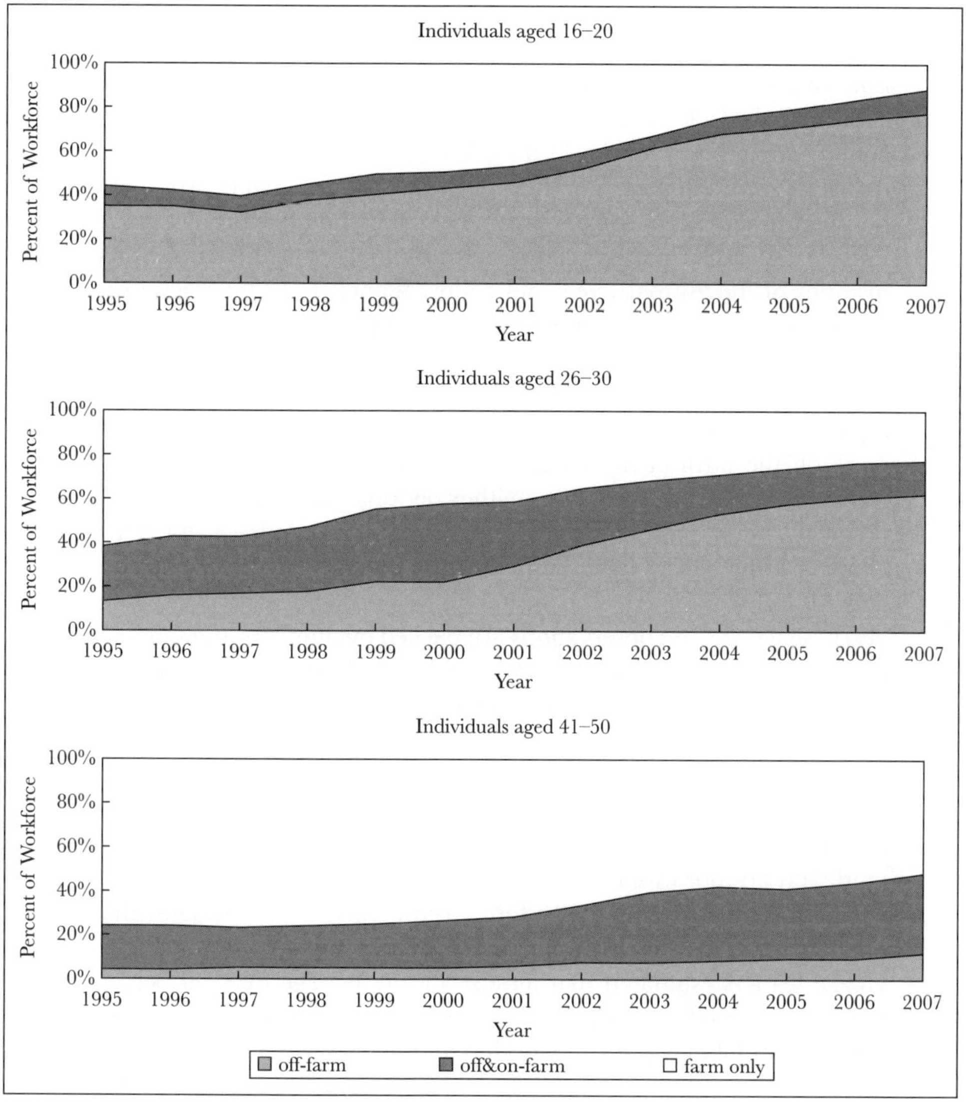

Note: See Figure 9.1 for description of figure.
Source: Authors' survey.

Figure 9.3. Percentage of Rural Labor Force Engaged in Non-Agricultural and On-Farm Employment, by Range of Ages.

By 1995, the first year of our data, already only less than 20 percent of the youngest cohort who worked non-agricultural spent any time in agriculture. By 2007 (when almost all of those in the young cohort worked off the farm) only around 10 percent of the youngest cohort worked *only* on the farm. Clearly, this generation is one very unlike those in the past. Very few of them have experience working in farming at all (except for perhaps as a child when helping during the harvest). A similar pattern can be seen by looking at the employment histories of the 26 to 30 year old cohort (Panel B). In interviews with young migrant workers in Beijing today, almost none of them say that they have any plans to ever return to farming. Many of them say they have no way to do so since they do not even understand the basics of agriculture. In contrast, of those in the 41 to 50 year old cohort who work off the farm (a much lower number), over 80 percent of them were still working in agriculture either on a part-time or seasonal basis (Panel C). Our data illustrate an overwhelming tendency for young workers to live away from home and be increasingly less engaged in agricultural work.

These figures and observations are backed by numbers and interview findings from an independent part of our 2008 survey work (focused on collecting 2007 data) in the same 101 villages. To elicit independent information on this phenomenon of young workers, we asked the village lead respondent and accountant (a team of two) to give us an estimate of the number of able bodied men (that were between 18 and 35 years old) that have their residency permit (*hukou*) in the village (and who are not in school or sick). On average, we were told that of the total estimated male labor force in the village, 777 persons, there were 215 men in the 18 to 35 year old labor force cohort. Of these, village leaders estimated that almost all (on average over 90 percent) were working off the farm and more than half (64 percent) were in the migrant labor force and working and living away from the village. In a follow up question, we asked (almost as a redundancy it turns out) if all able bodied young men in the village could find an off farm job. In more than 95 percent of the villages in which the question was asked, the answer was either "yes," or a slightly qualified, "yes, as long as they put a bit of effort into their search." Although village leaders estimated that fewer women in this same age cohort were working off the farm (it was harder for them to estimate how many of them were: working; searching for work; or not searching—because they were raising a family), they were able to estimate that more than 56 percent of the women in this cohort were in the migrant labor force, working, and living away from home. Note that these estimates from the village leaders are close to the estimates produced from our household data.

The trends that are emerging across China's provinces are also striking, and illustrate vividly the changing nature of labor markets and the nation's emerging development path. In the analysis of de Brauw et al.,[31] it was clear that in the richest province in their sample, Zhejiang Province, non-agricultural participation rates were both historically higher and grew faster. Although significantly lower, participation rates also grew rapidly in the provinces that were inland (Shaanxi, Hubei and Sichuan). Moreover, in these provinces, the percent of workers that left the province and now work full time off the farm was highest. In the other sample provinces, Liaoning and Hebei, the employment rates were lower and growing slower—especially in the 1980s and early 1990s.

When looking at the contours of participation rates by province over time with our data (from 1995 to 2007), one of the most remarkable features of the set of graphs is that almost all of the provinces appear strikingly the same (Figure 9.4). By 2007 the difference between the participation rate of the province with the most off farm employment (66 percent in Jiangsu) is only 13 percentage points higher than the province with the lowest rate of off farm employment (53 percent in Sichuan). Moreover, most of the growth rate in off farm participation in all provinces between 2000 and 2007 was from those rural residents that were working full time off the farm. Hence, the observation by de Brauw, et al. that, "if the trends of Zhejiang [which was growing the fastest in the early 1980s and 1990s] portend the future growth paths of China['s other provinces], we should expect to see continued strong and accelerating labor market growth in the coming years,"[32] appears to be coming true.

[31] de Brauw, Alan et al., "The Evolution of China's Rural Labor Markets during the Reforms," 2002.

[32] de Brauw, Alan et al., "The Evolution of China's Rural Labor Markets during the Reforms," 2002:341.

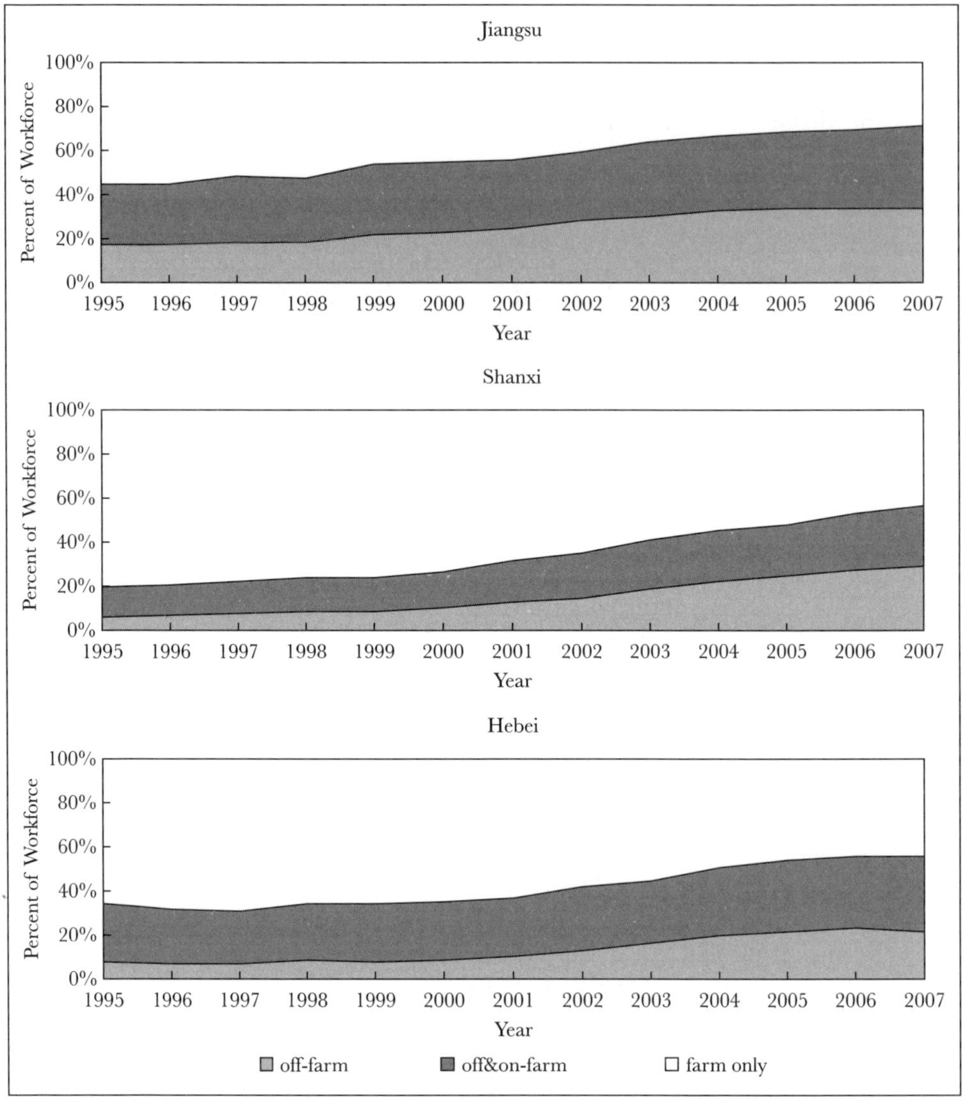

Figure 9.4. Rural Labor Force Participation by Province, 1995 to 2007.

IV. *Gender Implications of Rural Labor Market Development*

While emerging rural labor markets may have numerous effects on the fabric of rural and urban economies, we limit our descriptive analysis in this section to one of possible effects. Specifically, we examine how the development of labor markets has affected the level of participation of women in non-agricultural activities. We also examine the effect it has had on the participation of women in farming.

A. *Non-Agricultural Participation of Women*

Emerging labor markets have already begun to positively affect the non-agricultural participation rates of women (Figures 9.1 and 9.2, Panels B and C). Although women have participated at rates far below those of men throughout the entire study period, participation rates have risen steadily since 1995. In fact, during our sample period the participation rate of women in the non-agricultural sector has risen faster than that of men.

The rising participation rates of women have been driven by the entry of women into all job categories, although the most striking absolute gains have come from migration (Figure 9.2, Panels B and C). Throughout the entire decade of the 1980s, less than 1 percent of women left their homes to work for a wage.[33] However, since 1995 the rate of growth of the employment of women in the migrant wage earning labor force has been higher than any category of job types—for either men or women. Between 1995 and 2007, the participation rate by women in the migrant labor force rose by 7 percentage points, rising from less than 3 percent in 1995 (2.4 percent in the migrant wage earning labor force + 0.3 percent who are self employed migrants) to more than 10 percent in 2007 (8.9 percent in the migrant wage earning labor force + 1.4 percent self employed migrants).

The participation by women in the youngest age group demonstrates the most striking gender effects of the rise of China's rural labor markets (Table 9.4). In the 16–20 and 21–25 cohorts, the rates of participation are fairly similar; both are very high, especially in 2007 (rows 1 and 2). By the time women reach the 26–30 cohort, while the rates of participation are still high (about 60 percent), a gap begins to appear. However, when taken as a group (16 to 30 year olds), more than four out of five are working off the farm. In the female age group from 25 to 30 years old, the rates of participation, as might be expected, fall as women begin to have children. Men between the ages of 30 and 50 participate in the off-farm labor force at rates 40 or more percentage points higher than women.

[33] de Brauw, Alan et al., "The Evolution of China's Rural Labor Markets during the Reforms," 2002.

Table 9.4. Comparison of Labor Participation Rates in Percentage of Individuals that Participate in the Non-Agricultural Labor Force by Age Categories and Gender, 2004 and 2007

age cohorts	percentage with non-agricultural work in 2004 male	2004 female	2007 male	2007 female
16–20	84.8	66.7	97.1	83.4
21–25	90.2	73.8	94.5	81.3
26–30	82.9	54.2	87.9	59.6
31–35	85.6	43.5	81.2	53.5
36–40	73.9	32.1	86.4	45.0
41–50	61.9	28.1	75.5	33.6

Source: Authors' survey.

B. *Women's Changing Role in Farming*

While our current data set does not allow us to analyze this question for rural individuals using our 101 village study (since we did not collect information on hours in the farming sector), in a previous paper,[34] we showed that, surprisingly, the common perception that women are taking over the farm (as men push into the off-agricultural sector) is not actually true. In an environment in which a considerable amount of labor is moving off the farm—especially among the youngest group of male workers—it is not surprising that there should be growing attention to the study of those left behind. However, while other factors (e.g., composition of the labor force) are not held constant, the CHNS (Child Health and Nutrition Data, collected by the School of Public Health at the University of North Carolina) and the data used in de Brauw et al. (2002—henceforth, CNRS) also demonstrate that according to the measure of *work hours* there is little support for the labor feminization hypothesis (Table 9.5). During the 1990s, the average number of hours worked by men on their farms fell—as one might expect given the huge shift into the off farm employment sector—as did the overall number of hours worked on the farm (by 33 percent

[34] de Brauw and Rozelle, "Reconciling the Returns to Rural Education in Non-agricultural Employment in Rural China," 2008.

Table 9.5. Participation in On-Farm by Men and Women, China Health and Nutrition Survey, 1991–2000

	Year			
	1991	1993	1997	2000
Average Total Reported Hours of Farmwork	3682 (3211)	2851 (2510)	2420 (2207)	2023 (2177)
Share of Households Reporting Positive Hours of Farmwork	0.89	0.87	0.80	0.72
Average Hours of Farmwork Done by Women	1943 (1868)	1487 (1481)	1220 (1208)	1081 (1237)
Number of Observations	2149	2105	2216	2314

Notes: Standard deviations in parentheses. Year refers to the year survey was completed. Farm work is defined to include time spent "gardening" and "cropping," and omits time spent tending livestock or fishing.
Source: CHNS data cited in Zhang, Zhang, Luo and Li, "Does Education Still Payoff in Rural China: A Study on the Impact of Human Capital on Non-agricultural Employment and Wages," 2008.

from 1,528 in 1990 to 1,021 in 1996; and further to 963 in 2000). Surprisingly, however, the number of hours worked by women on the farm not only fell, they fell faster than those of men. According to the CHNS data, between 1990 and 1996, the number of hours worked by women fell from 1,542 in 1990 to 941 in 1996, a decline of 39 percent, 7 percentage points more than the average hours worked by men on the farm. Clearly, according to the "hours" criteria, there is not any evidence of agricultural feminization.

The participation of women in agriculture—especially as full time farm workers—also declined faster than that of men. This can be seen by measuring the shaded white part of the graph between the upper trend line and the 100% line in Figure 9.1 (Panel C). While the participation rates of men working full time on the farm is lower throughout our study period, due to their earlier and larger shift into the non-agricultural sector, the participation rates of women as full time farm workers declines faster. Since this measure of participation is complement to non-agricultural participation rate, this finding is not surprising, as the non-agricultural participation rate rises faster for women during the 1990s.

When we examine the proportion of farm work done by women over time in the CNRS, we also do not find evidence of labor feminization. Using employment history data, we created a measure of the proportion of farm work done by women in years prior to 2000. To do so, we estimated the fraction of a full-time worker that a part-time or busy season worker represents, for both men and women.[35] By aggregating the data up to the household level and measuring the proportion of farm work done by women in each household, we can estimate how the share of farm work done by women changed between 1990 and 2000.[36] We account for households that are formed after 1990 and for members of the household alive in 2000 that leave or return to the household. To generate a confidence interval around the mean, each calculated value was expanded by 1,000 times.

Figure 9.5 shows the estimated change in the proportion of the household farm workforce that is female over time. As suggested by the literature,[37] the proportion of farm work done by women appears to increase slightly during the early 1990s. However, it peaks in 1995 and then declines thereafter, falling by nearly five percentage points between 1995 and 2000. A drop in the percentage of farm work being done by women, on average, is certainly not consistent with a story of agricultural feminization in China. In fact, according to this, contrary to the common perception, agriculture has been gradually defeminized since 1995.

[35] In order to extrapolate the percentage of farm work done in each household by women back in time, we make some assumptions about these fractions. First, we assume that men and women work equal numbers of hours if they work full time on the farm. If they work part-time on the farm, we assume that they are equivalent to two-thirds of a full time worker, regardless of their gender (which is the fraction that is worked by part-time workers in 2000). Finally, men who work only in the busy season are assumed to be equivalent to one-third of a full-time worker, whereas women who work only in the busy season are assumed to be equivalent to one-third of a full-time worker (which is also based on the 2000 labor allocation data in the CNRS sample). We further assume that the fractions do not change over time.

[36] We only analyze the percentage of farm work done by women between 1990 and 2000, instead of over the whole period (1980 to 2000), because some individuals who may have worked on these family farms during the 1980s may have died. Since the share of respondents that were alive and for whom data were reported in 1990 is higher than 1980 (since there was more time for an individual to have died), this problem is not as substantial during the 1990s.

[37] E.g. Rawski, Thomas, and Robert W. Mead. "On the Trail of China's Phantom Farmers," 1998.

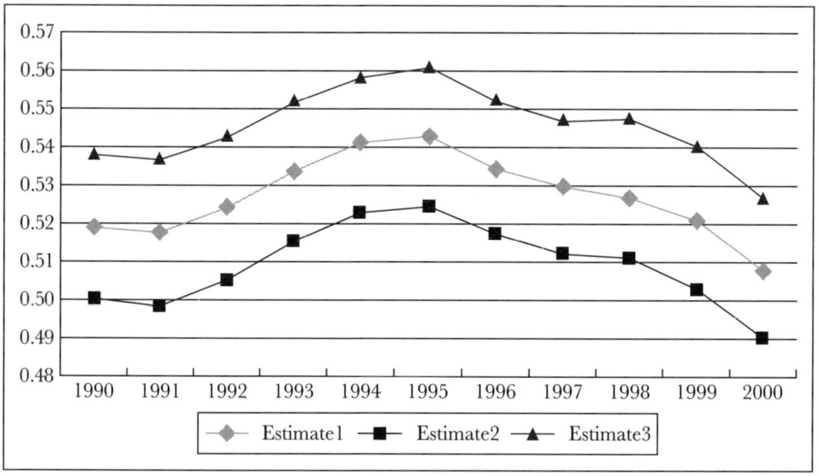

Source: de Brauw et al., "Is Feminization of Agriculture Occurring in China? Debunking the Myth and Measuring the Consequence of Women's Participation," 2008.

Figure 9.5. Estimated Proportion of Household Farm Labor Force That Is Female, 1990 to 2000.

V. *Women's Contribution in Agriculture*

A. *Impacts on Farming Productivity*

When assessing the impact of the reforms on women, one must address questions about whether or not their changing participation in agriculture can be associated with lower farm earnings. Internationally, women-headed households and women-cultivated plots have produced lower yields and revenues.[38] Women can be less efficient producers for a variety of reasons.[39] If true in China, then some of the gains women have received in the non-agricultural sector may have been offset by lower earnings in the agricultural sector.

Given that women are also much more involved in child rearing and housework than men, farms managed by women might be

[38] World Bank, "The Alleviation of Poverty in China," 2001.

[39] Saito, Katrine A., H. Mekonnen, and D. Spurling, "Raising the Productivity of Women Farmers in Sub-Saharan Africa," 1994; Quisumbing, Agnes R. "Improving Women's Agricultural Productivity as Farmers and Workers,"1994.

expected to be less efficient than farms managed by men in China. In order to answer the question of whether women-headed households are more, less, or equally efficient in cropping, we use a fixed-effects regression approach. Specifically, the logarithm of total cropping revenue for plot *i* farmed by household *h* in village *v*, y_{ihv}, is regressed on a measure of female management, Z_{hv}, a vector of household wealth and demographic characteristics X_{hv}, and plot level characteristics P_{ihv}.[40] The basic model is:

Formula 1

$$y_{ihv} = \alpha_v + Z_{hv}\gamma + X_{hv}\beta + P_{ihv}\eta + \varepsilon_{ihv}$$

To control for differences in growing conditions, prices, and other unobservable factors across villages, we include a village-level fixed effect, α_v.

Our null hypothesis is that the coefficient on the female managed farm variable, $\gamma = 0$, or that plot revenue is no different on farms run by women than on farms run by men. Since we lack a perfect measure of female farm management, we test four possible measures that are available in the CNRS. We initially use the indicator variable for a female headed household. Second, we use the nominal farm management measure, which is based on the employment history form, which was only asked in half of the sample households. To augment that measure, we also use a measure based on the reported off-peak hours worked on the farm by the husband and wife in 2000; if the husband either did not work on the farm or only worked on the farm in the busy season, while the wife worked on the farm either part-time or full-time (rather than peak season only), we code the household as a female managed farm. Fourth, we use the share of hours worked on farms by females.

Using more than 4,500 plot-level observations for the analysis, we find results that are at odds with the results from other parts of the world.[41] Regardless of the measure of female farm management, we find no evidence that female farm management is negatively associated with plot-level crop revenues, holding household and plot characteristics constant (Table 9.6, rows 1 to 4). Therefore, we cannot reject

[40] Plot level characteristics include its size (in *mu*), irrigation status, farmer-reported quality, topography, the distance of the plot from the household and whether or not a shock occurred on the plot in 2000.

[41] World Bank, "The Alleviation of Poverty in China," 2001.

Table 9.6. Regression Analysis of the Relationship between Female Managed Farms and Plot Revenues

	Dependent Variable: ln(plot revenue)			
	(1)	(2)	(3)	(4)
Female Farm management Measures				
Female is Head (1=yes)	0.071 (0.058)			
Nominal Female Manager, based on employment history		0.019 (0.041)		
Nominal Female Manager, based on hours worked			0.053 (0.039)	
Share of Hours Worked, Females				0.069 (0.050)
Household Characteristics				
Logarithm, Land Size	0.009 (0.022)	0.072 (0.026)**	0.011 (0.022)	0.011 (0.022)
Logarithm, Household Size	0.043 (0.042)	−0.034 (0.053)	0.038 (0.041)	0.032 (0.042)
Logarithm, Household Wealth	0.005 (0.010)	0.015 (0.012)	0.005 (0.009)	0.004 (0.009)
Education of Household Head (years)	0.002 (0.004)	0.002 (0.005)	0.002 (0.004)	0.002 (0.004)
Age of Household Head	0.0001 (0.001)	0.001 (0.002)	0.0004 (0.001)	0.001 (0.001)
Plot Characteristics				
Irrigated? (1=yes)	0.293 (0.031)**	0.328 (0.038)**	0.294 (0.031)**	0.292 (0.031)**
Distance to household (km)	0.004 (0.011)	0.002 (0.011)	0.003 (0.011)	0.004 (0.011)
Log, Plot Area	0.990 (0.016)**	0.989 (0.021)**	0.990 (0.016)**	0.990 (0.016)**
High Quality? (1=yes)	0.161 (0.026)**	0.163 (0.034)**	0.162 (0.026)**	0.162 (0.026)**
Plot is Hilly (1=yes)	−0.092 (0.031)**	−0.061 (0.039)	−0.093 (0.031)**	−0.094 (0.031)**
Plot is Terraced (1=yes)	−0.091 (0.060)	0.070 (0.069)	−0.087 (0.060)	−0.088 (0.060)
Plot had shock in 2000 (1=yes)	−0.146 (0.028)**	−0.178 (0.037)**	−0.145 (0.028)**	−0.143 (0.028)**
Single Season Plot	−0.321 (0.028)**	−0.362 (0.036)**	−0.321 (0.028)**	−0.319 (0.028)**
Number of Observations	4547	2437	4547	4540

Notes: ** indicates statistical significance at the 5 percent level. Robust standard errors in parentheses. All equations include village level fixed effects.
Source: de Brauw et al., "Is Feminization of Agriculture Occurring in China? Debunking the Myth and Measuring the Consequence of Women's Participation," 2008.

the hypothesis that women are equally efficient as men at managing plot revenue. In fact, the point estimates for all four measures are positive, which would suggest that women may be, if anything, better farm managers than men in rural China. However, since our measures of female management are all imperfect, these results should be interpreted as suggestive rather than definitive.

That said, despite the fact that women have taken on significant responsibilities and provided a large fraction of farm labor, plot level earnings for farms women manage are at least equivalent to earnings on plots that men manage. The most direct interpretation of this result is, of course, that women are at least as good at farming as men. However, the results in Table 9.6 suggest that we cannot reject alternative interpretations. It could be that since women-headed households are frequently (though not always) those in which the husband permanently works outside of the village, such households face fewer capital constraints and therefore are able to produce more (while in our study we hold wealth constant). It also could be that those farms that are women-run are not random. Rather, it could be that the only households that have farms that are women-run are those with particularly capable women.

B. *Impacts on Income*

One of the theoretical assumptions with female headed households is that they are less likely to earn as much income as their counterpart due to limited access to higher wage non-agricultural sectors. However, according to our data, families in which the wife takes over farming responsibilities do not seem to have lower incomes than other households. In fact, for some reason (perhaps because when the wife manages the farm, the husband can take a job off the farm) the income per capita of a woman-managed farm household is higher. The average income of a woman managed farm household in our sample is more than 3,000 yuan/capita; the average income of other households is around 2,000 yuan. So households run by women appear to be at least as well of as those run by men.

VI. *Conclusion and Major Challenges*

A. *Conclusion*

In this chapter, we have used the most recent rural employment data to show continuous expansion of non-agricultural employment in rural China. We have also shown that the general expansion in non-agricultural employment has benefited all groups in rural sector, including women.

The role of women in the labor force also is changing dramatically. The rise in participation rates is faster than men (although starting from a lower baseline). In some of the lower aged cohorts, there is little difference between the participation rates of men and women. One interpretation of this rise in the participation of women is that, as labor markets have become more competitive, the ability of managers to exercise their discriminatory gender-based preferences has declined, therefore opening up new employment opportunities for those who had previously not been able to participate. Alternatively, the rise in women's work could have occurred as the types of industries that have a preference for the skills of women rose. It is also possible that employers have been willing to hire any type and are searching for all types of workers—either male or female—and since a smaller share of females were employed in the late 1990s and early 2000s, they have been the ones drafted into the labor force most often in recent years. To the extent that working off the farm increases incomes and raises status, women have benefitted. Interestingly, there is little evidence that labor markets have pushed women into the role of managing China's agriculture. They still do a lot of the farm work, but their share of farm labor, in general, has not increased in recent years.

Hence, in this chapter, we have provided evidence showing how labor markets are performing in a way consistent with an economy that is in transition from agriculture-based to non-agriculture-based. The population is one that is shifting from rural to urban. It appears safe to say that, in the future, wages will continue to rise (assuming GDP continues to expand). In the next section we will discuss a few challenges facing agriculture, rural development, and the upcoming transition of the whole economy, especially whether rural education system can meet the challenges.

B. *Major Challenges*

1. *Agricultural Feminization among the Middle-Aged Cohort*

Although the discussion on women's participation in farming in the previous section in general did not show any trend of feminization, when we computing the hours of farm work done by each individual in 2000 (using the previous dataset), we can describe which demographic groups within households are farming, and the intensity by which they are farming (Table 9.7). The data indicate that, although men are still more likely to do farm work than women (70 percent of men do at least some farm work; only 65 percent of women do—rows 6 and 12), there are differences among cohorts. For example, among the youngest cohort of the household labor force, both males and females are much less likely than others to perform farm tasks, and they work less hours when they do work on the farm. Women of ages between 16 and 25 are less likely to work on the farm than men in the same age cohort; only 32.8 percent of these women did any farm work, whereas 39.5 percent of men did (rows 1 and 7). Likewise, women in the older cohorts (46–55 and over 55) also participate much less in farming (86.0/40.4 percent) than men in the same cohort (90.3/69.2 percent).

Table 9.7. Farm Hours Worked and Percent of People Working on Farm, by Demographic Group, 2000

Demographic Group	Percent Working on Farm	Mean Hours in 2000	Standard Deviation
Men aged:			
16–25	39.5	550.8	523.5
26–35	76.5	792.9	677
36–45	86.7	860.7	696.1
46–55	90.3	891.9	697
over 55	69.2	832.6	665.5
All Men	70	803.3	671.9
Women aged:			
16–25	32.8	543.7	533.9
26–35	81.2	849.2	684.9
36–45	91.2	944.1	698.5
46–55	86.0	911.1	688.6
over 55	40.4	574.9	503.2
All women	65	827.1	673.7

Notes: Means and standard deviations are measured only among individuals working on farm. Sample size is 3794.

Source: de Brauw et al., "Is Feminization of Agriculture Occurring in China? Debunking the Myth and Measuring the Consequence of Women's Participation," 2008.

In contrast, women in the middle-aged cohort participated in farming at higher rates than men (Table 9.7, column 1, rows 2–3; 8–9). For example, women in the 36–45 age range participate at rates that are somewhat higher than men in the same cohort. Significantly, the on-farm participation rate is highly correlated to the gaps among the cohorts in the off-farm labor trends. When cohorts of men are participating in the off-farm labor market at higher levels (and they are doing so increasingly) than cohorts of women, women are participating more back on the farm. The reverse is true for the younger cohorts. In the older cohorts, as shown in Pang et al.,[42] the participation rate among women falls faster than the participation rate among men. As we explore in more detail below, this difference is related to elderly women's participation in non-paid housework and grandchild care.

Therefore, while there may be no general move towards agricultural feminization in rural China, it may be that what social scientists are observing and describing as feminization is actually a phenomenon that is happening only to middle-aged women. The trend of agricultural feminization by middle-aged women is consistent with cohort effects in the non-agricultural labor market. Whereas young men and women appear to obtain non-agricultural jobs in similar numbers, middle aged men are far more likely than middle aged women to work non-agricultural.

To understand the difference in the hours spent by middle-aged men and women, it is instructive to compare the effort expended farming by the intensity of work reported in the labor history for 2000 (Table 9.8). Men who report only working on the farm work, on average, slightly more—just over 1,000 hours per year—than women who report only working on the farm (943 hours; row 1). The same pattern is found for part-time and busy season farmers (that is, men work more hours than women). Meanwhile, not surprisingly, full-time farmers work more hours on average than part-time farmers, and part-time farmers work more hours than those who only farm during the busy season. Therefore, these averages make it clear that middle-aged women do not work more on the farm than middle-aged men because women outwork men who are doing the same type of work, but rather middle-aged men are more likely to have non-agricultural employment than women. As a result, they are more likely to be part

[42] Pang, Lihua, Alan de Brauw, and Scott Rozelle, "Working until You Drop: the Elderly of Rural China," 2004.

Table 9.8. Farm Hours Worked by Level of Involvement in Farming, by Gender, 2000

Level of Involvement	Men	Women
Farm Work Only	1022.4	943.3
	(682.7)	(672.0)
Part-Time Farmer	711.9	598.6
	(570)	(555)
Busy Season Only	378.4	197
	(408.9)	(172.2)

Notes: Standard deviations in parentheses. Sample size is 1620, and only includes the subsample for which employment history data is available.
Source: de Brauw et al., "Is Feminization of Agriculture Occurring in China? Debunking the Myth and Measuring the Consequence of Women's Participation," 2008.

time farmers (and work less farm hours) than middle aged women. So while there is evidence of agricultural feminization among middle aged cohort, it is important to note that the typical middle-aged man is working slightly less than middle-aged women on the farm because they are also working off the farm.

2. *Livestock Sector and Future Feminization?*

The involvement of women in the livestock sector may mean that feminization, while not happening currently, may still occur in the future. In fact, our data—coupled with the sectoral shifts that have been occurring in the overall agricultural sector—provide evidence that there has been feminization in livestock production and that women's participation in the livestock sector has contributed to overall feminization (however, not enough to outweigh other forces that were defeminizing agriculture in China). Specifically, the argument is built in part on the findings in our data that both the participation in the livestock sector and the hours worked in the sector (conditional on participating) are far higher for women than for men. In fact, the CNRS data show that 59 percent of those that were involved in livestock activities in 2000 were women. Furthermore, 64 percent of the hours input into livestock activities were by women. It appears that the livestock sector in rural China is heading towards feminization.[43]

[43] Although an even higher percentage of hours of livestock rearing were performed by women according to the CHNS—85 percent—it is not changing over the early to mid 1990s, which would argue against a feminization of the livestock sector. However,

The effect of women's participation in livestock on feminization becomes evident when looking at the nature of changes in the composition of agricultural output. Statistics published by the National Bureau of Statistics in 2006 show that in the early 1980s, livestock accounted for 18 percent of total agricultural value added. The share rose to 30 percent by 2000 and to 34 percent by 2006. These figures are consistent with the simulation model detailed in Huang and Chen,[44] who suggest the share of livestock output in the total value of agricultural output will reach more than 40 percent by 2020. If men do not begin to raise livestock, it can now be seen how the change in the structure of China's agriculture—over the past decade and into the near future—means that the high rate of participation by women (assuming it will continue into the future) could increase the pressure on agricultural feminization in general. Feminization may occur gradually through structural change, rather than women taking over tasks that men had previously performed.

Even though women seem to be doing more work managing the farm and running livestock operations, men still control key phases of marketing process, a phenomenon that will dampen any conclusion that managerial feminization is also happening. Whereas women contributed 64 percent of the production work in livestock, men control 59 percent of the marketing work. This is a sign that as far as the traditional female-dominated livestock sector is concerned that feminization is more labor feminization, and not, according to the earnings-control measure, managerial feminization.

3. *Educational Challenges*

Studies[45] have found that investing in education still receives high return in rural China. The key to people earning higher wages in non-agricultural sector is to have high level of education. Many of rural China's strongest and most able laborers are not in villages anymore. They are already working in the cities and among the young there is really no one left in China's villages that is not already employed.

---

to the extent that the livestock sector is growing, the overall amount of farm work done by women could be increasing.

[44] Huang, Jikun and Chunlai Chen, "Effects of Trade Liberalization on Agriculture in China: Commodity and Local Agricultural Studies," 1999.

[45] e.g. Zhang, Haiqing, Linxiu Zhang, Renfu Luo and Qiang Li, "Does Education Still Payoff in Rural China: A Study on the Impact of Human Capital on Non-agricultural Employment and Wages," 2008.

Moreover, according to a paper by Huang et al.,[46] when there are young people in the village engaged in agriculture, they are mostly engaged in high-value, relatively capital intensive activities, such as horticultural production, dairy farming, etc. All these require a rural labor force with a higher level of education.

In fact, in China today there are many signs that the transition out of the no- and low-skill industries into industries that demand more trained and trainable workers is already beginning.[47] There are reports of low-wage firms closing down. International and domestic firms are frequently reported to be exploring investment opportunities in places that still have low wage rates, such as Vietnam and South Asia.

While the loss of jobs is always worrisome, there is also a potentially positive side. Losing industries that require sweat-shop working conditions is never a bad thing. However, to adjust to the shutting down of low wage firms, it is necessary that enterprises are able to shift into higher productivity economic activities. In other words, as wages rise, China will have to move itself up the productivity ladder. In fact, according to Szirmai and Ren,[48] this transition has already begun. Although the wage has risen at 10 percent per year between 2005 and 2007, labor productivity across the nation has risen at 15 to 20 percent per year. If true, this means that China already has begun the transition to an economy based on an industrial structure that uses more sophisticated technologies and management approaches.

While China's firms have largely been able to remain profitable during the first several years of rising wage rates, the real challenge is still in the future. Can the nation's manufacturers and service sector firms become competitive in quasi-skilled and skilled industrial sectors? To do so, this means that firms must either develop their own higher technology enterprises or to continue to induce up-scale factories to move from other nations, such as Taiwan, South Korea, Malaysia, and Mexico.

Does China have the ingredients in the country to do so? Certainly many of the components already exist. China obviously has the entre-

---

[46] Huang, Jikun, Yunhua Wu Huayong Zhi and Scott Rozelle, "Small Holder Income, Food Saftey and Producing China's Fruit," 2008.

[47] Park, Albert, Fang Cai and Wang Du, "Can China Meet Her Employment Challenges?" 2008.

[48] Szirmai, Adam, and Ruoen Ren, "Measuring Labor Productivity in Chinese Manufacturing: Statistical Problems and Solutions," 2007.

preneurial talent to do so. The logistics of the economy are improving dramatically. After the nation's accession to the World Trade Organization, trade and investment policy has improved dramatically.

Despite all these bright spots there is one fundamental outstanding question. Will the labor force, which will be coming in no small part from China's poorer, more remote provinces, have the skills and abilities to live up to the challenge? This labor force's average number of years of schooling is less than seven years.[49] More than 20 percent of the labor force cannot read or write. While illiteracy and poor numerical skills are especially characteristic of those in older age cohorts, the average education level is less than nine years for those under 30. Such low levels are almost unprecedentedly low in rapidly growing economies like China's. When Japan, South Korea, and Taiwan were at the same point in their development, they had a rigorous, high-quality K-to-12 education system. High school was free and nearly universal in all three nations. Any work force that is supposed to take on the challenges of computerized manufacturing, precision machinery, highly-complex logistics, and first-tier service and global orientation, almost certainly needs the numerical, literacy, and foreign language skills that are taught in a well-structured high school system.

Bibliography

Chan, Anita and Robert A. Senser. "China's Troubled Workers." *Foreign Affairs* Vol. 76, No. 2 (March–April 1997): 104–17.

de Brauw, Alan and Scott Rozelle. "Reconciling the Returns to Rural Education in Non-agricultural Employment in Rural China." *Review of Development Economics* Vol. 12, No. 1 (2008): 57–71.

de Brauw, Alan et al. "The Evolution of China's Rural Labor Markets during the Reforms." *Journal of Comparative Economics* Vol. 30, No. 2 (June 2002): 329–353.

——. "Is Feminization of Agriculture Occurring in China? Debunking the Myth and Measuring the Consequence of Women's Participation." *China Quarterly* No. 194 (2008): 327–348.

Huang, Jikun and Chunlai Chen. "Effects of Trade Liberalization on Agriculture in China: Commodity and Local Agricultural Studies." United Nations ESCAP CGPRT Centre in Bogor, Indonesia (1999).

Huang, Jikun, Yunhua Wu Huayong Zhi and Scott Rozelle. "Small Holder Income, Food Saftey and Producing China's Fruit," *Review of Agricultural Economics* Vol. 30, No. 3 (2008): 469–479.

[49] de Brauw and Rozelle, "Reconciling the Returns to Rural Education in Non-agricultural Employment in Rural China," 2008.

Jin, S.Q., S.D. Rozelle, J.K. Huang, and R.F. Hu. "The Creation and Spread of Technology and Total Factor Productivity in China's Agriculture." *American Journal of Agricultural Economics* Vol. 84, No. 4 (2002): 916–930.

Lohmar, Bryan, Changbao Zhao, and Scott Rozelle. "Rural to Rural Migration: New Channels of Non-agricultural Employment in Rural China." University of California at Davis Department of Agriculture and Resource Economics Working Paper (1998).

Maurer-Fazio, Margaret. "Earnings and education in China's transition to a market economy—Survey evidence from 1989 and 1992." *China Economic Review* Vol. 10, No. 1 (1999): 17–401.

Meng, Xin. "Regional Wage Gap, Information Flow, and Rural-Urban Migration." Paper Presented at the Conference on Rural-Urban Labor Migration, Beijing, China, June 25–27, 1996.

Mohapatra, Sandeep. "The Evolution of Modes of Production and China's Rural Economic Development." University of California at Davis Department of Agricultural and Resource Economics Working Paper (2001).

National Bureau of Statistics. *Zhongguo Tongji Nianjian* 中国统计年鉴 [*China Statistical Yearbook*]. Beijing: State Statistical Bureau, 1990 to 2000.

Pang, Lihua, Alan de Brauw, and Scott Rozelle. "Working until You Drop: the Elderly of Rural China." *The China Journal* No. 52 (2004): 73–94.

Park, Albert, Fang Cai and Wang Du. "Can China Meet Her Employment Challenges?" Oxford University Working Paper (2008).

Parish, William, Xiaoye Zhe, and Fang Li. "Nonfarm Work and Marketization of the Chinese Countryside." *China Quarterly* No. 143 (1995): 697–730.

Perkins, Dwight. "Completing China's Move to the Market." *Journal of Economic Perspectives* Vol. 8, No. 2 (1994): 23–46.

Putterman, Louis. "Dualism and Reform in China." *Economic Development and Cultural Change* Vol. 13 (1992): 467–493.

Quisumbing, Agnes R. "Improving Women's Agricultural Productivity as Farmers and Workers." World Bank Education and Social Policy Department Discussion Paper No. 37 (1994).

Rawski, Thomas, and Robert W. Mead. "On the Trail of China's Phantom Farmers." *World Development* Vol. 26, No. 5 (1998): 767–781.

Renfu Luo, Linxiu Zhang, Jikun Huang and Scott Rozelle. "Elections, Fiscal Reform, and Public Goods Provision in Rural China." *Journal of Comparative Economics* No. 35 (2007): 583–611.

Rozelle, Scott. "Stagnation Without Equity: Changing Patterns of Income and Inequality in China's Post-Reform Rural Economy." *China Journal* No. 35 (January 1996): 63–96.

Rozelle, Scott et al. "Leaving China's Farms: Survey Results of New Paths and Remaining Hurdles to Rural Migration." *China Quarterly* No. 158 (June 1999): 367–393.

Saito, Katrine A., H. Mekonnen, and D. Spurling. "Raising the Productivity of Women Farmers in Sub-Saharan Africa." World Bank Discussion Paper No. 230, Africa Technical Department Series (1994).

Solinger, Dorothy. *Contesting Citizenship in Urban China: Peasant Migrants, the State, and the Logic of the Market*. Berkeley, CA: University of California Press, 1999.

Song, Y., and Janice Jiggins. "Feminization of Agriculture and Related Issues: Two case studies in Marginal Rural Areas in China." Paper presented at the European Conference on Agricultural and Rural Development in China, Leiden, The Netherlands, 2000.

Stark, Oded. "Rural to Urban Migration and Some Economic Issues: A Review Utilizing Findings of Surveys and Empirical Studies Covering 1965–1975 Period." World Employment Programme Research Series Working Paper. Geneva, Switzerland: International Labor Office, 1976.

Szirmai, Adam, and Ruoen Ren. "Measuring Labor Productivity in Chinese Manufacturing: Statistical Problems and Solutions." Mimeo, 2007.

Todaro, Michael. "Internal Migration in Developing Countries: A Review of Theory, Evidence, Methodology and Research Priorities." Geneva, Switzerland: International Labor Office, 1976.

West, Lorraine and Yaohui Zhao. *Rural Labor Flows in China*. Berkeley, CA: University of California Press, 2000.

Wan, Donna. "Women in China and Off Farm Employment Decisions." Unpublished Senior Honors Thesis. Stanford, CA: Stanford University Department of Economics, 1993.

World Bank. "The Alleviation of Poverty in China." Washington, DC: World Bank, 2001.

Zhang, Haiqing, Linxiu Zhang, Renfu Luo and Qiang Li. "Does Education Still Payoff in Rural China: A Study on the Impact of Human Capital on Non-agricultural Employment and Wages." *China and the World Economy* Vol. 16, No. 2 (2008): 1–16.

Zhang, Linxiu, Renfu Luo, Chengfang Liu and Scott Rozelle. "Investing in Rural China: Tracking China's Commitment to Modernization." *The Chinese Economy* Vol. 39, No. 4 (July–August 2006): 57–84.

INDEX